Fires in Many Hearts

Doris McKay around 1980

Fires in Many Hearts

by
Doris McKay

in collaboration with Paul Vreeland

GEORGE RONALD
Oxford

George Ronald, *Publisher*
Oxford
www.grbooks.com

© Doris McKay 1993
ALL RIGHTS RESERVED

First published privately 1991
Published by Nine Pines Publishing 1993
This edition 2021

A catalogue record for this book is available
from the British Library

ISBN 978-0-85398-645-4

Cover painting and design: Jaci Ayorinde

Contents

Aknowledgement   vii

Preface   viii

The Burning Log   1

Tilbury Tenement   141

Joy Gives Us Wings   203

Go Thou Straight On   263

Dedicated to Howard Colby Ives

A lighter of fires in many hearts: his spiritual sons and daughters, impregnated with the love of God, spread first over eastern United States and Canada. His spiritual progeny have multiplied through the generations to become an army. I am one of his daughters and, to me, he will be always "Daddy Howard".

Acknowledgements

Fires in Many Hearts was encouraged first by Dr Abbas Afnan during a visit he paid to me in Vernon Bridge. Gail Bowles assisted in the typing of the early drafts, which was then entitled *A Record of a Bahá'í Life*. Theresa Maloney helped me to sort through paper mountains and John Ward kept the copies of my manuscripts together. Roger White was one of the first readers and, through his brief notes, conveyed a supportive enthusiasm for my continuing efforts. Ann Boyles introduced the manuscript to an appreciative public when she produced a dramatic reading, *Excerpts from the Memoirs of Doris McKay: A Life of Service, A Life of Love,* at the Bahá'í Arts Festival in Lennoxville, Quebec, in the summer of 1989. I am grateful to Don MacLean who took an editor's fine-tooth comb to the work, also to Alanna Robertson Vreeland, Eric Maloney and Rosalind Cross who proofread the final draft. Paul Vreeland is truly my collaborator. It is his labour which carried *Fires* through to publication. I hope each one of you knows of my boundless appreciation. It cannot be contained in these few, brief comments.

Preface

Her years of devoted service will long be remembered by the countless believers whose lives were touched by her manifold activities on behalf of the Cause. Her steadfastness and obedience to the beloved Guardian in remaining at her pioneer post will serve as a shining example of devotion for generations to come.
The Universal House of Justice
December 4, 1992

Doris McKay was, quite simply, one of the most important people in my life. When I was a little girl, she was my art teacher for six years in elementary school in Charlottetown, Prince Edward Island. I remember that I loved her intensely and followed her around, volunteering to clean the paint brushes or anything else. . . whatever it took to be near this wonderful woman. I'm sure I didn't know consciously what attracted me to her; I just knew that I loved her fiercely, in a way I had never loved anyone before.

That love blossomed when I turned nineteen. Returning home from my first year away at university, I fell in with a group of Bahá'í youth and ended up somehow at a Bahá'í deepening. I wasn't particularly interested in this strange religion, but I liked the people who called themselves Bahá'ís, and so I went along with them. I can still remember the moment I walked into that house and saw, sitting at the other end of the living room, my beloved Mrs McKay. The first thing I knew, I was standing in front of her, and she was saying my name. She remembered me! I was in seventh heaven! Then, joy of joys, she was inviting me to her apartment the following evening for supper. I felt I could die of happiness.

After we had eaten that supper together, Doris suggested that we have our tea in the sitting room. With the teacups and cookies, she also passed around prayer books. I began to feel distinctly uncomfortable. The nerve! Asking someone to say a prayer! I began to wonder if I'd been wise to come at all. Perhaps Mrs McKay was some kind of religious fanatic. But when she said a prayer, I thought, "That wasn't so bad." The young man who had brought me said a prayer, and it wasn't so bad either.

Finally, it was my turn. I remember leafing through the prayer book with great concentration, determined not be a hypocrite, determined not to say a prayer I didn't *mean*. Eventually I came to one that looked alright. I took a deep breath and began to read aloud. Before I had gotten through the first three lines, I knew three things simultaneously: first, that this was the most beautiful poetry I had ever read in my life; second, that it was true; and third, that now that I had found it, I had to do something about it.

So you see, I owe my life, my spiritual life, to Doris McKay. She ignited the fire of divine love in my heart, and for that I will be eternally grateful. She continued to nurture me for over nineteen years after that eventful evening. From my earliest visits to her farm in Vernon Bridge, she would tell me the stories of her life in the early days of her Bahá'í career. She would talk about Howard and Mabel Ives, about Harlan and Grace Ober, about Louis Gregory and the racial amity work, about May Maxwell, Martha Root, and Dorothy Baker. At first, these names were just a blur – friends of Doris, some of whom had been lucky enough to meet 'Abdu'l-Bahá during His visit to America and all of whom had had stirring adventures of the spirit that changed the direction of their lives. Gradually, though, I began to realize that these names were people who had played a significant role in the history of the Bahá'í Faith in America. I dimly saw that my own beloved Doris had a part in that history, too.

I was overjoyed when she began to write the stories down. I remember going out to the farm and listening, spellbound, to the latest page, and sometimes searching frantically for lost pages. (Doris was a chaotic housekeeper; things would mysteriously fly out of her hands and into the ether without provocation.)

It took her a long time to write. Often, she would rework certain passages many times, concerned about conveying the most accurate impression possible of an event or her memory of a person in a given situation. When she began to work on the Tilbury Tenement section of the manuscript, she fretted over whether or not it was proper to discuss the difficulties she and Willard, the Obers and the Ives had had in Pittsburgh. We, her eager audience, urged her to be honest, to describe the tests and trials they suffered, because we could identify with them; they showed us the humanness of these heroes and heroines. They gave us hope that we, too, could overcome our weaknesses and arise to serve the Cause in spite of them.

Doris' work continued over the years, usually accomplished late at night (Doris was a nighthawk), on a small manual typewriter set on the dining table at the farm. Of course, the writing was interrupted quite often by hordes of visitors who flocked to visit Doris from all over the globe – people to whom she had taught the Faith and who now returned from faraway pioneering posts to lay their victories at her feet; people she had never met before but who had heard of her and who wanted to meet her for themselves; old friends with whom she worked in the earlier days of the Faith in Canada. And so the rhythm became established: visit and write, write and visit.

I think I always believed somewhere in the secret recesses of my heart that Doris would live forever. I certainly thought she would not leave this world until her manuscript was finished. I also noticed that she seemed to be working at it rather slowly. We joked that she was stretching out her days. But God stepped in and changed the situation.

Doris suffered a stroke in May 1989. At first, it looked like she would not recover enough to continue her work on the manuscript, and indeed, she was partially paralysed for the rest of her life. But her mental faculties were soon again as sharp as ever, and that was when Paul Vreeland stepped in and began to work intensively with Doris on the project of finishing the book. He and his family had returned from their pioneer post in Haiti and Paul assisted Doris in editing the manuscript. Doris would dictate and Paul would transcribe, bringing the pages he generated back on his next visit for Doris' additions, corrections or deletions. Without this time-consuming process, the book would never have reached its end.

When it was finished, there was the problem of publication. A "Doris McKay Consortium" sprang into being, composed of a number of her friends who felt that her wonderful book must be printed and who contributed their skills, labour and money to see that come about.

Herb Lee, pioneering in Macau, arranged for the volume to be printed in Hong Kong. There were times when Doris despaired of ever seeing the book in print, but finally, in the fall of 1990, the first copy arrived.* Paul rushed to Doris' bedside to give it to her, and she was overjoyed. Subsequently, she was also overjoyed to receive fan mail from all over the world – letters from people who told her, for example, that the book had inspired them to set off for a pioneer goal, or letters telling her that the book had been the basis of a fireside in a particular community or a course of guidance with a personal difficulty.

We wondered how long she would live, now that the book was done. In retrospect, it seems to me that she stayed with us long enough to enjoy some of the fruits of her labour, to bask a little in the notoriety that the book brought to her, after having spent so many years in an isolated pioneering post. When she passed away just a few days after the Second Bahá'í World Congress in New York, in November of 1992, having heard exciting news of it from someone who had just returned and felt impelled to go and tell her about it, that seemed appropriate, too. The Faith was embarking on a new era in its development; the heroes and heroines about whom she had written were, I am sure, calling to her from the next world, urging her to come and join with them in supporting their efforts to assist those still in this world. I believe that Doris, realizing that now she could do much more from that world than from this one, finally answered the call of her beloved Willard, of May, Dorothy, Martha, Louis, and particularly of "Daddy Howard", to join them there and carry on the eternal work of the Kingdom.

PREFACE

I admit that at times I miss her severely. The bond that joined us will not be broken by time or space; it never has been, since that day in 1973 when she presented me with the most precious gift I have ever been privileged to receive, and it never will be. When I am lonely for the sound of her voice, I pick up her book – and once again I am in the farmhouse in Geneva, or the tenement in Pittsburgh, the house in Jamestown, or at Vernon Bridge, enraptured by her voice, her life, her faith. Listen, and you too may find your life forever changed, your heart aglow with a mysterious and beautiful flame kindled by her words.

Ann Boyles
Halifax, March 1993

Publisher's note: This refers to the original edition privately published by the friends in 1991.

The Burning Log

It seems to me that my chief distinction in the Bahá'í Faith is that I have lived so long. At this writing (1983[1]), I have lived fifty-eight years in the Paradise of Abhá which is, for me, the knowledge that the Chosen One of God has, in the ascended Glory of the Sun, revisited the earth.

Throughout the years this certainty has been the cause of rapturous joy, my charm against disaster, my password to the hearts of others. This is the reason for the little smile that I wear on my lips at the thought of my treasure, my talisman, "my phoenix egg" that I carry in the warmth of a symbolic hand.

Was it an accident that someone had given my father a book of Persian poems when I was fifteen, and that when he saw I was in love with it, he had given it to me? The book went with me through High School, Teachers College, and Art School and after that out into my teaching world. I grew up, then out, with my perceptions widened and coloured by the songs of Omar Khayyam, Hafiz, and Jal'u'din Rumi. I drew illustrations in the margins. I wore the cover off the book. I asked a young friend of mine, a great pioneer in the far reaches of the world, "What would have happened if you had not heard the Name, Bahá'u'lláh, on the boat that day?" She replied, "I would have been lost. That is literally true."

Yes, people do get lost in the Valley of Search. I too, walked in that Valley with a pack of "isms" on my back when I was young. Like my friend, I travelled alone seeking I know not what, until, by a miracle, I grasped the meaning of that Word. I, too, was lost.

---

[1] This book was six years in the writing, and Doris celebrated her ninety-fifth birthday just a few weeks before it was completed (September 29, 1990).

Lost, yet I thought I was found when I met Willard McKay and we fell in love and were married in June 1923. After the years of teaching and living in different places, I started a new life on that beautiful fruit farm in the Finger Lakes country of western New York state. There dwelt love and compatibility, and, for a setting, there was the old house with its antiques, and the lavish plantings of roses and flowering shrubs on the grounds. The nook by the brook was planted with violets, bloodroot, hepaticas, bluebells; sweeping arbour-vitae hedges sheltered the orchards. Family and friends were nearby and there was an inner atmosphere of conversation, music, and books. Every deep wish seemed granted.

The remembrance of my early marriage has remained, floating in memory like an iridescent soap bubble. It seemed that we were at the peak of fulfilment and security. I wrote a poem in those days which conveys my deep sense of satisfaction then: "THIS IS ENOUGH!"

With a mild sense of nostalgia, I have taken out the diary of our first year. It began in January 1924. Here are the pages of a life we would later leave behind – a life bent on pleasure exclusively, an almost pagan excitement with Nature. Thronging through the pages are many casual friends with whom we played cards, picnicked, skied and crouched around fireplaces and discussed our "isms". Each day in the diary tells of the weather and what we had to eat.

Did I really say, "This is enough!" I ask myself today, "This?" The romantic bubble is burst. Any Bahá'í who has lived more than half a century in the altitude of spirit would have suffocated with boredom with that life of 1924!

In the late fall of that year there was a slight erosion in the pattern. We felt flattered to be invited to join two older couples on Sunday nights to read a newly published book called *Bahá'u'lláh and the New Era* by Dr J. E. Esslemont, a book left by someone named Howard Ives.

The two or three evenings were social; stimulating because

they gave us an opportunity to talk about our religion or lack of it. And the talk was so interesting with the Doctor and his wife (both orthodox Christians), the Collisons (atheists) and Willard and I, discussing "New Thought". Actually, we did not open our minds to the book, although we were curious about the title.

But there came the day when three words that we read stayed with me. I did not welcome them, but they persisted to crowd my consciousness. They were: "SERVICE IS PRAYER!"

On an Indian summer day Willard and I climbed the hill at the back of the farm and looked down over the cherry orchard to Seneca Lake. The trees were drab now, the cherries picked, and the sixty or seventy Italian pickers paid off. I spoke timidly on a subject we had avoided. "Everything seems so heavenly the way it is, but in our lives we have no service and we have no prayer. . . So, if service is prayer, as the book said, perhaps we should invite your mother and sisters to move out here with us."

How gladly Willard assented, as if he had been waiting for me to say this! Thus it happened that, before Christmas, the farm truck came out from town, riding high above the frozen ruts in the lane with Willard's dignified and erudite mother in her wheel chair. Our family, including Marguerite and Christine, would now be increased to five.

The old house looked very welcoming. Fireplaces in two rooms were crackling with blazing apple wood. Candles were burning in their sconces and the lamps with golden and rose china shades were alight. Our old furniture, given to us by my mother, had been accepted as an addition to the beautiful antiques of the McKays. A baby grand piano had found its wall in the bookroom. The wide planked floor was painted orange with dark blue borders. Every surface was polished bright. Kim, the old sheepdog cum collie, went rushing out to greet the truck.

1925

Thaya, a Bahá'í teacher, writes today, "How to convey to those unbelieving souls out there, the wonder of being a Bahá'í!"

My story begins with that wonder – a wonder that was given to us on an evening in January 1925. The seven of us who were invited to meet Howard and Mabel Ives that night were like a handful of travellers, strangers to one another who had met on a bus. Actually, we were taking off for a whole new world together, although, had we known it, we would have resisted that very thought and perhaps have left the bus. We had in common that all of us were adults who had found a certain pattern in our lives. We were people with strong opinions and curious minds.

I suppose the others were feeling as Willard and I were feeling, excited for some deep reason, but resolved to be critical and wary. Sales resistance we could call it today. All of us would appear to have been among those who were least likely to become Bahá'ís.

We Meet Mr and Mrs Howard Ives

The call had come soon after New Year's day. "Would you like to come to a baked bean supper at the Collisons' tomorrow night and meet the Ives?" Tomorrow was Sunday, and late that afternoon Willard and I stepped into our Model A Ford and charged down the lane to the main road. In fifteen minutes we were stepping into the fire-lit room.

Over the handshakes we caught the message of Howard Ives' eyes. Most eyes are veiled at first contact, the first meeting. Perhaps some are veiled always. But these eyes spoke. They said, "My dears, this is a meeting of souls. We cannot hide from one another." The moment passed and we saw his eyes to be deep set and brown under bushy brows. They were set in a lined face with strong features. He had a mobile, speaker's mouth. The man was spare, a little bent. Close to him stood his wife, Mabel, his physical opposite, not very tall, exceedingly pleasing and pretty with blue eyes and dark curly hair. She looked both merry and wise.

We began to enjoy ourselves. The aura of the two guests enhanced the atmosphere of the room, imparting an expansion of mind to a level above the merely rational. It was an unfamiliar elation, a response to a sense of intimacy – a sense of somehow being known and cherished. There was laughter, and stories were exchanged. We made a semicircle around the fireplace, with plates of Mary's baked beans on our knees. It could have been the food of kings!

The Bahá'í Message

We sat away from the fire and became quiet and expectant as the Ives' were introduced to speak. We were to see the skilled operation of an experienced team of husband and wife. Mabel spoke first on the world aspects of the Bahá'í Faith, stressing its call to universality. She listed and explained the Bahá'í Principles derived from the Writings of Bahá'u'lláh – revealed over a century ago. Among these were a list of concepts. In those early days they were challenging, even explosive – far reaching in their call, not to a locality, but to the whole world. For example, mankind is one, the religions are one, all racial, national and religious and class prejudice must be abandoned. There must come universal education, a universal language, a world court, a world administrative body. By eliminating the roots of dissention, she said, universal peace would ultimately follow.

"How can we achieve such a state of mind?" somebody asked.

"By still another Bahá'í Principle," she responded. "The independent investigation of truth."

There was a thoughtful silence. We had all been seekers, each in our own way. We had remained cool to the insistent dogmas of the church, the weird statistics of psychical research, the egoistic goals of the modern cults into which we had probed. Had we perhaps been perishing for a firm belief in something reasonable, something scientific, and at the same time something warm?

Mabel's strong confident voice laid every treasure before us in dazzling array, and somehow, truth could never again be piecemeal. In our minds a new thought exploded: the concept of oneness – a concept to be loved as a reality, for itself!

In that flash of illumination, we accepted the integration of our ideas and of our world.

Speaking quietly, Howard told us of an Entity, veiled in light, whom he called "the Manifestation of God". This being had born the name of Zoroaster, Krishna, Buddha, Moses, Christ, Muhammad, and, in recent times, the names of the Báb and Bahá'u'lláh. Their words were the Messages of the Holy Spirit made vocal, each in its own day.

In their dual station, the Manifestations or chosen Intermediaries between God and Man were men – and yet, more than men. Their messages were from one Source: God – the Unknowable Essence. All taught the singleness of God, Whose laws they brought. All taught the love of God and love of "thy neighbour". They brought the laws and ordinances of God that differed with the changing times. Now, at the summit of the long cycle of human history and evolution and in a time of great danger to the human race through world strife, not one, but two exalted Beings had appeared. The Message for this day was Justice, and through World Order, peace.

Here, indeed, was a new idea, a Christ returned! "Like a thief in the night," said Howard. When he invited questions, our instinctive need was to relate to our previous beliefs the supreme fact that he had revealed. But how could his answer be reconciled to such a group as were gathered before him? The agnostic and atheistic scientists, the churchman, the searchers in the humanistic cults.

Sometimes it seemed as if Howard had left us when, with open palms and head thrown back, he sat in silent prayer. Then he would rise up, his deep eyes flashing, his white mane vibrant on his head, and the answers would come through an electrified atmosphere.

He told us, "Instead of giving up Christ you will find Him. Yes, God spoke through His prophets. Did He not say to Moses, 'I am the Lord, thy God.' Yes, this is in fulfilment of prophecy. The prophecy of all the prophets foretold this Day."

"Science?" asked Rex Collison.

"Science and religion will enhance and prove each other.

How can one truth contradict another truth?"

"Reincarnation?" That was my question.

"It is true that we are born again after leaving this world, but not in the sense of reincarnation. In the next world we will continue to advance into higher stations, if we so desire. Births will be necessary to attain to these, just as tonight a new world and a new birth lie before you. Your first birth was from the womb. Even in this world, a 'second birth' is available to the awakened soul."

"Proofs of the prophet?" Here was the challenge to investigate truth, Howard told us. "The life of the Prophet and His Teachings are the unassailable proofs."

"How do we know that They were sent by God?"

"Whence came that dynamic power to uplift humanity of the world religions that bear their names?"

His voice stopped, as did our questions. We sat silent, amazed by another and personal proof. We had beheld a man communing with an Unseen Power. We had watched him bring inspired, reasonable, and acceptable answers back from another realm.

Such was the power in the room, our eyes, too, were suddenly opened to it. A place of spirit had, somehow, signalled us. The man, Howard Ives, had become a part of his message, had become something more than the flow of words, the voice, the movement of hands in prayer. More than his eyes looking into ours with a compassionate comradeship. Our defences dispersed. The Message flowed into our separate worlds like a sudden flood. I believed. We all believed.

It had been a happening. There are different ways of saying it. For example, a boat on a sluggish, weed-hampered stream enters a main current that effortlessly speeds it along. A painting, obscured by dust, is restored to the artist's original colours. A fish, floundering on the beach is returned to the sea by a kind of ninth wave; a half dead person is revived by oxygen. Many times when the early Bahá'ís were with us, our spirits were to feel this release. Tonight, this night with Howard and Mabel, had been our first.

I had one last question for Howard as he held my hands in a goodbye: "How does one pray?" Howard and Mabel exchanged the look of conspiring parents.

He said "Dare I?"

She nodded, and he slipped into my hands his own worn prayer book to take home.

I tried to sleep that night, but I had to give it up because I found myself spiritually awake for the first time in my life. Of course, I had had lovely thoughts before, induced by some book or other that I was reading, but these had been passing thoughts that had made me feel comfortable, like a church service does for some people.

I asked myself, "What had I learned from contact with the passionate sincerity of Howard's words?" That there was a world of spirit and that there was an Essence there – a knowing and responsive ENTITY. That Howard had addressed this Being and had been inspired in the answering of our questions. That it followed that we, too, could pray, establishing a kinship with this Power, with Bahá'u'lláh as an intermediary.

Yet, marvelling at this new dimension of my understanding, I was miserable. The intonations of Howard's voice seemed still to ring out, "Mankind is one! All prejudices must be abandoned." How could I, with my own two or three choice prejudices, qualify as a Bahá'í? In the searchlight of these teachings, how ugly my faults were! Were the doors closing? For a few hours I had thought that I belonged to "the new creation" mentioned by my teachers. Now I was a little less secure.

I arose and lit a candle, turned the pages of Howard's prayer book and prayed, almost with fear, that these hindrances might be removed.

My prayer was answered overnight. In the morning I awoke with a free, unsullied soul. This I knew through an experience of faith – a positive knowledge of things divine.

Mary Collison telephoned to ask, "Are you still up in the air?"

"Yes, I am," I replied, "and I never want to come down!" Neither Mary nor I ever did come down.

We Meet Other Bahá'ís

In the days that followed, the ground had vanished and yet we had no wings. There was now a bewildering sense of unreality about the human plane. Sometimes we did not seem real to each other. When I look back today, only the days since our acceptance of Bahá'u'lláh seem real. As our new life began to grow, the old receded.

Howard and Mabel guided us with parental concern, returning as often as they could to instruct and to inspire us. We were soon to meet their closest friends, Grace and Harlan Ober, for we were invited to attend a "Feast" at the Obers' home in Buffalo and to spend the night.

We took flight like seven young birds following their parent birds to a clime where always the sun shines and roses bloom. Those who rode in the Ives' car had the added advantage of a tour, with Howard as guide, through *The Seven Valleys*. On we flew through the spiritual landscape of the Valleys that symbolize the seven stages of the progress of the soul: the Valleys of Search, of Love, of Knowledge, of Unity, of Contentment, of Wonderment.

"Now," proclaimed Howard, "we come to the seventh Valley, the Valley of Annihilation." Just then a heavy truck tore past with a screech of doomsday – missing us, it seemed, by only half an inch. "Praise be to God," said Howard, watching the road a little more carefully the rest of the way.

"Why is the Seventh Valley described as the one of 'annihilation'?"

"Bahá'u'lláh describes it this way: This station is the dying from self and the living in God; being poor before God and rich in the Desired One. It is a stage corresponding to the unitive life of the Christian mystics."

We arrived at the Obers' house on a pleasant Buffalo street. Close together in defensive formation, our country group filed into the hall and on into the oval of people which occupied two connecting rooms. I was conscious of my new hat, a large blue scoop lined with lavender shirred silk, a hat I had bought to fortify my ego for this occasion. For a moment all eyes turned toward us. Then the reading continued and several people spoke.

Only one speaker do I remember. She was a slim young woman with smiling grey eyes, her pallor and luminosity set off by a wine-coloured velvet dress. When asked to speak, she told a simple story to remind us that we were "all children of one God." The impact of her personality was stunning. I was so stirred by her, that when I was invited to say a few words, I stood up and said merely, "I am speechless!" and sat down.

When the closing prayers were said, this vision of a person moved down the room, stood before me and took both my hands. She looked deeply into my eyes, nodded, and said, "You are the one!" I knew by my excited heartbeat that this was no casual meeting.

Her name was Dorothy Beecher (later, Dorothy Baker). Her job was to tell stories to children in the Buffalo schools. Her grandmother had been named "Mother Beecher" by 'Abdu'l-Bahá, but at the time her parents were not Bahá'ís.

Dorothy Beecher had seen right through my hat and veil of acute self-consciousness. Such was not true, however, of my hostess. We laughed, at our next meeting, when Grace Ober confessed that she had classified me as a person "just going along for the ride." This was far from the truth because I had been talking deeply with Howard, and I had been reading. And I had been intrigued by the unsolved mystery of prayer. No, Grace had not seen through me. At breakfast the next morning the conversation deepened, and Grace looked with concern at my impassive face. Later, when I asked, "Where do our prayers go when we pray? Do they go to the Supreme Concourse?", Grace said that she had the surprise of her life.

Willard Gets "Up in the Air"

Although called away by many duties, the Ives did not leave us alone. And the Obers began coming over on weekends. They were another team of husband and wife as inspired and as strong as the Ives. 'Abdu'l-Bahá had married them in 1912, with Howard, then a Universalist minister, officiating.

Sometimes Grace would stay over for a week, visiting among us, answering our questions and, with magnificent designs appearing in outline, weaving for us a new life.

One night Grace and I sat praying by the fireplace in the dining room. Willard, still intellectual in his approach, had asked Grace, "Is it alright for me to be a Bahá'í if I give it only my academic approval?"

With a twinkle in her eye, Grace responded, "Yes certainly Willard, that will be fine."

That night Willard went to a dinner meeting of his University Club to sit with the learned professors of our two local colleges. The subject for the evening was, for them, an unusual one: "Concept of Deity". Being younger, Willard had never spoken before at the Club discussions. That night, however, after listening to the dryness and limitations of their academic minds, Willard rose to his feet and told them about the Manifestations of God and that from them alone, could one learn of the Unknowable Essence. He rushed home to tell us, as "up in the air" as any of us had been. He loved to tell the joke on himself – about his "academic approval". From that night on, he was a most ardent Bahá'í.

From Grace we learned more of the early teachers and the reason they were not like other 'good' people we had known. "Walk thou above the world by the power of the Greatest Name," 'Abdu'l-Bahá had told them, and this, following His footsteps, they had learned to do. In His presence and through His teachings they had found a new range of spirit – an altitude of station beyond the human kingdom. It's a higher plane of existence that I call "the plus level" that is open to them. 'Abdu'l-Bahá called that level "the Spirit of Faith". Thus uplifted, the early teachers had surged forward in a small band, the apostles of a new Day. They were to learn in their human moments, that "the steed of the Valley of Love is pain." The rising and falling between the higher and lower levels of Nearness is part of the process by which maturity is won. It was their firmness of intention that never wavered. Even while swept by emotional tests, they remained firm as a rock.

More About Howard and Mabel

From their friends we learned more about Howard and Mabel. After meeting 'Abdu'l-Bahá, Howard had given up his ministry and his security. His marriage broke up and his little daughter, Muriel, remained with her mother. Howard travelled and taught and tried to make a living.

In 1920 he married Mabel Rice Wray, an equally devoted early Bahá'í teacher who also had met 'Abdu'l-Bahá in 1912. After an unsuccessful business venture, they faced the fact that there was no easy way to find the freedom to teach to others the principles of their religion. They sold their things and accepted a joint selling job in Pittsburgh, peddling a course of literature for people who had not gone to college. Together they sold the books and Howard gave a course of lectures on them.

The selling of books would be followed by a six-week course of lectures requiring two or three months. At the end of the lecture series, the Ives advertised free public talks on the Bahá'í Faith. Usually, study classes would follow and from them, Bahá'í groups would form.

By living very frugally, the Ives managed. One wondered how they could have done it. Recklessly they burned themselves out and only through stressed concentration, were they able to balance their Bahá'í activities with keeping alive. They were truly heroes, but they did not pretend to be saints. They kept their enthusiasm all through a life made up of crises. There would be good food and good times. Always the Ives were human. Always the Ives were fun. Certainly, this is a high station: to appreciate the good things that God has given us and, yet, to give them up gladly – to be detached.

Mabel, in her remodelled handed-down clothes, was dainty and feminine; Howard, in his shiny grey suit, was distinguished. Together, they were an aristocracy of spirit.

Lessons in Prayer

Looking back on our early efforts to deepen in the Faith, I realize that one cannot learn how to pray. One can learn about prayer, but actual prayer, as "conversation with God", comes as a "grace" or a gift, unexpected and undeserved. A feeling fills one's heart. Should this take place and, with it, a glimmer of love for that unknowable Being called God, one is ready and eager for another step – the discipline of prayer.

"I know the Manifestation is the Intermediary, but He too, seems so far away. How can I know God?"

"There is no knowledge of God except through an experience of the Holy Spirit emanating through His Manifestation," one of our teachers replied.

"What is the Holy Spirit?"

After a moment's thought, "It is a stepdown transformer of God's love."

The Nineteen-Day Fast was approaching, and Grace Ober agreed to visit Geneva during the first week to "teach us to pray". On the first day of the Fast, Willard and I ate before dawn and drove to the Collisons'. Grace had planned for us an order of prayers: The Greatest Name ninety-five times; the long and beautiful Dawn Prayer with its refrain, "Thou seest me, o my God, holding to Thy Name, the Holy, the Shining, the Precious, the Greatest, The Highest, The Abhá . . ." (This was the translation in use at that time); then a prayer for spiritual qualities; nineteen prayers to the "Remover of Difficulties"; and healing prayers.

There is no ritual of prayer in the Bahá'í Faith. This we knew. But Willard and I, remembering our first Fast, adhered long afterwards to this program of prayers as planned for us by Grace.

The Night the Ice Went Out

The Tioga River was nearby. As the later days of winter lingered, we longed to see the river flowing openly again. With consternation and hope we longed for that annual event when the pistol-like cracking would signal the break-up of the ice which would be cast up in five- to six-foot-deep chunks on the roads and lawns and would damage some of the houses. It was the irresistible response of the river to the pressure of warming weather – to the coming of spring rains. When the ice went out, the landscape changed. That night was an event to be talked about and noted in diaries. Our first Naw-Rúz was like that.

We carried a social self-consciousness into our Bahá'í lives; a self-consciousness distant from an awareness of the "real" people inside others. We had each our private store of thoughts and a fear of "what the others would think". There was a desire to protect ourselves through self-concealment. This was our build-up of ice – an accumulation of low temperature responses.

With the Fast and its dawn prayers over, we were a little more aware of the spiritual forces playing about us, but we were still the searchers, the scientific investigators. Our knowledge was deepened, we had accepted the Message, and our emotions remained shallow.

Grace, with Harlan, drove back from Buffalo to make us a Persian pilau which she had learned from Maḥmúd, 'Abdu'l-Bahá's cook. She brought with her a large tray of burnished brass that had held so many feasts in the past. When Willard and I arrived at the home of Dr and Lucy Heist, the food was already cooked and waiting to be arranged on the tray.

We saw built before us an amazing structure of baked, buttered rice, a crown of carrots cut lengthwise, the space between filled with chopped nuts and olives, peas, and whole onions. This was the first layer. There was another layer of rice, with a decorative design of dates, sliced peppers and tomatoes and French cut green beans. The brass tray was hidden by a mounded edifice of blended foods. Today we would call it "gourmet".

The Feast, earthly symbol of spiritual bounty, was eaten in the big kitchen of the Heist home, where floated the odours of the cooked food. We ate, much aware of the significance of this, our first, Naw-Rúz Feast. Then, regaled, we sat at the table and listened to Grace talk. While she spoke, her radiance made us aware that the presence and remembered face of 'Abdu'l-Bahá was with her. She quoted his words, saying that "food prepared with love is healing for the body, the mind, and the soul," and that this food tonight had been special because it was offered with His hospitality.

As she talked, Grace lived again in those days of 1912 when the Master had visited North America. While speaking of the food, she recalled that Maḥmúd had prepared dishes like this. He had come as a cook and she had noticed him as he came off the boat from steerage, wearing a turban on his head and a ground-length black robe. On his back he carried a featherbed, or mat. Little had Grace realized just how intimate would become her relations with this elderly man who spoke only Persian.

On this occasion all eyes were drawn to 'Abdu'l-Bahá with his silvery white hair, fez, and oriental robe; fragile looking but taking long steps; not tall, but looking tall. He was making welcoming gestures with His hands. Walking behind Him would have been His small entourage of interpreters and aides.

When news arrived that 'Abdu'l-Bahá was coming to America, Grace had offered her services. She had thought of herself, she admitted, as a hostess, arranging flowers and extending gracious welcomes to guests. When the arrangements were made, Grace was assigned to a much different station – that of helping Maḥmúd in the kitchen. This was, she told us, an example of 'Abdu'l-Bahá's humour. "He sends us tests to burnish our souls."

Grace confided that her weakness had been pride of family, talent, and attainment. Now, with the Master actually under the same roof, her task was to clean the pans stuck up with rice cake! She described the slow baking of the rice in the oven and the golden crusts that adhered to the pans. Poor Grace! The pots and pans became monsters. And, worst of all, the Master had not singled her out for praise and attention.

Then one day, all the happy, shining-eyed people were leaving with the Master for the West Englewood Picnic. The pots were standing in the sink and Grace could not leave her kitchen. This was the climax. She hid herself behind the door and began to cry. Suddenly, swinging open the concealing door, 'Abdu'l-Bahá was in the kitchen. With love and laughter He paraphrased her name. Instead of Grace, He called her Grease, rolling the G so that the word was "Gggrease". The weight rolled off her heart and she laughed. She was soon to learn that 'Abdu'l-Bahá had arranged for her to go with the others to the picnic.

We ate the Master's food from the big brass tray that night. Then listening to the many loving stories, we were all laughing and crying like little children. Somehow, Grace had brought into that kitchen the irresistible charm of the Master, His penetration of the mind, His bubbling spirits, His fatherly concern and His eyes that made souls transparent. Such love was transmitted to us. It melted the ice of pride or resentment and the congealment of constraint and fear. These negative feelings, often called "human," did leave us that night and we were happy and unburdened as never before. We were unified with each other.

We had come to our first Naw-Rúz Feast as people not very intimate with one another. We had accepted, but intellectually, the Bahá'í Teachings and we were not in the habit of knowing anyone well. The atmosphere of this Naw-Rúz had the effect of sun on ice. We saw one other for the first time as real people. We ceased to hide from one another and began to care truly. Grace Ober had, through her association with 'Abdu'l-Bahá shown us how He cared about everybody.

Never again did the ice re-form as it had. Not only had we laughed; we had wept. We would never forget "the Night the Ice Went Out".

Our First Assembly

We formed the Spiritual Assembly of Geneva, New York in May 1925. Included in our "community" were the couples of the original group that had been introduced to the Faith at the Collisons' bean supper. There were, also, Willard's mother, Edith; his sisters Marguerite and Christine; and two youth members, Elizabeth and Lucille Heist.

The manner in which Edith McKay became a Bahá'í was a triumph of human lucidity. A typical lady belonging to a church for many years could, at that time, be expected to recoil in alarm from statements that challenged not only her ideas of organized religion but, also, offered a dizzy perspective of world affairs. But Edith McKay was not a typical lady. She was actually a pioneer in higher education for women. She was among one of the first classes of women to graduate from Cornell University.

We told her one morning about the Cause as Marguerite, Willard and I hovered anxiously beside her bed. We waited. Why didn't she say something? When she spoke it was to tell us, "You haven't told me a thing that doesn't make common sense." On hearing the message, she had become a Bahá'í.

The formation of the Geneva Assembly took place around the fireplace in the book room at the farm – the room adjoining Edith's. She listened from her bed to the proceedings and sometimes her voice joined in. That night, she listened with us to the reading of letters from Bahá'ís across the country, letters which welcomed us with such love, into the Faith. Our hearts were thrilled with the knowledge that there were people reaching out to us. This special welcoming into the family of Bahá had been arranged by our spiritual parents, the Ives, who had written to several friends.

I am sure that we were all stirred deeply by the importance of our commitment. I know that I was. The next morning, I sat in a deck chair by a flowering syringa bush, an open Bahá'í book in my lap. (It was the old Bahá'í Scriptures.) The acres of cherry trees were in white bloom, the apple and pear trees were budded and all their fragrances blended. I envisioned before me, two paths: one, relatively smooth, was tracing to the present familiar ways of my life; the other had turns around which I could not see, a rough, steeply ascending path. That I have remembered for more than fifty years this setting, this occasion, marks that morning as a Moment of Truth. I rejoiced in my decision to take the upward winding path.

Conflict of the Old and the New

The early summer brought a conflict of old and new personal relationships. A weekend was planned, with the Ives and Obers coming, and the Bahá'í friends were invited to a large meeting. I received from Isabel a telegram telling me that she was coming from Washington to spend several days at that time, too. I had known Isabel in Art School and we always looked forward to our get-togethers.

Isabel arrived. All went delightfully well until it was time to prepare her for the coming of the Bahá'ís. As we relaxed on the lawn, I took a long breath and began.

"Isabel, do you believe that Christ will come again?"

Her response came from a Georgia Baptist background, "Oh, yes, indeed!"

"Well, what would you say if I told you He has already come?"

"I wouldn't want to hear another word about it!" She left me, stalking proudly into the house.

"Just let her meet Harlan Ober," I prayed. Especially Harlan. I had absolute faith in his powers of persuasion. He had, along with the arguments of his fine Harvard-trained mind, all the endearing social virtues. "He will talk to Isabel," I told myself happily. "He will make her understand."

That night twenty-five Bahá'ís came to the meeting. All were intoxicated with the wine of the spirit, loving and embracing one another. All except Isabel, who was in bed with a raging headache.

"I'll run up and say some prayers for her," decided Grace, who made for the stairs. I followed. Grace perched herself on the bed and put her hand on Isabel's head. Isabel moaned and turned her head aside, muttering, "Please go away."

The next morning my indisposed guest was leaving by train. Twelve or more people were serving themselves breakfast and eating close together at the kitchen table or in the breakfast nook. Isabel would not speak to me. Standing, she looked around helplessly. I brought Harlan downstairs and begged him: "Harlan, you must help her! You will know what to say. This is serious!"

Harlan found Isabel a corner in which to sit down, consulted with her about her choice of breakfast, served her and then sat down with her and engaged in intense conversation. Presently they came to me, and Harlan announced, "I'm driving Isabel to the train, will you come with us?" Isabel, smiling now, affectionately took my hand.

We saw her off and I could see by her smiles that she had "gone with a gladsome heart". What had Harlan said to cause this transformation? He explained it. "The Master told us we must serve every soul – but we must find the plane on which the person can be served, whether material, intellectual, or spiritual. I found that plane with Isabel and I served her. I served her breakfast."

"But I saw you talking. What did you tell her?"

"I asked her about her interesting work in Washington. If we are to serve with love, we must serve with understanding."

Those were impressionable days. More and more were we conditioned to accept the infinite variety manifest in the Bahá'ís and to feel respect for the family bond that united all of us as Children of the Kingdom. We were told, "You will find that there are human faults in the most devoted Bahá'ís. We are enjoined to humility, and what can make a person feel more humble than to acknowledge before God his own failures and faults?" As in a garden, while hoeing the weeds, we are cultivating the plants.

It is part of the balance of our natures – the silhouette of light against dark – man in his lower aspect wrestling with the angel of his higher self.

In the teachings of the Faith, we are not to mention the faults of others, and we are to speak of our own faults only to God. But we must not be egotistical in our self-abasement. Only with self-forgetfulness are we free to concentrate on God. Why have we not learned this? "Make your will a door through which the confirmations of the spirit come," 'Abdu'l-Baha had said.

We were helped to see that "use of the will" meant not to experience an expanded consciousness, the quest of so many seekers. Rather, we were to learn and to relearn that the practice of will is a love response experience, a self-forgetfulness because of an absorption in God. Even when we fail to achieve the absorption, our trying is itself a means of maturity and growth.

Grace's Station of Servitude

Our greatest lesson had been to see and to hear Grace pray on our behalf. When she prayed, the strong, capable, assertive Grace became a beggar. We would steal glances under lowered eyelids at her pale oval face, ordinarily so animated, cast now in a line of passionate entreaty. Her outstretched hands were urgent in their appeal.

I can see her now, a harmony of rounded lines. She had large green-flecked hazel eyes, heavy lids and a wide curved mouth; sloping shoulders. She could make herself irresistibly comical, turn herself into a clown. In her younger days Grace may have been a strawberry blonde. Now there were tints of burnt sienna in her greying hair. Her artist's training was reflected in her choice of clothes: tans, yellowy greens, reddish browns, and oranges predominated. Her wardrobe brought forth the appearance of a strong and compelling personality. The effect was one of both inner and outer unity.

Sometimes my poetic temperament found Grace a bit hard to take. One spring morning I took her to a treasured retreat near our house – a little grove where a brook lazed over mossy stones. The path leading there was edged with white and purple violets. "You must come and see the violets," I urged. Grace came, talking about the Teachings while her sensible flathead shoes stepped blindly on the flowers!

Grace and Mabel were, at this time, twin engines in the advancement and organization of the Cause. They were, as 'Abdu'l-Bahá would have called them, true "maidservants of the Merciful". But it was for Howard and Harlan that I had felt romantic affections. Such is the waywardness of the heart.

A Talk with Mabel Ives

While Howard was carrying on business that spring, we invited Mabel to stay with us for a rest. She delighted in the respite from exhausting efforts to make a living and from her strenuous teaching activities. Her habit had been to "keep going" until she was ill. She would take a rest, and then throw herself back into the grind. Those days of her visit in 1925 were welcomed for this restoration of "strength to serve the Kingdom". This time, Mabel was not ill and Nature's energies fed the flame of her soul.

Mabel could never get enough of the sun or of being outdoors. She partook wholeheartedly of nature to a degree that only Willard and I could appreciate. One morning, a farm helper passing nearby saw our dignified leader of meetings suspended upside down from a tree and chanting loudly the Greatest Name. "God is the Most Glorious." She came down laughing.

Especially helpful for me were our talks. It was a hopeful time. The world was then sandwiched between two wars and we and our friends actually believed that, by his League of Nations Treaty with its Thirteen Points, Woodrow Wilson had "made the world safe for democracy". Had not Mabel, herself, said that Wilson's daughter was a Bahá'í and that the President kept on his desk, a card with the Bahá'í Principles?

It was one of those beautiful days and Mabel and I sat drying our hair in the little formal garden that Willard and I had built. I observed, "The Bahá'í World is sweetness and light and soon the whole world will be transformed."

"I wish that could be true," replied Mabel, "but further trouble will beset the world." Threatening dark clouds drifted over the garden bleaching some of the radiance from the flowers. I shivered.

She continued, "How else can the established institutions of the world be ultimately destroyed so that new ones can be built in their place? How can we build the New World Order on a foundation so obviously defective? She quoted Bahá'u'lláh, 'Abdu'l-Bahá and Shoghi Effendi.

The dark clouds drifted away and sunshine returned to the

garden. Mabel assured me that, after a darkened period, the world itself would come back into the full light, like our garden. "Are not the affairs of the world," she observed, "in the hands of Divine Providence?"

The "Practice in Speaking" Class

While Mabel was with us, she started a "Practice in Speaking Class". The purpose was to train the Collisons and the McKays to chair meetings and to make short talks on a variety of subjects based on a study of the Writings: the "Two Natures of Man," "Can Human Nature Change?", "What is Truth?" among others. We were businesslike. We made outlines on filing cards and we explored the few Bahá'í books that were available in those early days. Most of those books are available no longer today, books like *Divine Philosophy*, *The Wisdom of 'Abdu'l-Bahá*, and the *Bahá'í Scriptures*. Mabel would drill us. One of us would act as chairman and the others would take turns in giving ten-minute talks. We would stand and address an imaginary audience. After each talk, the chairman would ask for questions. Despite the fact that all of us had been schoolteachers and should have been at ease on our feet and comfortable before a group, the fun of the Practice in Speaking Class was that, with our bright-eyed teacher observing us so closely, we were very nervous. After Mabel left, we continued the practice by ourselves.

Teaching

We were learning so much during that first year and, even more important, we were learning to teach! All through the spring, Lucy Heist taught her Sunday School class. ("I don't see why I can't," she said. "I believe in Christ even more now that I know that He has returned.") There were actually two classes, each for adult women. One Sunday nobody came to Lucy's class. She sat for an hour in an empty classroom, her Bible opened to the verses she had intended to read. In silence she sat and prayed. When the hour was over Lucy stood by the church door and greeted warmly her students, who had gone to the other class. Only one woman came back to speak to her. "Mrs Heist. We all like you, but we can't stand your teaching."

"What is wrong with my teaching?" queried Lucy.

"We believe in the Devil and you don't." Thus ended a church relationship of many years.

Jimmy Tollis

There is the story of Jimmy Tollis. He was Italian and the manager of a local fruit farm. One night Rex Collison brought him to our group. He listened very attentively but said almost nothing. On a later visit, becoming more communicative, he told us his story.

When Jimmy was a little boy in Italy, he was sent out one morning to pick dried beans. A stranger came walking down the road with a pack on his back. He approached Jimmy and said, "If you will give me a handful of those beans, I will give you one of these books." He drew a book out of his bag. Jimmy accepted it and the stranger went off munching the beans. The next Sunday Jimmy took the book to the priest. (Apparently it was a tract of *The Gospel According to St. John*.) The priest ripped out the pages and gave back to Jimmy the now empty covers. "These are for you," he said, and proceeded to tear the pages themselves into pieces which he threw out the church window. Jimmy vowed that, someday, he would read the other Bible – the Protestant one.

At twenty-one Jimmy emigrated to the United States. As he walked up an Ellis Island street one Sunday morning, he saw people entering a Protestant church. He followed them in and never returned to the Roman Catholic Church. In time Jimmy learned to speak English and joined a Protestant church but never did he find the answers he was seeking. This is not strange, for he did not know what questions to ask. Like many of us, he was starving for a truth he could not find! When he read in the newspaper the word "Bahá'í", he went to Rex Collison's desk at the New York State Experimental Farm. Rex told him about our class. It was uplifting to our spirits to feel that our classes were really teaching. Jimmy never missed a meeting. He would smile and nod as he listened, but what was he thinking? We asked him about his wife, Mary, would she like to come? "She will come – sometime," he would say.

One night his smile was wider. He had talked to Mary. He had begun by telling her, "Mary, these people say that Christ has come again."

"What is His Name?" she asked.

"Bahá'u'lláh."

"I knew it," she exclaimed. "A few weeks ago I saw that Name written in letters of gold across the sky. I had forgotten it, but I know it began with a 'B.'"

Mary accepted the Faith at once and came with Jimmy to the next meeting.

A Nervous First Meeting with Louis Gregory

Louis Gregory was going to visit our new community and it was arranged that he would stay at our house. With the exception of the Ives and Obers, he was our first Bahá'í guest. Louis was in vigorous middle age and he seemed to my inexperienced eye, like an elongated being from another planet: long legs, long arms, long neck. His head was so very far above mine. The physical qualities pointed, as it were, to a lofty altitude of integrity, courage, and resolution. His brown skin veiled from me his face. It was like being introduced to someone in a dark room while being conscious of a magnetic spiritual attraction and power. I thought to myself, "This man is integrated from his roots; from the subsoil of his ancestry. He shot up like a straight young tree towards the sun, the source of his growth." His face appeared affable, yet so self-contained and quite unreadable. At that moment of meeting, I was not prepared for anyone like this.

Louis took a brief rest in his room and I heard him coming down the backstairs. I was still feeling very rattled and worried about saying the wrong thing. He asked me about our group activities, of which we were proud, and about the different members. I complained about the backwardness of one of them. Louis sprang to his feet, snapped his fingers like a firecracker and, saying not a word, retired to his room! I had been backbiting, of course; praising myself and feeling superior, committing a whole category of insidious Bahá'í crimes. I was left to think of Grace Ober's oft repeated words from 'Abdu'l-Bahá, "All voices are from the King."

Later that afternoon, when the sunlight in the long low room was beginning to wane, I saved myself from walking into Louis. He was prostrated on our Khasak rug, flat in prayer. With agility and grace he arose, smiled and said, "There's a little of the oriental in me, I think." There was no reference to our first little talk.

I was to meet Louis Gregory again and again over the years. He was ever an example, always serving the Faith with wholehearted devotion. He comes in and out of the story of my years, but I shall never forget the lesson that he taught me on his first day in my life.

Green Acre, the Convention of 1925

"July is the time to go to Green Acre," declared Mabel. "The National Convention of the Bahá'ís of the United States and Canada will be held there. This will be your opportunity to meet the administrators and the teachers – to see what the Cause is really like. May Maxwell will be there. Wait till you see HER!"

When I talk about that first Convention, some dear friends have protested, "But there had been other conventions before 1925." This is true. But while I can say that this was my own first Convention, it was also the first Convention, under the Guardian, of the National Spiritual Assembly of the United States and Canada. With Shoghi Effendi guiding the development of an unfolding world administrative order, this Convention was unique. It was not an isolated national event; it was part of an new international initiative.

We drove with the Collisons. The Heists would be coming too and Jim Harlan and his wife Anne. We wound our way through the White Mountains and now, late in the afternoon, as we neared the old seafaring town of Portsmouth, New Hampshire, we caught the tangy scent of the marshes. We were but four miles from Eliot, Maine and Green Acre. The car was silent now. Each of us was excited in our own special way. My own feelings were of anticipation, bordering on a fear of coming into contact with the spiritual voltage of the great Bahá'ís whose names were familiar to us. A mole-like part of me feared the light and a moth-like counterpart wanted to rush blindly towards it. Both the mole and the moth rolled on swiftly.

We first saw hallowed Green Acre in the slanting rays of the late-afternoon sun. We could not mistake the corner where we were to turn, marked by a gift shop and tea-room and, by the road, a large flower. Now we saw the white three-storey inn on a rise of ground overlooking the Piscataqua River. A breeze stirred the silky pink and gold grass on the slopes.

The veranda fronting the inn was empty but animated voices emanated from the dining-room. The crowd from Geneva gathered around the desk before slipping into the dining-room to order a New England dinner of baked beans, hot biscuits and blueberry pie. Our shy arrival was disrupted as soon as Howard and Mabel discovered us. They greeted us warmly, with loud welcoming cries and engineered the moving of tables so that we could sit together. Later they whisked us down the long veranda to a room called "the Hall". In it was a raised platform trimmed with garden flowers and lights. Piloted by Howard and Mabel, we stepped into a constellation of brightly shining people – people who would become, with time, intimate and dear to us – Doris and Horace Holley, Jessie and Ethel Revell, Hebe Struven, Harriet and Curtis Kelsey. Then, there was May.

May Maxwell seemed to be a person set apart by an almost visible aura; outwardly, she was a being of such beauty and poise and of such a power of attraction that we had to restrain ourselves from staring at her. Years later in attempting to describe her, I wrote that the memory of her was a "perfume that could not be contained in a bottle". And it was years later that she was to conquer my shy withdrawal from her.

The next morning, I awoke early and slipped out by myself to look around Green Acre and to inhale its atmosphere. As I walked, I meditated: "What had Howard meant when he had talked about 'The Meeting'? What had I seen in Dorothy, that strange, beautiful girl in Buffalo, and now, in May Maxwell? What were the stations of the human soul and how was it that some people seemed to be mysteriously nearer to God?"

After a long look at the garden, a stroll along the lane past the tearoom, I came to Fellowship House. I found myself in a handsome living room that opened onto a veranda overlooking the river. A tall, red-haired lady appeared. She embraced me lovingly. While still in the arms of this radiant being, I said, "But I don't know you." "That makes no difference," she declared. "You soon will." She was Mariam Haney, mother of Paul Haney who would become later a Hand of the Cause of God. How true was her statement! Through correspondence and occasional meetings we became close friends. It was through her encouragement that I was able to write numerous articles for *Star of the West* and later the *Bahá'í Magazine*, which she co-edited with Stanwood Cobb.

Back at the Hall the chairs were arranged for the Convention. A quartet of Black singers had been hired. Their rousing spirituals brought the hundred or so delegates and friends to their seats. Montfort Mills, who had been recently with the Guardian, opened the meeting. The roll of delegates was called and their alternates acknowledged. In those days of long train journeys from opposite sides of the country, alternates were accepted.

Today, there are more than one hundred National Assemblies in the World. In 1925 the National Spiritual Assembly of the United States and Canada was the eighth. The structure which now is called Bahá'í Administration was set up in accordance with the Guardian's plans for world growth of the Faith. We were there to see it happen.

Did our Geneva Bahá'ís grasp how historic was this occasion? Only dimly. I wrote down the words of the Guardian as spoken by Mr Mills. The message said:

> "It is difficult to break with some of the customs and traditions of the past and familiarize the vast number of Bahá'ís, so diverse in their outlook and conceptions, with the necessary changes and requirements of this new phase of the history of the Cause."

The stir among the assembled Bahá'ís was in the womb of a promised New World Order. Across the world the beloved Guardian was saying, in effect, "it is incumbent to live the life and spread the Teachings, but in this day, more is required; to step into the Formative Period of the Faith and become imbued with its spirit."

In my state of immaturity, I could imbibe only milk. I was quite incapable of digesting such solid food as our new Administrative Order. It was in my more sensory impressions of the spirit of that meeting that I found the nourishment to encourage my growth.

Mr Howard MacNutt

The road that ran along the Green Acre property passed a dense grove called "The Pines". Among the tallest trees was one called "'Abdu'l-Bahá's Pine". Beneath it, in 1912, the Master had addressed a circle of early believers and had chanted prayers. To the Bahá'ís that spot was sacred, and ever since, the friends would slip away to this place to pray there.

It had been arranged. The group from Geneva was to meet with a very great Bahá'í, Howard MacNutt, who would talk about the deeper Teachings of the Faith. Mr MacNutt had learned Persian and had translated some of 'Abdu'l-Bahá's American talks. He had assisted also in the early translation of Bahá'u'lláh's majestic *Kitáb-i-Íqán*. Mr and Mrs MacNutt had been believers since 1898. Well aware of our great privilege, we sought the MacNutts in the pine grove.

For several afternoons we would meet at two o'clock and trail along the path through the pines to the giant tree. There we would find waiting for us, the white-haired MacNutts and their little dog. We would sit at their feet on a carpet of pine needles and open our hearts to Mr MacNutt's words as he set forth the teachings of 'Abdu'l-Bahá: unity, love, God, the Holy Spirit. The sun would slant down through the branches, releasing the scent of the pines. Mr MacNutt's face was radiant.

On our last afternoon, Howard MacNutt took out a manuscript roll of prayers that he had translated while in 'Akká and in the presence of the Master. The passion and power in the prayers, seemingly beyond the power of those in our prayer books, was more like those in the Tablets 'Abdu'l-Bahá revealed to the Persian Bahá'ís – more mystical and more poetic. With 'Abdu'l-Bahá's permission, Howard MacNutt could keep and use the prayers but could not publish them. It was our appreciated bounty to have him share them with us.

Our Geneva group was not entirely on the receiving line. News of our Practice in Speaking Class had been spread by the Ives. So, one morning, after one of the sessions, we found ourselves before a large gathering assembled on the veranda of Fellowship House. The four of us sat frozen in the front row while a very bland Louis Gregory, describing himself as a "deacon in the Baptist Church", introduced himself as chairman. He called upon us to present the arguments of the Faith as we would address them to orthodox Christians, scientists, agnostics, and any one of the modern cults such as Christian Science or theosophy. After our talks we were to answer questions. Our knees were shaking. I remember how the rigid line of Rex Collison's jaw revealed his stress, and I can hear my own creaking voice. But our beautiful audience of star Bahá'ís were praying for us as we plunged into our talk. The question period was uproarious. Thunderous applause rewarded our efforts and our audience crowded around to embrace us. It had been an emotional experience for the practice speakers: first to be abjectly helpless, then to be raised up by unstinted praise. Not so hard to be a martyr after all!

Dr Susan Moody

At one of the evening meetings Dr Susan Moody spoke. She was seventy-five years old, a small, intensely vibrant personality who had returned after fifteen years of service in Teheran. Her pioneer work was in education and health for women and children and it lasted until the government closed the schools. Accompanying her was Lillian Kappes, her companion and co-worker since the early 1900's. I seem to remember Dr Moody in a black-and-white checked dress.

One of her stories was so exciting that the passage of time has not erased it. She told us about a night in Teheran, the last night of the Moslem month of Ramadan, when an aroused mob, ignited with the windup of their fast, raged through the city attacking "foreigners". They came with flares and firearms, roaring down the road to the Bahá'í school. Dr Moody and Lillian were just the kind of prey for which they were looking; two Bahá'ís, and American women at that. They decided to leave the building and to hide behind the bushes. With hearts beating fast they prayed the *Tablet of Ahmad* for "one who is in affliction or grief". The mob approached the gate and the two ladies crouched in the dark reciting, "solve our difficulties ... O God, remove our afflictions." The gang stopped at the gate and fell into violent argument. Distracted from their original intent, they turned away. The Bahá'ís and the school were saved by "the Merciful, the Compassionate."

On the last morning of Convention, after the last prayer, the hired Black singers stood up. They had been listening to Bahá'ís talk all those mornings. Now the last word was theirs. With wide grins they sang most lustily, "The Old Time Religion Is Good Enough For Me". The Convention cheered and people trooped up to shake their hands and to thank them for their songs.

The Pilgrim House

The return of Grace Ober ended any desire to relax after the Green Acre experience. When Grace was around, there were few inactive Bahá'ís. As an instrument of Bahá'u'lláh, she aroused people to activity. She said, "What about the little house? If you have no other use for it, perhaps we could turn it into a Pilgrim House."

We unlocked the door and explored. The largest room was the big square kitchen, which had floor-to-ceiling cupboards. There was a sink with a pump and square paned windows looked both east and west. Downstairs were an old-fashioned sitting room and a small bedroom. Upstairs there were two more bedrooms with sloping gable walls.

Grace's enthusiasm was contagious, and the Pilgrim House became the summer project of the Geneva Assembly. Our two technicians, Rex and Jim, following specifications from a Cornell bulletin, built a fireplace of native stone. After days of ardent labour, with everybody working and contributing, the sad little tenant house came into bloom: scrubbed, plastered, the walls tinted yellow, the woodwork creamy white. The bedroom walls were papered with bright rambling designs. The broad planks of the floors were painted blue and there were blue checked curtains at the windows. The house was nicely furnished, too, with pieces of cast-off furniture. The deep pantry shelves were stacked with white and yellow dishes and shined-up pots and pans. From our house came forks and an old oil cook-stove named "Florence". To the little garden on the east side Willard added dwarf fruit trees.

The Bahá'ís brought food for an opening supper party. By this time, it was early fall, a little cool on that day, and a light rain was falling. We had a perfect opportunity to try the fireplace. The apple wood flared into a splendid draft and the fire warmed and lit the room.

We were told, in the midst of our preparations, that Dr Heist was bringing Mr Siegfried Schopflocher. He entered delightedly into our party and it was an amiable experience to meet him. Since part of the meal was on the cook-stove in our own kitchen and had to be brought to the Pilgrim House at the strategic moment, I found myself running back and forth in the rain. Our guest accompanied me and I was still calling him "Mr Schopflocher". He was calling to me, rather out of breath, "Call me Fled!"

"What did you say?"

"Call me Fled! Fled!"

That was the end of the "misters", although we never did call him "Fred". "Freddie," I think.

Several weeks later another guest arrived. Mother Beecher was to spend the winter with the Collisons. We found her to be a very endearing lady, eighty-five then, very neat and trim, alert and full of humour, authoritative and precise, very perceptive. She spoke clearly, enunciating her words with a precision that she had acquired by listening to and practising oratorical addresses on wax Victor records. We were not allowed to mumble, because she was hard of hearing and did not want to miss a single word. She exhorted us often. "Speak for the edification of all," she would say. It is quite embedded in my consciousness. Mother Beecher – she was also the grandmother of Dorothy, the girl who had claimed me in Buffalo. Mother Beecher had grown up at Clifton Springs, about fifteen miles from Geneva.

Dedication of the Pilgrim House

November 26th, the Day of the Covenant. Twenty-four people made a double semicircle before the fire in our little meeting place and hostel, our renovated Pilgrim House. We had company from Newark, New York, Buffalo, and Rochester. All were making extemporaneous talks under Willard's persuasive chairmanship. The meeting began and ended with prayers of dedication for the House that had been achieved by the unity of our efforts. Before we separated, I brought out a new Guest Book bound in green leather and asked Mother Beecher to be the first to inscribe it. She wrote:

Thanksgiving Day, 1925

The opening and dedication of this Unity Home today will never be forgotten by those who participated in its festivities, both spiritual and material.

Being the Day of the Appointment of the Center of the Covenant, suitable exercises were observed for commemorating that very important event.

Conferences and soul-stirring talks showed the results of deep research and understanding of the inner meanings of the Revelation.

This blessed gathering will no doubt prove to be an inspiration to this group and a preparation for their future work.

May this home, opened by the General Assembly be an eternal blessing to all who enter its door.

With deepest Bahá'í love,

Mother Beecher, aged 85 years

1926

Another Bahá'í year. Naw-Rúz 1926. We went back to Buffalo to attend the Feast. Two carloads of us arrived at the banquet hall where long tables ran the width of the room. There were present a large gathering of Bahá'ís and invited "key people". I sat across the table from Dorothy. She and I had been chosen to give brief talks. I was representing the Geneva Assembly. I was going to be nervous. My hands were icy cold. How could I face this big city knowledgeable crowd? A pot of tulips sat on the table and Dorothy's radiant face swam on the other. I called to her, "Dorothy, there are so many people here, how can I get up and speak? Help!"

She laughed as if it were at a delicious joke. "It is really so simple," she said. "Pretend that you are speaking to just one person and you will never be nervous." So I did. I spoke to one person – Dorothy. Her eyes were twinkling and she was smiling at me, sharing our foolish little joke – the joke that I could be scared! I did make a happy talk and the people applauded with loud cheers. I still remember Dorothy's advice when I need to.

Leonora Holsapple

The Macintosh apple orchard was beginning to show its pink and white bloom, so I know it was in the month of May that Leonora Holsapple came. The enormous seringa bush on the lawn was fragrant and buzzing with bees. Leonora was spending a day with us and we were camping on a Mexican serape spread out on the grass. Leonora had been a class mate of Willard's sister, Marguerite, at Cornell University. She was home now, on a visit from her pioneer post in Bahia, Brazil.

She laughed, "Do you remember, Marguerite, how tongue-tied I used to be? I couldn't raise my voice to speak in class, not even to read aloud!"

"Yes, I do remember," recalled Marguerite. "It was a real affliction, wasn't it?" They talked over old times. Both had had scholarships, both had been bookish and shy, and this had helped to make them friends. Now, through separate channels, they were Bahá'ís. What a difference it made in the basis of their friendship!

We begged this new Leonora to tell us about her decision to pioneer in South America.

"I was at the Convention in New York City when 'Abdu'l-Bahá's *Tablets of the Divine Plan* summoning 'the armies of God,' were revealed. Here are some of His words that stirred us to such a pitch of excitement. I know them by heart:

> Each one is holding in his hand a trumpet, blowing a breath of life into all regions . . . Any soul from among the believers of God who attains to this station, will become known as the Apostle of Bahá'u'lláh.[2]

---

2 'Abdu'l-Bahá, *Tablets of the Divine Plan* (Wilmette, IL: Bahá'í Publishing Trust, 1974), p. 17.

Leonora paused, searched our faces, then continued. "I felt the call to go, but there was every reason why I should not have. It happened to me in this way:

"I had a dream of a comet flashing across the sky with a tail that swept over the whole world. The tail was made of sparks. And now I was a spark rushing with the wind in the wake of the comet. I knew then that I would offer to go to Bahia at the southern tip of Brazil. The language was Portuguese but I would apply myself and learn it. I chose Brazil, remembering 'Abdu'l-Bahá's words that the christening of the city 'Bahia' was through the inspiration of the Holy Spirit."

"What happened after you arrived?" we asked.

"I gave English lessons but this was not enough so I took my savings and bought a house. I take in roomers and give meals. Finally, since I could find no one to listen to the Bahá'í message, I adopted nine orphan girls. When I take in washing and ironing, the girls help me with the work and we make a living. We have a happy household. The girls are taking care of things while I am gone. There are enough of them to make a Spiritual Assembly when they become a little older. They are only teenagers now."

Leonora was our age, still in her early thirties; a woman no longer retiring, but competent and strong.

Convention in Montreal, 1927

The third Convention of the National Spiritual Assembly of the United States and Canada was held in Montreal during the winter of 1927. Willard went as a delegate. He must have come back on a night train because I remember hearing the rattle of the 'tin Lizzy' and the dogs' joyous barking as Marguerite and I were having breakfast. Soon he was standing in the kitchen doorway, tall, slim and ruddy, wearing his old overcoat and without a hat. His excitement was as full of oxygen as the air outside. We settled him with coffee and pancakes and then we asked him, "How about the Convention?"

Willard reported that Montford Mills had been a wonderful

chairman – "an iron hand in a velvet glove", courteous in his handling of the sometimes bewildered delegates who had wakened to find the Cause in a transition state, different from the old days of "the Baháʼí Temple Unity". They were now to share in building the foundation of a new administrative world order on which would be built later, the institution of the Universal House of Justice. The clear vision of this overwhelmingly solemn trust was brought to this early Convention by Montford Mills, who had been in consultation with Shoghi Effendi.

That Convention elation – how well I was to know it in the years that followed! It was a world outside time, a world that Willard was trying to share with us. He spoke of a friendship he had made with Mrs Hebe Struven, sister of the early teacher Lua Getsinger. Hebe herself had visited ʻAbdu'l-Bahá in the prison city of ʻAkká – had been smuggled in under a load of vegetables!

Hebe had accepted the mission of inspiring Willard, the young Baháʼí, and how well she succeeded! They talked at great lengths about living the Baháʼí life and, as they talked, they drove in a hired carriage up Mount Royal. It was a deepening experience, and one that changed the accent of Willard's life, and of mine, for always.

The theme of it all was universal love. "We are not required to love everybody personally," Hebe had explained, "but we must love everybody universally, for the sake of God."

She said that it was asked during ʻAbdu'l-Bahá's stay in New York, why everyone came out from His presence with a shining face. He explained that it was because He had seen in each one the Face of His Father.

"He saw the beauty of the soul in every person. The people responded and became uplifted. The Baháʼís need that transforming love," said Hebe, "and we must give it to one another. It is the Holy Spirit, as in the days of Christ – Baháʼu'lláh has placed His attributes in every soul. We will seek Him in these souls, if we are seeking God."

"Willard," cried Hebe, "while you are here at Convention, look for someone who needs it. Then try it."

Willard knew who that would be. It was George. George was

a man of classic beauty with a high patrician nose. His large grey eyes looked out contemptuously, so it seemed, from half-opened lids. His face was impassive. He looked bored and lonesome, especially with the group of delegates. When he joined them, the talking fell away. Said Hebe, "What most of the friends do not realize is that being made to go to war has immobilized his face. He has been shell-shocked."

So, while asking inwardly for help, Willard joined George at lunch. The eyes opened for a moment and looked searchingly into Willard's. As the two talked, a lively mind and a devoted Bahá'í heart revealed themselves.

If Willard had held back, through indifference, from his experiment in "universal Love", the rewarding personal relationship we both had with George Spendlove, honoured and beloved teacher of the early Toronto Bahá'ís, would never have developed.

Green Acre Revisited

That summer Marguerite and I drove to Green Acre. We were to stay with Ella Robarts in her cottage near the Inn. One day while we were relaxing on a rug on the grass, our peace was shattered by the arrival of a shaky elderly lady from Boston. She disappeared into the house, scolding Ella in a loud complaining voice. "You did not tell me that you had invited others to stay here. You know I am too nervous to stay with people. You knew I would be upset."

Marguerite and I exchanged knowing glances. This lady needed "universal love"! So, when we met her to be introduced, we proceeded to "love her for the sake of God". Like magic, this poor lady became loveable, her nerves relaxed and, before long, her spirits were exhilarated. By bedtime, we were all out in the kitchen eating Ella's food and our dear little old lady was showing us how high she could kick!

For this, I thank Hebe for first pointing out the potency of "The Elixir of Love."

At that time two or three morning classes were held at Green Acre: one in Fellowship House, another on the inn's veranda and, perhaps, another under "The Pines". In the evenings there would be talks or reports from teachers or returned pilgrims.

We gathered one evening to hear Mrs Elizabeth Greenleaf, a much-loved teacher, tell us about her trip to Haifa and, especially her meeting with Shoghi Effendi. Not many had visited the Holy Land then, and we were eager to know more of the Guardian.

Elizabeth, tall and stately, a person of presence and beautifully poised, began her talk in this way: "I felt like an ELEPHANT when I met the Guardian!"

After we had stopped laughing, she explained that it was his perfect equilibrium, the balance of his qualities – rational, spiritual, and practical – that had produced in him such grace and harmony of being. Were we, the lopsided Bahá'ís with too much or too little of the needed qualities, his co-workers?

Jináb-i-Fazil

We were told that he had been persecuted in Persia by being forced to ride backward on a donkey followed by a jeering mob. This was but a detail of what had happened to this dignified man and renowned scholar, Jináb-i-Fazil. I can see him now as he sat on a platform waiting to address us. His head was bowed and he was slipping through his fingers prayer beads made of rose petals. He seemed to be in a state of abstraction. Then he rose and began to speak in fiery Persian. His wife, who sat beside him, was asked to chant a prayer. Looking like a shadow, emaciated and pale and covered with a black garment, suddenly she enveloped us in a stream of passionate prayer that left the room vibrating.

We were stunned by the forces emanating from these people from whom the self had been burned away. Examples of abject self-effacement until arising to speak, they resigned themselves to a power that shook them. The Persian husband and wife were remnants of an earlier and darker Persian era of the Faith.

The magical influence of Green Acre was around us that week – a deepening in the Faith, friendships, a picnic on Mt. Salvat. Sometimes we would slip away to the beaches, take walks along the shore of the Piscataqua River, or visit The Pines. We would never again see Mr and Mrs MacNutt under 'Abdu'l-Bahá's pine. While engaged in interracial teaching in Miami, both had been run down and killed.

Several of the friends owned cottages along the road. Names that I remember are Roushan Wilkinson, the Thompson sisters, Julia Culver and Marion Jack.

Marion Jack

In those days, "Jackie" was just another pleasant person. I never heard her talk about herself, except on the day when we were invited to her cottage for tea. She told us about her stay in Haifa and showed us some of the paintings that she had brought back. Actually, there were too many to show in her small house, so some were propped up around the walk outside. They were in oils, faithful to the buildings and the landscape. We looked eagerly at all the colours, knowing that they were like the colours there. Over tea Jackie's words embellished the beloved scenes to which her paintings had transported us.

At that time, it would have been irrelevant to ask about Marion Jack's story. If we had asked the Thompson sisters, Julia Culver, May Maxwell, or Mason Remey, we would have been told that she was born in the Canadian Maritimes, in Saint John, New Brunswick, and that this laughing, vigorous person we were meeting was, in fact, seventy-two years old! Her story would place her in 'Akká, teaching 'Abdu'l-Bahá's grandchildren in 1908, and later, travelling and teaching in foreign lands until she returned to North America in 1914. In 1919, in response to the Divine Plan, she went to the Yukon.

After another summer, Jackie would say a final farewell to her Green Acre cottage, for she would be spending the rest of her life in Bulgaria – behind the Iron Curtain, as, much later, it was to be called. When she died in her nineties, Shoghi Effendi was to call her "an immortal heroine" and "a shining example to pioneers of present and future generations".

But, on this day our emblem of steadfastness seemed so ordinary. There seemed to be so little to remark about her appearance.

We returned to Geneva, where Howard and Mabel joined us for a few weeks that summer, accepting the hospitality of our Pilgrim House. In the fall, their business took them to Ithaca and we kept in close contact with them. They would return for weekends, sometimes bringing with them Genevieve Coy and Amy Dwelly, then graduate students at Cornell. Genevieve and Amy would later become Bahá'ís of brilliant service. Through another Bahá'í, Forsythe Ward, the Ives were introduced to the Cornell Cosmopolitan Club of which Willard was a former member and, together, they invited us to a banquet at the Club. Willard and I were delighted to accept.

I was intrigued by the variety and brilliance of the members who represented the cream of their Indian, African, Oriental and South American cultures. Their faces were a garden of hues. Beaming paternally, Howard brought us to Chun Chuan Cheng, whom he introduced as someone we would meet again.

I mentioned an Indian poetess, Madame Naidu, to my partner at dinner and asked him to recite one of her poems.

"Certainly," he agreed courteously and began to chant in a resounding voice a poem that seemed never to end. The conversation at the long table fell silent. A little flushed when he finished, I murmured, "Thank you!" I was the insular and ignorant one. No one else in that glorious gathering of foreign and American students saw anything remarkable in the interruption.

Later, Forsythe Ward took us on a tour of the Club's quarters, even up to the dorms at the top of the building. He turned on the light. To our surprise a large bare foot stuck out of the rumpled sheets on one of the beds and a startled head looked up from the pillow.

"I forgot," whispered Forsythe, "that he was sleeping here."

He turned off the light and we retreated, laughing. The owner of the foot was not the only one startled. We all were!

That winter the members of the Practice in Speaking Class arranged, with the permission of the Local Spiritual Assembly, to hold six advertised meetings in a hall which we rented for two dollars a night. We were fortunate in our publicity because the *Geneva Times* gave us a column each week to review our talks. It was too bad that fear kept most enquirers away.

But not so Leslie and Ruth, a young couple who had recently arrived in town and were very lonesome and bored. They came to one of our meetings, listened attentively and, when we adjourned, came with us to a fireside at the farm. We found that we had interests in common. Leslie Hawthorne was a friend of Forsythe Ward and when I related the story of my Cosmopolitan Club banquet and tour and the disturbed foot, Leslie exclaimed, "That was my foot!"

Leslie and Ruth soon became treasured friends. They attended all our meetings and gatherings throughout the fall and winter, and in the spring of 1928, they stood up and announced to an assembled roomful that they wished to become Bahá'ís. The year 1928 proved to be significant for Leslie. He graduated from university, married Ruth, became an American citizen (he was from Great Britain), and joined the Bahá'í Faith. The Hawthornes' lives continued to be eventful and full of distinguished service. They moved in a few years to Texas, where they attracted a group of Mexican and American believers. Then followed some years in Utah, for Bahá'í work with the Mormons. Leslie became a specialist in his own field of agriculture, and Ruth found her degree in Home Economics valuable in her approach to the wives. In 1962 the Hawthornes pioneered to Uganda.

"I shot an arrow into the air, it fell to earth, I know not where..." wrote Longfellow. From Geneva, New York, to Uganda! We were to learn by repeated experience over the years that Divine Guidance directs the flight of those arrows.

The Tests and Visions of Agnes Parsons

Our Dr Albert Heist had been gaining fame since he became a Bahá'í. He seemed to have an uncanny ability to diagnose and heal. He was an osteopath, although other degrees hung on his office walls. A number of Bahá'ís from away came to stay for a while in Geneva and to take treatment from him. In January 1928, Mrs Agnes Parsons came from Washington, D.C., to benefit from his recently acquired equipment for recuperative exercises. This would be, also, our opportunity to know a particularly rare and special servant of Bahá'u'lláh. Mrs Parsons was the wife of a United States Senator when she first heard of the Bahá'í Faith in 1908. One afternoon, over a cup of tea, we begged her to tell us the story of "How did you become a Bahá'í?"

She opened her book at the beginning, telling us the story of her meeting with 'Abdu'l-Bahá and how it had changed her life. Her pilgrimage in 1910 had been prompted by a blend of curiosity and hope. Her meetings with Lua Getsinger had aroused in her a longing for the ideal. She had not yet met 'Abdu'l-Bahá and could not accept the fact that anyone of His description could be "real". She determined that she must see Him with her own eyes and that she would judge the Faith by what she found in Him. Agnes Parsons had a perception that the Faith would set upside down her ingrained values. She fortified herself for the meeting. She would challenge the claims of 'Abdu'l-Bahá and then decide.

She went to 'Akká and was annoyed that 'Abdu'l-Bahá kept her waiting for what seemed like an age. When finally summoned, she entered His presence in that mood. He looked at her. The first thing she knew, He was courteously raising her to her feet. She had fallen flat on the floor. Why had she been overcome? Because a blinding ray of light had passed from His eyes into hers.

This meeting notwithstanding, Mrs Parsons was still doubtful. The next morning, she visited the tomb of Bahá'u'lláh and asked for a sign. She said that not a breeze was blowing, but when she asked for her sign, the flowers at the entrance of the tomb blew vigorously back and forth as if in a gale, and a little bird flew into the bosom of her dress and nestled there for a moment. She accepted this as Bahá'u'lláh's answer.

Neither she nor we understood the meaning of the third supernatural sign. We knew that 'Abdu'l-Bahá was called by Bahá'u'lláh "the Mystery of God" and that He was a moon-like reflection of the identity of Bahá'u'lláh, Who was the return of the Spirit which had spoken before through Jesus. The early believers, some of them, thought that 'Abdu'l-Bahá, too, was a Manifestation, until Shoghi Effendi's writings dispelled this fallacy. However, when Mrs Parsons said, "Are you Christ?", the form of 'Abdu'l-Bahá disappeared into a cylinder of light that looked and cracked like the trunk of a tree on fire. The vision passed. There was no verbal answer.

She reported that her acceptance of the Cause was now wholehearted and complete. She returned to Washington, D.C., and became an active member of the Bahá'í community there, teaching the Faith and opening up her home to the believers. She was to see 'Abdu'l-Bahá again two years later when He visited North America. In anticipation of His coming, she built a new house. For eight days, from April 20 to April 28, the Master and His interpreter accepted her hospitality, although His usual policy was to maintain separate quarters in a hotel or rented house. Her beautiful new home, besides affording a base for His activities, provided the setting for meetings with many of Washington's elite. Adding drama to the situation was the fact that, in Washington, as in the deep South, there existed two worlds – one White and the other Black. 'Abdu'l-Bahá's theme throughout His stay with the Parsons was, with an emphasis on the elimination of prejudice, the Oneness of Humanity. Unity of Race was His challenge to that city.

Notwithstanding the encouragement to make use of first names, we younger Bahá'ís called Agnes Parsons "Mrs Parsons". We would never address her by her first name for she was a lady of inherited dignity, "to the manor born". With us, Mrs Parsons was never familiar, certainly not demonstrative, and yet we knew that this reserved and gracious lady sought for and maintained a humble relationship.

On another winter's night, we sat around the dinner table at the farmhouse: Willard's mother in her wheelchair, Marguerite, Mrs Parsons, and Louis Gregory. The atmosphere was genial, almost intimate. Willard and I were again on our subject of personal and universal love. We asked Mrs Parsons and Louis which they preferred. To our surprise, Mrs Parsons said rather quickly, "personal," but Louis replied, "universal, it's safer!" Their choices revealed to us the searching heart of Mrs Parsons, whom we had thought to be unapproachable, and, for all his geniality, the disciplined detachment of Louis.

In that rare moment of closeness, was Louis recalling the first time he had dined with Mrs Parsons? During 'Abdu'l-Bahá's stay in Washington, a formal luncheon was arranged to which a select group of "important" people were invited to meet Him. The Master and Louis were conversing in another room when His host, the Senator, came to summon Him to the dining room and the waiting guests. The table was laid beautifully with its silver and china, but 'Abdu'l-Bahá pushed some of the dishes aside and requested that beside His own, a place be set for Louis.

Our supper that night ended in a burst of laughter. Willard suddenly called out, **"DOWN** GREGORY!"

"I beg your pardon," responded the surprised Louis.

"Oh, excuse me," exclaimed Willard. "The cat was clawing my pant leg." From under the table ambled a big, jet black cat with the markings of a formal white tie under his chin. "He is named Gregory," disclosed Willard, "after you."

"For nearly three weeks the Master stayed at the Inn in Dublin, New Hampshire," Mrs Parsons related on another afternoon. "I invited a large dinner party, wondering what my friends would think of a person so different from themselves." It was then that 'Abdu'l-Bahá produced for His concerned hostess the second of His dinner-table tests. The cultivated representatives of the political, artistic, scientific, and philanthropic circles waited courteously for the guest of honour to begin His meal, and 'Abdu'l-Bahá commenced to eat with His fingers!

"But oh, with such delicacy and grace," she noted. The people were fascinated. Then the Master told a funny story. Everyone was relieved because they had expected a formal lecture. They told funny stories in turn, and 'Abdu'l-Bahá told them, "Good to laugh!"

"He told them about His life in prison," she added. "A captive most of His life, sometimes with a sword suspended above His head. Still, He and His fellow prisoners had been able to laugh. Joy, He said, was not the result of material comfort or wealth."

Elizabeth Greenleaf's Ham and Eggs

Elizabeth Greenleaf's stay at Geneva must have overlapped Mrs Parsons', for her entry in my guest book is dated February 6th.

> His loving care and kindness surge even as the eternal billows of the sea, and His blessings are continually showered from His eternal kingdom.   'Abdu'l-Bahá

At the time of her visit, those blessings had showered down on Elizabeth for more than thirty years. She had been a channel to the hearts of many. It seemed as if particles of light irradiated her physical atoms. She was sparklingly radiant.

It was on this visit that she told us the story of the white ram. In a dream, a powerful white ram was destructively butting and dispersing people. He seemed to have the face of Dr Ibrahim Khayru'lláh, a declared follower of Bahá'u'lláh. Dr Khayru'lláh had been teaching the Faith for many years and had gone with the first party of pilgrims to the Holy Land to visit 'Abdu'l-Bahá. Charles Greenleaf urged his wife to forget the dream, but the impression lingered. When Dr Khayru'lláh returned from his pilgrimage it became evident that he had brought with him strange teachings. Disappointed that 'Abdu'l-Bahá had rejected his vain-glorious plan to become the guide and administrator of the Cause in the West, Khayru'lláh became a Covenant-breaker and allied himself with the enemies of the Faith. However, the core of confirmed early American believers, such as Thornton Chase and the Greenleafs and many others before my time, became even more united and dedicated. The ram separated the sheep from the goats; the Cause grew and the violators were ineffective.

One day Elizabeth said, "Some of the friends were so in awe of 'Abdu'l-Bahá in those early days after His arrival in New York that they hid from Him."

"I can understand that," I admitted. "I, too, might have done that."

"Well, that is what I did," said Elizabeth. "After longing for more than fifteen years to meet Him, I could not bear to make myself known to Him. Until one day Grace Ober, tired of arguing with me, opened the door of His audience room, pushed me inside, and shut the door."

There was to be no escape. The Master motioned her to take a seat and continued conversing with His guests. She sat there, red-faced and head bowed, really quaking. Then, at the apex of her embarrassment, 'Abdu'l-Bahá did a strange thing. He came over to her seat and, in English, whispered in her ear, "ham and eggs".

"This was a secret joke between me and Charles. If either of us got upset, the other would say 'ham and eggs' and the trouble would end in a laugh. Nobody else in the world knew this, but 'Abdu'l-Bahá did! So I laughed with Him and my fear vanished forever."

Keith Ransom-Kehler

On March 4th, 1928, Keith Ransom-Kehler came for an unexpected flash of a visit – just an overnighter. We were instantly electrified by her personality. She was the privileged kind of person who becomes the centre of any group merely by being there. She was tall and straight, intense, with wide-open brown eyes and white hair wrapped like a turban around her head. I remember her in a dress printed with large white daisies on a brown background. This may be a trick of my imagination because Keith herself was such a "daisy". Added to that, she was a "looker" and a firebrand, too!

We were ready at sundown to break our third day of the Fast. Ruhi Afnan was there and, I think, Louis and some young people. Keith, to amuse us, began talking about horoscopes and we sat around for an hour after we had eaten telling our birthdates and laughing at Keith's remarks about us. One completely uninhibited person spreads the pleasant infection; we were so relaxed in Keith's company. She asked for another glass of water to take some medicine, whispering to me as if confiding a private joke, "The doctor says I have Bright's Disease, you know."

She left the next morning but not before I had brought her my guest book. "Write your favourite quotation, Keith," I asked. This is what she wrote:

> O our God! Lead us to the ocean of Thy graciousness and immerse us in Thy Name, that our thoughts may not grieve us and whatever happens to us in Thy Cause may not afflict us.

The words were tragically appropriate. They were a portent of what was to come to Keith in the Path of God. Within only four years, Keith, beautiful in face and form, poetic in her written word and eloquent of speech, died in Persia after a long, exhausting mission. Like Ṭáhirih, she was proclaimed a martyr, the first from the Western world.

This was our fourth spring in the Cause. My opportunity had been providential in that my daytime care of the invalid in the house kept me at home except when Marguerite or Christine spelled me. This meant that there were many hours of quiet daytime calm in which to study the Writings of Bahá'u'lláh and 'Abdu'l-Bahá. There was not then the wealth of reading material that we have today. I read, reread, and meditated on the creative Word found in the few books available. I was beginning to use the Bahá'í Writings as the criteria with which to measure the truths claimed by popular science and other sources. I reviewed my study of Christian mysticism, really searched the Bible, and, for the first time in my life, dipped into the Koran. Our neighbours, too, the Collisons, were absorbed in the Writings. All of us were. It was a fertile period of assimilation and growth – of great value and appreciated in our later Bahá'í life, when activities claimed more of our time.

A week after Keith's brief visit, mother Edith McKay's illness reached a climax and within days, she ascended to the Abhá Kingdom. The last weeks of her life gave us further insight into the mysterious forces of prayer.

Aside from the stress of advanced arthritis, six weeks ago she had seemed well. Then one day she had a talk with Grace Ober about making a concentrated prayer effort to bring relief from an immobility which she found unbearable. She agreed to accept God's answer to the prayers – should it be either "yes" or " no." For the first time in her illness, she gave up her will to God. Every morning at eight-thirty, Willard, Marguerite, and I met beside her bed to say the Greatest Name and the prayers for her healing. From the day we began, Edith McKay began her departure from this world. Her decline was obvious and swift. Her high colour faded and her bodily functions weakened. At her own insistence, we continued the daily prayers beside her bed.

The end came while Ruhi Afnan was with us. In our house, he served us selflessly. He was, at that time, the Guardian's representative to the North American believers and his future defection would then have been unbelievable. The week wore on until, as if from a dream of the unreality of this life, Edith McKay's soul took flight from its outworn body. A benediction, marvelled at by neighbours and friends, descended upon the house. A Unitarian minister and friend of the family had come from Ohio, and he and Howard Ives shared the service. Afterwards it was as if we held a reception, very joyous. We passed around cakes and sandwiches, and her old-time friends lingered by the fire. It was early March, and the family was still keeping the Fast.

I was free now to travel. April saw me taking a night train for Chicago on the way to Wilmette as a delegate to the 1928

National Convention. I spent the first day in Chicago riding around on the tops of busses in the bright spring air. I wanted to see the city too, to prepare myself for the event ahead. I had not changed much. I felt as I had on my visit to the 1925 Convention, dreading somewhat the spiritual impact of the intense emotional atmosphere I would find there and yet impatient in my desire to be present. In the evening I checked into the Evanston Hotel and met my roommate, Katherine Cole, from Cleveland. The next morning, with a group of friends, I rode to Wilmette.

There it stood, a vast circular construction less than one storey above the ground, its walls covered with a dark grey paint or plaster. A path led to a single recessed door. A line of joyous spring-clad people were strolling up the path and entering.

Inside was a wide main corridor with small adjoining rooms and welcoming double doors entering upon a large nine-sided audience chamber known as Foundation Hall. As with the progress of the soul, we had come in by the straight and narrow path and entered into glory. The impression was of many lights, walls hung with fabulous Persian carpets, tables laden with flowers and ferns, and a semicircle of folding armchairs placed around the focal point of the Convention business to come. The delegates and friends revolved around the centre of the hall like electrons around a nucleus, sometimes adhering to one another as if drawn together by magnetic forces of mutual attraction. I stayed close to my new friend, Katherine Cole, whom I would treasure over the years ahead.

Lovely singing called us to attention, and we took our seats. There were prayers and opening remarks and then the Convention was underway. Horace Holley read from the correspondence of the Guardian, which called us to take an urgent and unified step forward into new and ordered growth. As in the three previous Conventions, there flowed two streams representing two ages of this World Faith: the old "Heroic" age and the new "Formative" age. The Guardian was calling upon us to become one wide river. There were still two currents because some of the staunchest believers did not understand as yet the requirements of this new phase in the growth of the Cause. It seemed as if only a few were poignantly aware of the drama taking place at the World Centre in Haifa where the young Guardian was given the guidance to formulate with a master hand the plans for the future growth of the Cause. Shoghi Effendi was in the extremity of an ordeal and it was out of his grief, pain, and exhaustion that the flawless structure of the new World Faith was being outlined and its foundations laid.

Only a few, seemed, as I recall, to be fully involved. The delegates were engrossed with their local assemblies and intent on making reports. They moved around in a rosy haze enjoying the reunion with their friends. Like myself, they listened to Horace Holley, Montfort Mills, or May Maxwell, all of whom were in close touch with the Guardian. Everyone took down a few obedient notes for the people back home.

Katherine and I were invited to dinner parties every night. They were given by older and more affluent Bahá'ís, I think, to foster a spirit of love and unity. After dinner, usually at the Evanston Hotel, we would go back to the Hall for an evening program. When we retired again to the Hotel, we visited one another in our rooms or said prayers. The main purpose of the delegation had been accomplished on Saturday afternoon. We had elected, by secret ballot, a new National Spiritual Assembly.

I was tired when I left Geneva and now I was in a physical condition that I recognized as "light" tired, a floaty feeling with a weak heartbeat. On the train home I went to sleep in my berth. I was awakened by someone twitching at my pillow. It was a very big and Black porter.

"Thought you might like to wake up, Missus, and look at Niagara Falls. We will be here fifteen minutes while taking on water at the Suspension Bridge."

I groaned, "If you had asked me, I would have told you that for two years, I taught school in Niagara Falls. We even used to come out to this very place for picnics."

My too-kind porter thought this was a most delicious joke. He told everybody in the coach. "I woke her up and she used to live here!" Laughter rippled in his wake. I did get up, however, went out on the platform and saluted the dear old Falls at sunrise.

At home, Willard and Dr Heist were determined that I needed a rest. I made my Convention report to the community and then arranged to visit Hornby for a few days. I wrote:

> I am on the Lehigh Valley train headed for Beaver Dam, New York. The little train runs along the east side of Seneca Lake.
>
> As I peer out of the window, I see the mist rising over the river which is lavender with a shine like silk.
>
> What memories I have of this little railway! I came this way to Rochester at the age of ten to be a city child; I rode this train to Geneva to teach, then to meet Willard. One morning my mother and I took my father back to Lindley to be buried. We had taken this train and at this time of year only five years ago.
>
> Before we were married, Willard and I spent a day hunting trailing arbutus in Beaver Dam . . . Now I am going 'into retreat' with my mother's old friends five miles from the station . . . Straight up, behind a horse and in an open wagon."

Will and Clare Underwood welcomed me back to the small unpainted house that their pioneer ancestors had built a century ago. After a pancake breakfast, I went out, as in my girlhood days, to range the woods and fields. It was still April and the wind was chilly, but the earliest wildflowers were budded.

The Convention uplift rose again. I had with me the small black prayer book and, as I was memorizing 'Abdu'l-Bahá's Tablet of Visitation, I rambled. I was in a special, sacred, spot with oak trees grouped on a sheltered southern slope. Dead leaves were heaped in a natural depression in the ground. In that nest of leaves, I prayed, "'Abdu'l-Bahá, it is my desire to serve Thy Cause."

In the prayer book, now out of print, there was another prayer. It began, "He is the Listener and the Answerer!" I was aware that He listened at that moment.

I had been restored by my stay at Hornby and returned home. I engaged my cleaning lady, Mrs Moses, to clean the house and the Pilgrim House. I helped to plan the garden and I waited to see what form the answer to my prayer would take.

I was not surprised when a letter from the National Spiritual Assembly arrived and, with it, a package of blue paper that pleased me very much. It was National Teaching Committee stationery with a letterhead that filled two or three inches. At the top of the letterhead was the symbol of the Greatest Name, and on the left, the names of the nine members of the Teaching Committee. On the right were the names of a newly established Outline Bureau: Reginald Collison, chairman; Doris McKay, secretary; and Marion Little. Marion was from New York City and her duties were consultative.

The letter from Horace Holley suggested that we prepare outlines on the subjects of Christianity, Science, and Bahá'í social teachings with compiled references from all the available Bahá'í books. We were encouraged to get help from other believers, and Willard, Marguerite and Mary Collison became "associate members". A date was set for us to present and to discuss our plans with a quorum of the National Teaching Committee. We would leave to meet with them soon after the weekend of our Blossom Picnic in May.

The apple and cherry trees were raining perfumed snow when the guests from Rochester and Ithaca arrived for the Blossom Picnic. I had arranged a Saturday night dinner for eighteen. On that day I had undertaken to make six pies, now sitting on a shelf. I sat down with fatigue and cried a little. A few hours later I was back in the kitchen cutting up vegetables. Howard Ives was with me then, leaning his elbows on the table and talking sonorously about the mysteries of the Cause. My knife slipped and I cut my finger. With a rather absent mind, I bandaged it. Observed Howard, "I have been watching you. My daughter, you have grown. Love in action is how 'Abdu'l-Bahá has described the Bahá'í life," Howard reminded me once more.

Ali Kuli Khan

Dr Khan once came to visit us. He gave a marvellous talk to two rooms packed with an eager audience. No one in Geneva had ever seen anyone as glamorous as Dr Khan, who looked like the hero of one of Scheherazade's tales. After breakfast the next morning I took our guest for a walk around the farm lanes. With Dr Khan wearing spotless grey spats, we were mindful of our steps. He showed interest in everything, especially Old Joe, the gander who was approaching us, his funnel-shaped head low to the ground and his great wings flapping. Old Joe had no well-wishing intentions. "Excuse me just a minute, Dr Khan," I implored. Before he could answer I took off through a bordering field. Joe, screaming and hissing, continued to follow me. I knew the proper technique and was not alarmed. I took a sharp turn to the right and Joe, borne by his own momentum, flew past me and into the next field.

Gregory, the black cat, had a brother – a striped tiger that answered to the name of "Little Alí". When Dr Khan and I returned from our walk, Little Alí was waiting at the house, his topaz eyes fixed on a tall evergreen tree. Soon Alí was off, climbing to the very top. When I called, "Come down Little Alí. Come down," I explained to Dr Khan that the cat had been named for him. "Khan" was positively delighted. When the cat ran up the tree again, our gentleman in grey spats boasted with appropriate gestures, "See what my namesake can do! VERY GOOD!"

Committee Work: New York, June 1928

Rex and I met with the Teaching Committee at one of the New York Hotels. May Maxwell, Harlan Ober, Marion Little, and Ruhi Afnan were there. We listened to a review of the journeys taken by Bahá'í teachers throughout the country, and Rex reported on our plans for the Outline Bureau, which were accepted. The leading spirit was May Maxwell. She was, as I had seen her at the Convention, very keen, quick-thinking, informed, and exacting.

Consecrated to the service of Shoghi Effendi, her efforts were intent and single-minded. Outside of a business meeting, May was a different person. But Rex and I had not met that person – not yet!

On the morning our business was completed, we went to see Ruhi Afnan off on the little merchant ship he was taking to Haifa. He wore a stiff dark suit, and his face was grim. His return to the Holy Land was overdue: in fact, he had received a cable urging his return while he was at our house for a second visit. His mood at that time was rebellious and his retort was "No!" Now, he was returning obediently. In the bright sunshine at the wharf, he passed out of sight like a cloud.

A little group of New York believers were there to wave farewell, among them Doris and Horace Holley. Horace was looking exhausted, actually ill.

We were not surprised to hear a few days later that Horace was coming to Geneva to be treated by Dr Heist. That is how he and Doris came to stay at the McKay Farm from June 6th to June 25th.

The Holleys

Willard expanded in the companionship of the Holleys. In Horace he found a choice support for his "academic" mind which, most of the time, had to be kept in storage. Both men were knowledgeable, quick of wit and comeback. Horace was truly a genius with extraordinary gifts that could be released in a variety of meaningful and productive channels. He had written, when young, a beautiful book of poetry. He had been a newspaper man. He had compiled *The Bahá'í Scriptures*. Now his faculties were turned towards the Administration of the Faith and the enlightenment of the friends. He was indispensable in North America in this evolutionary period as a worker for the Guardian. Horace was unique, too. The amount of energy he ordinarily expended was fantastic. The work he did was superhuman. When asked about it, he referred to a "zone of energy" in which he sometimes operated – a more than normal strength that was available, sometimes, to him. At the time of his visit, however, he was run down. He was relaxed but not idle, and he would soon wind up again.

It was the Word that bound us in love to both the Holleys. Horace told us how it was the Word that first convinced him. He had graduated recently from university and was bound for Europe, perhaps for a walking tour of the Black Forest of Germany, when someone gave him a copy of a book that contained the words of 'Abdu'l-Bahá. He read the book while crossing the ocean and knew that he was a Bahá'í.

Both Doris and Horace had a passion for the Word. One could tell by the way Doris read the Writings aloud, every syllable infused with meaning. To read it was her way of teaching. She loved to read aloud, and I loved to listen to her. After a day of working outdoors, Horace would sink into the nearest chair, reach for *The Bahá'í Scriptures* and disappear into the world of the Word.

One morning we sat long over the breakfast table on the veranda. It was sour cherry time at the farm and the orchards were vocal with Italian pickers. Willard's job was to move truckloads of cherries to the cannery. The pickers moved in early, but it was not yet time to go to the truck so he was free to enjoy the relaxed and expansive conversation of our guests. That morning Horace told us of his meeting with 'Abdu'l-Bahá and the experience of "cosmic consciousness" that followed.

He noted that it had happened exactly sixteen years ago on this same day in June. The scene was a resort on the French-Swiss border to which Horace had travelled to meet Him. A fragment of Horace's own writing expresses his experience. He had seen a stately old man, robed in a cream-coloured gown. His white hair was shining in the sun.

"Without ever having visualized the Master, I knew that this was He. My whole body underwent a shock. My heart leaped, my knees weakened, a thrill of acute, receptive feeling flowed from head to foot. I seemed to have turned into some sensitive sense organ, as if eyes and ears were not enough for this sublime impression... In every part of me I stood aware of 'Abdu'l-Bahá's presence... While my personality was flowing away, a new being, not my own, assumed its place. A glory, as it were, from the summits of human nature poured into me... In 'Abdu'l-Bahá, I felt the awful presence of Bahá'u'lláh, and, as my thoughts returned to activity, I realized that I had just drawn as near as any man may to pure spirit and perfect being. I entered into the Master's presence and became a servant of a higher will for its own purposes."[3]

The two weeks of Dr Heist's treatment and counsel, the outdoor life, rest and the frequent games that we played were a successful cure. The Holleys left us, and Horace tapped again into his zone of energy.

Green Acre, 1928

Love, unity, prayer, sacrifice. These are strong words so imbued with meaning that they wield an inherent redemptive power. As I rode towards Green Acre with Rex and Mary Collison, my thoughts dwelt on the fact that somehow we were different people – different from the ones we had been when we drove over that road four years before. Our attitude in regard to these words had changed.

Our work on the reference outlines had brought us into hours of contact with the Writings. All of us had consulted on how best to fit the references together into a program of study. The magnificence of these studies had shown us a wisdom that gave us keys by which we could escape "the prison of self". We were now much more receptive to what we might find in the atmosphere of Green Acre. Perhaps we might glimpse life from

---

[3] Horace Holley, *Religion for Mankind* (London: George Ronald, 1956) p. 232.

the perspective of the Supreme Horizon mentioned by 'Abdu'l-Bahá.

The Inn was full. The Collisons engaged a cottage, and I was directed to a room in an accommodation on the road to the right of the one where Marion Jack's cottage stood. Between the two roads stood the Pines, edged by fields.

Mornings, I would take a detour through the Pines on the way to the Inn. It was a dream experience to walk through that hallowed spot while the dew was still on the spider webs. The birds, squirrels and rabbits carried on their sylvan commotions.

One evening Dr Glenn Shook, who lectured on Science and Religion, played the colour organ. I cannot explain its mechanism. All I know is what I heard and saw. The instrument looked like a small, modern parlour organ, but while Dr Shook played it, colours danced across a large white screen. The music was classical: Bach, Handel and Mozart. The colours on the screen were like northern lights, very brilliant and animated. They grouped and regrouped, frolicked and chased one another across the screen in obedience to the vibration of the music. The summer crowd was enchanted by it.

To conclude the evening, the moving pictures of 'Abdu'l-Bahá were shown. Seeing Him, I adored Him as I had never loved anyone before. The film was old and the camera so primitive that the movement was bouncy and overly quick. And the people looked so improbable, the men with cutthroat collars, the women with flounces and birdcage hats! But nothing was absurd or incongruous. Because of the Master's lilting presence, nothing but grace and beauty were there. I felt as if the screen were drawing me physically closer to Him.

I went back to my room alone, and I did a daring thing. I walked through the Pines in the dark of night. I became overawed, frightened and I began to run. My panic subsided as I came out onto the road, which was white with moonlight.

I slipped up to my room and wrote:

The Pines have seen Him,
Have felt the reverberations of His stride;
The ground has felt it through the carpet of pine needles
And reached up, as to rain. . .

I, who had not beheld Him
Feared to see His picture flung across the screen,
O faint of faith, to fear!
Tumultuous I stood – at sight of Him –
Too far! too far! that by the door I stood,
I longed to press my cheek against that screen!

In the summer of 1928, Marguerite and I were told that Lorna Tasker, a poetess, was working in the tearoom. After tea, one day, we went into the kitchen and asked for her. Our poetess, who was a history teacher in Beverly, Massachusetts, was making tea bags of loose tea and gauze. We had never before seen tea bags. Lorna was a little younger than we. Her small, pale, face was illumined by eyes that truly were "windows of the soul". Her accent was "down East," bespeaking the honesty and integrity of the early day pioneers who were, no doubt, her ancestors. At our request, Lorna read a few of her poems – beautifully.

I would look for her again, and when I found her, she was washing her white socks. I sat on the edge of the bathtub, watching the operation. As a surprise to us both, I began talking to her about the station of being an "Apostle of Bahá'u'lláh." I remembered Leonora Holsapple's visit and the words of Howard Ives. Howard had said, "To be an apostle is a state of mind." "At least, we could try," I said.

Lorna told me that she had picked up a book in George Spendlove's gift shop. It was *The Book of Certitude,* the *Kitáb-i-Íqán.* She had learned of the Faith through George, who was in charge of the shop that occupied the other half of the tearoom. Her eager reading of the Book gave her the "certitude" for which she had waited.

She said that the waitresses had teased George because of his British reverence for tea. From him they had learned to "take the pot to the kettle" so that not one bubble of the essence would be lost. She could appreciate and enjoy such nuances of taste for she had been blessed with poetic sensibilities. My books would have called it "low threshold". She was always only a step away from a plus-nearness spiritual realm of rapture induced by light, or the music of wind in the trees, incoming waves, or the whispered messages conveyed by touch.

Moved by the spirit of our meeting, I invited her to visit Emerald Hill, our name for the Geneva farm. She accepted and we set a date for the week of her school vacation in February.

We stopped to visit Hebe Struven in Worcester, Massachusetts, and then continued on to Geneva, where we resumed the patterns of our lives. In the warm weather we took our outlines up to the top of Emerald Hill, where a row of Black Tartian cherry trees still retained some stray fruit. Soon we would use the stone oven that we had built there to roast the first ears of corn. The crops of string beans and corn checkered the fields; the acres of apples and pears, fenced in by arbour vitae or spruce hedges, were acquiring size and colour. The slope of the hill ran three miles to Seneca Lake.

For the promised corn-roast, the Hawthornes brought Ruth's brother, Chester, and his wife, Sally. Sally stayed with us for a few days. She was a businesswoman, manager of a belt factory; very modern, restless and high-geared. We did not talk about the Faith but, for most of the night, we consulted concerning her problems. The next day she picked up *The Hidden Words* and asked, "What's this?"

I judged her and replied, "You wouldn't be interested, Sally." God forgive me.

Perhaps, after all, psychologically it was the perfect answer. When we returned from an errand in town, we heard loud, very lively music on the Victrola. There sat Sally, listening to the music, furiously chewing gum, and reading *The Hidden Words*. She asked questions and that same day she accepted the Faith. Her home in Rochester, New York, became a centre of Bahá'í activity. When I got to know her better, I learned that she lived by intuition; she knew, without being told, of events before they happened. Who had said, "We do not select the Bahá'ís, we find them"?

September brought Katherine Cole and her family from Cleveland, Chun Chaun Chen and, later, J. Krishna Lall from the Cornell Cosmopolitan Club. One was a follower of Lao-tzu, the other of Krishna. Alas, that each was entombed in the Faith of his ancestors. Entombed and tied to the religions of remote pasts. The Founders of those ancient religions, had They appeared in our own age, would have revealed the Words of a universal religion and taught the oneness of mankind.

"There is no flavour to American food," complained Lall. So we challenged him to cook an Indian dinner. He picked a variety of vegetables, combined them with a paste of farina, and then emptied into the mixture all my curry and most of my other spices. We invited twenty-five people to meet Lall and to share his dinner. Certainly, his food was not tasteless. There were full pitchers of water to cool our guests' tongues, and Lall was happy. He later sent me a package of Indian curry to prove that mine was inferior.

Lall's prophet, Krishna, was alleged to have said in the *Bhagavad Gita*:

> ... Whenever the world declineth in virtue, and vice and injustice mount the throne... then, come I, the Lord, and mingle as a man with men. And by my influence and teachings do I destroy the evil and injustice and re-establish virtue and righteousness. Many times have I thus appeared, many times hereafter shall I come again.

The *Gita* was a gift from our next visitor, Mrs Ruth Moffett. It was now October 1928, a year after Ruth's pilgrimage. Unlike most "pilgrim's notes," the Guardian had approved these taken during conversations with him. How eagerly we listened for the first time to a description of the three conditions of prayer: concentration, purity of intention, and, lastly, detachment from the outcome.[4]

---

4   Five years later Ruth Moffett published her detailed study of the dynamics of prayer, *Doʿa on Wings of Prayer*. On pages 15–17 of the 1974 edition (Des Moines, Iowa: Wallace Homestead Co.) she describes the five steps of prayer dictated to her by the Guardian:

One of our earliest lessons had been, "prayer is conversation with God". Now, with the Guardian's notes for a new era of the Faith, we asked ourselves and Ruth, "Conversation about what?" The ultimate purpose of prayer was for the advancement of the Cause; it became a discipline, an obligation, a thrusting step in the direction of the Holy Spirit. Were we disciplined enough, pure enough, courageous enough, to pray for such an outcome?

Enter and Exit the Whites

Mrs Ruth White and her husband, Leonard, appeared unexpectedly on the afternoon of Willard's birthday, November 1st. I had made a cake and had prepared a celebration dinner when, suddenly, the Whites, whom we had never seen nor heard of, knocked on the door. Ruth White, later described by Shoghi Effendi as a poor deluded woman, seemed at that moment the very opposite of "poor". They were Bahá'ís. They had been recently in Haifa. Could they come in?

Mrs White was prepossessing. A kind of stalwart personality that wore black and white with a small chic hat. They were world travellers, full of information and convictions of being right. Leonard was more modest and attractive in his manner, more of a listener. We all listened while Ruth told us of a new term, "Administration", that soon all of us would be using. She described the Guardian, the World Centre and said that she had seen the original Will of 'Abdu'l-Bahá.

With the meal over, Willard stood ready to cut his cake. The door banged open and our two large dogs burst into the room. They had had an encounter with a skunk and carried with them

---

1. Pray and meditate about the question or problem,
2. Arrive at a decision and hold to it,
3. Have determination to carry the decision through,
4. Have faith and confidence that the "right thing will come to meet your need", and
5. Act as though it had all been answered.

an odour both vile and overpowering. The dogs, frenzied and somewhat blind, charged through the house and, again, out the doors. We could think of only one remedy besides that of leaving open the outside doors. We had a box of incense in little pyramid capsules, but the smoke from these increased, rather than ameliorated, the problem of "airs". The Whites' conversation was never resumed. It was somewhat befitting to connect the foul smell that occurred with Ruth White's determined efforts, soon afterwards, to discredit the Master's Will. Her reason for doing this? A dream she had! A frightening example of the harm done by "vain imaginations".

Toward the end of the month arrived another Bahá'í who would become, many years later, the victim of vain imaginations. On the 28th Mason Remey telephoned and later appeared at our door by station taxi. He was a magnificent looking man, proud and born by tradition to rule. He had written books, travelled, been a prominent architect. The Guardian had often called upon him for consultations. The need to be first would deceive this man one day and he would become the cause of grief to the Bahá'í world.

We had a peaceful evening in the book room, the candles burning low in their sconces above the hearth. We read prayers and listened to Mason's stories of the Master. In the guest book, to commemorate the date of the Ascension of 'Abdu'l-Bahá, he wrote, "The seventh anniversary of the Great Sorrow".

1929

"I am a captive, rid me of my bondage." The cry rises from a human spirit that has glimpsed the freedom of the spiritual world. The entrance into a new year in the Cause was a time when, again, all the Teachings seemed new and a golden thread linked the jewels of people and events, each an unexpected gift that a more-than-human spirit had added to my life. With the new year, I counted and assessed those jewels: the night that Howard Ives invoked the Unseen Power and gave us our first experience of a new spirit and a new Faith; the moment I first met Dorothy; that spring morning when I saw the two roads and made my choice; the night I saw the movie of 'Abdu'l-Bahá; my moment of rededication in the Hornby woods. And, yes, the intensity of my conversation with Lorna Tasker had the same dimension as those other moments – not essentially emotional, not rational, but indicative of a higher faculty that 'Abdu'l-Bahá called "the Spirit of Faith".

'Abdu'l-Bahá said that the first faith comes in drops and increases to a shower. I saw the stages of my faith as upsurges of understanding and commitment, drops borne by sudden winds, or, as steps in a succession of stairs. These moments had not been a reward, but a grace from the bounty of Abhá.

The Burning Log

It was during the week that Lorna spent with us that I had my first experience of making a "covenant" as a promise to God shared with another. The saying "out of this world" was true of this strangely anticipated time together. We had a week of Bahá'í meetings where both of us had spoken. We enjoyed fine music and poetry and, on skis, climbed up the hill to shout the prayers of the Báb to the winter landscape below. Our talks revolved around the love of God, the Universal Love that Hebe had introduced to Willard, and the miraculous powers released by the unity of the believers. We had prayed for ourselves and for others to experience "the unity in the love of God," but still, the purpose of our week was, as yet, unfulfilled.

Silent and rather sad, we sat late one night by the embers of a dying fire. There was no electricity in the farmhouse, but we had the light of two blue candles set in my tall, brass wedding candlesticks. We sat on the floor with a pile of books beside us. I turned to "The Unveiling of the Divine Plan" in the old *Scriptures* and read again the second condition in the *Tablet to the Apostles of Bahá'u'lláh*.

O ye friends! Fellowship, fellowship! Love, love! Unity, unity! So that the power of the Bahá'í Cause may appear and become manifest in the world of existence.[5]

With the reading of these words the purpose of this visit dawned on us. What our covenant would be. Both of us promised that we would look for people of capacity and invite them to the unity of the love of God. We would love people and pray that they would taste of that unity. Knowing ourselves, we knew this to be presumptuous, but we made a covenant with each other.

Each uttered a simple pledge:

"I will try, Lorna."

"I will try, Doris."

While our two young souls sat scared by the solemnity of our vow, the embers of a burned-out log began to crackle. It began popping and showering sparks out into the room, sending up rings of grey smoke. This, it seemed, was a response. The unseen Presence was in the room then as was an overwhelming nearness to Love itself. "The Listener and the Answerer" had left us with a sign, our symbol of the burning log.

Lorna had been back at her desk at the Beverly High School only a day or two when Mabel Ives returned to Geneva. She announced, "An Interracial Amity Conference is to be held in Rochester on March 7th and I have been given the responsibility for finding a suitable meeting place, a White minister to share the platform with Louis Gregory, and of interviewing a list of prominent members of both races. All of these arrangements," she sighed, "will take several days. And several days I do not have."

Then came the shock. "Willard and Doris, you will be just the ones to do this for me, with Elizabeth Brooks to help."

Thus Mabel pushed us out of the nest where we had been as fledglings who had never known flight. We protested but would

---

5   *Bahá'í Scriptures*, p. 542, or more recently, 'Abdu'l-Bahá, *Tablets of The Divine Plan* (Wilmette, Ill: Bahá'í Publishing Trust, 1974), p. 19.

never dream of refusing. We were beginning to see that with each covenant we make, with each rededication of our spirits, comes a new challenge. Sometimes the challenge is an opportunity and at other times, a test. It turned out that with this challenge to organize the Amity Conference, there were confirmations with us all the way.

Over the Colour Line

"Remember," the Master's voice within me seemed to say, "the first time you prayed, you wished to cross this line. You are ready now, to cross the line with love."

How clearly I recalled the miracle that had removed my prejudice in a single night when, armed with Howard Ives' prayer book, I had undertaken my first experiment with the power of prayer. I remembered also my girlhood days in Rochester and saw a continuity. When my family first moved to Rochester from Lindley, New York, we lived on a city street that had an invisible line running through it – a colour line. People living on the east side of Caledonia Avenue were of one race, and those on the west, of another. Black, White. We averted our eyes from each other. An exchange of looks would have been considered an affront. The prejudices on each side of the line were leaden, like the walls of a casket. It was over the very line called "Caledonia" that the Bahá'ís were to move with their call to Interracial Amity.

Unlike myself, Willard was a born crusader against that social barrier. He was "lead resistant," a neutrino of the spirit. His life pattern before becoming a Bahá'í had been affected by his stand for oneness. He lost his job at the University of Texas because of his outspoken friendship with people of all races. "One of the students in our dormitory at Cornell," he had boasted, "was Black. He was my roommate." The remark reached the Dean's ears. Willard did not withdraw his stand. The family fruit farm had needed his help, so Willard became involved in its problems and gave up his university career.

"Too bad," some would say. "Willard was a born teacher!"

But Willard saw now that it was providence. He would say, "If I had not come back, I might not have become a Baháʾí – and I would not have met you!"

On Thursday morning, February 28th, we took the interurban trolley to Rochester to help Mrs Constance Rodman and Elizabeth Brooks draw up the plans for our campaign. We could not have done it without Elizabeth's lists of leading people and contacts with the newspapers.

Elizabeth had accepted the Baháʾí Faith from the Ives a year before we did and was a confirmed and dedicated handmaid of Baháʾuʾlláh. Her face is before me as if on a photographic slide in my brain. Round face and cheek bones like a yeoman of the guard, as indeed, she was. Straight, clipped iron-grey hair, level brows over steady grey eyes, a wide mouth, ingenuous, wreathed always in smiles. She was extremely tall.

Elizabeth later devoted her life to the friends over the line. She rented a house in a poor section of town and supported herself by taking in roomers. We had found an "apostle" of Baháʾuʾlláh.

If we had carried banners, they would have read: "Forgive Our Whiteness – Mankind is One – Join Us!" We visited churches, offices and homes. The people were guardedly polite, judging us with keen intuitive senses that necessity had developed. Praise God, they did not reject us. Perhaps they read the invisible banners we were carrying.

By March 2nd, our preparatory work was accomplished. We had travelled the city by day and spent the evenings praying in Mrs Constance Rodman's little rented parlour. At night we slept there behind a pale blue curtain.

We returned to Geneva and began the nineteen day Fast. I had come home with one nagging worry: I was to be chairman at this important meeting where I would introduce Louis Gregory and the young White clergyman, Mr Sanford, assistant in the largest Presbyterian church in the city. The planning of my part seemed taken from me. To Lorna I wrote: "I am nearly sick with a cold. It was wet and slushy in Rochester and I had a sore throat..." I had to admit, however, that what I really had was "cold feet."

A supper party was planned for the night of the conference. Louis, Willard and I had invited five of our Black friends to a popular downtown restaurant. Our friends did not relax at first. In 1929 this was a controversial, rather than customary, atmosphere. What a joyful experience to feel the difference melt into a true unity feast! A line from Walt Whitman comes to mind: "They came together to talk about the millennium, but their meeting together was the millennium." To the goggle-eyed astonishment of the supper crowds, we walked through the streets and up exclusive East Avenue to the place of our meeting, the Women's City Club.

From my place on the platform, I watched the hall fill to the doors. A triple line of chairs in an alcove facing the hall held the choir of the African Zion Church, their director Mrs Lee and their minister James Claire Taylor. Glorious voices opened the program with a Negro spiritual and I, as chairman, arose to address the hundred or so gathered.

Louis, eloquent and dignified, had spoken to organized interracial meetings all over the country. The Rev. Mr Sanford, young and idealistic, carried friendship to estranged and wounded hearts. The choir wound up the evening with the Negro National Anthem, and the audience, two-thirds of whom were Black, took up the song and sang the ringing, triumphant words. When it was over, the tide rolled up to the platform and we were one race.

To Lorna I wrote,

> What a fool I have been these last two weeks to worry over the part I had to play. You must have been praying for me in my hour of need, for I felt a sublime happiness, love, assurance, and power. I cannot describe the ecstasy I felt all through.

Willard and I spent the night with the Sanfords, met Louis and returned with him to Geneva. He would spend a few days with us before going to another conference in Buffalo.

The following night we left the farm. Louis and my mother washed supper dishes together while the three McKays drove to a public meeting at the Hotel Syracuse where the Ives were to speak. My mother, her roots very much in the old world order, was a little afraid to be left in the house with Louis. "Is he safe?" she had asked. We assured her that he was very safe.

About sixty people gathered at the Hotel, and many questions were asked. One man became angry with Howard and, making violent remarks, stormed out of the room. Marguerite and I tended the literature table, and Willard played the piano. It was two o'clock before we reached home again.

Louis and I spent the next afternoon cooking an enormous pilau. The meat in it was Joe, the gander. That ill-tempered bird had charged one car too many and, on this day, had been killed head on. To cook the elderly goose, we borrowed a large pressure cooker from the New York State Experimental Station. It took some extra cooking to soften up Joe's resistance. In those days, more than now, pilau, with variations, was a favourite food and always a festive dish. Louis was an experienced pilau cook and together we accomplished what went down in history as the "Joe-pilau". The visit was also an opportunity to invite our Sunday morning discussion group to meet and talk with Louis. We had, later, a splendid social evening. Everett, our fine musician, played the piano and we sat on the rug by the fire and talked till late. And Joe was compensated. His atoms had entered the human kingdom.

Mary Hanford Ford

Marguerite and I were polishing the house for the company we expected later when Mrs Ford arrived. It was Saturday, April 14th, 10:00 a.m., and she had not been expected until the afternoon. Looking like a small avenging angel, she entered berating our branch railroad whose agent had misinformed her about schedules and had let her start out late one evening. Soon afterward, in the middle of the night, she had been ousted from her sleeper for a two-hour wait at a country station. Not a pleasant stop for a fragile-looking lady in her seventies. She asked for a cup of tea and we put her to bed.

Anxiously we peered in at her door. We saw a woman who looked collapsed rather than asleep, and I was surprised when she appeared at lunchtime completely restored. She told us of her faith in tea as a restorative and also of her trained ability to revive herself through relaxation and prayer. We were beginning to find this new person exciting, adorable, and sprung up with vitality and love. We had beheld a miracle.

She stayed until Tuesday, her brilliant conversation going on for hours, day after day, on every sort of topic: history, art, philosophy, metaphysics, world events. Her fascination with the world of thought was a love beaming through the fireworks of a remarkable mind. She was ninety pounds of wit, wisdom and depth.

She told us that when she was a young person, she was left a widow with children to support. She became a professional lecturer on Art, travelling from city to city. In her Bahá'í talks she drew upon Art to teach religion – as she did one evening in Geneva.

On her first morning she entered with a heavy bag, which she requested be placed by her bed. It was full of books. She explained that 'Abdu'l-Bahá had told her to read five non-Bahá'í books for every Bahá'í book, and during her rest periods she would be reading them.

"How does she do it?" we asked ourselves. Perhaps the people of the New World Order, generations from now, will have evolved the powers of intuition by which she functioned. At this time, it seemed a secret knowledge; she had developed faculties that we did not possess. In Haifa, 'Abdu'l-Bahá had given her access to teachings not universally given and to Tablets not to be copied. She spoke of developing our intuition and hinted that there are additional senses possible to cultivate in this life, and for which the so-called "sixth sense" is but a preliminary.

On Sunday morning we asked her for stories of Bahá'u'lláh. Here is one of them:

> Bahá'u'lláh poured tea at sunset in the garden of Riḍván for a small gathering of His trusted followers, then poured forth utterances that enraptured their ears. Carried away by His exal-

tation at the Words pouring through Him, He danced with an ecstasy inexpressible by words. A pastel picture was made by an artist who was present. It was hanging in Haifa at the time of Mrs Ford's pilgrimage.

One who watched in the Garden was 'Abdu'l-Kareem, a merchant who, in order that he might visit the Blessed Perfection, had sold his goods and paid his debts. On the night he arrived, he was not met at the boat because the servant of Bahá'u'lláh had been told that a "great prince" was coming, and he saw only an old man in a three-cornered shawl. When the servant reported that the distinguished guest had not arrived, Bahá'u'lláh said, "I shall have to send someone with better eyes," and He sent Abbas Effendi ('Abdu'l-Bahá).

When Abbas Effendi reached the dock, He saw an old man hunched on a bench in the cold night; he had lost his shawl in the sea. No one had met him, and he was cold, lonesome and disillusioned.

Then Abbas Effendi appeared, wearing a long cape against the cold. Claiming 'Abdu'l-Kareem as His Father's guest, He enveloped him in the cape with Himself and the two sat on the bench and prayed till dawn, that he might be prepared for the soul-challenging experience of entering the presence of Bahá'u'lláh.

Mrs Ford said that 'Abdu'l-Kareem himself had told her these stories.

As I live again those days with Mrs Ford, I recall her spiritual and mental capacities. They were enriched, rather than diminished, by age. The day she left, Marguerite said, "There goes the youngest Bahá'í visitor who has ever come to us!"

We Visit Dorothy Baker

The Collisons, McKays, and Ruth Hawthorne starting out early for the 1929 National Convention, stopped for Bahá'í visits in Buffalo and Cleveland. Now we were on our way to Lima, Ohio to visit our own Mother Beecher and the Bakers.

My heart skipped a beat of excitement at the thought of seeing Dorothy again, and of seeing her in her own home. My "particles" had been windswept and swirled at my earlier meetings with her. I think both of us were aware of a hidden design by a God, "Who doeth whatsoever He willeth". At last spring's Blossom Picnic, Dorothy, her soul in a white fog, had asked me to drive with her for a half hour. During that time, we had been unable to exchange a word.

Later, that afternoon, we witnessed a transformation of spirit, the turning on of a light, a dazzling illumination emanating from a pale lamp shade. The circle of people who clustered on the lawn had never heard such words of eloquence, words released with such a radiance. The quiet girl of Dorothy had assumed a newer vitality and had captivated all hearts.

Mother Beecher, during her winters in Geneva, had spoken often of her adored granddaughter. She told us of taking the young girl to meet 'Abdu'l-Bahá when He was in New York in 1912. She told us, also, of an early teacher who, after seeing Dorothy, had a vision so astonishing that he sought out Jináb-i-Fazil for an interpretation. Jináb-i-Fazil replied, "Someday she will become one of the great teachers of the Cause." Mother Beecher began to pray and to contrive that this promise would be fulfilled.

In 1921 Dorothy had married Frank Baker. Frank was older than she and had two motherless children. A few years later they moved to Lima, Ohio, and Frank established a successful baking business. He was indeed Frank the baker! They started a family of their own, a girl and a boy. Frank was practical, honest and big-hearted. Dorothy had a structure of common sense and hominess as well as prettiness and poise. Inevitably, the social life of the friendly mid-western town engulfed them.

Dorothy's dilemma was that the voices of the "world" did not deafen her ears to the call of the Mystic Nightingale. She was alone. There were no Bahá'ís in Lima. Her husband and parents were not Bahá'ís, although later they became glorious ones. No one understood except her gallant grandmother, when she was there. The situation was unknown to Dorothy's friends who, although they loved her, did not know her.

When we arrived, we were welcomed into a prosperous household where the business of living was successfully carried on. The whole family ran out to meet us – Mother Beecher, then a spry ninety; Frank, hearty and kind; Dorothy, smiling; her mother, Luella; and the children. They swept the travellers into the house for a bountiful meal, and afterwards we gathered in the living room for an evening of good fellowship and some hilarious games.

When Frank took Rex and Mary to visit the bakery the next morning, Dorothy took the rest of us for a drive around town. "Connie goes to school there, and I am president of the Parent Teacher Association," she laughed. We visited the school, the golf course, then saw the homes of some of their friends, and returned by way of the bakery. We had seen all of Dorothy's outer world with Dorothy a delicate flower growing in a vegetable garden!

She had not shown us her whole world. For all her merry words, she had been unable to hide her depression. She said she had been ill. How ill, we would not know until later. Our own relationship in the inner world was a mystery known to God alone. As we were leaving, Mother Beecher drew me aside and whispered, "When she was so ill, Dorothy said to me, 'Grandma, if anything ever happens to me, I want to leave my children to Doris McKay.'"

She was coming to the Convention on Saturday. Perhaps there we would be able to talk.

First Days at the Convention of 1929

I do not remember any of the business, except that Shoghi Effendi had called for the next step in the building of the Temple – the raising of the steel structure above the concrete foundation. We were still functioning in our "cheese box" of Foundation Hall. We were delighted with the Temple's interior, but its outer appearance was a trial to the people of Wilmette.

Our continued sacrifice was always a discipline before us. Considering the smallness of our number, it seemed that the beloved Guardian had asked us to do the impossible, especially since we could not accept contributions from non-Bahá'ís, nor were we allowed to incur debts. Some of us would go home and sell stamp and coin collections, rare oriental prints; some would take extra jobs. Orcella Rexford gave each of us a little orange bag for the dimes and nickels we saved by small sacrifices. Jewellery was given up for sale; cheques were written and pledges made. The Bahá'ís would manage; they always did. Work would begin and the steel structure of the dome would be completed. Our mood was happy and independent of our material wants.

Dinner with Louis Bourgeois

Willard and I accompanied a number of others who were invited to a luncheon at the home of Louis Bourgeois, architect of the Wilmette Temple. His house seemed to be in accordance with his spirit of Temple building and although small in area, there were three levels; an effect of airiness and space was created by a living room two storeys high with a mezzanine balcony around the sides, stairs leading to the second floor.

I sat next to Mr Bourgeois at the long table where our meal was served. He told me that he used to be a vegetarian until, at a meal with 'Abdu'l-Bahá, the Master took a small roast chicken and put it on his plate, saying, "Eat. But in the future the foods will be fruits and grains." Mr Bourgeois then asked, "Would you like to see some of the designs for the ornamentation of the Temple?"

Soon our host was taking us downstairs to his studio. He shuffled dozens of long, tubular blueprint cases. He selected several and began displaying, on a vast drawing table, the prints that they contained. He threw them onto the table with a twist of the wrist that would start them unrolling. We saw before us a fairyland of intricate stone designs.

Mr Bourgeois said that the inspiration for the Temple was from another realm and that he had been conscious from the beginning that Bahá'u'lláh was the creator of the building. With such luminous words, the architect displayed roll after roll of designs for a building that was yet to be built. He showed us where he had arranged for jewels to be placed in the ornamentation.

We were dazzled. Assured that already the "Temple of Light" rose above us in the world of conception, Willard and I returned to the lowly Foundation Hall for the afternoon session.

On the last morning, Willard and I went over to say goodbye to our luncheon host. "I love you, Mr Bourgeois," said Willard, and the warm-hearted little Frenchman seized Willard and saluted him on both cheeks. We floated to our waiting car. Mr Bourgeois died that year, before the structure rose.

Dorothy takes her First Steps

Saturday morning my thoughts had strayed from the Convention business. "What does God want from all Bahá'ís?" I pondered. "What can I offer to Dorothy? Only what Lorna and I had promised in our covenant – to listen, to love, and to pray. Yes, I could do that."

I looked over my shoulder to the door. Dorothy stood there silhouetted faintly in her light summer dress and small white hat. Face and lips were pale, eyes grey. At that moment, the strong soul of the Convention and the ardent concentration of the people rose up around her and she swayed. I arose and went to her. She asked if I would walk with her, and we slipped out. I was four years older than Dorothy and at this moment I was the counselling friend whom she had chosen. Neither of us knew why. She had that star quality that never, perhaps, would find its equal in a friend.

We climbed down the stairs behind the architect's house to the shore of Lake Michigan and walked close to the water. Then we returned and walked around the streets of Wilmette. I knew already the causes of conflict between her life and the forces of her destiny. These spoke to her through her grandmother's pressures, the prayers of her friends, and her own feelings. When she was with Bahá'ís and speaking for the Faith, she knew that the Power used her. She could see the faces of the people made astonishingly beautiful by the words that came to her and her manner of offering. As we walked, an irresistible overflow of pent-up waters washed away the protective barriers of excuses and self-justification upon which she had relied. Had she put it off too long? Had she thrown away her destiny? She was drowned now in her own grief, beating herself with guilt.

We circled back to the Hall and Ruth Hawthorne joined us, her face alight with her prayers. We drew Dorothy into the little shrine in a cubby-hole off the corridor over the cornerstone of the Temple. Here was a little oasis in the structural wilderness of columns and beams.

We found there a small circular table spread with a gold and black cloth and a vase of pink roses. Near the table was a bench covered with a Persian rug. We sat, and Dorothy wrapped herself in the spirit of worship. She listened to the prayers uttered by a young Black couple who shared our nook, and she remained as still as a statue.

It was over. The inner light shone through. Never again was I to see Dorothy's face without that light. In that little alcove shrine, something had happened and the troubled spirit had found peace. At dinner that evening, we sketched out her new life. She said, "I thought I was lost forever."

Back home, I received from Dorothy these words:

And now may I tell you something? At the Convention and during your visit to Lima you have given me unbounded strength! What you did, I do not exactly know. The few minutes at the shrine will never be forgotten. How my throat ached! And when I looked up I saw you looking at me so serenely and oh, so sweetly. Ruth was looking at me too, and it startled me for I had never really seen Ruth before. But what those moments at the shrine taught me cannot be put into words. I think my heart was laid at the Master's feet there.

Don't forget that I have joined your 'Unity in the Love of God' and am anxious to pray for you and to work with you.

Through the grace of God, Ruth and I had been permitted to ease the agony of birth for the most gifted of our Bahá'í teachers and a future Hand of the Cause of God in the Faith.

We were beginning to notice that any Bahá'í decision made with prayers opens a sequence of events. Some of these events are like ripples made by agitation in a stream – ripples which reach the ocean and are caught up by the waves. Decisions are fateful. I see now that my whole life is composed of ripples of events begun by decisions, one leading to another.

This is true, especially if, after making a covenant to serve the Cause, one makes a move with that intention. Another example goes back to February 1929, that fateful month of "the Burning Log". The decision was this: to answer an article in *The Atlantic Monthly* entitled "The Passing of the Prophet". The author, a Unitarian minister, had stated that the day of belief in the prophet had passed. There would be no more prophets.

This was the one and only time in my life that I have answered a magazine article. I wrote to inform the author that, indeed, there had been two Prophets within the last hundred years Who claimed to be the Word of God as it had been spoken by Muhammad, Jesus and the other Founders of world religions. I told him that in 1844 the first Prophet had announced the coming of a universal Manifestation of God Whose teachings would unite mankind. I wrote of their persecution; how one was martyred and the other exiled and imprisoned. Thousands of their followers were killed and their Cause had become worldwide. That was the substance of my letter, as I recall. I did not mention names or places and, of course, I hoped for an answer.

The answer came from the editor! Did he have my permission to publish the letter? Gladly!

I heard again from him. He was swamped with questions from his readers and sent me forty letters to answer and asked for a second letter telling more about the history of these Faiths. The May issue of the *Atlantic* came out before I left for Wilmette.

It was because of the sudden publicity that I was asked to make a report on the Convention floor. The writing of the letter led directly to two friendships as well as to a widening of McKay horizons. May Maxwell and Loulie Mathews, both dynamic people, were brimming over with natural enthusiasms. Together the two ladies began to make plans for us which, at the moment, seemed like daydreams. Willard and I returned home encouraged and sustained.

I attempted to describe my feelings:

> It is like comparing an ordinary electric light bulb to a forest fire. This is the problem I face as I try to describe the difference this Convention has made in me. Bahá'u'lláh spoke of His 'particles'; mine have been transfused and have lost their identity – as in the interior of the sun, dense matter becomes a molten mass. Ripples of energy seem to find their way to the surface carrying heat and light – and my heartbeat has been to the rhythm of spheric music.

It was to be an early spring, forecast by the appearance of buds on the cherry and pear trees and bright-pink peach blossoms. The brown cases on the apple buds were already swelling. Our second Blossom Picnic was set for the weekend of May 11th and 12th.

We had been home a day or two when May Maxwell called to invite me to New York for a brief meeting with the National Teaching Committee. I left the picnic plans to other Bahá'ís, took a night train to the city and arrived for breakfast. I was early for the meeting and had a day to myself – a day to spend in a city that I had come to love when, for two years, I taught on Long Island. I seemed also to be guided to telephone Willard's friend, a secretary of the YMCA, who suggested a tour. "There are young 'Y' students taking a series of bus tours to ethnic neighbourhoods. This week they are visiting Harlem. It's called the Reconciliation Fellowship Tour and you can catch it if you hurry." He named the street corner and with hasty thanks to the beneficent powers, I managed, just in time, to board the yellow bus.

We, the bus travellers, were to learn about Harlem as it was on that day in 1929. We visited a church and talked to an earnest young organist; a modern library, where we chatted with a librarian about a new housing project. We saw, too, endless grimy streets and neglected shop window displays. The people were wearing shapeless and drab clothes that were shoddy and cheap.

But there was an idealism and a hope here which were described in our next visits to the Urban League offices and the headquarters of the NAACP (National Association for the Advancement of Colored People). The secretaries enlightened us with stories of poverty and legal injustice that left the White students mute. During the question periods I dared to raise my voice and speak of Race Unity as a program. "What," I asked, "is being done to further friendship and unity between the races?"

With Harlem streets as a witness, the question seemed banal. I expected scorn from the informed workers, but I added the word "Bahá'í" and referred to my recent experience in Rochester. I was encouraged when, detained at the doors, I was asked for further information about the interracial work of the Bahá'ís. Mr James Hubert, Secretary of the Urban League, invited me to have lunch with him the next day. Of course, I went.

Mr Hubert was waiting for me at the subway entrance, wondering, I suppose, if I would have the interest to return. He was a fine-looking gentleman – a light brown suit flattered a complexion of pastel mahogany. His face was both sharply keen and meditative. We walked to a restaurant which was situated in a corridor of an old brick building. There were small separate tables with lights in orchid shades and small vases of artificial flowers. The food was delicious, and as we ate, we talked.

Mr Hubert listened politely as I held forth on amity, oneness, association through mutual experience, then friendship.

He said, "I wish it were true, but it can't be done."

"But it has been done," I insisted. "You can see it with your own eyes!"

"I won't believe it 'til I see it done," said my host.

I replied, "Then come to our Blossom Picnic this weekend in Geneva, New York."

The Second Blossom Picnic

Quite a challenge to a key man like Mr Hubert to rush off to a picnic a hundred miles away in upstate New York! But he came that Saturday, by the afternoon train. He stepped down at the weather-beaten, country-looking station. Perhaps he was feeling a reaction, a return of mood to the bitterness and frustration that pushed him on with his work, the work on which he had closed his office doors eight hours ago. His face inscrutable, he accepted a seat in our open Model "A" Ford car.

After a drive of two miles, Willard and his quiet guest turned at the entrance and crossed over "The Bridge of Sighs." (Howard Ives thought it ought to have been called "The Bridge of Larger Size".) A crowd of boys were playing ball in a field. They were of both races, Black and White. Here was something that Mr Hubert had never seen before.

Guests had been arriving since noon. Late afternoon found me in an orgy of rice cooking, twenty-five pounds of it, Persian fashion. I had washed the rice through several waters and, to preserve some crispness, cooked it rather sparingly. I spread it with butter and baked it on cookie sheets in a slow oven. Meanwhile, carloads of our Black friends from Rochester arrived and were taken for walks in the orchards. More of the Geneva friends arrived with their consignments of prepared food – boned chicken, rolled dates, cooked whole onions, carrots, chopped nuts and olives, green peppers and tomatoes. Mr Hubert mingled with the crowd, and I saw him deep in talk with Tom Bolling, Secretary of the Rochester coloured 'Y'.

The big kitchen was now full of helpers. We started to pile the large platters, constructing pilaus similar to the one we shared "the night the ice went out". The old dining room table with all its wide leaves was opened and trimmed with flowers and lighted candles. Great platters were placed at each end, and lines formed. We served eighty that night. After the plates were passed back to the kitchen, we called a meeting.

Willard had trucked a load of chairs from the funeral parlour. Some people sat on the stairs and the children sprawled on the floor. The evening was mostly musical. Mrs Lee and the members of the Zion Church choir furnished some of it. Our beloved Bahá'í teachers were there to bring the presence of the Master. Howard and Mabel Ives attended, as well as the Obers, Louis Gregory and May Maxwell. It was a beautiful, enchanted moment engraved on the tablets of eternity. The scent of lilacs and apple blossoms wafted in through open doors and windows.

The guests, reluctant to break the spell, lingered late, and the younger children slept on the floor. Eventually, those who lived nearby drove home, while others were entertained in Bahá'í homes. We had thirteen overnight guests at Emerald Hill, some of whom slept in the Pilgrim House. Willard and I slept rather precariously on a red plush sofa in the dining room. In the early hours of the next morning, we were startled by a resounding CRASH. The four Black teenaged youth brought by Bishop Shaw were sleeping upstairs in our bedroom, and their weight became too much for the antique bed. The wooden slats broke and deposited the boys on the floor. We rushed to the scene, spread out the mattress and put the sleepy and bewildered boys back to bed.

Blossom Picnic – Day Two

Sunday morning. A self-serve breakfast for seventeen: popovers, scrambled eggs, fruit and mugs of coffee laid out on the sideboards. Other guests began to flow back, and a carload of the varicoloured Cosmopolitan Club students arrived from Ithaca. All the young people gathered in the Pilgrim House for a meeting conducted by Mary Maxwell, who had been wading in the brook the day before with a goose under each arm. Mary was beautiful, tall and graceful, lovely in a rose-coloured dress.

It was a relaxed day. One on which to enjoy the country and wander around the acres of fabulous beauty. Today the friends provided a great picnic lunch that we ate on the lawn. That evening we held another meeting with music again and talks by the guests and noted Bahá'í speakers. The seventy who attended tasted the Paradise of Abhá. One lady, a Mrs Edgecomb from Binghamton, remarked, "I have the feeling of a vibration in the top of my head." I told her that I had known it, too.

The tide of the Blossom Picnic receded and left a drift of pearls along the shore. The friendships begun with the Black community of Rochester were sustained through the following week by meetings with three Black ministers, Elizabeth Brooks, Louis Gregory and a local interracial group. Bert Jackson of Geneva became a devoted Bahá'í. A janitor, he was the least pretentious. Of those who had been called, Bert was the one chosen.

Elizabeth Brooks was a vital link in our follow-up efforts in Rochester. She arranged meetings in several homes where Willard and I gave firesides on Sunday nights. Often, we spent the night in homes of our Negro friends. Old church and social ties held fast, although we were grateful for the privilege of sowing the seeds of love on both sides of the colour line, and more grateful still, to be accepted as trusted friends by so many. I remember one woman who exclaimed, "If the Bahá'í movement makes you love us like this, it must be the return of the Christ spirit!"

I thanked Bahá'u'lláh that the "Caledonia Avenue" of my young girlhood had become, through His bounty, a phantom barrier. Soon two families, the Lindsays and the Greens, joined us to become a firm foundation for the Faith in Rochester.

I thanked Bahá'u'lláh for our Blossom Picnic. During those two days, besides the oriental students from Cornell, fifty members of the Black community had been with us. Mr Hubert said, on leaving, "I had to see it to believe it!"

Returning home from the picnic were three carloads of people from Binghamton, New York. The Ives had conducted their lecture series and had formed a Bahá'í study class. Those who had come to the picnic had set out in the same spirit of adventure as had Willard and I when we travelled four years earlier to Buffalo. Perhaps one of those carloads had had the privilege of having Howard recount *The Seven Valleys*, too. But it was the meeting with other Bahá'ís that was a confirming step.

For Willard and me, as well as the Binghamton group, the steps were planned by the Ives.

How did it feel to be a Bahá'í in those early days? I wrote in my diary in June 1929:

> Diditte, my cat, is what Ruth Moffett would call a 'planetary mother.' She worries fiercely about her young. She is always bringing them back or taking them away. When they are away, they are usually to be found in a hay loft in the barn – a place of ancient timbers with the sunlight falling on the yellow of last year's hay. To go there to adore the kittens is to step into the world of yesterday.
>
> The other day as I stood there watching the gaiety of the kittens dancing in the hay, I felt nostalgia for the time when I would have unblushingly taken a love story and a sandwich and sat half a day with the kittens.
>
> I can remember when it used to fill me with well-being to sit down by a pink-shaded lamp and play bridge with some friends, the tinkle of teacups and the rest. Some of them are still there, playing. To me, after being four years a Bahá'í, they are like the kittens in the hay, dancing in the sweet, warm, care-free earth vibration. For us, no more. Instead, we have these other delights and a certain immunity from the pang and fears of mortals."

In June, Ruth Moffett and her husband Robert spent their wedding anniversary with the Geneva friends. The occasion expanded into a triple Bahá'í wedding. The Heists, the McKays and the Moffetts all had anniversaries in June. The rooms at the Heist home were decorated and a sumptuous feast prepared. The "brides" were quite radiant in their white dresses and enormous bouquets of mock-orange blossoms. Our husbands may have been a little more self-conscious.

What had seemed like a play, at first, had taken on significance for us and our invited guests. Had not all the grooms asserted in the presence of the others their pledges to God: "Verily, we are content with the will of God." And we, the brides had given the rejoinder, "Verily, we are satisfied with the desire of God."⁶ This, I knew, was my first real marriage, my Bahá'í one. Throughout the next day I felt lifted above the ground to the height of my own knees. I was disappointed that my more down-to-earth husband did not share in this sensation.

Ruth had had a letter from Shoghi Effendi, and she shared the priceless statement that God, although the Unknowable Essence, is not an abstraction – but cognizant, loving, responsive, although forever beyond our ken.

Chun Chuan Cheng comes to Emerald Hill

We had been introduced to Chun Chuan Cheng of Canton, China, at a dinner of the Cosmopolitan Club. He had come with the other students to the Blossom Picnic and later had written to us asking permission to spend the summer on the farm: "I am going to you to have experience, home life, and manifold learnings on your farm."

Cheng made arrangements with the Agricultural Department of Cornell University to receive laboratory credit for his summer's work. He would learn the care of fruit, how to drive a car or tractor, to milk a cow. He would work for no salary.

On the first morning I asked him of his plans.

"First, I meditate fifteen minutes. Then I do my washing [his bath], then I practise my violin, eat breakfast, go work 'till four, then I wash again." The rest of the day was for his "manifold learnings".

The advent of a Chinese student into our rural environment invited, fifty years ago, more comment than it would today. It did not take long, however, for all to acknowledge Cheng's superiority. He had won a university scholarship in Tientsin, in a competitive examination and had scored first among hundreds of others. His test with us was to adapt to a different style of life,

---

6 *Bahá'í Scriptures*, ibid., # 840, p. 457. The pledge of marriage, as found in today's prayer books, is translated as "We will all, verily, abide by the Will of God."

and, in so doing, to win the people over from their prejudice.

I found my grandmother removing one day, a treasured quilt from his bed. It was one that she had given me as a wedding present. When I persuaded her that Cheng was very clean, she agreed to leave the heirloom where it was. The morning he went out to work with the Italian women in the cherry orchard, the three male workers were in near panic. They called Willard aside and whispered, with appropriate gestures, "He bad. He eat people!"

But when my grandmother became ill, it was Cheng whom she asked to bring her lunch tray. Often he would sit by her bed and tell her stories. Once, on the way home for holidays, he told her, river pirates had kidnapped some young students of the rich. Cheng was among them, but his parents were poor, and they could not pay the ransom. He was left on the riverboat, in a sort of cage. He said, "It was then that I taught myself to meditate. I became changed."

His captors put him ashore, eventually, and he found his way home. He said that the experience was good for him because, with his increased power of concentration, his studies were made simple and he was able to win his scholarship. He had been referred to the Chinese Consulate in Washington, D.C., and was their ward. Cheng came to think of us as his parents and on his school vacations, came "home" to us.

The summer of 1929 passed sweetly. For more than a month, the Sicilian cherry-pickers came and worked at the harvest. The orchards were gay with their cries. Even the little children were put to work picking up the fruit that had fallen on the ground. This was fruit country and hundreds of pickers from the cities flocked in. The fruit and vegetable harvests would continue in the area until late in September when the apples and pears were put in. The pickers would camp in barracks provided by the growers in the neighbourhood. The sound of outside activity was an overtone for the life going on in the house. That summer I cooked for a household of seven, to which numerous visitors were added. I would write to Lorna,

We will have twenty-two overnight, including Dale and Katherine Cole from Cleveland . . . There were fifty-five for dinner at the Heists', many from Binghamton. I must go now and make a million beds. . . We have had a big picnic for each of four days. Barefoot dancing on the lawn, Oscar Wilde stories by firelight, 'Abdu'l-Bahá's Tablets at sunset on the hill with a young moon rising.

On July 19th I had another telephone message from May Maxwell calling me to a National Teaching Committee meeting in New York City. She would engage a room for me in her hotel. I would be with her in the evening and meet her for breakfast, then we would spend the day at Committee work with Mason Remey, who was chairman. Harlan Ober and Marion Little would also be there. In the absence of Rex, I represented the Outline Bureau. I recorded the notes and made a report for Horace to put in the Newsletter.

Visit to the Kinney Apartment

I went to New York, and in the evening, May took me to the Kinney apartment, her spiritual home. At our tap the door was flung open by Mr Edward Kinney, whom 'Abdu'l-Bahá had named 'Saffa'. My first impressions were that he was not tall but expansive both in girth and in his gestures of welcome. He had generous features, impulsive movements. I recall his rich baritone voice as he invited us in.

In the living room a full-length painting of 'Abdu'l-Bahá faced, with the assurance of His presence, whoever entered. There were a number of people in the long room. Carrie 'Vaffa' Kinney greeted me. There was the intimate circle of friends who seemed, like May, to be members of a spiritual family linked by bonds of remembrance of the Master. Some of those memories would date before His visit to New York. To step into this company gave an uplift to the soul. Among us moved our host. Of him, I wrote, "He is full of spiritual fire. His heart is afire and he sets others aflame."

We spent the evening until midnight reading Tablets and listening to anthems that Vaffa had composed. The Greatest Name, "Ya Bahá'u'l-Abhá", was the refrain. I took refuge in a black oak chair with a tall carved back and listened with closed eyes to the mention of the Name of God. To conclude the evening May recited a prayer which she said was the Guardian's favourite.[7]

Saffa Kinney arose and impressively addressed the room. "All prayer is a covenant with God," he said. "By that prayer we have all made a covenant. We promise to do our part to carry out what we have prayed for."

"Everything stopped," I wrote later. "The people in the room just looked at one another. We looked and looked until all our personalities seemed to fall away and there was only the shining of an inner light, beautiful and clear."

Toward the end of August, two or three carloads of Bahá'ís from Geneva were on their way to Binghamton, a large manufacturing town about one hundred miles south of Geneva. Wheels had been rolling between our two towns since the spring picnic, but this promised to be an event of special importance. Through the summer months the Ives had been staying nearby in a cottage at beautiful Quaker Lake. All of us were invited now to an overnight house party and to stay with them or with some of the Binghamton people. Mabel and Howard were excited and joyous. We knew their mood. It had always something to do with the advancement of the Cause. Lorna Tasker was with us. She acknowledged later that she was "in a state of strange excitement", which she felt others were sharing. The Obers arrived from Buffalo and lastly, the Binghamton people. Baskets of food were taken down to the pine trees by the lake and after reading a selection of 'Abdu'l-Bahá's words on the subject of love, we feasted. Following the meal, a number of people spoke, and Lorna remembers that Mary Collison told the story of Bird Gadoon. Lorna recounts it this way:

---

[7] The prayer, revealed by 'Abdu'l-Bahá, begins "O Lord, my God and my Haven in my distress! My Shield and my Shelter in my woes..."

The Story of Bird Gadoon

The bird Gadoon was of unusual plumage. She could fly higher and farther than other birds and her eyes were turquoise blue, whereas the eyes of the other birds were brown. The other birds were jealous, and whenever she tried to build a nest, they drove her away and destroyed it. So she was forced to use some other method of raising her brood. Unknown to the others, she laid her eggs in their nests, one in each nest. When the little birds were hatched, in each nest there would be one unlike the others – one that felt within him a strange restlessness, a yearning for something he knew not what.

And then, one day, the mother bird flew over the forest and called her young. Aloft she soared in the great freedom of the sky, and from the forest the young birds rose and followed her.

So, all who are born in the nests of the world bearing in their hearts the yearning for a deeper brotherhood, children of a dream yet unfulfilled, will rise, hearing the call of divine love and mount on wings to join the others.

Lorna continues her record,

As we listened, dusk came, and night. The party broke up, but no one went home. We went around by the light of bonfires greeting one another, laughing, talking, being glad together. I forgot my usual reserve, my uneasiness on meeting new people. We were all old friends, comrades in the love of God.

The next morning about forty people sat down to breakfast. The picnic tables were moved together, white cloths laid and the food spread out. Everyone was in the highest spirits, and beyond the hilarity was the feeling that this was a special moment. Howard Ives stood up and read a prayer with the power that was in his voice. Next, he called for talks, starting with Harlan and Grace Ober. The magic of that team of Bahá'í teachers who had known the Master became the air we inhaled. They spoke of the reality of servitude. The Geneva guests, too, spoke from their hearts.

We cleared off the tables and returned to find that Howard had placed on them a long sheet of paper and a pen. He said: "All those from Binghamton who wish to become Bahá'ís, write your names on this paper." Nineteen signed.

We had been exchanging letters with Loulie Mathews ever since our meeting at Convention. Now a date was set for another meeting with her. She was inviting us to spend a week in New York City, beginning on December 5th. We were to speak at public meetings, be passed around among the Bahá'ís and to stay at the Woodworth Hotel, where we would be near the Kinneys.

More letters came from May. Those two dear people who had conspired at Wilmette, Loulie and May, had added now a teaching trip which they had planned for us – a trip to Philadelphia, Washington, Baltimore, Boston, Portsmouth and, finally, Montreal, where we were invited to spend Christmas week with the Maxwells.

Well, the fruit money was in and we could think about clothes. I bought a blue velvet suit and tam in Rochester, and Mayme Rapelje, our Geneva dressmaker, made me a pretty, flaring, blue silk dress. This was the nucleus of my wardrobe. When Willard dressed up, he was aristocratic in appearance and I was vain about his looks and aplomb. Cheng's opinion of Willard's appearance was quite different. He once said, "Willard, he is poet and peasant." Marguerite and Christine were left in charge of the house and the two dogs and five or six cats. The tenant farmers looked after the farm animals, including our three mules.

We had now a little time after our busy summer to rest, to prepare some talks, to say some prayers. Then we were off again for our first scheduled stop, New York City.

We were the most unlikely people in the world to be making a tour of big cities, but the doors flung open and through them we went! For the next month we were to lead an enchanted life. Loulie Mathews was our fairy godmother and May, our guardian angel. Our talks were not brilliant. No Dorothy Baker eloquence came to our aid. But then, Martha Root was not brilliant either.

A strong magnetic power sustained her. That same power showed through our public talks. We could tell by the concentrated attention of the faces we looked into. We were upheld by the certainty that our friends were praying strong prayers for us. Our recognition that "of ourselves we can do nothing" was answered by the companion statement "God doeth whatsoever He willeth." This helped.

New York City and Richard Harrison's Fish Fry

Loulie, our hostess, did not intend that the visit of "the children", as she called us, should be an ordeal. She planned delightful diversions and came with us whenever her busy life permitted. One matinee afternoon she indulged Willard's fondness for Wagner by taking us to a performance of "Die Valkyrie" and, another time, to the current hit, *De Green Pastures* with Richard Harrison in the role of "de Lawd." At the opening curtain, "de Lawd" is seated on a cloud, hurling thunderbolts upon the people of the earth. He is prevailed upon by the all-Black cast to give the world another chance. All ends with a triumphant fish fry in heaven tended to by "de Lawd" and His angels.

After the final curtain, Loulie said, "Would you like to go backstage and meet Mr Harrison?" She piloted us through aisles, passages and doors, and soon "de Lawd" was shaking our hands and calling for the Black angels to come and be introduced, wings, stars and all.

That night when Willard and I were relating our experience at the Kinneys' dinner table, May said, "Why can't we invite Mr Harrison here with some of your Harlem friends, for a pilau dinner tomorrow night, Doris?"

We telephoned Loulie. She was enraptured with the plan and she agreed to pick up Mr Harrison and bring him to the Kinneys' and, later, to take him back for the evening show.

"This is great," said Vaffa, "but remember, I have to be away all day."

"I will go shopping and buy all the makings," May volunteered, adding, "Doris and I will make the pilau."

The next afternoon there was a commotion in the hall. May arrived with a boy who was carrying large bags of provisions. We put on aprons, wielded knives and other utensils, and performed the ritual of preparing the food of the Master. May, with her usual go, turned out to be an excellent cook. Meanwhile, we kept on telephoning to invite friends from the Black and White communities to our Feast. These included the Huberts and the Allens from the Urban League, Mr Harry T. Burleigh and Marion Little. There were five of us from the Kinneys' and some visiting Bahá'ís.

Reinforcements came. The table in the long narrow dining room was lengthened and places set for eighteen. In the kitchen, the gently baked rice was taken from the oven and the pilau made. When Loulie arrived at six-thirty with Mr Harrison, we stood waiting behind our chairs, the place at the head of the table being reserved for him. Looking back in memory at that table and the beaming welcoming faces, I seem to see it through Mr Harrison's eyes. He stood still for a long moment, then said: "Some FISH FRY!"

I recall another dinner of that time, one with Mary Hanford Ford. Her apartment was like herself, small, compact and stocked with the treasures of a lifetime. She had made herself comfortably at home at the farm. Now, we were to see her in her own world. In the afternoon she whisked us away to have tea with a Baroness. The Baroness, imposingly large, bejewelled and well-draped, was deferential to Mrs Ford. The minds here were sophisticated, world-travelled, interested in metaphysics. With them, our Mrs Ford took her rightful place in the centre. I think it was compassion that brought her there.

But it was in the company of Bahá'ís that Mrs Ford became a tiny queen. How they adored her! That night at the Feast of Masá'il, our hostess, Marion Little, just picked her up like a small child and swung her around. In her green velvet dress, she was all of ninety pounds. The merriest of all was our wise, clever, famous Mary Hanford Ford.

Then there was a luncheon hosted by Loulie. Loulie had written once a book, *My Friendly Enemy, Life*. She had had her ups and down of fortunes and had arrived now, with her husband, at a cycle of affluence. I paused in wonder at her living-room door. Over the fireplace hung an original Corot! I was so mesmerized by it that I did not see the other paintings. But I do remember being impressed by the bright peasant tiles of the imported Italian cook-stove.

Loulie's friends were an experience for Willard and me. Perhaps they were from a world related to the Baroness's domain. One gentleman, brother of a famous dancer and fresh from the Parisian art colony of the Left Bank, had a fringed white toga, a silver fillet in his long white hair and wore sandals. It was all very casual. Loulie's little white dog persisted in licking the gentleman's bare toes. The atmosphere was artistic and bookish and Willard and I, although feeling rather "upstate", got on quite well. One lady was especially interested in prayers at dawn when, according to Muslim lore, the inverted sun over the horizon showers bounties on the earth.

Saffa's Story

There was a knock at the Kinneys' door. "Excuse me," Saffa begged, "I have a music pupil. Don't leave unless you want to." He introduced his pupil as the star of a current musical show. I had not known that Saffa was a trained musician and composer, an organist and choirmaster, and in demand as a voice teacher. Within half an hour he was back again and we resumed our talk.

When I asked him to speak of 'Abdu'l-Bahá, his eyes twinkled. "Do you, too, want me to tell you of the time He carried me up the steps – and me, nearly 300 pounds?"

One day during 'Abdu'l-Bahá's visit of 1912, they had returned from a trip in the city and 'Abdu'l-Bahá lay back in the car, His eyes closed. He roused Himself, descended from the car and stood with Saffa looking up a flight of steps they would have to climb. Saffa made a worried remark, his eyes on the Master's frail form. Suddenly, 'Abdu'l-Bahá hoisted the weighty Saffa in His arms and ran lightly up the steps with him.

"It was as if I had no weight," Saffa explained. "'Abdu'l-Bahá, who has been called by Bahá'u'lláh, 'the Mystery of God', had summoned the Power of the Great Ether. This power, shared by the Manifestations, is supernatural. In our lack of understanding we call it a miracle – and so it has always been, for us, a miracle."

'Abdu'l-Bahá had meant this as a joke on Saffa, for having worried. The Master's laugh had been hearty.

Philadelphia and Mrs Revell's Kitchen Sink

The week in New York was over, and Willard and I were alighting from the train in Philadelphia. We had been told that we would be within walking distance of the Revells' home. We stepped out, inhaling the air of a new city. We saw that the houses were built in compact blocks with nothing to distinguish the separate homes except their trimmings – details such as doors, railings, steps and window curtains. I do not remember any grass or trees. We clutched our slip of paper with the street and number.

We arrived safely and were drawn into a long connecting hall by an angel disguised as a tiny little lady of seventy. She had snow-white wispy hair, brown eyes, a strong nose and the sweetest and most sensitive mouth we had ever seen. She was Mrs Revell, the mother of Ethel and Jessie. Here was another who had known the Master and had received His blessings during His visit to North America. She was shy with us. We sat down at the table with her and she poured tea. Then she wondered why, although we ate her cookies, we drank no tea. She sampled hers. All we had in our cups was hot water!

"Oh, my goodness, I forgot to put in the tea. I get so excited!" She grabbed her teapot, hurried to the kitchen and soon returned with the tea. By this time, through laughing about the tea, we were well acquainted with Mrs Revell. She told us her story of 'Abdu'l-Bahá.

Mrs Revell had been at a meeting in a Philadelphia hotel

when 'Abdu'l-Bahá said to her, "I will be at your house tomorrow at nine o'clock."

"I came home walking on air," she said. "The Master in my house!"

She began to clean and polish and worked to make the whole house befitting for the Master. "But there was one thing I could do nothing about: the kitchen sink. It is porcelain, stained and cracked. I thought, if the Master should ever see that, I would be disgraced."

"The next morning," she went on, "I made refreshments. I looked again at the house. Everything was spotless. We had a screen in one room, and I moved that out in front of the sink."

"Sharply at nine, the Master came and with Him ever so many people. Even the stairs and hall were full of people standing. But why was the Master passing through the people to the dining-room and kitchen? He strode straight over to that screen, pushed it to one side and looked at my sink. Then He laughed as if it were His joke on me. I laughed, too, as I am doing now, and kept on smiling all through the wonderful talk He gave. This house was the only home in Philadelphia that He honoured by His presence."

"But you are not drinking your tea!" exclaimed our hostess. Dear Mrs Revell had given herself the fresh tea and had forgotten to pour ours. The three of us were laughing hopelessly at this second incident.

"It was the Master who made me forget. And, you know, that day He was here, I forgot to pass the refreshments."

We had our charming hostess to ourselves that afternoon, until Ethel and Jessie came home from work. Their brother was there, and in the evening he took us sight-seeing around Philadelphia, and we saw the famous Liberty Bell.

Washington, D.C.

Looking very elegant, Mason Remey met us at the Washington station and took us to breakfast. For over fifty years, I have remembered that we had chocolate walnut waffles.

Our sight-seeing trip began with a visit to Arlington National Cemetery and the grave of the Unknown Soldier. Eclipsing this in importance, it seemed, was an imposing monument that marked the grave of Mason's father, who had been an admiral in the United States Navy. It was impossible not to see in our guide an overwhelming pride of family. Yet he was genial and kind, taking us to see the Capitol and the White House. This was the man whom, one day, the Guardian would appoint as a Hand of the Cause of God and who, later, would fail in his allegiance to the Covenant because he thought he had the right to rule.

We were charmed by our tour and were delivered to the home of Allen McDaniel, Chairman of the National Spiritual Assembly. Our hosts were gracious, although a little formal, as was their home. We did not see much of the McDaniels, what with meetings being held every evening and the friends claiming our daytime hours.

When she had hugged me at Green Acre, I had protested, "But I don't know you." She had replied, "We will know each other sometime." Since that time, four and a half years earlier, Mariam Haney had maintained a friendly relationship through correspondence. She was one of the first who had encouraged my Bahá'í writing. One morning during our stay in Washington she called for us and took us for a drive around the city. She said, "I remember taking 'Abdu'l-Bahá on this drive in 1912. Paul was a little fellow and he cried the entire time. I could do nothing with him."

Mrs Haney asked me if there was anywhere I would especially like to go. "The Corcoran Art Gallery," I replied. We stopped there and saw the paintings, all of which I have since forgotten. I do remember a line from a poem of Rumi. "I am bound for heaven. Who has an eye for sightseeing?" It was so then.

After luncheon at the Haney home, we went to see George Spendlove, who had an antique shop on P Street. George and Willard met like brothers, after their friendship at the Montreal Convention. At George's shop we saw some beautiful European furniture. We had dinner with him and went with him to the rooms where we were to speak.

The mingled group of believers, representing the Black and White races of the city, were the variegated fruits of the tree of Oneness that 'Abdu'l-Bahá had planted with such concentrated intention during His visit. Mrs Lua Getsinger had nourished the ground from which that tree grew, and a distinguished band of early Bahá'ís, headed by Mrs Agnes Parsons, had tended it with courage and dedication. It was our precious experience that night to be in the radiance of that circle.

Faces along the Path

As I sat in the kitchen of a boarding-house in Baltimore, a busy Bahá'í hostess served me a bowl of delicious stew. One of her boarders was a tall, strong man in working clothes who introduced himself as John Reddin. He told us that he was from Halifax, Nova Scotia. How far away that seemed! He was a Bahá'í, too, and had lost his arm in the Halifax Explosion. In years to come I would learn more of that disaster. But now, we enjoyed a hurried visit before speaking at a downtown hall. The rain poured and few people came. The next morning, we were on our way to Boston.

Lorna met us at the Bahá'í Centre and, after a meeting, we went to Beverly, Massachusetts, to spend the night. When we returned to Boston the following morning, we called on Mr Matthew Bullock of the Urban League. I offered him a letter of introduction from Mr Hubert. Mr Bullock's manner was polite but reserved. We had, at least, made a gesture for racial unity.

We were surprised to hear much later that he had become a Bahá'í and, still later, gratified when he became a member of the National Spiritual Assembly. I believe that our visit with him and whatever effect it had was an example of Bahá'u'lláh's guidance. It illustrates our need for alertness in taking the initiative with the knowledge that our actions may be the keys to an unknown yet unfolding destiny.

The Gregorys and a Marriage Prayer

"There he is!"

Yes, there stood Louis Gregory waiting for our bus with a look of boyish eagerness. We walked briskly with him to a small house on a side street.

"Yes, we certainly are in residence," he said triumphantly. Louis and his wife Louise had been married for eighteen years; yet only occasionally had they lived together in a place they could call home. Their marriage was "made in Heaven". They had met while on pilgrimage, and 'Abdu'l-Bahá had suggested that they marry. In spiritual attune, they did, through devotion to Him. Soon they were to discover the bounties of intellectual compatibility and the growth of human affection. They were truly married on every plane. But, by agreement, they had, for months of each year, gone their separate ways: Louise to teach in Europe and Louis to promote racial unity in the United States. Here, in Portsmouth, New Hampshire, they were together for a time.

When we stepped into the kitchen, Louise, small and dark and with a red scarf wound around her head, was bending over the stove and stirring the contents of an iron pot. "I hope you like okra," she said anxiously as we shook hands.

The hospitality was southern. The stew, featuring the okra, was a blend of meat and vegetables. Time passed dreamily, while we floated on Louise's solicitude and Louis's gaiety. We shared with them the details of our trip and for Louis, who knew all of the people we had met, it was family news.

The neighbours, both White and Black, came and we sat in the neat little parlour which must have come furnished with the house. The intimacy we had known at dinner was extended now to the guests. We sat there, somewhere beyond our usual selves, secure in love. Willard and I had been making many talks which were planned in advance. Here, we could carry on a conversation with the inner reality of the people who had gathered. So we relaxed into a paradise of the blend of races, as in those remembered meetings in Rochester. We talked about prayer and the answer to prayer.

I told them, "God will answer every sincere prayer, 'Abdu'l-Bahá had said."

Another person contributed, "When we pray for spiritual attributes, we will be answered, at least by tests!"

"And our material needs?"

"Yes, those prayers are answered, too, although in the wisdom of God, the answer is sometimes 'No.'"

"Relating to attributes," said Louis, "let me tell you that, in my youth, my greatest sin was pride."

We were amused to hear this admission, for Louis was a most humble and self-effacing man. So humble was he that we all laughed heartily at the "monster of self" that we imagined him to have slain. Louis laughed, too, and mocked the situation by getting down on his knees and begging for help. He continued, in a more serious vein, "We have to look at ourselves first and bring ourselves to account so that we will know when we are 'standin' in need of prayer.'"

We slept that night in the Gregory's house, deeply aware of the privilege that was ours. In a prayer revealed for their wedding 'Abdu'l-Bahá had said, "Verily, they are married in obedience to Thy command. Cause them to become the signs of unity and harmony until the end of time. . . "[8]

Montreal

We arrived in Montreal on Christmas Eve. The climate in Washington, D.C., had been mild, and I was wearing over my velvet suit only a cloth coat. Frost crystals sparkled in the light from the high leaded-glass windows of the Maxwell house as we waited at the door of 1528 Pine Avenue. It was opened soon, and we walked into May's embracing arms. Sutherland and Mary, with welcoming smiles, were standing nearby.

The place was already a shrine. The Master was still there. His holy presence breathed to us, emanating from May's greeting like a strain of music or the scent of attar. The beauty of the

---

8 *Bahá'í Prayers*, p. 107.

house, created by Sutherland for the service of the Cause, soon enveloped us. We passed the door of a formal parlour or library, and the chair where 'Abdu'l-Bahá had sat was pointed out to us. We entered the living room where we relaxed and answered eager questions about our trip and listened to some of the plans for our week in Montreal. I absorbed the atmosphere, but I retain no memory of the room except for its elegance, taste and comfort. Only one object do I remember well: a small oil painting of a beautiful Scottish girl of another generation. Her name was engraved on a brass plate mounted on the frame: "Mary, Duchess of Sutherland."[9]

As the ringing of church bells proclaimed Christmas Eve, we were shown upstairs to our room. A collection of Japanese prints was displayed along the stairway and hall. We slipped off to sleep in an unreal and dreamlike world.

Lying awake the next morning, I had a flash of understanding. I had mistakenly called our impressions "dreamlike", but we were the ones who were disoriented from reality. "The real life is the life of the Spirit and not the life of the body." Loulie Mathews had been right. We were the "children" born rather recently to the Bahá'í Faith. We were also, however, the ones who, for the past three weeks, were welcomed into the intimacy of mature Bahá'ís who had known the Master.

"This is too much for me," my lesser self complained. I was to suffer in the days ahead, just as I had seen Dorothy Baker suffer from the conflict of the two natures within. The test turned me inward for days, and I was saved from embarrassment only by Willard's pleasure and excitement of being there. I could not talk, and I found it difficult to raise my head. Any display of composure had to be achieved through will power.

The events of the day were casual enough. While we sat at the breakfast table, we heard music from the street. French-speaking carollers were outside, and we ran to the window. Sutherland went outside to give them some money and they sang again. I think there was, too, a violin or fiddle. The carollers were bundled in rough coats, thick scarves and worn caps.

---

9 She was the second wife of the Third Duke of Sutherland.

As they strode along, the snow creaked under their thick boots.

Relatives were coming for Christmas dinner and May, Mary and the maid were very busy in the kitchen and dining-room. Mary wore a blue, silk morning gown bound by a metal belt around her slim waist. I recall the quick rhythm of their movements as she set the silver around the long table.

The traditional family dinner had ended in a blaze of glory, a great ball of flaming plum pudding. In the afternoon the McKays excused themselves and went upstairs for a rest before setting out for "tea" at the home of Ernest Harrison. We did not know yet that tea is a time of day in British Canada. This tea turned out to be another complete turkey dinner. Such was the munificence showered upon us that Christmas that we ate two turkey dinners.

We spent the evening with Ernest and his family. His handsome children, having returned from skiing on Mt. Royal, were flushed and excited. Mrs Harrison was polite but reserved, and conversation was difficult to maintain. Soon, refusing help, she retired to the kitchen to cope with the dishes. It was obvious that Ernest, in his intense inward devotion to the Cause, was in but not of the life of the house. I thought, "He stands erect on a hill, a weather-beaten monument to God." Years later, his wife gone, Ernest came alone as a pioneer to Prince Edward Island.

We spoke seven times in the six remaining days of our visit. As in our meetings in New York and the other cities, our efforts were confirmed by a power other than our own merit. There was no doubt in our minds that during our week in Montreal, May's prayers clothed and protected us even as the furs in which she wrapped me warmed me in the below-zero temperatures. We followed the schedule made for us until, on Sunday, we spoke in the pulpit of one of the two churches where 'Abdu'l-Bahá had spoken. From my seat in the carved pulpit chair I looked down into May's eyes – eyes that shone with an electric light. We were in the full focus of her prayers. Their strength parted the veils between earth and the heavenly forces. To rise and speak, well, what else could we have done? After the meeting in the church, the little group of the very first Bahá'ís in Montreal went to the Maxwell house and laid out a community supper.

The life of the household flowed pleasantly around us. Mary's young friends, called "The Youth Group", came and went. Most were students at McGill University, where Mary was enrolled in special classes. Several were of mixed racial background. One student, for instance, was of Irish and Japanese parentage. Mary's tutor in Arabic was Turkish. There was a Black in the group, too; Eddie Eliot, an electrician. Emeric Sala and Roland Estall were youth then, and Rosemary Gillis, a rare, dark, Scottish girl, very striking with high cheekbones, full features and jet-black hair. A lifelong friendship with Rosemary began the afternoon that May sent the three of us for a sleigh-ride on Mt. Royal.

As we rode, we saw spread below us the St. Lawrence River with its bridges and the vista of the city of Montreal. Our views were split by the looming back of the driver. With his bushy fur coat and great cap, he resembled a bear. It was a crystalline world we rode through, and we talked about ourselves. Rosemary said, "My greatest test is Mary. She is so far above me that I feel quite dumb. She is so lovely, such a teacher, so gifted. I never can think of anything to say when I am with her."

I smiled at the description of my own ego plight. "Rosemary, how well you have described my own feelings since coming here and, more than that, my experience of 'nothingness'. I feel that May is calling where ordinary mortals cannot follow." Willard listened indulgently but made no remark.

In the evening we were invited to meet with members of the Youth Group. Because it was Christmas week, a feeling of gaiety was in the air, and I wished I had something to wear besides my veteran blue silk dress. As I started downstairs, Mary called from her room, "Would you like to wear this? I think it looks like you." It was her glamorous Spanish shawl; blue roses embroidered on a square of white silk, with a fringe of shaded blue at least eighteen inches wide. Mary draped this over my "Alice blue" shoulders and joined me in a rapturous gaze in the mirror. Instantly, I had become a somebody! Enchanted, I wore my blue finery with the flair of a Spanish lady.

When I returned from the meeting, I stopped at Mary's room

to return the shawl. "Why, Doris," said Mary, "the shawl is my gift to you. It is perfect for you."

The joy of the Maxwell house had been showered upon me, yet I was still captive of a gloomy withdrawal of spirit. With May, my wings were of lead. I had remained dumb during those hours she had talked with us about the Cause, the presence of the Master illuminating her words and physical being. I thought ruefully of the early story of Elizabeth Greenleaf running away from 'Abdu'l-Bahá yet lingering in a contradiction of love and fear. My Montreal visit was drawing to a close. On the last day May came into my room to find me cast down on the bed, crying. She had to know why. I told her how the week had been agonizing for me, "as if a part of myself has been burning away".

She suggested that now I could begin to understand Shoghi Effendi's anguish when called to the station of Guardian. She had known of his pain. She explained, "To the extent that we elect to carry that cross ourselves, will he be relieved of his burden."

"Is this," I asked, "what is meant by the station of martyrdom?"

"Yes," she responded.

At last I had spoken, and May had answered. She stayed with me awhile, comforting me by pouring heavenly love on me. She had become my spiritual mother, and that is how I still think of her. A tenderness not of this world was communicated to me, and my self-thing with her was banished forever.

We would return again to our administrative duties on the Teaching Committee, but now there would be a difference. Willard knew this when he came back from his walk. He knew that he was stepping into a new heaven. May had taken us into her heart and now was spiritually related to us. The glow of that warmth has never cooled in the forty years since she left this world.

That night May moved into our room, and Willard and I slept in the bed of 'Abdu'l-Bahá. She had made the bed with green sheets and over us spread the gown of the Greatest Holy Leaf. It was called the "Robe of Bounty". I lay awake many hours that night, aware of the unusual lightness and insubstantiality of my physical body; sometimes, I seemed to be floating above it.

We stayed close together on our last day and May spoke of many things. It was then that we learned about the Robe of Bounty. The Greatest Holy Leaf had given it to Lua Getsinger and Lua had given it to May. Shoghi Effendi had said its presence in Montreal was most portentous. Its counterpart existed as a spiritual reality, a mystery and a bounty like the Tablet of Aḥmad.

May told us an intimate story that helped to explain her constant reference to the Guardian. She had been prostrated with grief at the death of 'Abdu'l-Bahá and for months had remained ill in bed. When she was called to visit the Guardian, she arose and went in a wheelchair. In Haifa, she experienced the shock of the Master's absence and suffered the realization that she would never see Him again. The thought of losing Him forever overwhelmed her, and she lost the strength to leave her bed again.

In her most despairing moment, the youthful Guardian, then twenty-six, came and stood by her bed. As their eyes met, it was 'Abdu'l-Bahá Himself who stood there, as if He had never been away. As the vision faded into the form of Shoghi Effendi, her startled recognition of his conferred identity with the Centre of the Covenant restored her spirit. She had once more contacted the spirit of the Master and had been given evidence of His presence and His nearness to her.

The next day Shoghi Effendi wheeled her chair to the tomb of the Báb, which is also the burial place of 'Abdu'l-Bahá. He helped her to stand and asked her to walk with him around the Shrine. Supported by his arm, she took the first faltering steps and then walked slowly around the tomb.

May's healing had begun, and ultimately she was restored both in body and in mind. She had glimpsed the reality of the Guardianship, the Valíyy-i-Amru'lláh (Defender of the Faith), and her devotion was complete.

After a New Year's party in the ballroom with Mary's Youth Group, Sutherland drove us to the train. In parting he clasped around my neck a silver chain with a blue butterfly pendant.

1930

We left the noise of the cities and returned to the stunning silence of the Geneva countryside. The orchards were asleep now, tucked under a blanket of snow. Falling snow blurred a soft stillness.

On the first starry night we put on skis and went up Emerald Hill. Willard seemed to know all the stars by name, as had my father. I could never remember them so I would ask him about the constellations. We skied down the Hill and back to the house where the old dog, Kim, was waiting. We piled more applewood on the fire and talked about our teaching trip. May's spiritual intonations echoed through memory with the clarity of a silver trumpet.

Jimmy Tollis was looking well and unusually happy when he breezed in one day. He had been depressed for weeks, and I had included his name in the healing prayers that we said at the Revells' house. Jimmy had been suffering from stomach ulcers.

We asked him about his health and he was pleased to tell us, "Why, I got well all of a sudden. One day I was working in the field, and then, one moment, all the pain in my stomach was gone. I knew the moment because I actually felt the pain stop." Jimmy laughed. "I ran home shouting to Mary, 'I'm well! Mary, I tell you I'M WELL!' And I've been well ever since."

Willard asked, "Do you remember the date?"

"Yes. It was so strange, I marked it on the calendar. December 17th."

Willard took out his little black book and showed us where he had recorded the healing prayers for Jimmy. The date and the hour corresponded.

Night School

In the days of a deepening Depression, the Bahá'ís had fallen into step to achieve the latest objective in the construction of the

Temple – the raising of the steel structure above the foundation. The challenge was to find extra ways of making money. Mine was to teach a night-school class in the high school. I had given a course the previous year, but attendance was so close to the minimum that should anyone drop out, I was always in danger of losing it.

On registration night I sat in the auditorium, quaking and praying. To a hall half-full of applicants, the principal described my class as one in elementary design. It stood apart from the many other utilitarian courses offered. I repeated silently the prayer for the Remover of Difficulties and did not pause. When all the courses had been described, the applicants were told to report to the rooms to which the courses of their choice were assigned.

"Oh, God, let there be at least eight," I prayed.

I hurried upstairs to the art room. Fifteen easels were there. Providence looked down on me with a smile, I think. Had I been too urgent in my petitions? Thirty-five crowded the room and less than half had anywhere to sit. I noticed that the students were quite young and very talkative.

The class was moved to the chemistry laboratory and I began, three nights a week. When my grandmother became ill and was dying in Rochester, I went to her and, until her death on January 27th, commuted to class.

I suffered from that loss and felt a built-up exhaustion fall upon me. I returned to Geneva very ill with a cold. My Monday-night class was disastrous. On Wednesday night I was even more ill. The infection was in my sinuses, throat, chest and kidneys. Then a beautiful thing happened. Like Jimmy Tollis, I had an instant cure. On that night I went to my class, my symptoms disappeared quickly and all of us worked in an absorbing harmony. There were wings over that class that night.

Outside in the chilly weather, Willard was waiting to take me home. "Something miraculous has happened," I told him. "I am actually well, and my class and I have been in heaven." I was sitting beside my miracle. Willard had not gone to the library as was his habit; instead, he sat out in the car in front of the school praying that I would be healed.

We were happy to have another confirmation of one of the promises in 'Abdu'l-Bahá's writings. This is my favourite:

> When you call on the mercy of God waiting to reinforce you, your strength will be tenfold.[10]

To believe such words was to have our powers expanded.

> There is no doubt that the forces of the higher worlds interplay with the force of this planet.[11]

> The truth is that God has given men supernatural powers . . . in man there is a power that is bestowal of God.[12]

Our friends and teachers who had known the Master had lived, through the inspiration of His presence, in the realm of the spirit. The class the night of my cure was for us yet another glimpse into the vibrant world of a level of super consciousness that is available to us, do we but wish it!

Mr Ivanoski Paints a Portrait of 'Abdu'l-Bahá

"I have decided to commission Mr Ivanoski to paint a picture of 'Abdu'l-Bahá," announced Mrs Francis Esty. She, Willard and I were looking at the portraits of family members in the Esty home in Buffalo. The paintings were in the style of the Impressionists, vibrating with flecks of light-diffused colour.

"Mr Ivanoski spent some time with us before he painted the portraits," she explained. "No one sits for a portrait. He tries to

---

10 'Abdu'l-Bahá, *Paris Talks* (London: Bahá'í Publishing Trust, 1969), pp. 38–39.
11 *Wisdom of 'Abdu'l-Bahá*, p. 167.
12 'Abdu'l-Bahá, *Foundations of World Unity* (Wilmette, IL: Bahá'í Publishing Trust, 1971) p. 62.

catch the essence of his subjects by studying them in different light and in different moods, noting their changing expressions. When he is ready, he excuses himself from the world around him and becomes absorbed in his painting."

"Painting is a form of meditation," I offered.

"Painting is prayer," she added.

From the vibrating colour on the walls, we followed our hostess into her Bahá'í garden. "I built this garden when my husband died. I commune with him as I work here and I know that 'Abdu'l-Bahá is with us."

She took us to a tea-room in the afternoon. A woman psychic was there, moving about and reading teacups. She stopped at our table, turned my cup around, looked grave, and said, "I see you leaving your home."

I exclaimed, "Oh, no. No! I plan to spend the rest of my life there. I never want to live anywhere else!" But the woman replied, "Time will tell if I am correct."

The first visit to Mrs Esty's came at the turning of summer into autumn and while the late summer roses were vying with her budding chrysanthemums. She was pleased when my article "The Garden of the Heart" appeared in *World Order*. In March, she invited me to go with her and her daughter to the Annual Flower Show in New York and to see Mr Ivanoski's portrait.

On the drive to the artist's home in New Jersey I learned that for weeks, Mr Ivanoski had 'lived' with 'Abdu'l-Bahá, studied photographs of Him, read stories of His life, absorbed His words.

"I have planned this," said Mrs Esty, happily, "hoping that Mr Ivanoski will see the light and become a Bahá'í."

A servant opened the door into an unfamiliar world, an old world of polished luxuriance. In the centre of this environment was the superlative personality of the artist himself. His courtesy put me at ease after my shock of being served a formal luncheon by an attending footman.

"Yes, I returned to Poland after the First World War," our host was saying. "I was to be with Mr Paderewski when the League of

Nations appointed him Premier of the Polish state. I came here last year with him."

I ventured that Willard and I had heard Paderewski play at a concert in Aeolian Hall after his triumphant return and that he wore over his shoulder a wide scarf with the colours of Poland, red, green and white. He opened by playing Chopin's *Polonaise*.

"I, too, was there. A great occasion," said Ivanoski. After our return from Poland, Mr Paderewski turned to his music and I to my studio. Shall we go there now to view the painting?"

The walls were high and there was a skylight. A large area of the wall facing the door was curtained in a soft neutral-hued material like velour or velvet. We took chairs, well back, and to the right of the curtain. Mr Ivanoski pulled a cord and the curtain opened wide. There was a brief breathlessness. In silence, we beheld a large, illuminated canvas.

It was superb. Mr Ivanoski was, indeed, a master painter. A prophetic figure sat on a bench in a garden, the details subordinated to the figure and, especially, to the face. The effects were gentle and beneficent. We knew that the artist shared our reverence.

I had second thoughts, however – thoughts that I kept to myself. The picture, prized as it was, had been painted by someone who had felt the warmth of the Master but not the heat which I see in some of His photographs. In them I detect a bit of the "Mystery of God". His eyes are a reflection of two realities: the right eye speaks a compassion for humanity and of an intimate understanding; the left eye is unfathomable and as untameable as a falcon in heaven. These are some of the things that I see.

Tea with Marjory Morton

Mr and Mrs Max Greenvan and Montfort Mills were there. The Greenvans had been away for eight years to Haifa, Japan, India and some of the European countries. Marjory had been to Haifa six times. While we sat eating pâté sandwiches and sipping a smoky Souchong tea from Chinese cups, we talked about the Words of Bahá'u'lláh and later of World Administration. Marjory began to tell us about her first pilgrimage.

On her first voyage to Haifa, she had been very sick. The sea was rough, and she had to be carried to the small boat that took the passengers ashore. Later, at the Master's table, she had to refuse food. But 'Abdu'l-Bahá placed a plate in front of her and said, "Eat." She accepted, although she was so miserable she thought that it would kill her. When 'Abdu'l-Bahá brought her a second helping, she thought, "It is certain now that I will die. But if it is the Master's will, I will die for Him." She ate the second plate of food.

She was healed, of course – not only of her present ills, but also of a chronic stomach ailment.

How impatient I was in those days in New York! There were so many things I wanted to do. Certainly not to spend so much time shopping with my companion or making the daily visits to the Flower Show. I prayed, "O God, make me free and without desire." I became resigned and at last I recognized the test and accepted it. Of itself, that recognition was important. During the last two days, other plans developed for Mrs Esty and her daughter, and I was free of my social obligation. Like an arrow, I shot to May and Mary's hotel and was accompanied by them on another visit to the Kinneys'. I met Millie Collins then and shared a room with her for the night.

When I think of Millie, I am flooded with descriptive phrases. A small, love-animated hurricane will do, for a start. She had grey eyes and wispy hair and wore dark business-like clothes. She was unpretentious, efficient. Her jewellery sparkled, as did her fun. "I want you to help me write for the Convention, a report of the National Spiritual Assembly meeting," she asked. The next morning, we wrote the report while she packed her bags for the trek west.

After Millie left, I returned to May's hotel for farewell prayers. While I settled in her room, she crossed and took something out of her suitcase. It was the Robe of Bounty. She spoke again of Lua and wrapped the robe around me so that I was covered with its faded apricot pinkness. We said the prayers and talked about teaching. Then I left for an appointment at the Kinneys' with Mr Hubert. I was delighted to hear his promise to study the Faith and to speak of it to his associates. He drove me back to join the Estys in taking a night train to Buffalo.

National Convention – 1930

Katherine Cole and I had taken the long road from her home in Cleveland to Wilmette. We went via Flint, Michigan, where we picked up Helen Whitney. On the next day of our journey, we held a meeting in Detroit and spent the night with Bahá'í friends. Lou Eggleston was at the meeting. I had been introduced to him by the Obers the year before in Buffalo. Lou was pensively reserved tonight. His mind and heart were at odds, he later told us, battling the decision to become a Bahá'í. He put his struggles into questions during the meeting and we were able to give him convincing proofs. His inner conflict was resolved, and he accepted the Faith academically, as Willard had done, and followed us to Convention the next day.

The Bahá'ís were dressed in last year's clothes, the brightness of their faces making up for the absence of new spring finery.

On one wall of Foundation Hall hung the fabulous rug from the tomb of Bahá'u'lláh. It was sent by the Guardian with the suggestion that it be sold for the benefit of the Temple Fund. It had not been necessary to make this sacrifice. To our own efforts had been added those of the friends in other countries and actually we had on hand the $400,000 required for the erection of the steel framework. We did not have to sell the carpet. We had responded to the Guardian's call, and during the first gaunt years of the Depression, we had achieved "the impossible". WE HAD WON! The work would begin in August. Mr Bourgeois' plaster model of the finished Temple was displayed on a rotating black velvet mat on the speaker's table. It was in the Temple that our dreams had taken shape.

We watched for Lou. He had come and then disappeared. We

were to learn later that for the best part of two days, he walked the shores of Lake Michigan making up his mind before taking the final plunge – not into the lake, but into the Bahá'í Faith. He had found rather shattering his initial entrance into the Convention. He was overwhelmed by the variety of personalities, the mixture of nationalities and races and our uninhibited cries of greeting. Most disturbing of all, he said, was the experience of being an alien in a new dimension. The rest of us, it appeared, had somehow arrived in another world.

When he made his appearance, his friends were waiting for him – the Obers, the Geneva group and Helen Whitney, who bore him away under her wing. I am telling this story because it is history. Lou and Helen met again at Green Acre and in due time they were married. The Bahá'í summer school at Louhelen Ranch is one of their fruits.

The spirit of the Convention was joyous, triumphant, high. During the reports of activities, I was called upon to tell of the interracial work in Rochester. I smiled at Mabel Ives, who was as excited as a little mother hen, entranced by the peeping of her chick. Rochester had been Mabel's plan in the first place. Mabel was always more than a teacher; she was an organizer.

The newly elected National Spiritual Assembly appointed Rex Collison as chairman and Doris McKay as secretary of the National Teaching Committee. May Maxwell, Dr Heist and Louis Gregory were the other members.

I drove back to Cleveland with Katherine Cole, and Louis Gregory joined us. 'Kay' invited her friends to come and hear about the Faith and to share in Louis's vegetable pilau – a pilau festooned this time by a wreath of fresh spinach. I continued to Rochester where Elizabeth Brooks was in heaven over the formation of a Bahá'í study class. Sally Reynolds was an ignited teacher there. I wrote, at the end of the trip, "The fire of the Love of God has been at white heat and many veils have been consumed along the way."

Convention of the Urban League

James Hubert kept his promise. I was invited to Buffalo to attend as an observer, the convention of the Urban League. It was an all-Black convention with delegates from forty-three states.

I was so with them, in body and soul, that I forgot my whiteness. When I stepped out to do an errand, I experienced the shock of re-entering a world of white majority.

I was given ten minutes at the end of the last session in which to introduce the Faith. I spoke on the abolition of prejudice, emphasizing our meetings in which racial unity was practised in our homes. There was warm applause from the audience. One member, a minister, told me that my talk had been a benediction.

My Harlem friends, Mr Hubert and Mr Allen, drove me home. We stopped for dinner at a wayside restaurant. This act, in itself, was a bold step over a social frontier. A well-dressed birthday party occupied the tables by the windows. I smile as I recall the double row of startled faces; the ones with their backs to the entrance turned around to stare open-mouthed. They beheld a rather wispy-looking me, escorted by two aggressive-looking members of the darker race. At our side table, after ordering the choicest food on the menu, we were treated with a dazed deference. We made a noteworthy exit, too. My friends stopped to buy cigars. There, next to the desk was an advertisement for another dining place. Three, two-foot-high capital letters, "KKK", stood to represent the Ku Klux Klan, which was active in these parts.

Exhilarated and talkative after our successful foray, we drove on to Geneva. Mr Hubert and Mr Allen stayed the night, and the next day, the Collisons came and we all went to Seneca Lake for a picnic.

Cheng Returns

Cheng was being admitted to Leland Stanford University for doctoral studies in the fall. Before he went there, he returned to spend the summer with us on the farm. He planned, when he completed his studies, to return to China. It was a duty to his people, he explained, although he would prefer to have stayed in America. "I have now come to stay, except next week, when I will be driving to Pennsylvania to visit a friend."

Cheng now considered us to be his adopted parents. Our "son" had come home to us on all of his school vacations and we attended his Cornell graduation. To his professors, he had introduced us as "my family".

Cheng was a follower of Lao Tzu and always had with him a precious little leather-bound book, *The One Thousand Sayings of Lao Tzu*. It was, of course, in Chinese. He and I translated a few pages into English, and I found that it contained the familiar triad of God, Manifestation and Man.

Cheng's bright face was always at our Bahá'í meetings. He indulged our emotional response to the glad tidings of Bahá'u'lláh's appearance in our own day as if he felt himself to be an "older soul" with a heart of mandarin antiquity.

On Sunday night, Ali Kuli Khan came to speak. Our spirits were so elevated. Cheng rose to speak, complimenting us respectfully, but stating with an unusual emphasis, "But for me, I am a practical man, a philosopher." On the next morning, he left us for his Pennsylvania holiday.

On Tuesday morning the telephone rang and a voice asked, "Are you the friend of the Chinese student, Chun Chuan Cheng?"

"Yes, but why?"

"I am a Dean of Cornell University and I regret to inform you that Cheng was killed in an automobile accident in Pennsylvania."

Thus, the dramatic exit of our "practical man". How soon was he to learn the ultimate practicality of preparing for the life to come. Dear Cheng, the love of so many people followed him to the next world. We prayed that he would be "one of the fruits that ripen best when plucked from the tree".

We had been functioning that summer as a Bahá'í community. Young people had converged on the farm from different directions, asking to stay and work for their board. Goldie and Frank Haffner from Pittsburgh, eighteen-year-old Otto from Germany, and Sabri Jamal from Baghdad, sent to us by Horace Holley. Everett Bosch came with his gift of music, and Lorna was a guest.

The summer of 1930 was the nearest that I ever came to an ordered routine. I arose with Willard at five-thirty or six and vanished into a secluded porch behind a curtain of vines. My typewriter was there beside files of correspondence for the Outline Bureau and the National Teaching Committee. After writing three or four hours, I would go in search of breakfast. In the kitchen, the serving trays would have been prepared and waiting for the boys hours before. Fruit, jam and bread would be put out on the table, and the house custom was to help oneself and eat wherever one liked.

Later, with Goldie's help, I would prepare a simple lunch. The workers would come in, bathe and help themselves to sandwiches, salads and cookies. We would carry our lunch out to the porches or to the picnic nook or sit inside and listen to Everett play the piano.

For the evening meal, we became civilized. We would dress up a little for a seven-o'clock dinner at a table set with candles and flowers. Willard served with high style. After dinner, the boys carried out and washed the dishes, and we would have conversation and readings, sometimes games and dances. It was a party every night.

Unity is a Light-Giving Essence

I had experienced a succession of "covenants" and over time, I was to see their effect on the motives that pushed me forward. There WAS a power in the promises made to God, especially when those promises were made in the presence of other Bahá'ís who were activated by the same resolves. Foremost among those covenants were the promises that Lorna and I had made on the night of the burning log – promises to practise universal love. The vows of Bahá'í marriage represented another covenant. I had experienced another, with May Maxwell, when she asked us to join in a prayer triangle, each begging divine guidance for the mission the Guardian had given her – "to the extent that we elect to carry" the burden, will the Guardian be relieved of his. She helped me to realize that, indeed, we do elect to become believers, elect to assume spiritual responsibilities and elect to become living martyrs. Lastly, there were the prayers of dedication called for by Saffa Kinney. The motive for all of these covenants was UNITY. At one of the conventions, Elizabeth Greenleaf had called unity "a light-giving essence". She had said that unity must change the believer before the believers could change the world.

On June 25th, 1930, Howard Ives wrote me a letter. Howard would usually begin a letter by describing recent events and his health or lack of it. He would preface his remarks by saying that the letter would be short. More often than not, by the time he finished describing his health, he would be struck by a train of inspiration streaming gold. This is what he wrote on that day:

> Unity is the great key to spiritual progress. The unity of believers must be of such a character that never, NEVER, must one single thought of anything but love and sympathy and kindness and reverence enter into such a heart. 'Abdu'l-Bahá says that when we see even the slightest traces of love for Bahá'u'lláh in any soul, we must reverence that soul. How great then must be the reverence we have for those souls who are fully confirmed in the Cause of God and have arisen for service...
>
> But our great task, as individual believers, is to see that in the group in which God has called us to serve, never does the slightest breath of anything but love arise. And that constantly, at every moment of our spiritual journey, every selfish desire, every human attachment [must be banished and we must] find our greatest joy in becoming 'as dust beneath the feet of the friends.' ... This is the station of unity in this Day to which the believers of God are called...

Upon thee be glory and peace! Upon thee be all the confirmations of holiness and sanctity!
In His Name and love,
  Daddy Howard

Such was, in part, the letter from my spiritual father.

We continued to assist the Cause in Binghamton and Rochester, but Geneva, too, needed attention. As individuals, we were all growing spiritually. We were close, like the children of one family. There were ties that bound us together, and yet we did have conflicting qualities. We needed administrative growth, too, and the mysterious quality of unity was eluding us. The "perfect unity" as the standard set by 'Abdu'l-Bahá and the hope of Shoghi Effendi did not exist. At least, not in Geneva. Willard, Lorna and I prayed for our unity, and Lorna, Ruth Hawthorne and I were encouraged further by May's promise to share with us a prayer covenant. Regardless of the physical distances that separated us, every morning each of us prayed the dream of unity that we shared.

One late afternoon I was in my room, praying for a sign from Bahá'u'lláh, and the inconceivable happened. I was suddenly in His presence. The attempt to describe my entrance into that emanation calls for a host of inadequate similes. Still, I must try. It was as if I were struck by a scattering wind, an explosion within my soul. I tasted the Cup of Bliss and had a frightened premonition of loss. Grief overwhelmed me. The Presence would not stay but, like a rainbow, faded from me. Perhaps even in the next world I would not be worthy of this unearned Grace from God, this Gift of the Meeting!

    I fled downstairs to Lorna and Goldie, who put their arms tightly around me as if to save me from flying to pieces, but I could not stop crying and shaking. I could not tell them what had happened. Then Lorna had an inspiration. She found our black cat "Dido" and put him in my arms, and I paced the lawn in my bare feet. Eventually, I came back to the comfort of this earth.

That night I wrote on a scrap of paper that I have kept through all our moves:

> His darts, thrown from afar
> struck deep within my heart.
> Yet I wept not from pain of the jagged wounds
> that cut my Self away –
> but that the Hand which held the darts would not be mine to hold,
> perhaps, till time was old.
>
> Yearning, desire, despair! His Beauty,
> shining like a Sun!
> It was as if my Dearest Love –
> but never known –
> had passed me by,
> bound for eternity.
>
> His Beauty had not been a scourge.
> His Heat an endless drought;
> Had thirst and pain not been His call to me?
> His way of telling me where shade lay deep
> and balm grew near the spring.
>
> He passed;
> But left His handmaids with me.

I went that evening to the Assembly meeting, a meeting I had been dreading. The gentle impact of the Presence was with me still and I sat quietly. For once I was not over-zealous and outspoken. I was not forcing my thoughts upon this group. And in that way, I saw at last my aggressive spirit subdued. I was no longer a test to any of this group. And the prayers of the maidservants, in the covenant that we shared for unity, were answered. I record this because of the great lesson He taught me.

An Early Teaching Conference

What was Bahá'í teaching like fifty years ago? When we became Bahá'í, most teachers were like the apostles of Christ. They had arisen to travel and to teach while the Master was still living. As long as these teachers were alive, they were here to train and inspire us.

Now, the Guardian had issued a call. There were three goals: teaching, completion of the Temple, and the growth of the Administrative Order. On August 16th, Lorna and I arrived at Green Acre for one of the earliest teaching conferences. Teachers came. Some were members of the National Spiritual Assembly or the National Teaching Committee. Others were members from the eastern Bahá'í communities.

Rex Collison, as chairman, opened the meeting by reading beautifully from the Writings. Someone rose to suggest that all of us might, at least, learn to read the words effectively, as Rex had done.

Our program was aggressive, yet practical:

> How to Confirm New Groups
> How to Attract Youth
> The Personal Study of the Teachings
> Inter-Assembly Cooperation

There was consultation on the importance of the Guardian's statement that the Bahá'ís should visit one another. In the evening, the Ives spoke on "How to Do Bahá'í Work in a Large City" and "How to Follow Up a Big Meeting."

Mary Collison reported on the success of the Outline Bureau's project. Questions and assignments were added to the study outline that we had prepared and referenced. Together they formed a new correspondence course, for which close to 300 had applied. Mary commented on the question "How to deepen in the Cause?" by quoting the Guardian: "To deepen in the Cause means to read the writings of Bahá'u'lláh and the

Master so thoroughly as to be able to give it to others in its pure form."

On Sunday morning Lorna was asked to speak on "Inspiration" and to read a number of her poems.

The conference was an enjoyable three days full of enthusiasm and resolve, and there was time to be with our friends: time for a supper in Portsmouth with Jessie Revell, a trip to Ogunquit with George Spendlove and Rosemary Sala, a picnic on Mt. Salvat. I remember an evening with George and Lorna. We had spread a carpet on a bank above the river and, by the light of the headlamps of Lorna's car, read from *Bahá'í Scriptures*.

The Green Acre Teaching Conference spawned others in several communities. Teaching was on the move. So was racial amity. The Geneva conference was held in October, on the 19th. Louis Gregory and Juliet Thompson were there, along with forty others.

I went with Juliet to show her where to put her coat and hat. A bed overflowed with the outer garments of our guests. At this first meeting, she seemed to be without the accents of personality which most of us rely upon. Yet, I am sure that if she had slipped quietly into a crowd, no one would have failed to recognize her distinction. Only a few of us knew that she had been singled out by the Master for a tender and special love. It was Juliet who had been the distinguished artist that had painted His portrait. Unlike Mr Ivanoski, Juliet had experienced the warmth and the transforming heat of the Master's love.

Juliet Thompson

Louis and I had gone to Rochester a few days earlier, to meet Juliet at Sally Reynolds'. Sally was out of town and was leaving the house to the three of us. We visited in the afternoon, cooked our dinner and planned a meeting for the evening. A "fireside" is what we would call it now. Elizabeth Brooks was with us to help. In that radiant and carefree atmosphere of the spirit, I thought, "Actually, in ordinary life we are only half alive. A person becomes a keyboard with two extra octaves: one, childlike and free, balanced by the deeper notes of a self we never plumb."

Seventeen came to hear Juliet speak that evening. To be with Juliet was to find the beloved Master. His qualities radiated from her as naturally as her breath. A small divan was set at an angle in Sally's living room and Juliet sat there, relaxed and loving, waiting to begin. She rested her notebook on her lap and read excerpts from it. It was her diary of the days that she spent with 'Abdu'l-Bahá, first meeting Him in the Holy Land, then with Him during His visit to New York. She told of the moment when He appeared at the blue door of her room, and as she recalled the event, words deserted her. Silence spoke instead. She was overwhelmed by her own unworthiness, just as she had been then. She implored us to understand. We watched her eyes, reading in them the message she had come to bring us of a divine love and a supernatural awe of the "Mystery of God". "About my shortcomings," she smiled, "I was taking them too seriously. I was afraid to meet the Master, forgetting that He would understand and forgive me."

The next morning Juliet was bubbling with high spirits. She and I blew around in gales of laughter, getting breakfast for Louis. "Oh, come on, Louis, break your rule and have a cup of coffee with us," she teased. "Very well," said Louis, "since it is you who asked. One teaspoon of your coffee in a cup of hot water, please." I wish I could remember the conversation of these two young/old apostles of Bahá'u'lláh. He had said, "Drink thou with a healthy relish, O people of Bahá."[13] This we did, with joy and exultation.

When Louis left, Juliet and I tackled a sinkful of dishes. "This is a good time, Juliet," I said, waving my dishtowel, "to tell me about your life as a young Bahá'í in Paris. How did it begin?"

"It was the artist, Mrs Alice Barney, who opened the door for me to go to Paris and study at the Sorbonne. Through her, I met her daughter Laura who took me to May Bolles' apartment. There, on the wall, was a picture of 'Abdu'l-Bahá. I had found the Person

---

13 *Gleanings from the Writing of Bahá'u'lláh,* Trans. Shoghi Effendi (Wilmette, IL: Bahá'í Publishing Trust, 1949), p. 46.

whom I had seen in my dream as a young girl. That was the beginning. May answered my questions and I became a Bahá'í."

Her story sounded like the opera *Manon* or the romantic story of *Trilby*. The life of the artist on the Left Bank. Through her story she wove the names of Sutherland Maxwell, Hippolyte Dreyfus Barney, Thomas Breakwell, Mason Remey. They were all young then and studying in Paris. May Bolles' apartment was where they met.

"At the Beaux Arts Ball," Juliet laughed reminiscently, "Laura, Jackie and I vowed to give the Message to all our dancing partners. What a magical evening – fancy dress, lights, music, youth and dreams, and our glorious Message given to listening ears."

Urban League Speakers in Geneva

The building had the facade of a Greek temple with imposing pillars. The hall was large and, on this day, packed to the doors with a mixed small-town audience who had come with equally mixed emotions balancing between racial prejudice and curiosity.

It was Mary Collison's idea. She had persuaded the Women's Club to open their fall program with talks by the Urban League secretaries Mr Hubert and Mr Allen. As a special attraction, Harry T. Burleigh would sing.

As a famous composer and singer, Mr Burleigh strode onto the stage and, with the magic of his voice, dominated the gathering. His charm was irresistible. He gave us all the humour and pathos possible of the Negro spirituals. He opened with a personalized rendition of "Deep River" and wound up with one of his own compositions, "The Gospel Train". He even simulated the whistle with his voice. The audience, enchanted, called him to sing it again. The first lesson of the evening was that music is a universal language. Our little band of Bahá'ís exchanged proud glances. In turn, Mr Hubert and Mr Allen spoke about the dramatic upward struggle of their race and how the League was organized for social and economic advance. Their talks were informative and appealing.

The Geneva audience looked somehow changed, as if relieved from their cramping thoughts. They had been raised to think of Blacks as their "enemy". They found now, that the "enemy" had stirred their love and their respect. For many it was a bewildering experience. Some of them might have been members of the Ku Klux Klan, which had threatened to burn a cross on our farm.

Sam and Lois Allen stayed with us, as did Louis Gregory. We ate breakfast outside when we could and I remember one morning when I was shocked to watch Sam stack a large tray with coffee, cream and sugar, popovers, jam, butter, the dishes and silverware. He picked it up, balanced it above his head, and ran through the house. "No worry," he said. "I got my training as a pullman porter."

Sam and I were old friends since the Urban League convention in Buffalo. But Lois was not so easy to get to know. For all the fun and intimate talks we shared, Lois had to make a conscious decision to trust us.

The invitation to the Urban League was reciprocated. The Collisons and the McKays were invited to Harlem on November 8th and 9th. We were asked to bring as many as thirty friends, who would be entertained in Harlem homes. Actually, only fifteen Bahá'ís stayed in Harlem. The Ives came from Hartford, Connecticut, the Obers from Pittsburgh, and there was a carload each from Geneva and Binghamton. Louis Gregory joined us. Generous hospitality was bestowed upon us and our hosts showed us the town, introducing us to notables and to other people's homes. I like to think that the minglings were under Divine auspices – a foretaste of the "fruits of one tree".

Willard drove back with the Geneva friends, but I stayed over another day with the Allens. Lois confided in me her deep-seated racial prejudice. She was well-educated. Her father had been a graduate of Princeton. It was not an ignorant prejudice. She said, "I can't help it. If there is a knock on the door and a White man stands there, my heart sinks. Whoever it is, if he is White, I feel the same."

When I asked her if she would take me to the Museum of

Modern Art, she was self-conscious about going out on the street with me, but she was game and we fared forth together. In the Museum, everyone was White. Then Lois called me over to where she was sitting on a bench against the wall. She whispered, "A Black man just came in!" I laughed, and said, "So did a White one!" She got the point.

The Allens' had said, "Come any time," and in a few weeks I was back. Their third-floor apartment over the League office was, for the three of us, an island in the sky, a place of safety and understanding love.

Perhaps it was the foreboding innate in us at the approach of winter, but accounts of the Great Depression, now in its second year, would seem to explain the gloom of Willard's older brother Cecil. He would draw Willard aside for consultation about the affairs of the farm and would leave, his face closed and grim; Willard, after one of these talks, would be suspiciously cheerful. The Macintosh apples, each wrapped in a square of purple paper, polished and flawless for the New York market, still waited in the old iron barn, hundreds of barrels of them. The earlier fruit had gone at a disastrously low price.

By the fire, with the small iron kettle hung on its ancient crane, we faced the moment of truth. We would have to dismiss the tenant farmers, store or sell our heritage of antique furniture and leave for wherever we could make a living. Cecil, maintained by a job in town, would assume the affairs on the family farm.

"Gregory, our cat?"

"Lorna's mother would take him," I said, and arranged it through correspondence. Our beloved black cat, with his big six-toed feet and his triangular head with unusually large ears, was to take the trip by train in an apple crate. Cooked liver was nailed to the walls.

"The cat is lucky," I thought. "He has a place to go to." Disrupting thoughts intruded into the bubble-like dome of my security. Suddenly, at one with the refugees of history, were we not, ourselves, the dispossessed? My separation from this beloved spot, the scene of early married life, my Bahá'í childhood, and the present base of a very active Bahá'í life, would not come easy. But Willard, mature as always, assured me that my depression would soon pass.

The Providence of May Maxwell

"My calamity is My providence..."[14] Bahá'u'lláh had said. My own quick release from such a passionate attachment was yet another sign of His loving care. As my world began to fall apart, May Maxwell returned and took a room at the Seneca Hotel. She was then in delicate health and would rest in her room for days on end. Those of us on the Teaching Committee would go to her for our consultations. We would be transformed by what Rex Collison called "May's chemistry." I was soon able to write,

> A great peace has come over me and I have stepped into the larger perspective of the Faith. I lapse out of it occasionally but, for the most part, I am cheerful and not regretful of the overshadowing change.

The creativity of the Committee meetings contributed to my revival, but May would do more to transform our spirits. Willard and I would go up to her room in the evening. She and I would prop ourselves up on pillows and Willard would hover nearby. We did not talk about our problems, which now seemed unreal. Rather, we read prayers and listened to May talk about the love of the Master. Our "providence" was that she poured out on us the healing power of that influence, telling us how much she loved us and inviting us to be "in amity" with her. This meant that she was asking us to make a "prayer triangle" with her – a prayer covenant that each of us would pray to aid her in the accomplishment of a mission that the Guardian had given to her. She said there was a special power in the prayers of three people who were in unity – a hidden mystery to be guarded and worn next to the

---

14 Bahá'u'lláh, *The Hidden Words of Bahá'u'lláh*. Trans. Shoghi Effendi (Wilmette, IL: Bahá'í Publishing Trust, 1971), No. 51 of the Arabic, p. 15.

heart like the keys of a treasure-house. She added, "We should strengthen the ties of unity for the sake of unity itself."

There was unity in our triangle on those nights in the old hotel. We were led by May into a new dimension. Some souls are like hollow reeds through which pure music can be piped, reeds cleansed of self. Such souls, the writings tell us, may be the mediators of God's help to us in this life as well as in the next. "Ye are the angels," 'Abdu'l-Bahá says, "if your feet be firm, your spirits rejoiced, your secret thoughts pure, your eyes consoled, your ears opened, your breasts dilated with joy. . . ."[15] Because of the ministrations of such a soul, Willard and I, in that soft-lighted room, tasted a life-giving essence. Nor was May alone in helping us. On more than one occasion she spoke of her teacher, Lua Getsinger.

"Sometimes I feel that Lua is with us," she would say. "Lua was great because she never deserted a soul to whom she had given life."

Our committee work was done, and May left. I sent Horace Holley nine pages of reports for publication in the Newsletter. He responded, "Your teaching reports came yesterday. I think this whole activity is the greatest we have done and will lead to the public success of the Cause."

December passed and the landscape, like the minds of bewildered people, was subdued with greyness and fog. A visit to Elizabeth Brooks in Rochester found her aghast at the state of business in that city. Mabel Ives wrote, "I am ill and can trace my illness to a spiritual condition. I must try to find the key. All Bahá'ís must seek and find spiritual illumination through the vitality of their inner being at this truly dreadful period of confusion." Louis echoed, "The Bahá'ís are suffering. I have to keep busy every second or I will fall into depression."

On January 31st, 1931, Willard and I went to Rochester

---

15 Bahá'u'lláh and 'Abdu'l-Bahá, *Bahá'í World Faith* (Wilmette, IL: Bahá'í Publishing Trust, 1976), p. 360.

to ask my former high school principal, now president of the Board of Education, if there were any jobs for us. His reluctant answer was "No".

We began looking for school or agricultural jobs, first near home, later in the west or the south. If God had a plan for us, we did not have a clue, but we seemed strangely preserved from the expected anxiety.

"We are waiting in the dark," I wrote, "yet with trust. No one ever had poorer prospects. We ought to be congealed with apprehension, but somehow we are being set free by this breaking loose from security."

May and I Test Each Other

May returned about this time and committee work resumed. From my notes: January 29th:

> We have just returned from an evening with May. She has been talking about the elimination of self in teaching, about being humble, letting others do the talking. She says that this she can never learn! When the ego shows up, the other person loses interest.
>
> We have had dramatic experiences of prayer with May. She is very powerful and brings down to us a little of heaven's fire. Yet, some of the time she has been out of sorts. She would like us to understand that the call to the early Baháʼís was to be heroes. It did not follow that they were always saints.
>
> Last night, a test surprised me. After returning home from one of those exalting evenings, Willard went to bed; I stayed up, praying in the room downstairs. Perhaps May was praying, too, for it seemed that suddenly I was invaded by her presence. Body, soul and mind were rocked by the entrance of her being into mine. I did not have the capacity to contain such grace. So this is what May meant by her oft-repeated phrase, 'interpenetration of spirit'. I was afraid and then, surprisingly, angry. It was a defensive response to my troublesome lower nature.

After dawn prayers, wisdom expressed itself in this way: 'To contain May's love, you have to be a receptacle without sides. The celestial unity must flow through, and not be contained by you; otherwise, it will shatter you.'

Today she told me that she had been unhappy all day and could not tell why, except that 'half of herself was gone.' It was because I had separated my spirit from May's. I had sat by her bed and complained of her 'wasted relationships' with a number of believers in Geneva, people who were in awe of her, and shy. They were awkward with her and did not know what to say. I spoke of the Master, Who, she had said, instructed her to be 'the centre of the love of God in the Western world!' What of those faithful but unnoticed souls? I left May and went to sit in a chair by the window to cool off.

The incident that precipitated my complaint was this: I was painfully aware of a wall between May and the Geneva people. That wall was built on a sense of personal inferiority experienced by the friends. There were, in particular, two sisters. They were physically unattractive and had little to offer in the social graces. They made their living making fishhooks. When these sisters came into contact with the charm and magnetism of May, they sensed a pathetic inferiority and wilted. I took May to task for this. I said to her, "Are you thinking about these people in Geneva as being as full of potential as ordinary Bahá'ís? Why is it they are not elated by your presence as we are? For those of us who know you, we can share friendship, inspiration, love and talk. But to them you are a great lady, and they are not at home with you. They are not at their best. They feel awkward. Why are these sisters depressed? They should be sparkling too." I had such a nerve to do this. I was wrong in every sense of the word. My notes continue:

> How could I have forgotten that our darling May had expended all her strength to make those difficult winter journeys to Geneva? I had forgotten that Willard and I were absolute nobodies in comparison to her, and that unity with her loved ones was

the oxygen she breathed. In a few moments she called me, her voice weak and very tired, asking me to say healing prayers for her. Holding her hands, I said the Greatest Name and the healing prayers. She told me that life began to pour into her then.

May had made us feel so at home that we could reproach her. She responded to my observations by planning a big party in the hotel. It was to be like a feast with lots of things to eat. She gave a personal invitation to the sisters, who felt as though they were being summoned by royalty. We went, all of us dressed up and inclined to be a little nervous. May greeted everyone with hugs and kisses, and we tasted of the unity in the love of God. People forgot their fear of her and became expansively happy. The next day she was gone, on her way back to New York.

In a few weeks' time she wrote:

> You must know, Doris, without a word of mine, the strength and spiritual depths I have drawn from my association with you since I left. This second meeting has only served to intensify the spiritual interpenetration of each other's being in the mysterious alchemy of divine love. Almost every night when we are together in communion we seem enveloped and embraced and lifted up into the tangible part of the Supreme Concourse.

Around the 25th of February, Alfred Lunt invited the Teaching Committee to meet with the National Assembly in New York. I went a day early in order to visit Mabel and Howard Ives in Newark, New Jersey. It was beautiful how they carried a sense of "home" with them throughout their continual changes of location! It was a homecoming to be again with them, especially with our sleeping arrangement that night. They slept in one twin bed and I in the other! The next morning, I went back to New York and took a room in the Pennsylvania Hotel, where May was staying.

That night the telephone rang in my room. May told me that she was very ill and asked me to come down to her room and say healing prayers. I sat on her bed with my hand on her heart and said the Greatest Name, seeking to synchronize its rhythm with the irregular beat of her heart. When she was better I stayed there, lying by her side. We talked and it seemed to me as if my atoms were dissolving into an intense healing ray. When I rose to leave, her heart protested, so I waited a little longer until she slept.

Alfred Lunt came from the National Spiritual Assembly meeting greatly concerned about May. She was weary now, but over her attacks. After a day's rest in bed, she was strong enough for our meeting, which we held in her room, with a quorum of the National Assembly.

The last evening of my stay in New York I spent with Millie Collins. She was returning to California in the morning. I was delighted when she rerouted the first part of her journey so that we could ride together as far as Geneva. We rode, hand in hand, all day, telling each other about ourselves and our lives in the Cause. Millie, I remember, was wearing her beautiful rings, one a large moonstone, the other an emerald, each with a gold inlay of the Greatest Name. These were the gift of her husband, who, she said, had made a fortune in copper. Millie had been a miner's wife. Her husband was not a Bahá'í, but in his unselfish love for her, he left her free to spend weeks away every year travelling back and forth across the country by train. When the train arrived in Geneva, at eleven o'clock, the friends were waiting on the platform. Millie left the train and rushed out to embrace them.

Our last two weeks at Emerald Hill. We witnessed the disintegration of our material home. We were selling our books, the piano, my grandmother's dinner set. Our old dog, Kim, was put to sleep. We discarded our country clothes and took on city ones. Our feelings, mercifully, were still detached and unreal. I wrote, "Sweetness and softness are being taken out of our lives. And the joy we have known here. Our sense impressions are sharpened to poetry, our awareness lifted to the cosmic."

I was alone in the dismantled house on the last afternoon, saying the "Remover of Difficulties", when I passed into an unconscious condition – not a sleep, just a blankness. It was dark when I emerged. I knew at once what wonderful help had come from the Compassionate Spirit. With Bahá'u'lláh's celestial aid, I had been granted a final severance. My attachment was wiped clean. Unlike Lot's wife, I forgot to look back when we drove away at dawn.

We were going to join the Obers in Pittsburgh, with the expectation of a place to live, a job for Willard, and an abundance of Bahá'í work. The Obers' pleas made it a mission. The date of our exodus was March 10th, 1931.

We were driving an open Studebaker car, 1923 model, which we had bought from Howard Ives for $25.00. Its buttoned side curtains offered some protection from the March wind and on the floor was our own invention, a lighted farm lantern under a blanket, cosy for the feet. Packed in the back were our overflowing earthly goods. There were chains on the tires to prevent skidding on the icy roads. By the time we arrived in New York City, the public seemed to view us with astonishment as we wound our clickety-clanking way around Riverside Drive.

A visit was planned for us in New York, similar to the one of the year before. We were the invited guests of Loulie, although she was still very ill with pneumonia. She had arranged somehow, for us to attend a matinee at the opera, a play, and a dinner out. We were permitted to see her only once and we found her vital, the life of her body rallying for even greater services to the Faith, although the door of death was still slightly ajar. There were meetings planned for us and visits with the friends – Mrs Ford, the Holleys, Curtis and Harriet Kelsey and Mrs Marie Hopper.

We found these friends kindly as ever, but subdued. There was something else effecting this community, something more than Loulie's illness and the necessity of moving her to Colorado, something more than the advancing might of the Depression. New York City, called by 'Abdu'l-Bahá "The City of the Covenant" was being infected by the virus of disunity.

Now we knew what May's unexplained mission had been. It related to the problems created by Mirza Ahmad Sohrab, who persisted in his disobedience to the Local Spiritual Assembly of New York City, of which he was a member. That disobedience extended to his violation of the authority of the Guardian. The devoted early friends had known Ahmad when he travelled with the Master as interpreter in 1912. Later he had been chosen to present 'Abdu'l-Bahá's Divine Plan in 1919. The Guardian, deeply saddened, had asked May to keep contact with Ahmad and "to make efforts to save him from his own acts." Awaiting the Guardian's final instructions, May had complied.

While we were in New York, a cable was received from Haifa. It was over. Ahmad was declared a Covenant-breaker and May was instructed to carry the message to the friends. She asked us to go with her. There was unrest in the hall and some of the people left to follow Ahmad. Thus, at times, are the believers sifted. There was a hushed silence when May, dignified and pale, stood before the assemblage and read the cable. A Bahá'í friend sitting near me whispered, "Did you see a white light around May as she stood there calling us to steadfastness?"

We were welcomed again to Harlem. James Hubert called an interracial meeting in the rooms of the Urban League with Mary Hanford Ford and me as speakers. Willard was called upon to speak from the floor by the chairman, Sam Allen. It was a distinguished meeting of known Black leaders and devoted Bahá'ís. It was standing room only.

That evening we went with the Holleys and the Allens for dinner at the Huberts' home and, later, spoke about the Faith. The next Sunday, the New York Assembly returned the courtesy of the League, inviting some of the Black leaders to speak. There was an interracial luncheon at the Women's City Club.

We were preparing to leave again, and we went to May's room to say prayers and our final goodbye. We were putting behind us a life we had known, and we were enveloped by May's tenderness. We shared in 'Abdu'l-Bahá's mystical presence and were inspired by May's words. Then, suddenly, she announced. "I am going with you as far as New Jersey."

She bundled up in her fur coat and joined us in the front seat of the car, sharing the warmth of the lantern under the old lap robe. This was the May of delicate health who could not face the Montreal winters. Over the long bridge into New Jersey we rode. We said a last 'Alláh'u'Abhá', put May into a taxi, and drove away to the next phase of our Bahá'í life.

In the Susquehanna Valley we sensed the change of climate and put our farm lantern out for the last time. We stopped for the night in a Pennsylvania Dutch village and ate sauerkraut and pigs' knuckles at a church supper. On a bright morning we passed from the immaculate cleanliness of that village to the coal mining valleys of the Alleghenies, which eventually led us to our destination. The miners were plodding home from their shifts, tunnel lights still burning in their caps. Home they went. Home to rows of small square houses planted down in the shadow of steep hills. We could see at times a browning grey cloud light up with an orange glow. It was from the blast furnaces in the environs of Pittsburgh. "Abandon hope, all ye who enter here," I murmured, recalling Dante's *Inferno*.

Soon our attention was focused on the posters advertising St. Philomena's Raffle. The date was for that night. The side curtains of the Studebaker were open now and flapping. We steered through the impatient traffic until we saw the old church with its soot-blackened bricks. It was bedecked with coloured lights, and loudspeakers were announcing the coming event. We had entered the section of Pittsburgh called Squirrel Hill and had no difficulty finding the Obers' apartment. It was but a short step away from Philomena's. In the din of the loudspeakers, the door flew open and we were in the Obers' welcoming arms.

A New Life

The nationalities of the Ober household spelled the name of Grace: German, David; Russian, Mary; American, Harlan; Canadian, Grace; English, Aziz (Ronnie). The way of life seemed comfortable, even luxurious to us. Harlan's business of distributing fire extinguishers seemed prosperous. Grace went to the office each day with Harlan. Louise, the Black maid, came in daily to do the housework.

We ate dinner that first night, then yielded to the insistence of the loudspeakers and joined the crowds at the raffle. We looked in at the little booths and were jostled by the avidity of the mob. The noise and excitement were overwhelming and we soon returned to the apartment, found music on the radio and had a tall glass of "Grace juice" – hot tea with a slice of orange. A round of prayers for our combined service placed us together as co-workers in the plans of God.

With our coming, the house was overflowing and we were to sleep on cots in the sunporch. That part was fun, like camping. In the morning Willard was gone with Grace and Harlan. Louise came and, with that exception, I had the day to myself and for settling down to my letters and reports.

The Bahá'ís of Pittsburgh were coming to meet us that evening. I drew the shades over the arched inner windows of the sunporch and took out of our baggage my prettiest dress, one handed down to me by Mrs Esty. It had a white silk blouse embroidered with a wreath of flowers of tiny beads. The skirt and jacket were black velvet. Willard dressed, too. He looked rosy and trim in his one suit of blue serge.

The Bahá'ís swept in and took us into their hearts. This beautiful community was an example of unity in diversity. It appeared, even at this first meeting, that the McKays would be a moderator of its extremes. Without representing an extreme, we stood somehow at the central point of a group that ranged from the brilliant minds of the academic world to near illiteracy, from those with economic security to poverty, from Black to White. We had our vow to practise universal love, and here was ample opportunity. At this meeting I felt for the first time the impact of our dramatically changed environment. A sudden let-down after hovering on the 'heights' is, I suppose, to be expected. How often we tread the "Valleys", the stages or cycles of growth! In my thoughts I rebelled against the travail of passing from the "Valley of Love" to the "Valley of Knowledge", of which Bahá'u'lláh said,

"He in this station is content with the decree of God."[16]

Had I said during those sublime days of uplift with May that I was free from attachment? On the morning ride with her to New Jersey I had asked her, "How does one attain maturity in The Cause?" She assured me, "Someday, you will know."

Now it was time to remember things said in our farewell talk with her. She had told us, "The Cause of God is not child's play." She had told us that one day when ascending Mt. Carmel, an American believer had tried to call Shoghi Effendi's attention to the marvellous warbling of a bird. The Guardian had replied, "I have no time for birds."

In our changed circumstance, I saw a need to change my attitude. "It means," I wrote, "reports, not poems; it means responsibility, not rapturous dreaming; it means Pittsburgh, not Geneva." In crossing over this grim mountain, I was loaded down with a hard cold, hundreds of words to write, no place to retire to and the Easter vacation with two young boys for a rainy week!

On Easter morning Bahá'u'lláh granted my spirit a resurrection. After a time of tears, I awoke joyous and whole. The battle over, Howard Ives appeared unexpectedly, "like a knight in shining armour".

At breakfast Harlan said to Howard, "They are happy and joyous in spite of the fact that we have had to 'hang them on a peg.' They have adapted themselves to the children, in spite of the fact that they are not used to children." Only God and Willard knew about those storms out of a falsely smiling sky.

With the return of the sunshine, Ruth Randall Brown called to take me to see the city. In the spirit of adventure and elated by the opportunity to get acquainted with that vivid and exciting personality, I clothed myself in a dress given to me by May and altered by my dressmaker in Geneva. It was carefree in colour with brown flowers set in a gold background. A surprise box containing a spring coat with a cape in a soft green had come from New York. May's note read:

---

16 Bahá'u'lláh, *The Seven Valleys and the Four Valleys*. Trans. Marzieh Gail (Wilmette, IL: Bahá'í Publishing Trust, 1978), p. 12.

I found this in the basement at Klein's. I go there sometimes to look for things for Mary. It was very cheap.

Don't worry,

May

So I was ready for spring. I went with Ruth and we drove several miles to Schenley Park in the heart of the city. I saw the Carnegie Library and the two centres of learning, Carnegie Tech and the University of Pittsburgh, where Bishop Brown taught Business. Then we went to the great stores in the triangle made by the three rivers. To cap the day, we visited the Heinz Pickle Factory to join a tour of their enormous plant and to sample some of Heinz's "57 Varieties".

National Convention 1931

Ruth Brown and I met Katherine Cole in Cleveland and drove with her to Wilmette. We swept along with happy laughter and talk, exhilarated by "the Convention feeling" – a sense of keen anticipation. We would see the newly erected framework of the Temple and we would meet Martha Root, back from recent travels.

The House of Worship had, indeed, risen from the ground. It was still bare of its ornamentation, but the structure was very encouraging. At its dedication I stood with Dorothy Baker. Prayers and readings were enunciated from an upper balcony. A strange echo took up the voice and the intonation of Bahá'u'lláh's *Tablet of Wisdom* reverberated throughout. A beautiful Persian voice began to chant. Dorothy and I, arm in arm, stood under the glass dome rising more than a hundred feet. The sunlight seemed to be amplified by the great bowl above our heads. Around us circled the variegated throng of people whom Bahá'u'lláh had called, mysteriously, to advance His Cause in this Day. In the echoing music, we felt our bodies sway. Others later mentioned how they, too, were moved. With the recitation of Bahá'u'lláh's *Tablet of Visitation,* the solemn dedication was over. We filed quietly down to Foundation Hall with its oriental carpets, bouquets of roses and the folding armchairs arranged in semi-circular rows around the speakers' table. That morning a new goal was set before us: the ornamentation of the framework of the Temple. Defying the world depression, we dreamed of our next advance. It was May 1st, 1931, nineteen years from the day that 'Abdu'l-Bahá had set the cornerstone.

First Meeting with Martha Root

After the day's closing I was invited to meet Martha Root in a local hotel suite. I opened the door into a roomful of people. In the midst of a rather dense circle of friends was the silvery grey head. The radiance of the people shone like a ring of gold around a single pearl. Each face, each form, was bent toward her.

My name was called. She rose and came towards me with outstretched hands and with what seemed to be her usual greeting of "Alláh'u'Abhá". Our eyes explored each other and she smiled. A chair was found for me and I joined Leroy Ioas in the outer circle near the door. I recovered from my first stunned impact of Martha's spiritual magnetism to observe that all the joyous people were eating ice cream from little cardboard trays. Leroy whispered, "The Master said that the Bahá'ís should all eat with one mouth." A spoon was given to me and Leroy and I ate from his dish.

At one time during the Convention, Martha was speaking in Chicago. Although she was not visible, we, in Wilmette, were not deprived of hearing her. A loudspeaker was set up and we were able to hear her over radio. It was a perfect delivery, every word clear and powerful, a stirring experience to hear the name of Bahá'u'lláh mentioned in that way, resounding throughout the Hall in Martha's steady voice.

I recall that many of us found the 1931 Convention puzzling. Why could not the Bahá'ís be more realistic about the emphasis on the Administration? The growth of the administrative functioning of the National Assembly was now under the Guardian, something that some of the delegates had difficulty in accepting. Some of the most loyal believers were too rigid.

Montfort Mills, who had been with the Guardian, told us that the time will come when the word "administration" will be so accepted and so familiar that it will be seldom mentioned. It will just BE, like the laws of a country, a way of life.

This was the morning on which, from the Convention platform, Elizabeth Greenleaf confronted our flushed faces by saying, "Unity is a light-giving essence. And without the light of Unity, how can we say we see?"

I was kept very busy between sessions with committee meetings in which we planned the journeys of our travelling teachers, Louis Gregory and Albert Vail. I was later on the floor with my report of the work of the National Teaching Committee and of the interracial advances made by Louis. I reviewed the year's work on the Study Outlines and the regional teaching conferences. Mariam Haney lifted my spirits by telling me that I had a "trained mind and a trained heart". Why, indeed, should that not be true with all the training bestowed on our Geneva group, since our spiritual birth six years ago, by the more mature and dedicated followers of the Master?

The Princely Cloak

It was the last night of the Convention and the third Feast of Riḍván when George Latimer, the chairman, was putting together an informal program. Dorothy's seat was next to mine and had been empty for a long half hour. When she returned, her white shoes were grass stained and her hair windblown.

"Walking again, Dorothy?" She nodded to my whisperings. "You look as if you had seen a ghost."

"Yes, Doris, the ghost of my former self," she smiled, her eyes gently apologetic.

George Latimer was looking our way. "We all remember Mother Beecher. Her granddaughter is here, and she will say a few words to us." Dorothy rose obediently and walked to the platform. I think it was her first time before so large an audience. I wondered if she were feeling as I did the first time that I stood to report before a sea of faces – the gust of their regard flowing from their eyes, bright like sunlight shining on the waves. She stood there a moment, perhaps overwhelmed by the impact of that sea.

She told me later that a word had swept through her mind: "Guidance". She had been asking for guidance to solve the problems of her life – her three children, her ailing grandmother and Frank, her kind and sociable husband. These were her loved ones, whom she yearned to serve. But there had been the dreadful weariness. The doctor had told her that she was "very" ill. She stood there now, gave herself up and plunged in. She spoke in that sweet carrying voice of hers. "Blessed are those who follow guidance." She began to speak from a station unknown to herself. There was a hint of the miraculous in her manner and choice of words.

Could it be, I wondered, that the oft-promised Holy Spirit was inspiring the pure soul of Mother Beecher's granddaughter? Perhaps, too, inspiring the hearts of the believers and bringing them back to unity? The atmosphere was so beautiful. It begged a doubt. Dorothy felt it. "I felt as if a princely cloak were being placed on my shoulders," she confided later.

What might have been the thoughts of the people to whom she spoke? There was the Guardian, the much-loved link to the Master. But there was also the National Spiritual Assembly which, because of the disunity of some of the members, they did not trust. There was also the world depression and thoughts of doom. Above their heads stood the framework of the Temple dome, unfinished and undecorated. It was a time of change and confusion.

"There was a time," said Dorothy, "when confusion fell upon the disciples of Christ. Then came the hour to go forth and teach. The Holy Spirit was there. It was the time of the Pentecost and the disciples were filled with a humble but vitalizing power, guided by the Spirit to go forth and spread the Word."

"What the Cause needs now," she was saying, "is the Pentecostal spirit to bring the believers together and enable them to appreciate the Administration as a warehouse of the Spirit, not as a machine to be operated, as some have said, but an instrument of guidance. She repeated her refrain, "Blessed are those who follow guidance."

The audience had been spellbound. As if on air, Dorothy walked to her seat. She sat down, a little light-headed, amused at herself for "feeling like a priestess," and still wearing the "cloak".

I could not wait to ask her. "Something has changed, Dorothy. What happened when you were out walking in the dew?"

"I was crying," she whispered back, "when I met Albert Vail. He told me what I had guessed – that I might not be here next year. He asked about my family and, then, 'Have you no fear for yourself?' I said, 'No, but I would like to leave some service as a monument to the Cause.' He advised, 'Then work as if your illness never existed.'"

When George Latimer rose to close the meeting, Dorothy asked me to slip away with her to the Temple Dome. Our seats were on the left side of the hall and the stairs were just outside. A single light swinging from a cord cast eerie shadows on the walls of the big nine-sided room. Our steps on the unfinished stairway seemed to be leading us up to the climate of nearness. We sank down on a bench, with the structure of the skylight arched above our heads. From this spot of ultimate refuge, Dorothy's voice rose in supplication for the Faith and for her dear Bahá'í friends.

"May they open their eyes," I quoted the prayer revealed to the Northeastern states, ". . . by beholding the light and be freed from the darkness of ignorance. May they walk around the lamp of guidance. . ."[17]

---

17   The translation with us today is, "May their eyes be opened to behold the light, and may they be freed from the darkness of ignorance. May they gather around the lamp of Thy guidance. . ."

"I am the Listener and the Answerer," the Voice in the small black prayer book told us. Up here it was a loving presence on Dorothy's Night of Wonder. Taking turns, we said many prayers before re-joining our friends below.

Blossom Picnics

Ruby (Hebe) Struven

Seigfried Schopflocher

Kenneth and Roberta Christian who were named Knights of Bahá'u'lláh for Southern Rhodesia (now Zimbabwe), with their son, Roger

Mabel Ives

Harlan and Grace Ober in 1911

Dunduzu Chisiza with Rex and Mary Collison who together were named Knights of Bahá'u'lláh for Ruanda-Urund (now Rwanda and Burundi)

Martha Root

Dorothy Baker

Louis Gregory

Horace Holley

Keith Ransom Kehler

National Convention at Green Acre 1925

1. May Maxwell
2. Stanwood Cobb
3. Marion Jack
4. Elizabeth Greenleaf
5. Louise Gregory
6. Dr Susan Moody
7. Mary Maxwell (later Rúḥíyyih Khánum)

May Maxwell and Jeanne Bolles

Doris and Willard in 1935

Doris in Vernon orchard shortly after pioneering to Prince Edward Island

Doris with Peggy Ross from Toronto in 1953

The McKay/Geary farm in Vernon Bridge, PEI, sometime in the 1960's. Left to right: Willard McKay, Grace Geary, Doris McKay, ?, Irving Geary, ?.

Tilbury Tenement

During the two weeks that I spent in Cleveland and Wilmette, Willard and Grace moved the Obers and the McKays out of the prosperous facade of Beechwood Boulevard and down the side of the hill to Tilbury Street.

Bishop Brown had come over to Cleveland to pick up Ruth and me. Now, having arrived back in Pittsburgh, we stopped at a three-storey double house of weathered brick. Our neighbours were sitting outside on their square of lawn, where it was cooler in the shadow cast by the house. Their eyes rested on Bishop's immaculate small car and the distinguished appearance of the Browns as they escorted me up the steps to the pillared brick portico. The door opened and Grace ran out, as usual, her arms flung wide to embrace us. We said goodbye to the Browns, and Grace drew me into "Tilbury Tenement" and up two flights of stairs.

"Oh, Grace, I love it!" I warbled as I looked in at the large treetop attic she had prepared lovingly for us. It seemed as if the room had everything: space (the whole width of one side of the building), two windows making a cross draught, and odds and ends of convenient furniture – a table to write on, plain kitchen chairs, shelves for books, a wide old fashioned iron bedstead, and a small electric fan. Grace had hung yellow curtains at the windows. There were watercolour paintings on the walls and Bahá'í quotations, lettered and framed. Grace said, "This is your room, Doris, yours and Willard's. Welcome to the 'Palais Royale'!"

When Willard came home we unpacked our few boxes, hung up our clothes and put our books on a shelf.

"I am not working for Harlan," Willard announced. "All business is at a standstill. Did you know that five Pittsburgh banks failed while you were away?"

"What shall we do?"

"I have a job," Willard said brightly, "soliciting funds for a bread line. An old Roman Catholic church in 'the Strip' is handing out bread and soup to a hundred or more homeless men who live in shacks made out of packing boxes and cardboard. 'The Strip,'" he explained, "is that pitiful little village of those shacks. It's on unwanted land between a cliff and the Ohio River, with a city streetcar track running through it. Set at one side there is this soot-stained old church. The City allows the men to squat there, and the church feeds them twice each day, the church paying a small percentage for solicited donations." This was Willard's job.

Next door in the attic that corresponded to ours, an old Jewish mother made moaning accompaniment as she chanted a mournful song from her homeland.

That night we sat with the Obers in the large, meeting-sized living room. "How did you manage such a look of freshness?", I asked, "with all this soot lurking about?"

"Cleaners," said Grace, "You rub the wallpaper with a pink dough that looks like the kneaded erasers we used in Art School. The rugs I cleaned with a scrub brush and the foam from a pail of hot suds. The Master enjoined us to purity," she added.

We talked and planned our lives with the move to Tilbury Street – our seismic slide to changed conditions. We agreed that Grace and Harlan would continue to devote their time to office sales and collections. Grace would be the office girl and I, the housekeeper. Willard would find ways to make a little money.

The four of us, feeling very exalted, prayed that night, the first of hundreds of community prayers, voicing our appeal for assistance, renewing our covenant to work for the Cause in Pittsburgh. We prayed, too, for the completion of the Temple dome. "We must turn to the Guardian, offer ourselves to him."

"It will not be easy," warned Grace. Then she made one of

her unforgettable statements, reminiscent of the Master, "We must not think of difficulties as tests, but as opportunities for the power of the Holy Spirit."

I awoke to the sound of a lost voice, my own, saying, "Who am I?" I would like to have heard Willard's answer but he was already up.

In an hour I would be serving breakfast to the six of us, including Aziz and David, the boys adopted by the Obers. As I made coffee, I heard a knock at the door. The man peering through the glass looked harmless and I opened it a few inches. He thrust in an arm, holding out to me a pair of brown shoelaces. "Here, take these for a cup of coffee," he urged. Harlan's voice responded, "Would you like to come in and sit down?" I put the food, whatever we had, on a tray. The man wolfed it down and disappeared through the door.

Harlan and Grace were dressed to leave but there was time after breakfast for them to explain to me the complexities of the washing. "I don't know anything about electricity," I confessed. "There was none at the farmhouse. We sent the washing out." Grace and Harlan went down with us to the basement. I carried an armful of shirts. They watched while I soaped the collars of the shirts with a bar of yellow soap called "Sunshine" and left them to soak in the tub. I learned the levers on the washing machine and was rewarded by the vibration of the motor. Back upstairs again, we watched the Obers leave.

Our friends, smiling and waving, looked invincible as they drove out to their daily ordeal. After seeing the two boys off to school, I washed the dishes and found places for them in the cupboard. With Willard's help I started the vacuum and cleaned the rugs and the furniture fabric, then did the dusting with an oiled cloth. Later, in the basement again, I scrubbed the collars with a stiff brush and started the washer. Soon Willard's voice was heard using the telephone upstairs and the monotonous words given him to say: ". . . you will admit the necessity of coming to the aid of these hungry men with a generous contribution, or even a small one..." If people agreed, he wrote down their names, addresses and the amounts promised. At the end of the week, he would collect his small commission.

About three in the afternoon, I climbed up to our treetop 'palais'. I needed it. "Fresh soot will fall every day. It is a constant," I murmured, adding, "and constant, too, is the upright perfection of Grace and Harlan. They really live up to the laws of Bahá'u'lláh, especially cleanliness!" The easy-going McKays would have to accept a new standard for that attribute, and discipline would call for supreme effort. Fate had brought us here, and there was no retreat.

That night Grace taught me how to fold and iron shirts, collars smartly pressed, sleeves crossed in the back. The second morning I ironed the shirts as if my salvation depended upon doing a perfect job. As I worked, I intoned lines from 'Abdu'l-Bahá's Tablet of Visitation: "Give me Thy grace to serve Thy loved ones," I whispered. "Strengthen me in my servitude to Thee. . . "

When the ironing was done, I stacked sixteen shirts and the piles of sheets and towels neatly on the ironing board. When Grace and Harlan came home that evening with bags of vegetables for me to prepare for supper, I called them to come down and see first the display of my work. Harlan inspected a shirt that the new laundress had ironed for him. He told Grace that I had done better than my predecessor, Louise, the maid. He said, "Doris is an artist in life, as well as in other things."

So I had learned the art of ironing a shirt! I wanted to cry. I wanted to fly!

The Crimson Ark

From my present perspective, our year with the Obers (later to be joined by Howard and Mabel Ives) is an "Epic" in the Faith. I have only the scraps and pieces of journal entries, and letters to my friend, Lorna Tasker, to aid my memory. I shall try to work them together to describe all that was 1931.

When I think of that time, I think of the Crimson Ark, "the ark which Bahá'u'lláh hath prepared for the people of Bahá". The movement of the ship is erratic: it seems to flounder, then to dart ahead on a planned course. There is no fear of capsizing, for the believers aboard are praying. Their chants still the pounding of the waves.

Harlan was steering our ship. He had challenged us to come. There was Bahá'í work to be done, a Local Spiritual Assembly to be united and inspired. There would be a way to make a living because Harlan would employ Willard. Through unity and prayer, we would make a powerhouse.

May 1931

From my notes:

> I am alone in the house and talking to myself about the upset in our lives. 'Abdu'l-Bahá has said there are two natures in man. In me, these natures hold converse. I know now who I am. I am nobody. Already, I am run-down, shabby, inclined to be on the defensive. We have no money and my service in the house is below par. I do not tell the Obers that my back and feet are killing me.
>
> 'But remember last night,' says my inner voice, 'you were awake in a thunderstorm and began to worry about money, and finally you slipped out of bed and began to wander around the room. The flashes of lightning were lighting up two photographs of 'Abdu'l-Bahá and one of the Most Exalted Leaf so that their eyes looked into yours, you thought, knowingly. And, you said, 'You are my Family, my People, and your presence is sweet.'

I thought of Harlan, resenting his rule of the house. "But the material of which a Bahá'í is made is rugged," I had written, "because strength is needed in the Formative Period of the Faith." There is something unbreakable about the early Bahá'ís. Only occasionally are they as gentle as Louis Gregory is gentle. (That quality, says Louis, has to be acquired.)

I remember the uplifted faces under the dome at the dedication of the Temple. They were strong faces, modelled by the thumb of God, the Fashioner. On that day their faces were alight. "If sometime that light should dim in an airless and unspiritual atmosphere," I noted, "the breaths of the Holy Spirit will revive it on some other great occasion."

"In the tavern of this mortal world the bile of the man of God is not removed."[18] My life as a bride on a farm has shed light on these words of 'Abdu'l-Bahá. I had found the little sac of bile in the chicken and, had it not been removed, the meat would have been bitter.

Harlan too, that man of God, was tasting the bitterness of failure. I was so absorbed in our own material downfall that, at the time, I did not relate myself to Harlan's crushing financial plight. As well as supporting three adopted children and ourselves, he had taken upon himself responsibility for his destitute salesmen. From his New England ancestry, Harlan must have absorbed some of the idealistic dreams of Emerson and Thoreau, for deeply implanted in him was the concept of an exalted communal relationship for the unity of mankind. Clearly this had been his thought when he urged us to come. This fantasy was now threatened.

We could offer no material help except our work in the house. Our bank account was down to one dollar and all of Willard's life insurance was withdrawn. We were selling the heirlooms we had left in Geneva. Even my diamond ring was in and out of pawn.

The Steed of Pain

There came days at Tilbury when, on the "steed of pain", we rode four abreast through the Valley of Love. The true cause of our depression, I brooded, was that our Bahá'í community was being pulled and stretched between earth and heaven. It was like the agony of the rack in medieval Europe. Tension was the sharp pain, depression the dull throb.

The prayers that we gathered to say at night were spoken with such power (especially those uttered by Grace) that the Gates of

---

18 *Tablets of 'Abdu'l-Bahá*

Heaven were assailed by them. Why did not intercession come from on High to relieve us? Why too, the question persisted, had not the all-powerful Spirit come always to Bahá'u'lláh's aid? Sometimes, when the winds of God were blowing in our Tilbury community, it was as if we stood on the edge of a pit. We were very quiet, because if we stirred, we might fall in and take the others with us. Our one security was that we were united in holding on to the Cord of the Covenant.

The symbol of "the cord" reminds me of the day that I met Harlan in the hall upstairs. He had been ill and was wearing his old bathrobe tied around with a long cord. Smiling shakily, he said, "This cord I am wearing belonged once to Bahá'u'lláh."[19]

The inconsistencies of our moods was a test which made us doubt one another. Who was the real person? This one with the darkened face? Or the irradiating teaching soul? Our avoidance of one another would seem like disapproval, even rejection. This was true especially for the McKays because our financial contribution was nil. I could not bear this. I was to learn later, from Howard Ives, that it was my pride.

Yet, our prayers for assistance were answered and blessings of great munificence came. Although there was no material help, we would find ourselves, when teaching, uplifted to that different world of being that 'Abdu'l-Bahá called the Spirit of Faith. At such times we were 'awake' again, the nightmare over. We spoke without notes and attracted people through love.

It was still May when I wrote:

> As I adjust myself to the requirements of the work in the house, the members of my body protest. There used to be a myth about my not being strong, and I learned nothing about hard physical work. My muscles aren't ready for it and my few pampered ailments feel themselves challenged.
>
> Yesterday I was upset all day. I wept and raged and when my work was done, I wept and walked. In my green coat, its cape flying, I went out into cool damp weather and followed

---

19 I discovered later that it had been lent to him by Bahíyyih Randall (Lindstrum).

Beechwood Boulevard round till I came to a place where country began. I looked down into a valley where the town of Homestead lies and watched the mist of smoke and the tracing of a muddy river under black iron bridges. Sometimes, like Dante's idea of Hell, there would be a flashing of lurid light from the blast furnace.

And yet, in my notes of June, there were signs of growth.

I do not want to put my tests on record. It is absurd for me to complain of my lessons, for I recognize in them the guiding Hand of Bahá'u'lláh.

My faults are all on trial. They are being torn out of me like unsafe tumbledown houses along a street. . . If I were only a bigger and braver person, this training would be glorious.

Later,

To choose humility and meekness had been once like the choice of a grey rag of a garment instead of a flaming robe. I've come to love the luminosity of humbleness, the grey wing of a moth that has sacrificed itself to a flame.

God has thrown in my way storms to test my strength: restlessness, resentment, discouragement, fatigue. I have shared my feelings with Willard, who is so detached and wise. But one night he comforted me so tenderly that I became hysterical with self-pity and shed a flood of tears. In the morning Grace said, 'Doris, you have been crying. You must tell me why.'

'It is the feeling of being trapped,' I said. 'Of no future, no solution. It's being smothered with soot and sticky heat and not knowing what will happen, and being so terribly tired. And it's hiding ourselves from one another.'

How could I say this to Grace, whose fortitude encased her feelings like a polished shell? But Grace said, 'I know, Doris, because I feel exactly the same way myself,' and she opened her arms for a hug.

Louis Gregory gives me Five Dollars

Louis was in town and was invited to the house for dinner. Other guests were there, and the evening took on the genial mellowness of Louis's presence. I was surprised when he called me aside, looked understandingly at my wan face and said, "Experience has shown that it is not always easy for Bahá'ís to live together." And he gave me a five-dollar bill. FIVE DOLLARS!

How many days would beloved Louis go without his dinner because of that gift? He slipped it into my hand and before I realized what he was doing, he was gone to the other side of the room. By what power of intuition had he read my problems so sympathetically?

But, oh, the brilliant pictures against the troubled background! On most nights when we did not have guests at home, the Obers' car, named "GoCart" (G and O standing for Grace Ober), would drive out for meetings. There were weekly meetings at Alice Parker's, business and Feast meetings, meetings with our Black contacts, made through the YMCA, church and other service groups; and there were the meetings of a new national Bahá'í committee called "Bahá'í Study", consisting of Ruth Brown, Harlan, and myself.

Mr Joseph Douglass

One night the "GoCart" turned towards one of the better residential streets in the Black section. Friends of Grace and Harlan had invited us to meet Mr Joseph Douglass, a concert violinist from Washington, D.C. Friendly hosts greeted our delegation, as did a thin dark man of cultivated and gentle voice, his eyes alert in a quiet face.

Magically, all of us were soon in the special Heaven of the Unity of Race, that same heaven that we had entered with Lois and Sam Allen in our visit to Harlem in the spring of 1930. The felicity of meeting on a plateau between two ethnic worlds, with souls discerned to be kindred, is to experience rapture stored in the world to come, really beyond description. It is an experience and a discovery, a finding of completion. The Baháʼí principle of the Oneness of Humanity, no longer merely an exalted concept, becomes an emotion near to the heart.

I remarked, "There is a statue of Frederick Douglass in Rochester, New York, where I come from, in the Square by the Central Station. The inscription says that he was an orator for Abolition at the time of the Civil War. Are you related to him?"

"I am the grandson of Frederick Douglass," he replied.

Do you ask a violinist on tour to play for you? Willard did, most humbly. Mr Douglass took out a precious old violin and played simple melodies with magic, as Kreisler would have done. Willard, transported, asked for the "Goin' Home" melody from Dvorak's Ninth Symphony. This was the high note of the evening. Soon we said goodbye and we too, were "goin' home".

The four of us drove through the drab streets, feeling as if we had been celestials welcomed in a stately mansion – such had been the elevation of our experience of true rapport.

At Tilbury Tenement I ran upstairs to write one of my first poems. I had things I had to say to Mr Joseph Douglass. Urged by Grace, I sent it to him with a note of appreciation. He responded with hope of another meeting.

Enhancement

I watched the face of the coloured violinist
As he drew forth melodies, filched from Dvorak,
From the time-honoured wood.

And I saw that for which I had been searching,
The sign of the lovely sequestered people,
Of the people sealed away;

Of an island inundated by a roaring white population
Where full-throated songs are sadly muted,
Whispered to dark ears only;

Of a world which my fancy longs to enter,
Exchange glance for glance with heavy-lidded eyes,
Dally with purple-shadowed hair;

Of a continent waiting for discovery,
A place of heartbreak, prayer and laughter,
Invisible, but near.

When shall a few of us go to seek our kindred,
Riding intrepidly over the white crested waves
With our garlands of greeting?

Our Fellow Believers

June 5, 1931

At the Feast of Núr (Light), Willard and I saw again our fellow believers. In those days, there was one community of Bahá'ís over a sprawling area. If you had taken a picture of a human heart and cut it into pieces for a jigsaw puzzle, the separate pieces would have been the boroughs of Pittsburgh. The Bahá'í community, too, seemed made up of pieces because it was a cross section of the social life of those boroughs. It was unique, and in my memory, prized.

Somehow our delightful group – the Browns, the Obers and the McKays; Leila Payne, the statuesque wife of a Black undertaker, her white hair braided around her handsome head; Henry Seker, the paper hanger, and his wife Bessie, who had been a nurse; Braydon Black, a real estate man and a bachelor; and Eve Kerin – all of us would that night find places to sit. It was a gracious room, embellished with Miss Alice Parker's old furniture, books and pictures. There were bowls of fresh flowers. Alice, a distinguished educator (so the column in the newspaper said), was sixty-four now and had every admirable quality in excess: mind, initiative and a warm, loving heart. She had been one of the four hundred people who had heard 'Abdu'l-Bahá speak in

1912 at a meeting arranged by Martha Root. Now, in her apartment, in this meeting nineteen years later, lived the miracle of Unity, even Oneness. Everyone knew its value. Alice drew a grateful breath, leaned back, and relaxed.

We find Hidden Treasures

I had known that night of the Feast that Eve Kerin was a cryptogram waiting for a key. I had been attracted by this silent, white-faced woman with blunt features in a high-boned face. She had intent dark eyes under heavy black eyebrows, an effect accentuated by a white blouse and plain black suit. Her immobility was relieved only by the nervous movements of her hands. A communication sprang up between her eyes and mine, but what was she saying so silently?

She invited us to spend the coming Sunday at her home in suburban Emsworth, fifteen miles of trolley ride away. Their street was inclined on one of the Pennsylvania hills with coal deep down underneath. We climbed up steps to reach their small house. We were introduced to Eve's frail husband, Charlie, and to their children, Joe and Sue. At first their shyness seeped into us and we all sat down, enigmatic and stiff. Then there was a little cry from the kitchen and the family took us out to see a nest of kittens under the stove.

All at once we belonged to the Kerins and they to us. We knew that we had found an essential comradeship. They had not been to school, and we had. They had had hard knocks since childhood, while our way had been relatively easy. They had no artful words with which to converse, and we had too many. But soon they were eagerly telling us their dreams and how they felt about nature. They brought out their favourite poems to read to us – poems that we enjoyed too. We not only had dinner but stayed for the evening meal and on until after eleven o'clock before leaving for the long ride home. They had asked us to stay the night.

That day we had been uplifted to the grace of God. I think even Charlie and the children realized that something was different. Later I wrote, "Something happened up there at the Kerins'. Something happened yesterday to all of us alike. We did not talk about the Cause. We WERE the Cause."

The Kerins, locked up in their own worries, had found again their true selves. And so had we, especially when we all went out to climb a hill. My light-hearted spirits were effervescing as in former days. Sue told her mother, "I never saw a grand lady so like a little girl!"

The Key

The next week brought an understanding of Eve's cryptic behaviour on the night of the Feast. Grace met Eve in town and brought her home to dinner; to meet again was a reunion. The Obers stared when the erstwhile stony Eve advanced on both Willard and me and kissed us soundly. After a happy meal I asked Eve up to see our treetop room and we had a visit and prayers.

"We need your prayers," Eve began abruptly. "Charlie is out of work and scaring us with his depression. And he is drinking, you know. I haven't had an easy time, myself, breaking the drug habit. It was the opium they gave me at the hospital while I was having my operations."

"Sometimes, still," said Eve, "my mind takes strange flights, psychic maybe." (I think of a later time when an experience she had would be called extrasensory.) "For example," she explained, "the first time I saw you, I saw some part of you that was not your outward self. It is almost a child, otherworldly and rather delicate. It occurred again that night at the Feast. Didn't you see me looking at you?"

So many sides to us all. I had recognized this elusive quality in myself and even had a secret name for it, which now I shared with Eve. She said of that part of me, "That person has something to say to me." Later when we were talking about giving up our will to God, Eve brightened and said, "I think that is what she wanted to tell me."

NAACP Convention

July 6th, the convention of the National Association for the Advancement of Colored People (NAACP) opened in a large auditorium. Grace and I were there. She pointed out to me Dr W. E. Burghardt DuBois, chairman of the five-day event. He was a noted author and editor of *The Crisis* magazine. It was said that this intellectual Black person disliked the White race. I felt nervous when I watched Grace, with her arresting look of spiritual dominance, go up the aisle to speak to him. He rose politely and accepted from her (horrors!) the folds of blue paper on which my poem "Enhancement" was typed. He bowed and Grace came triumphantly back to her seat whispering to me, "He's going to print the poem in *The Crisis*."

Throughout the week, the convention sessions would find Bahá'ís beaming, nodding, shaking hands. We knew already some of the delegates and now we met many more. At the close of the last morning's session and after an exchange of words with Dr Dubois, Grace was granted a few minutes on the platform. She extended to the delegates an invitation to stop at the Tilbury address for a cup of tea before leaving for home that afternoon.

Grace hurried home with her news. For racially prejudiced Pittsburgh, it was a one-woman Declaration of Human Rights. First, she made telephone calls to the other Bahá'ís; then she went out ringing neighbours' doorbells, telling the people to look out of their windows at four o'clock if they wanted to see some very distinguished people. She promised them that they would be surprised. Later she made other telephone calls for sandwich rolls and ham, cupcakes and cold drinks, and asked Eve Kerin to come and help make sandwiches for thirty. Then she returned to the afternoon session to talk people into coming home with her.

At four, the street began to fill with parked cars and the NAACP delegates, dressed now for a social occasion. They who moved on in the direction of our door, were some of the most impressive people in the nation. We had expected thirty. Sixty came.

Eve and I scurried to the kitchen where our sandwich rolls were arranged on trays, and we cut them all neatly in two. The neighbours stared out of their windows – eyes on the overflow of our guests on the steps and the lawn, paper plates and cups in their hands. Our visitors were in an expansive mood. Evidently, they considered this a "peak experience" after a week of discussing the wrongs and ills suffered by their race. They were relaxed and jovial. Grace, at her best, moved among them – a messenger of light, magnificent.

Visit to New Castle

Two days later we spent the night at a farm near New Castle, Pennsylvania, where the Ives were spending the summer. We arrived late in the afternoon and had supper and an evening of talk before being tucked away in country bedrooms. In the morning I beheld an orchard from our window.

To be on a farm again in summer sent me back a year in time. My spirits rose and I felt my cork blow with an excess of joy. At the first opportunity after breakfast, I slipped out alone into the orchard, touched the old trees and talked to them. I had been reading a life of Emily Bronte and I mused, "What would Emily's life have been like without her heather-covered moors?"

No one had seen me go, but soon they would be calling me. I felt as furtive as a wild creature in the woods, sniffing the air for human scent. Like the snapping of a twig warning it to bound away, their first call would alert that sensitive part of me to flee.

"Doris, where are you? We want a consultation with Howard and Mabel."

Dear cognizant Eve would have understood. I did not join the others immediately but slid around to the back porch and communed with the cat. The voices called again. When I appeared at the front porch, they said, "Where were you?" I sat down with the others and began scribbling on a piece of note paper. Howard wondered, "What are you writing?", but I shook my head and would not let him draw away my arm. It began,

"The twigs are snapping in the forest that I call MINE." I am sure Grace and Harlan were aware of something opaque in me. I did not tell them – could not. But I could give myself to Bahá'u'lláh, because HE knew my heart.

To the picnic in the afternoon Howard and Mabel had invited the country people and some of the connections that they had made in town. From New Castle came Edith Burchard and Ethel Kelly, two high school teachers who later opened the way for us to hold meetings in that city. They had heard of the Cause from Martha Root. (Edith's people had been settlers with the Roots at Cambridge Springs two generations back.) Chairs and rugs had been placed outside in a shady field where we held a meeting after the picnic lunch.

We talked about prayer, and the guests were invited to take part. For many, "conversation with God" consisted of special requests, but I still remember what one sweet little lady said. She had found that God would answer her prayers for spiritual growth. THAT she could depend upon – although not often had she been confirmed in her prayers for material needs. "God," she said, "sometimes answers 'no', but how His spiritual gifts have changed my life!"

When we opened the door to Tilbury Tenement there was a strange fragrance in the house and a trickle of liquid on the stairs. Aziz had been making ginger ale and before he left had stored the bottles in a case under his bed. In the heat, the bottles had 'blown their corks' (as I had), and the house was awash with quarts of the bubbling beverage, although bubbling no longer. (Nor was I.)

It had been possible, in that quiet field in New Castle, for the Depression to seem unreal. Now we were on our way to the Kerins' for a picnic on the Fourth of July. Leila Payne also had been invited and Mr Payne, massive, dark and noncommittal, drove us out to Emsworth in his undertaking limousine. (Later we would come home on the trolley.) A picnic basket had been packed and Eve, the children, Leila and Willard and I set out to walk to a favourite spot. Willard, laden with the basket, walked with the older ones, but I ran ahead with Sue and Joey, out of myself in the sun-dappled woods.

Charlie had remained behind to read his book, although he joined us in the evening to watch the fireworks.

At a meeting two weeks later Eve told me, "You came to see me last week. Do you remember?"

"Certainly not last week," I said.

"Oh yes, you did. At three o'clock in the morning. You came and stood beside my bed and looked at me and smiled. I put out my hand to touch you and you vanished."

"You were asleep and dreaming, Eve."

"How could I be asleep when I was sitting bolt upright in bed and screaming prayers at the ceiling?"

She said that one day she had gone out to purchase cyanide tablets to disinfect a sore on her arm. Afterwards, she put the tablets high up on a shelf in the bathroom. On the night she called, she had found Charlie in the bathroom with one of the deadly tablets in his hand. She took it from him, caught him when he collapsed and helped him back to bed.

In her own bed Eve tried to pray. But because of the ceiling, she thought, the prayer would not rise through to God. It was in her panic that, remembering my promise to pray, she cried, "Doris, Help me!" Somehow my spirit came to her while I slept. Does not our spirit often linger invisibly near those for whom we pray? This, perhaps, was a rare instance in which it was visible. I have heard of other situations where the spirit showed itself in order to reassure another.

Eve slept. She awoke on a high spiritual level that she maintained for days. She was able to rescue Charlie from his despondency and brought him to the next meeting. There was a new look in Charlie's eyes that night. As he was leaving, I said, "Charlie, have you ever thought of becoming a Bahá'í?"

"I might do just that," he responded. That night, with us all there, he enrolled.

When we arrived back at the Kerins' for Sunday dinner, we found a transformed Charlie. A wonderful bounty had descended upon our friend. With his finger in a prayer book, he met us at the door, wrung our hands and returned to his chair to continue reading. He had vanished into that land which he had found. Eve's face was alive, eyes smiling, lips in a curve.

When we sat down to Eve's chicken dinner Charlie said, "Wait, we are not ready yet." He pulled out his book and read prayers while the dinner cooled. Not that anyone minded. Even the children breathed the atmosphere and waited patiently. The food was delicious. That day was a real love feast, and the Host was 'Abdu'l-Bahá.

Emily Craighead

The Bahá'ís were in an atmosphere of unity at Alice Parker's, praying for souls to arise whom we might teach. On the second floor of her hotel apartment, the sounds of the street seemed far away. We began saying, in turn, the Remover of Difficulties – to the number of nineteen. Our voices, in different keys and inflections, made strange music: the cultivated voice of Alice, raised in earnest petition; the baritone of Harlan and the tenor of Willard; my own voice, high and chirpy. Leila Payne invoked God like a priestess; Henry and Bessie said the words slowly and with difficulty. Ruth's and Bishop's accents were from New England.

The door was ajar that warm night. We heard an indrawn breath and then a timid knock. Alice rose and opened the door to admit the one who would be the answer to our prayers. We were introduced to Emily Craighead, another retired teacher and an acquaintance of Alice. She was nervous and quailed visibly at the roomful of assorted people – all of us with our eyes so bright and looking as if we would like to swallow her.

"Have I interfered with your meeting?" she faltered. "Should I have come? Oh, please excuse me. I felt I had to."

She had waited in the hall for us to finish our prayers. The intoned words were like a spell calling to her. Through the partly opened door she had seen that we had not bowed our heads but had raised them, as if awaiting an answer. By the time Emily sat down with us to hear about the Teachings of Bahá'u'lláh, she had responded already to the call of the Holy Spirit that she had heard in the hall. This was the power of the Word itself; its syllables, when sincerely uttered, it was promised, would "cause the heart of every righteous man to throb".[20]

I cannot remember how she looked, except for her brown eyes and the white hair that once had been auburn. She was very tall and fragile looking – an elusive wisp of a person with a gentle and eager spirit. Her old church, old Pittsburgh family would cause her anguish when she joined the Bahá'ís.

Such is the power of the spoken Word that, in the time of Muhammad, Omar, who had come to slay the believers in the house of his sister, lingered outside to hear the Koran read. He had come to kill, but when won by the music of the Word, he sought out Muhammad, fell at his feet and offered up his soul to the new Cause.

Meeting at Mrs Payne's

The Payne Funeral Home looked very inviting. A stage was illuminated on each side by incandescent white globes on tall standards, and an arrangement of scented, artificial flowers was placed in front of a purple backdrop. Leila Payne, Willard and I sat in armchairs at the front of the stage.

At the right stood a beautiful little cabinet organ. Onto the stage and toward the organ ran a tiny ancient lady, her face the colour and corrugation of withered walnut meat. She sat down and began to play. It was a song that my grandmother used to sing when I was small – one that I loved. "Come, Birdie, come and live with me," sang the woman, "you shall be happy, bright and free. Come, Birdie, come! Come, Birdie, COME!"

The people did come when they heard the music, most of them habitual funeral goers with long faces. They looked unbelievingly at the gala decorations and at our beaming smiles. "You

---

20 *Bahá'í Prayers,* frontispiece.

shall be happy, bright and free," sang the lady. Mrs Payne rose and graciously introduced us as her dear friends who had come with a 'message' for them. The audience began to fill most of the chairs. When we told them, "Mankind is One and we are all children of one loving Father, God," they stared dumbly. Only one face, in the front row, seemed alert. When we asked if there were any questions, that person said, "Yes, I has. What makes White folks treat cullard folk the way they do?"

Happy no longer, I answered, "I am ashamed of all those white folks. They don't know what they're doing. Will you try to forgive us?" She smiled – yes, she would try. All the people smiled, and we came down off the stage and shook their hands.

In the latter part of August, the Ober family drove to Eliot, Maine, to visit Green Acre and to see a little farm that belonged to them. If the Pittsburgh venture failed, they might have to take up residence there; perhaps even take our community with them. It was a port in a storm – one that already had been considered seriously.

Willard's soliciting for the bread line was not doing well. People were not paying their pledges. With the failure of fifteen banks, they were not inclined to make promises. But he had some pay coming that he would collect on Saturday night. We looked forward to that day. For the while, our food was reduced to potatoes and boxed breakfast food.

During this time came the invitation to hold, on Friday night, a meeting in New Castle. It was from Edith and Ethel, the schoolteachers we had met at the Ives' picnic. The meeting would be advertised and held in a public place and we would spend the night at the home of friends.

Willard had housed somewhere in a shed the old Studebaker that had brought us to Pittsburgh. It was entitled to permanent retirement because of its advanced age and the life it had lived. But Willard picked me up in style Saturday afternoon, and with high spirits we started the sixty-five-mile drive to New Castle. After buying gas for the round trip, we had thirty-five cents left.

"We will have to pray for the right rear tire, said Willard. "It has a very doubtful patch."

"The spare?," I questioned.

"That, too, is patched."

The meeting was held in a tearoom rented for the evening. The tables were pushed back and the chairs arranged in rows. Our audience, friends of Edith and Ethel, was intellectual, academic. It was a splendid meeting. Today we would have called it a proclamation. I introduced the Baháʼí Faith and Willard gave his talk on 'Science and Religion.' No one knew how hungry we were.

We went home with a kind lady who said, "You must want something to eat after your efforts this evening." She brought out a large bowl of crackers and a pitcher of lemonade. Light-headed now with hunger, perhaps we showed too much enthusiasm for the crackers. "These are delicious crackers," said Willard, taking a second handful. "What are they called?" I asked, helping myself. "Oysterettes" she replied. We finished the bowl and drank the lemonade. For breakfast our hostess provided hot muffins and jam, bacon and eggs. We parted with hearty good will.

The Studebaker took us to the edge of the city. Then it happened: 'pshssssh', followed by a jolt. Glory be to God, there was a service station across the street! Willard ran over and said to the attendant, "See, here. The patch has blown off my tire. Can you help me? I can pay you thirty-five cents." They came back to the car, smiling broadly at our "joke." The attendant put the patch on and accepted our coins. Penniless, we pressed towards Pittsburgh and Willard's earnings at 'the Strip' – not for a moment forgetting to pray.

I watched from the car as Willard went into the office to draw his pay. To open a road, a mountain of rock had been chiselled in two. A steep grey wall rose there, its shadow, black. The crazily laid streets and cross streets of the shantytown were on the flats above the river, and there the old church, with its square steeple, stood in coal-sooted dignity. It was noon. A queue of men stretched from the box-built shelters to the door of the church kitchen. Each was handed a bowl of soup and a chunk of bread. All the men were stamped with desolation – the same hunched shoulders, the same dull eyes staring at nothing, the same avid acceptance of the soup. Willard was returning now with his quick step and square shoulders. He did not look at the lineup. He had learned that they wanted to be left alone.

"Yet they cling to life," I said. "Why, when it is so easy to die in these days?"

Willard said, "They are afraid to die. Their childhood religion spoke too little of a Compassionate God."

We opened the pay envelope: fourteen dollars and a few coins. We gently urged the Studebaker through six miles of congested population to the Borough of Squirrel Hill and Tilbury Street. It was Saturday, the Jewish Sabbath, and most of the stores were closed. We found one with an open door and spent two dollars of our money on the first real meal that we had had that week: two T-bone steaks (25 cents each), tomatoes, milk, butter and pumpernickel.

How happy and secure we felt now, elated by being so wildly extravagant and grateful for being brought safely home by the Help in Peril after carrying the Message to new people. After supper we prepared for the Obers' return by cleaning the house.

We were relaxing in the living room, listening to the Pittsburgh Symphony Orchestra. The air was redolent with a blend of cleaner fumes. The floors had been scrubbed with kerosene, the rugs sponged, and the windows washed to sparkling. The car doors slammed and, followed by Grace and Harlan, Aziz and David roared into the room. Grace halted, sniffed deeply and cried, "This house smells CLEAN." We sat down and exchanged our news, laughed about our New Castle excursion and absorbed the messages that our Green Acre friends had sent to us. The spectre of food was banished at the evening meal. Our milk, bread and tomatoes were added to the blueberries and home-cured ham the Obers had brought from Eliot. A homecoming – our community bond was a true reality.

The thought of fall and the turning of August into September brought change to the seeming endlessness of summer. Harlan invited me to go with him to New Castle to visit Howard. With his characteristic enthusiasm, Howard had fallen in love with some beautiful (lucrative, he said) white rabbits. We went with him to the farm where they were for sale. Certainly, the rabbits were beguiling with their rich white fur and shining pink eyes. They were, Howard pointed out, an investment. Their fur was valuable, their offspring saleable and, Howard hesitated, their meat would be there should there be an emergency. He had decided to buy all that he could afford – sixty.

"Where will Howard keep his rabbits?" I asked on our thoughtful journey home.

"In an old barn near Tilbury Street," said Harlan. "The Ives have decided to move in with us this fall and Mary will be coming home to enter high school. Our embryonic Bahá'í community is growing."

We were entering a time of even greater testing of our courage and resolve – more so than in the four months that had passed. The Depression was deepening in the city. Guards were being posted at night in the food stores. There was even some talk of closing the schools. Willard and I were almost penniless; Harlan's funds were diminishing. The miasma of desperation, constantly combatted by prayer, seemed to drift into our minds like polluted air infiltrating a house through chinks, crevices and keyholes.

On September 28th, 1931, I wrote:

> It seemed as if the tension of these four walls had tightened to the point of torture: the tension of stronger wills and personalities, the tension of noise, of ideas, the tensions of the city, the tension of waiting for winter to end and of getting enough money to live on.
>
> I walked four blocks to Murray Avenue to buy a stamp. The air was unusually clear of smoke, the sun was shining and a cool wind was blowing. I came back and began to run the vacuum cleaner. I was crying and 'holding on to the Cord' of the Greatest Name. The sweeper had sounds like the whine of a hurricane, a hissing of wind and a shrill cry. I found it glorious. I was caught up in the energy of a self-answering prayer. I did not have any feelings when I finished except those of physical fatigue.

Tomorrow the Ives are moving in with us and Mary returns after a six-week absence.

The Rabbits

Country and an unpaved road were only a short walk from the populated area of Tilbury Street. On this road Mary and I found the barn where Howard kept his rabbits. We stood in the doorway, saw Howard there, and went inside. He proudly displayed his neat rabbit crates, stacked in twos and threes.

"Aren't your rabbits rather small," said Mary pertly, her high-boned Slavic face animated.

"I bought the small rabbits because they were cheaper, more of an investment, I thought," replied Howard.

At breakfast a week later Howard announced, "I am ready to mate the two largest rabbits, to set them up in a home of their own in a nice, new crate. I have named them 'Grace and Harlan,'" he told us. After that they were a great source of fun – until the morning when Howard joined us with a disturbed face.

"I found Grace and Harlan's cage full of white fur this morning," he said. "They have attacked each other. I am very much afraid that both Grace and Harlan are male rabbits."

The rabbit tragedy then unfolded. Every morning Howard went to the barn. The bags of food grew smaller in proportion to the increased appetite of the rabbits. Could he afford to buy more feed? He tried to sell the rabbits, putting a sign on the barn and an ad in the newspaper. The day arrived when Howard came home in mid-afternoon a broken man. He had slain his rabbits, skinned and dressed them and put the meat into cold storage. A murderer would have had no deeper line on his brow. Howard's spirit dwindled into gloom.

The forecast of meat for the winter was fulfilled. My lot was to cook all the rabbits, two at a time, on the weekends. I searched for recipes and for variety. We had rabbit stew, baked rabbit with stuffing, minced rabbit with spices, rabbit "a la king" with white sauce and pepper rings and cold rabbit salad. I would enhance their attraction by calling them hazenpheffer or jugged hare. "When it is skinned," observed an interested onlooker, "a rabbit looks like a baby." Said Mabel, "Those rabbits should be grateful. They have entered the human kingdom." Rabbits taste rather like chicken and were a prized addition to our diet.

The rabbits even made a contribution to the Temple dome. When a plea came for sacrifice to the Fund, we invited all the Bahá'ís for a baked potato and rabbit gravy dinner. The friends were to contribute the cost of a normal dinner at home. We collected fourteen dollars for the Treasurer to send. Henry and Bessy Seker asked us all to their place, the next week, for another economy dinner.

Glad Tidings for Charlie Kerin

It was the first Sunday in October and the McKays were free to spend the day with the Kerins. We made our light-hearted approach up the steps to their house on the hill. Eve waited for us in the open doorway.

"Charlie is not well today. He is upstairs asleep now," she announced. "Wait till we have dinner," she said. "Then we will go up and see Charlie. The doctor says to just let him sleep."

I remember sitting in the kitchen with Eve while she cooked lamb chops. It was a subdued meal. Eve and the children were all silent until Eve said, "I may as well tell you what happened. Charlie has been fighting a battle, you know. Last night he lost. He came home late, and he'd been drinking heavily."

Eve had helped him to bed, and he had slept. In the morning he awoke and stumbled down the stairs. Trying to light the kitchen stove, he fell, hit his head on it and fainted. Joey and Eve carried him back to bed. The doctor came and said to let him sleep, leaving some pills for him to take when he awoke.

We went up to the bedroom to say healing prayers. Willard sat beside him on the bed, touching him with his kind, firm hands. Eve and I sat together on the other bed, our eyes on the frail form and pale face, our love pouring out to him. For many minutes we sat there, peaceful and strangely happy, praying for Charlie: "Thy mercy is my healing and my succour, both in this world and in the world to come...."[21]

In those moments, Bahá'u'lláh, the Wise, the Compassionate, released this soul from its dilemma in this world. Charlie, who had imagined himself lost, slipped into "the world to come".

From my journal, October 10, 1931:

> Yesterday we had services at Charlie Kerin's grave. I was appointed to speak for a few minutes and read a selection from the Bahá'í Writings. We drove into the bleak-looking Roman Catholic cemetery, which is on a hill surrounded by other desolate hills. I was so depressed that I felt I could not proceed. The people I was riding with were not in a good mood, either.
>
> Then I saw the river gleaming in a ray of sunlight and moving swiftly as if in answer to a Call. As the image brightened, there arose within me a sense of joyous nothingness which is also wholeness. When my turn came, I began, 'The Pittsburgh Assembly has extended its boundaries into the World of the Kingdom. We have a representative before the door of the Cleaver of Dawns.' I let the words pour out and the people began to weep.
>
> Later Bishop Brown said, 'If you would promise to do that for me, Doris, I would willingly lie down and die tomorrow!' That rhythm flows again through all this house, beginning with numbness and inadequacy, moving on to a call for help – then the answer, an inflowing grace, the promised strength of ten.

Later I would note in my diary:

> Today I sat down and faced Eve for the first time since Charlie died. We looked at each other and Eve said, 'You are like the girl in the poem who was quite plain sometimes, and again, she was beautiful. This is one of those times when you are beautiful. In fact, I have never seen you like this before!' Eve had come to tell me that Charlie had not gone.

---

21 *Bahá'í Prayers* (Wilmette, IL, Bahá'í Publishing Trust, 1982), p. 87.

'When I was crossing the street by the Fort Penn Hotel,' she said, 'I found myself standing still in the midst of two-way traffic.' (No red and green lights in those early days.) 'I thought I would be killed, when I felt his hand under my elbow, mysteriously guiding me safely to the sidewalk.'

There were brighter moments in my notes for the fall of 1931:

The Browns have given the household a truckload of furniture which they had stored in a basement. It looks as if the 'good fairies' had visited our room! We have a bookcase, a mahogany table and a little sofa by the window.

Ruth is taking an advanced English composition course at the University of Pittsburgh and she stops at the house to go over her notes with me. It is as if I am learning how to paint pictures with words. (They are studying description.) Art, they say, is to look at something so long that it looks to you so different from the way everyone else sees it. To express in simple words what you have seen is great Art.

I thought secretly, 'I have beheld you, dear Ruth, with that long, long, look. You are like my Lady Doll that someone gave me when I was a child.' Lady Doll, created by artisans in the middle of the century, belonged to a greater past. An artist had moulded the clay to cast her white china head with elaborate coiffure, straight patrician nose and staring, candid blue eyes. Lady Doll's hands and feet, long and slender, were made of the finest white kid.

No, I did not tell her what I saw. Lady Doll's delicacy did not invite personalities. Yet, we had intimate talks on those visits.

In 1912 when 'Abdu'l-Bahá was in America, Ruth Randall had been Mr Harry Randall's young wife, ill in bed with the disease better known then as consumption. She was expected to die. 'Abdu'l-Bahá visited her in her room and blessed and healed her. He told her that she would recover and bear another child. (A daughter, Margaret, had been her first.)

Twelve years later, while in Haifa on pilgrimage, Ruth pledged the financial support for the building of the Western Pilgrim House. When she returned home, she found that Harry's fortune had been wiped out. Over the years, his activities for the Cause had increased while his interests in the family firm of shipbuilders had dwindled. The fact that his name was often in the papers linked with the Faith and the teaching trips of Martha Root had disturbed his conservative Boston relatives and friends – advertising which hurt his law practice.

The Randalls moved to smaller Boston quarters and Ruth went to work as a clerk at the Jordan Marsh department store. In 1929 Harry died.

"How did you keep your promise to the Western Pilgrim House," I asked her later.

"I sold my jewels."

"And Bishop, where did you meet him?"

"We met at Jordan Marsh. We devoted ourselves to Harry in his last years of illness... Harry, too, loved him. Before he died, he joined our hands together. It was his wish."

Bishop Brown was offered a chair in Business Research at the University two years ago, and they moved here.

The Hidden Meanings

My writing exercises with Ruth opened my shutters to an increased intimacy with all that I observed inwardly. Words tumbled out of subconscious depths to surprise and delight me. My charmed discoveries seemed in accord with a book by Mary Austin entitled *Everyman's Genius*. I found it and another book, similarly entitled *Discovering the Genius Within You*, by Stanwood Cobb, in Alice Parker's wonderful case of books on psychology and religion. I hadn't read them then, although their titles were as evocative as a voice calling to me from a hidden room. I was intrigued now with the gathering of closer attentions and the discovery of essences of the familiar realities within my present life, such as the changing view seen from my attic window.

And this practice of observation I applied to other environments, persons. I recognized it as a form of meditation. "It is my spirit talking to my mind!", I heard myself exclaim.

I remember a short conversation with Dr Cobb. At Green Acre I stopped him and asked him for an explanation of "the Universal Divine Mind". Learned as he was, this beginner's question did not elicit a satisfactory answer. But now I read again the answer from 'Abdu'l-Bahá:

> But the universal divine mind which is beyond nature. . . embraces existing realities and receives the light of the mysteries of God. . . A ray of this light falls upon the mirrors of the hearts of the righteous, and a portion and a share of this power comes to them from the Holy Manifestations.[22]

My scribbling was one of my only diversions during the crowded days of fall and winter. There were other diversions, but not many so meaningful.

There were walks – the late midnight walks that Willard and I took together after coming home from meetings. We walked blindly into grandeur. Following a narrow footpath, we discovered once the great Frick Park. We had not known of its existence within the city limits. In the darkness we felt the woods by the freshness and cleanliness of their night airs, heard rippling waters and the sleepy monologues of unsettled birds. A cool, damp, and breathless night.

On another night we found ourselves on the grounds of a country club. I was so weary when we started our walk, I thought that I would have to be carried, but there was bounce in my step on the way back.

Such were the discoveries. In spite of the poverty of those days, it was quite safe out-of-doors at night. No one ever accosted us.

---

22 Abdu'l-Bahá, *Some Answered Questions*. Trans. Laura Clifford Barney (New Delhi, India: Bahá'í Publishing Trust, 1973), p. 253.

The Racial Amity Conference, October 1931

Louis Gregory had left Willard in charge of the arrangements for Pittsburgh's Racial Amity Conference. When Louis returned on the fourth, Willard had secured a free hall at the Frick Normal School, had enlisted the cooperation of the Urban League and had found an excellent speaker: a young and popular Jewish rabbi who would appear on the platform with Louis. The next ten days were spent in calling upon the great and near-great to arouse interest in the meeting. The conference would take place on the 14th.

Louis asked me to be chairman. It was four years since Willard and I had worked together with Louis. That had been the Amity Conference held in Rochester, New York – my first experience in speaking from a platform to a large meeting. About 175 people attended. Sitting near, Louis beamed encouragement to me. Later, when an elated crowd of us, Black and White, had supper at the coloured "Y", Louis said, "Doris, I wish you would be chairman at all my meetings."

During the week of the Racial Amity Conference, Tilbury Street was in its usual turmoil and stress. Of the situation I had written, "It is ever on, and on and ON with the alternative of NOWHERE!" A week later, Oct. 11th:

> We are, all six of us, making a mighty upward heave together. Tonight we went up to the McKays' room to call to Bahá'u'lláh, the Helper, the Help in Peril, using the ultimate invocation, 'Ya Allah el Mustagath!' The sloping walls of our attic tossed back the vibrations of our voices. The old Jewish mother, moaning and mourning in the attic room adjacent to ours, ceased her chanting.

The Guardian was sustaining us with his letters. There had been two. The one to the Local Assembly said, ". . . these difficult times would bring out the qualities of the sincere believers in the form of sacrifice and sustained effort." To us he wrote that we were a group of responsible teachers, adding, "Now we will see what you can do!"

Willard Hatch Visits

The Ives and the Obers were thrilled that their old time Bahá'í friend Willard Hatch would be stopping over in Pittsburgh on his way home from Haifa. He would be the bearer of news from the Guardian. There were so few visits to Haifa then. Only the Browns and the Obers had seen Shoghi Effendi.

While taking a leisurely teaching trip home from the Holy Land in 1920, Grace and Harlan were staying in Paris. They remember:

> We were in Paris on the way to England when Shoghi Effendi came through on his way to England to enter Oxford. It is a most precious memory... that he phoned us and came to breakfast. We asked him why he had chosen England, not France, to finish his education. He explained that it was the Master's choice that he become fluent in English.

On several occasions Grace had told the story of the glorified breakfast party with Shoghi Effendi, who was then twenty-three years old. She always added that she and Harlan were aware, even then, of Shoghi Effendi's nobility. They sensed that his destiny in the Cause would be very great.

Two years later the Obers were again in Europe, this time in Switzerland. One day while Grace was sitting in a tea-room overlooking a village street, a man in a black suit passed the window. "Who is that young man?" asked a fellow traveller. "He has the saddest face I have ever seen." Answered Grace, "Since the passing of his Grandfather, 'Abdu'l-Bahá, he is the Guardian of the Bahá'í Faith."

The solitary figure walked swiftly toward the mountains.

Willard Hatch was a tall figure with firm features and a raised voice. He was a seasoned and experienced Bahá'í of many years, now on fire with one idea: that of the Guardianship. On his pilgrimage he had been turned around to face new directions by an uplifting spiritual power. He wanted us to understand and to make efforts to tune our souls to this heartbeat at the core of the Cause, to reach toward the Guardian in our prayers, to say his name and to dream of losing ourselves in order to follow him.

Challenged by the ardent discipleship of Willard Hatch, I remembered how May Maxwell used to mention his name on all occasions – always the Guardian, the Guardian, the Guardian. I had been content to wait for understanding. I knew that he was human, but with a function more than human. And I knew that in his station he was "protected from error". Ali Kuli Khan had told me that he had prostrated himself before the Guardian and had been told to rise. Young Bahá'ís responded to the Guardian's loving messages. His letters terminated usually with "your brother, Shoghi." They marvelled at the decisiveness of his plans.

During these days, believers would read the Will and Testament of 'Abdu'l-Bahá and would know the words, "for he is, after 'Abdu'l-Bahá, the Guardian of the Cause of God... he who hath disobeyed him hath disobeyed God; he who hath turned away from him hath denied the True One...." This they would read before declaring.

Mr Hatch said, "He is the embodiment of an institution, the Guardianship." At last, I said to Willard Hatch, "He still is not real to me and some of my friends, although we love and accept him. But what is he like?"

But our visitor would not speak of Shoghi Effendi's personality, his charm, his humour, his struggle. He said only, "He is the Guardian, the orb of the Guardianship that is arising in this dark world."

I have always thought of myself as young, but I am two years older than the Guardian. May Maxwell had promised that, sometime, I would learn the meaning of maturity. It is a slow growth.

November

Surely the secrets of the hearts of the Baháʼís are events in the history of the Faith. I am moved to turn myself inside out to share with you the true record of those days in which we were revealed unto ourselves.

November. Willard Hatch was there no longer to lift up our spirits. Loose dirt blew in the streets or cold rains drizzled, allying with the people out there who had lost hope. There had been no material answer to our combined prayers offered two weeks ago. We were not relieved of the fear that we might become destitute.

I remember a line in the little black prayerbook that we used then. Baháʼu'lláh said, "It is incumbent upon you that joy and exultation shall be manifest upon your faces, that everyone may see in you the signs of forbearance and resignation." Our community at Tilbury did put up a radiant front to the outside world. At the time I noted:

> The collective power of this house is a dynamo – or a mad robot. When we sit down to one of our frequent consultations, telephone calls come from all over. We seem to attract the calls of weak people tuning in for power. We are all making great contacts with people in the city. Our Baháʼí teaching is being confirmed. Such is the mystery of God.

Grace used to say that our house needed rubber walls to stretch to hold us all. Harlan's abstraction and gloom were understandable with the pressures and tensions of the community he supported. Tilbury had become, through gradual stages, a ruled world, its standard of perfection fixed. Even for the children it had the rigidity of defence. And now the addition of Mary and the Ives to our number had pushed our household to a crisis of nerves.

Mary (Marusha) was a rebellious teenager, a fiery Slav, talented and beautiful and admired by the two boys. She was recovering from polio. Mary, Willard and I adhered to one another as a minority. And when Mary had another tantrum, she was welcome to sob it out in my arms.

Howard and Mabel had joined us. Howard had told me on one of his first visits to Geneva that the doctor had said his nerves were "stripped." Mabel, too, had chronic illnesses induced by stress. I wrote:

Those wonderful Ives. There is no one like them! It is their temperament to be either in heaven or in hell – nearness to God or separation from Him. The process seems necessary for the release of their special powers. Whatever their emotions in reacting to conditions, there is no variability in their passion to teach, never a cooling of their love for Bahá'u'lláh. It is only that they are sometimes in contact and sometimes disconnected from the Object of their love. They are always in a state of spiritual excitement and the people they reach are awakened and stirred, as we ourselves were touched and awakened the night we met them.

Spiritual Parenthood

My love for Howard is a transcendent emotion. We have always been close, ever since that fabulous spring of 1925 when he brought me and Willard into the Cause. Now I am privileged to see his reality shining through that tired, feeble body of his, and it is brilliant.

He wrote me a letter that first summer. He said I was the daughter of his spirit and asked me, as a bond of our relationship, to call him "father." I have never done this. It is too awesome. Besides, it is too sacred for others' ears.

Last night I sat next to Howard at a supper Feast. Under the cover of the general conversation, he said, "I have been wanting to tell you that your sweet spirit adds to the community consciousness." I almost cried because I knew the wickedness of my heart. I had quarrelled with Harlan over his interference with my working program in the house. I had slammed the kitchen door and refused to come back and talk things over. I had kept out of his way for days while I licked my wounds. One evening I wrote:

> It is 9:00 p.m. and I have just come upstairs. I have been in the basement scrubbing clothes and later, in the kitchen, cooking cornmeal to be put overnight in the fireless cooker. After a day of struggle with my duties I am walking crooked, like a half-opened jack knife. I am lying on my back and trying to think of how I can squeeze in an hour or two each day to carry on National Study Committee work. I am the secretary, and I am being buried by the correspondence that is stacking up.

Sunday evening. We were having a gay little supper party of creamed rabbit and mushrooms. Suddenly a wave of fatigue and depression swept over me. I ached in every bone. "If you will excuse me, I think I will go upstairs and lie down." Grace came over to me and put her hands on me, and I felt the healing begin. I said to her, "You could not do this if there were not unity between us." Again, she said something very profound: "Unity is renunciation." I did not go upstairs to lie down. I was completely revived.

Willard Goes to Washington

On the 10th of November, I wrote,

> Willard has been asked to speak in Washington, then to meet Louis [Gregory] in Atlanta for a two-week tour of the South. We had a letter from Loulie Mathews with her check for $60, and another one will follow from Roy Wilhelm.

The first of December, the time had come for Willard to go. I went with Harlan to see him off on a morning bus. I had been practically sleepless for two nights, missing him in advance. Sleep would not be induced, it seemed. On the looming last night before his departure, Willard even tried telling me stories about a character called 'Tinybird.' When that failed, he was inspired to suggest, "How about my practising the talk I'm to give in Washington tomorrow night?" I was asleep in two minutes – a joke that later we would enjoy.

Now I was sending him off with an artificially cheerful face and scolding him a little because he insisted on taking a cheaper and less comfortable bus. When the winds blew at Tilbury, I would not have him to hold onto.

That evening as I was doing the last kitchen chores, Harlan and I had a wonderful talk. It was wonderful because the Harlan that I knew was back – not the stressed and critical Harlan with whom I had had the argument. He said that I had arisen to a challenge in taking over the house. "It was a big O.K.," he said, "although we have a lot of adjusting to do, sometimes even to clash swords about how to run the house."

Grace came down and I owned up to my black wickedness. I told her that I was an Assembly problem because I had stayed away from two meetings because I could bear no longer to hear about "the life" without seeing it lived. Grace and Harlan had a good laugh and Harlan mauled me playfully, the way he does when the boys are naughty. This is what we needed: laughter and FUN.

But the night was not over. We talked about Howard's problem with nerves and of the need to keep the whole family hushed because of his condition. He was eating his meals alone in his room. Even I was keeping out of his way. At this moment he was sitting in the living room waiting for us to go to bed so that he could be completely alone. Even Mabel had been sent away. Grace thought Harlan ought to go to him – a mistake!

Harlan went in and I heard him praying, then talking. Howard began to shout, repeating over and over, "I want to be alone. I want to be ALONE!" Mabel came running down the stairs crying, "Oh, Howie," in an agonized voice. Then she took him away and held him in her arms the rest of the night. He told me later that he would have died had he not in his memory that night, the words of Bahá'u'lláh.

With Willard away, I went to bed alone, my teeth chattering from nervousness and the cold in our unheated room. I prayed and eventually went to sleep.

I awoke wondering if Howard had had a complete collapse and what the day would bring forth. I tiptoed down to the kitchen and was getting breakfast when Howard came in, dressed to go out. He took me right into his arms, called me his 'dear daughter' and love leapt between us. I slipped away upstairs, thinking my continued presence might be too much for him. In a few minutes he called me, made coffee for me and wanted to share breakfast with me. Mabel came along, and by the grace of God, all three of us stepped into the realm of spirit together and celebrated a great victory.

Later in the afternoon Howard returned, exhausted. His face was leaden and had terrible lines in it. He sent Mabel to ask if I would put my hands on him and perhaps put him to sleep. Oh, would I! I sat beside him with my hands on his head and neck, and I prayed. My whole personality was dissolved in prayer. The prayer had the effect of moisture on a hard crust it dissolved the shell that encased him. After a time, he caught my hand, kissed it and held it to his cheek.

I sat with him a long time, and sometimes he would speak to God or to me. I did not tell him what a test he had been to me as well as to the others. Yet I blamed myself for having withdrawn from him, my spiritual father, in those dark days. How shallow we were – how selfish and blind.

Soliloquy

To my friends of the Depression I wrote:

> This man has been a lighter of fires in many hearts; his spiritual sons and daughters are spread over the eastern United States and they have been impregnated with the love of God. In generations to come his spiritual progeny will have multiplied

and become an army. Three weeks ago, at a meeting, he prayed for a supreme martyrdom and because of this he has been in torment. He is making supreme efforts away from the earth, higher than ever before, and falling back on his face in water and clay. He is ill, perhaps because the community has been intolerant of him. We have all been tested. Only Willard, in his radiance, has been secure from test."

From my journal:

> Here is one of the things I have learned this year: no person is easy to live with. We all have our curious slants, annoying habits, inconsistencies. Why cannot we take, as we ourselves give, the bitter with the sweet, the drab with the vivid colour? What we know and love in each other, unchangeable, is the spirit.

Willard and I seem ordained to love deeply some of the kindred souls we have found in Pittsburgh: Eve and Charlie, Alice Parker, Ruth Brown. I have known about "kindred spirits" since Dorothy Baker, unaccountably, selected me to be her friend. But do we have a right to all this splendour?

One day I talked to Harlan about personal love. He said there is an individual love, sometimes developing out of universal love. It is part of the divine scheme. It does not make demands, does not fluctuate; it is not exclusive. The spiritual power generated by such unity is not for personal gratification but for the attraction of hearts to the Faith, a sacred energy devoted to the passing of God's love to others – a link with the Holy Spirit. It is a relationship belonging to married lovers and to dedicated friendships among the believers. As our perception of other souls increases through universal love, the number of those with whom we are united widens. This is the knowledge that came to Lorna and me on the "Night of the Burning Log". This, too, was the subject of our talks with May Maxwell: unity in the love of God.

At Tilbury Tenement there was peace after the storm. Howard

was weary but acquiescent. And now Willard's missive from Atlanta transported us out of the murkiness of the Pittsburgh scene. His talk in Washington had gone well. The people there had not gone to sleep, he teased. Arriving in Atlanta he had called at the white YMCA to ask if Mr Gregory had been there.

"Gregory was here," said the young clerk. "Black, isn't he?"

"He is called Mr Gregory where I come from," Willard said. "He is much respected as a speaker, a great traveller and a lawyer."

"You don't say. I sure would be embarrassed to call any Black man 'Mr.'" The clerk looked thoughtful and not a little shocked. He would have been incredulous if he had witnessed the handclasp of Willard and Louis at the Black YMCA a half hour later.

Willard wrote, "Louis thinks this is the first time a White man and a Coloured man have travelled together on terms of equality, riding on public conveyances through the southern states."

With Grace and Mabel

Grace and Mabel were home more often now. With a square-cut brush they were practising the drawing of curves and straight lines in the hope of making a little money at showcard writing. As we worked, we talked about our several ways of rejuvenating ourselves when exhausted:

Grace says that she flops down and thinks of herself as a tree sending its roots down, down, down, into the mineral world until some circuit of descent is satisfied. Then up, up, up into the air and out through all her limbs. Suddenly she feels free and leaps up with fresh energy.

Mabel says that she mentally detaches herself from her body, takes refuge in her spirit, touches its life, then returns with fire and assurance to her physical self.

I said, 'When I get tired, sometimes I am in contact with a throbbing flow that sets up a motion in my atoms and refreshes me. When I turn towards the source, it is there. I feel this in my hands when I say the healing prayers.'

One day Grace was sewing. I was reading aloud to her when she said suddenly, "I wonder if you know how much I love you?" I said, "Yes, I think I do," and she sat down for a talk on human relationships that would never have been found in the psychology books I had been reading. She said, "Our different personalities are only incidental, you know. Your attraction for me is elemental. We have been together before the Throne at another time, comparable to this."

"It sounds like reincarnation," I objected. "Not at all," she said. "The transparent glass that holds the wines of our separate individualities is preserved elsewhere. The bestowal of divine potentialities which we claim now may appear in another age, just as it happened in the days of the Manifestation. It is the return of the qualities."

"Does it mean," I asked, "that various kinds of personalities with certain attributes appear in different ages as species do in the lower kingdom? A certain kind of person accepts the Manifestation in a former age, another rejects Him? And that the apostles were a type of person appearing again in this day – that you and I are like those who followed Christ or Muhammad?"

Grace assented. "But remember," she added, "that the Master said it is not the personality or the rational mind that returns. Just as the Manifestations differed in personality but were one in their attributes, the same is true of their followers in different ages." She smiled. "When the Master was with us, we 'maidservants' spoke much of this, wanting to know what roles we played in former days, even arguing about it."

Visit of an Apostle

Martha Root was coming. At an excited meeting at Alice Parker's, we talked about the days when Martha lived and worked in Pittsburgh. Alice was an administrator and teacher in the Frick Normal School before 'Abdu'l-Bahá's visit in May 1912. Martha had been a successful newspaper writer and executive whose articles and lectures were well known. Certainly, these two career women knew each other.

"Yes, I knew her," said Alice, "but only in a professional way – at times when the Normal school was news. After the Pittsburgh *Post Gazette* published her article on the history and teachings of the Cause, we knew of her interest in the Faith. But I had admired her for years for her advanced ideas. 'Abdu'l-Bahá's appearance in New York had made a stir in the newspaper world and when He came here, about four hundred people showed up at the Schenley Hotel to hear Him speak. The meeting, of course, was arranged by Martha Root. The response of the audience was part of the magic of that evening. The contact with the spirit brought by 'Abdu'l-Bahá was truly a moving experience. And we saw a changed Martha Root, different from the practical, busy person known to the newspaper world. She was transformed by joy in the presence of the wonderful being who had come to Pittsburgh at her invitation."

"You know how I have always felt about the oneness of religion," Alice beamed. "Naturally, I was one of those who pushed up to speak with Him after the meeting. There were Bahá'í books too, which I purchased and took home to read... Then Martha was away again, finally around the world, meeting important people and writing articles for the press."

December 11th–15th

Eve and I were appointed to meet Martha on the evening of the 11th. Ink was raining from the sooty clouds that night and the glass dome over the station platform was leaking. The passenger train pulled in with a piercing squeak of wheels and reek of coal gas. Bold lights revealed the holes in the dome and the wet rises and cracks in the concrete.

Martha, a seasoned traveller on such trains, was alighting briskly from a coach two or three cars down. We could see the flurry of a small hurrying figure encumbered by bags and bundles. She was running to meet us and we were running to meet her when she tripped on a crack in the concrete hidden by a pool of water and went down. Before we reached her, she stood up, soaked and laughing. "What a lark!" she exclaimed. Carrying wet bundles and giggling, the three of us splashed over to the Fort Pitt Hotel, went up to a room and waited while Martha called room service to come for her coat. We had a prayer, embraced joyfully and said goodnight.

Martha's gleeful reaction to these circumstances was amazing to Eve. While we waited to catch our busses, we talked.

"Well, I never expected to see a sunbeam in a shower of rain," said Eve fervently.

"Eve, you have seen an Apostle of Bahá'u'lláh."

"Why do you say that?"

"Because in His Tablet to the Apostles of Bahá'u'lláh,[23] 'Abdu'l-Bahá defined their high station as the fulfilment of three conditions." I waited for her to ask me what those conditions were. "Firmness in the Covenant, fellowship and love among the believers, and travel to all parts of the world while proclaiming the Faith. Surely, Eve, Martha is a true apostle. There were a few in the time of Christ and many more are needed today. Bahá'u'lláh calls these souls the 'armies of God.'"

At two the next afternoon the Bahá'ís sat quietly at Alice Parker's, waiting for Martha. She came with the Browns, people she knew from the day when her great friend and co-worker Harry Randall was alive. She affectionately greeted each of us and went with Alice to remove her freshly cleaned coat. When everyone was settled, Alice welcomed Martha home to Pittsburgh, mentioning some of the far-off cities fabled in song and story – Cairo, Baghdad, Teheran – where Martha had sojourned on the return swing of her journey back to the starting place of her world tours: Pittsburgh. A cloak of romance rested lightly on Martha's dark blue shoulders.

---

23 'Abdu'l-Bahá, *Tablets of The Divine Plan* (Wilmette, IL: Bahá'í Publishing Trust, 1974), p. 17. This tablet begins, "O ye apostles of Bahá'u'lláh..."

"This morning," said Martha, "I was busy praying. Whenever I enter a city (I can't call Pittsburgh a new city), I pray nine times the Tablet of Ahmad, praying that doors will open to teach the Faith." She told us stories of near miracles that had followed that beginning formula. "'Abdu'l-Bahá was with me, opening the doors. We must never forget that, with God, all things are possible."

We sketched out the program we had arranged for her: tea at the University Club with some of her old associates, an evening talk at the Ebenezer Baptist Church, a tea and talk with an International Peace Society, a formal public speech in a lecture room at Carnegie Hall and some free time for Martha to renew her contact with the city she knew so well.

I went to all her meetings. I did not listen but looked at her with my mind relaxed and still, as in a refreshed sleep. In the bland atmosphere of her presence the moisture of the Holy Spirit was seeping down to my roots. It is impossible to explain in a logical way the effect that Martha had on people like me. She wove a spell. Her charm did not lie in what she said. She avoided brilliance, which can be a veil, however shining. Her person and her dress were without embellishment. "Nothing is needed," said Bahá'u'lláh in The Seven Valleys, "until thou canst become acceptable in the path of love." A divine economy was effective in Martha in moments of teaching. There was no obstruction of the Holy Spirit.

At the Ebenezer Baptist Church

The electric cross fixed to the steeple of the church lit up the street. Late, I climbed the stairs and entered. The people in the back row moved over and made a place for me. The faces of the White Bahá'ís in the audience looked ashen in the big Black congregation.

Martha was a small figure as she stood in the pulpit, speaking quietly of peace and unity and the One who had brought bright assurance to the world. The people sat, acquiescent, knit in a strange predicament, caught as they were that night with closed minds and open hearts. They stared at Martha, sometimes nodding and saying, "Amen." I thought to myself, "They are wondering why they are feeling this way when there is no rousement." "Rousement" was their word for the fiery, excited eloquence of their minister. It was love swelling up in their hearts and one was satisfied that the Spirit had come, that the Spirit was there.

When she was finished, the minister said a prayer and called for a second collection. Then the people stood and shook hands with one another over the backs of the seats. A brown hand clasped mine. Martha and the minister walked down the aisle to the door, where I joined them. The people surged around us, sometimes touching Martha, mumbling, "Praise de Lawd."

Martha had offered her soul to the congregation of the Ebenezer Baptist Church. At the tea given by the members of the Women's International League for Peace and Freedom she withdrew it. She could have entertained them as she had charmed her associates at the University Club, with a display of names and interviews with peace leaders in Europe. But Martha now chose to use the occasion to speak of the Bahá'í Principles containing the structure of a lasting universal peace. She chose to plant seeds rather than to regale the fashionable and vociferous crowd in this elaborate room with its raised speakers' platform. Her intuition had shown her the futility of trying to please them, for their cups were overflowing with a blend of foreboding, resolve, frustration and research into the conditions of Old-World ties. Their minds were stimulated by an eggbeater whirl of world crises. Our hostess, Mrs Norman W. Storer, took me aside to tell me of her disappointment. "Too philosophical, too detached," she said.

A woman's voice filtered out to us as we stood in the hall. "As soon as I heard that sugar was to be rationed, I bought two hundred pounds. I have it stored in the attic." A few lines from the Tablet of Manifestation (in the *Bahá'í Scriptures*) came to mind: "But thou beholdest the creatures and hearest that which proceeds from their mouths; therefore the bounty is restrained...."

December 14, 1931

My eyes had looked at Martha so many hours that week, what more had my "inner eye" beheld? It seemed to me that her personality was an arrangement of levels or planes, catching the eye like a piece of semi-abstract sculpture, each perspective demanding a change of focus: the Ebenezer congregation, the luncheon with the friends from the Press Club, the Peace advocates at tea, meetings with the Bahá'ís. Each event had brought out aspects of Martha like facets of light in a masterpiece – aspects of a soul who, in the act of teaching, was turned obediently to God for inspiration. Her personality was a work of art. Because of its simplicity, it was the essence of perfection.

On the night of her meeting at Carnegie Hall, her audience was banked in tiers of inclined seats: students, professors, professional friends of Alice Parker, the Bahá'ís and the guests that they brought with them. When Martha entered with Harlan, the people stood. She wore a lovely pale dress and a gauze scarf on her shoulders. Her hair, that night, was freshly coiffed and worn around her head like a silver helmet. Her face was a frame for brilliant grey-green eyes. She carried American Beauty roses. Martha stood forward on the platform and, with dignity and fullness of voice, proclaimed the Faith of Bahá'u'lláh. She spoke of World Order and Peace. When she was finished, the audience stood again and applauded. Their expressions were respectful, a little wistful, as if they had heard an ambassador from a king or from another planet. They came up to meet her, and lovingly, she gave away her roses. Martha was more than a personality; she was a presence. The reporters were baffled. They did not know how to describe her. On the 15th she moved serenely on to another city, Washington.

The quietness of unspoken thoughts settled now on Tilbury Tenement. It had been a month of emotional excitement and of widened horizons. First with the visit of Willard Hatch and then with Martha's. I, for one, was sunk in the emptiness of Willard's absence and was awash with uneasy feelings. It was as though the walls of the house ticked away like clocks, ticked away to mark the approach of some unknown doom. Or perhaps it was the drip, drip, drip of the steady leaking away of our funds. All of our foreboding was heightened. Winter was at hand. We had worked ourselves up to an orchestra of feelings, pitched from low to high.

At school the children had caught a wistfulness for Christmas. David was found to have taken money to buy a present for his teacher.

Willard's Triumphant Return

Quick steps and a lifting latch and Willard was home. The three children were first to reach him, and I had to scatter them to get my hugs and kisses. Cries of joy echoed through our household, now redeemed from gloom. In his shabby, red-striped bathrobe, Howard joined us, his face carved in a smile. "Is it my imagination, Willard, or do I detect in your presence the scent of magnolias and the warmth of the southern sun?"

"Unfortunately, a vain illusion," said Willard. "I had forgotten about weather in the south at this time of year. It rained almost every day."

"Did you have any encounters with the Whites?" Grace sounded hopeful. "It must have been a shock to some of them to see a White man and a Black man going everywhere together."

"I saw very few Whites after I left the desk clerk at the Atlanta Y. My trip with Louis was to demonstrate Black and White brotherhood as a Bahá'í principle. The Black students and their teachers were familiar with the Bahá'í social teachings brought to them on Louis's earlier visits. Understandably, they had listened to him then with a grain of salt. They had heard talk of brotherhood before. The mission of our journey was to demonstrate it. When we stayed a few days sharing their dormitory and eating with them at their table, they were amazed. One chap said, 'My father sure will be astonished when I write him about this; don't think he'll believe it at first.'"

"Why was eating together so important?" one of the boys wanted to know.

"Because it meant that I was equal with them. Eating together was a taboo. It was a revolution against the idea that the Black people were to be shut out from the Whites. That's one meaning. When Baháʼu'lláh said Oneness, He meant the end of all taboos. People are equal."

"Were there any bad feelings on the part of the students? You must have experienced some resentment against the White race."

"Absolutely none. There was a desire to be understood and loved by me that sometimes brought tears to my eyes. . . They couldn't help seeing that I loved them, so they loved me, too. It went beyond race."

Willard swallowed the lump in his throat in the pause that followed. He went on to say, "Louis introduced me to the chief administrators and their wives. We talked directly to them about the Message of Baháʼu'lláh. Will I ever be able to tell you enough about these souls, their learning, their wit, their penetrating thought! They opened their classes to us and their assembly halls. Louis and I addressed thousands of students, sharing the program between us. We had the confirmations of Baháʼu'lláh. And how we had asked for them, beginning with a prayer that Louis said every morning."

Willard looked across at me and our glances locked. "Would you like to say Louis's prayer now?" I asked.

We shut our eyes and moved into the alpha rhythm of the Word, Willard holding his hands upward as ʻAbdu'l-Bahá had done:

> O Lord, confirm me with Thy penetrating potency so that I may speak out Thy promises and glorifications among Thy creatures and my heart become overflowed with the wine of Thy love and knowledge.
>
> Verily, Thou art powerful to do what Thou willest and Thou art mighty over all things.
>
> ʻAbdu'l-Bahá

"The trip was Martha's idea, you know," he said. "She would have liked to have come with us. She sent me this, through Louis." Willard took out an envelope and opened a paper folder and said, "Here are two hairs of the head of Bahá'u'lláh, 'the one hair of Whose head is, before God, better than all there is in heaven and earth.'"

We touched the paper that held the gift of greatest value, united in our thrill of awe. Grace said, "When I was in Haifa, the Greatest Holy Leaf told us that she saved the combings from the comb of Bahá'u'lláh. That Martha gave you this great treasure was an expression of gratitude for the work you and Louis were accomplishing in the south."

When Willard and Louis left the Emery Institute in Atlanta, they went on to Tuskegee Institute in Alabama. Willard reported,

> "When I bought my ticket at the bus station, I asked the driver if there were any state laws which would prevent me from sitting with a Coloured friend with whom I was travelling. 'No, not if you want to sit on the back seat with the rest of them,' he replied. So we sat together on the back seat, although there certainly is more motion in the rear seats. After a while the driver came down to invite Louis and me to move up front – if we thought it would be more comfortable. This last lap of our journey lasted about four hours. We had time to talk over what seemed to us wonderful guidance to openings and remarkable confirmations of our efforts. Our faces must have been beaming. No wonder the driver wanted us to come closer!"

Mabel interrupted him by asking, "Certainly you met Dr George Carver at Tuskegee?"

"We called on him after breakfast on our last morning. We found him in his long room full of growing plants. That's also part laboratory but he says his real laboratory is in the cultivated grounds around the buildings. Boys, you can thank Dr Carver for the quality of your beloved peanut butter. He has experimented with over forty varieties of peanuts right there at the

Institute. Actually, he is one of the world's leading chemists. He has an international reputation."

"Does he know about the Bahá'í Cause?"

"Yes, Mabel. Dr Carver has been a friend of Roy Wilhelm for seventeen years and would like him to go there, to the institute. Roy isn't well, you know, and Dr Carver thinks he can heal him with some vegetable oils he has discovered."

"And what did I think of him? He is elderly, unpretentious and quite poor. And he belongs to 'Abdu'l-Bahá's 'superior race' who are the 'lovers of mankind.' He remains at Tuskegee from choice. He's turned down remunerative positions offered by the commercial companies because he's needed at the Institute to create revenue through his agricultural researches."

At the meeting with the Bahá'í friends that evening Willard reported that the presentation of the Faith and the spirit of universal love between the races reached more than a thousand students and teachers in the chief universities and technical schools in the southern states. His account was enlivened with human stories and repeated conversations. One of our newer members, Walter Buchannan, had once been with Booker T. Washington on the staff of A&M College in Montgomery, Alabama. Walter was incredulous.

"I would not believe anybody but you, Willard, that you and Mr Gregory had been asked to speak at the classes in Tuskegee and that chapel time was turned over to you. The chapel hour is the only time in the week in which the principal, Dr Moton, has the opportunity to speak to the student body."

"So he said," Willard agreed.

"How did you accomplish this miracle?" Walter wanted to know.

"Louis was our spokesman, of course. He talked to Dr Moton about the Bahá'í principles and about Bahá'u'lláh. He said that we were 'ambassadors for the oneness of mankind.' Dr Moton said he usually had fifteen minutes in the Chapel program, but that he would give us twenty."

Walter was still shaking his head. "But how do you and Mr

Gregory explain such a miracle?"

We waited for Willard's answer. "I think I have shown you that my experience was a profoundly emotional one, a mystical one. I was overwhelmed with love for what I sensed was the spiritual potency of the Black soul – in its moments of release, pure, close to the Source. The inmost reality of the White soul is its complement. When our two races united in this mission to spread the Word of Bahá'u'lláh there was a blending of qualities, a spiritual chemistry that overcame obstacles. Louis and I prayed sincerely every day. We love humanity. By the grace of God, we prevailed."

We came out to our waiting "gocart". It had seemed, for a moment, that the Breezes of the Merciful were flowing from the South. But this was Pittsburgh, and our second year of tests was about to begin. A man suddenly rose up in our midst asking us for money for food. He was an open-faced, naive sort of chap, light brown. He said, "I'm hungry. I tell you I'm HUNGRY." He showed us a rent in his trouser leg, almost to the knee. "Look at this, too!" We gave him a few coins and he vanished.

January 11, 1932

"Troubles are being intensified for all of us. Our great retreat is to His Fortress. Our spirits can be free. We are told to walk above the world by the power of the Greatest Name. We are the fortunate ones. Think of mankind in general!"

It was not Harlan who called us this time for a family consultation. It was Howard. "I have come to a turning point in my life, and I intend to waste no more time," he said. "Perhaps I will go away from you all and not come back." Mabel sat with her head back, eyes closed. My heart was thumping. "I had a letter from Washington," he said. "They want me on a two-week teaching stay. Perhaps I will buy only a one-way ticket, trust the Lord, and go about my business."

Considering his health, his age and his finances, his plan

seemed shockingly irrational. When we tried to reason with him, he became violently disillusioned with all of us and broke away to his room, shouting over his shoulder that he wished he had not confided in us.

He said we did not understand. But I did. That same week I had written in my private notes,

> I am bound with threads and ropes and ribbons, with everything that hurts and irritates and holds... I don't know whether I am accepted or rejected. My God! How I long for a change! Am I trying to run away from myself?

It was the tension in Tilbury Tenement that Howard wanted to get away from – our rack. We had witnessed his efforts and defeats since his earlier collapse. Repeatedly, he had disappeared behind a wall of silence and been in hell again with his nerves. His state was understandable and forgivable, but we could not let him go.

That night we called to the Guardian to take our prayers to Bahá'u'lláh, the "Remover of Difficulties" and the Healer. The next day Howard asked Grace if he could have a talk with her.

I noted:

> She [Grace] decided to tell him the truth; how everything in the house had had to build itself around his self-absorption; how the boys kept out of his way; how Mary at age seventeen was angry with him because he treated her like a tiresome child; how we deprived ourselves of food to give him special luxuries. Yes, it was Shock – and her treatment was inspired. She reached him and, as it says in The Hidden Words, he 'burst his cage asunder.'"

Howard's cure began at once, the change, a healing from on high. He came back to his loving friends. He won back the boys. He apologized to Mary. He let us play the radio at dinner... A week of recuperation and it was time for him to start for Washington where he would stay with Allen MacDaniel (then Chairman of the National Assembly). Howard would save souls there and everyone would come nearer to Bahá'u'lláh.

Later I would write, "He left in a blaze of glory after hugging me four times and calling me his 'precious daughter'. Never had there been such a victory. He said that never before had he met himself face to face in just this way. Dear Grace, our invincible heroine, said 'Praise be to God!'"

The joy-bells rang again in January of 1932:

> Emily Craighead has formally joined the Cause. Such love as I felt for her that night could not have been only my love. The Love of God beamed in all our faces. She sensed the divine Reality and became radiantly happy. It is wonderful to see a soul drawn out of its sheath through the power of Love." Emily, aged fifty-eight, entered the great adventure with the zest of a girl, although her family was persecuting her cruelly.

Weekly Public Meetings

In the heart of the old Duquesne Building there was a free room called Utility Hall, which was ours for a series of Sunday night public meetings. On this, our first night (February 4th), the Bahá'ís came early and scattered themselves among the rows of seats. Although we were yearning to turn around and face the door, our eyes surveyed the stage, its two armchairs, and a small oak table that held a potted palm. Behind us entered our friends from the Wednesday night Study Class and eleven new people who came in response to our newspaper ads.

Willard and Harlan ascended the platform and sat down in the two armchairs. I knew that they were making eye contact with the audience and praying inwardly. Willard introduced Harlan, who spoke on "What is the Bahá'í Movement?". It was a good talk, scholarly and with emphasis on the basic Bahá'í principles. Later there were interested questions from the floor. People lingered and felt at home. It was a good introduction by a pattern I knew well.

The second thrill of the evening for the McKays was the visits to the newspapers. First, "we took our notes over to Thompson's Lunch and ordered a mug of coffee, our first in weeks. Suddenly my mind began to click. I seized my pencil, spread my writing pad on the shiny white table, and the publicity wrote itself." Afterwards we made our way to the newspaper offices through a tangle of alleys, stealing around garbage cans and prostrate figures asleep in doorways. Scary, until I got used to it. "What about thugs?" I asked nervously.

"You don't find thugs in an alley. No money here to grab." Willard assured me.

"If the big streets are the city's arteries," I ventured, "these alleys must be its veins." I looked at the lights around the tops of the tall buildings. Illuminated front facades shone down into the ancient passageways which, it is said, once were trails for riders on horseback. By coming this way, we had saved walking half a dozen blocks.

Upstairs in the night room of the *Post Gazette*, I thought of Martha Root. That smoky, littered, masculine atmosphere must be tucked away in Martha's brain cells because she had blossomed there during her years of feature articles and news assignments with the *Gazette* and the *Pittsburgh Press*. We found the atmosphere exhilarating: deafening machinery, glaring lights, much shouting and running around – a glorious high-speed energy. We called for a typewriter and I dashed off my notes, remembering the proper heading, "For Immediate Release", a space for the editor to fill in a title, the arresting first sentence and the closing climax. We took the sheet to the night editor. He read it, initialled it and added it to the pile on his desk. Back to the network of alleys and on to the *Pittsburgh Press*.

Our publicity appeared, complete, in both the morning and evening papers.

Thirty-seven people came to our second Utility Hall meeting a week later. Twenty-five were visitors. A number of fine-thinking people joined in the discussion, including Dr Bryson, head of the popular "Pelley Group". Several other 'New Thought' members attended.

After the talk, the McKays found their way to "the Brass Rail". Before prohibition it had served beer, but now it was a snack bar. We ordered coffee and, like accustomed "hands", talked over our newspaper copy. Then, through the alleys to the press offices. This became our Sunday night routine in the months that followed, and our public meetings moved to a larger hall.

Finishing the Thirty-Six Lessons

Later that week I noted:

> Today all the lessons for the Study Outline Committee were finished and sent off to St. Paul for mimeographing. Harlan, Ruth Brown and I have been working since spring with the National Teaching Committee, the result being this offering of Thirty-Six Lessons taken from all available Bahá'í material and arranged with prayers and quotations for meetings. I have sent a descriptive report through the Newsletter to the Local Spiritual Assemblies offering the lessons for sale. They will be sent out from Pittsburgh – if Bahá'u'lláh allows us to stay here. "Affairs depend on means."

The Guardian's Letter to Emily

Emily had written Shoghi Effendi on the day of her entrance into the Faith. His answer came promptly. She started to read it to us but broke down and handed it over to me to read. The letter called her to the station of a Bahá'í teacher. The rest of the message was for every Bahá'í in the world. The Guardian said:

> If the complete destruction of our civilization is to be averted, if the world is to become a place of peace and good will where our own personality can become enhanced and developed spiritu-

ally, souls will have to arise who will first get imbued with the spirit of God revealed in this age through Bahá'u'lláh and then diffuse it in the consciousness of man.

Unless this happens, the darksome clouds that threaten a terrific storm to an already ravished society will not be dissipated and the era 'When the lion and the lamb shall lie down together' will never dawn.

"He asked me," marvelled Emily, "a new believer and not a speaker. What can I do right now?"

"Just be ready to serve," I responded. "To spread the knowledge of Bahá'u'lláh by word and deed. It is the fact that we TRY that counts. It is said that souls in the next world are gathered around to help those who have faith and who put forth an effort."

"I still don't understand why God needs our help," she said.

"Because the All Bountiful not only does things for us but does things with us; that is our part of the Covenant – to give ourselves for the operation of the Holy Spirit in the world. The Guardian implies that in spite of the smallness of our number, we Bahá'ís can save the world. There is an atmosphere around such exalted service. It is evoked by sacrifice, by unity and by love. These qualities are supernatural and miraculously potent. The Guardian's instruction to the Bahá'ís to rededicate ourselves and call on the help available to us is a desperate appeal. Those of us who listened to his message quaked at the power of his words."

"Unity. How can we achieve that unity? We are so very different."

"He is our unity," said Grace. "The Guardian, because he is the centre of the Covenant now. In him we are all united. That is our hope and the hope of the world."

We were confronted by the letter to Emily, and it became startlingly clear that the Guardian's message was addressed essentially to all who were only partially awake. I thought of the letters I had been receiving from Dorothy. How awake she had become, how steadfast in her search for someone to teach and how regular her study of the Word with Mother Beecher. Merely to think of Dorothy brought a lump to my throat. I had had two letters from her lately and I had not answered them. Had she won the struggle with self-doubt that had sent her out to roam the streets of Wilmette? Did she feel still the light touch of the "princely cloak" on her shoulders?

At this great moment, the appointed Centre of the Covenant is challenging us to arise and show forth our power as Bahá'ís. My introspective musings tell me that our only strength is in the decision to give up our lesser selves and offer to be used.

'Forget yourself,' said 'Abdu'l-Bahá, 'God's help will surely come. When you call on the Mercy of God, waiting to reinforce you, your strength will be tenfold. . . One must never consider one's own limitations, it is the strength of the Holy Spirit that gives the power to teach.'[24]

There is no such thing as self-sufficing. Of ourselves, we can do nothing. Will we ever learn that lesson? An impulse within me leaps, falls back, and leaps again!

There was an earlier letter from the Guardian to those of us in this house, calling us "a group of responsible teachers". He added, "Now see what you can do." Thank God we have some advantages: we are not young, but young enough; not very strong, but strong enough; not exceedingly well educated, but what we have will suffice. We have all the advantages that Martha had. The Holy Spirit could free us, too, if only the human spirit had the courage, the determination, the steadfastness to accept our role as she had done – whatever that role may be.

Sunday, March 20

"This morning was the beginning of a long day. Mary and I, accompanied by her little dog, Buddy, were taking one of our walks and were in a contemplative mood. I reminded her that a year ago on this very day, Willard and I had driven around that curve of Beechwood Boulevard for the first time. There was the apartment building where we had lived for the first six weeks.

---

24 *Tablets of 'Abdu'l-Bahá*, pp. 31–34.

"For Rent" signs were posted on it again. It rained and snowed on that day a year ago. I remembered driving down over the steep cliff of a mountain and into that pit of dense atmosphere, feeling a dark cloud settle on my spirit. Except for the occasional "scourings", it too had remained as grey as Pittsburgh woodwork.

"And now it is so different, Mary. We love this place and pray to remain here. We have a car with no tires or licence plates and, with luck, one room to live in. The 'security of our numbers' is gone, and yet, Mary, do you understand how Willard and I can be so light-hearted – and so scared we won't be able to stay?"

"Young-old Mary had acquired some wisdom in her life of feeling misfit. "Sometime," she said, "I, too, will be free to be myself."

Had it been the experience of other experimental communities that the sacrifice of individual persons had NOT been found in a storehouse of spiritual gains? Why had we felt so often a poverty of spirit? I remembered that Louis Gregory had warned me of this happening. Or is there a hidden inner treasury where all the copper that is lost is transmuted into piles of newly minted gold coins?

Naw-Rúz Feast

The lecture meeting and the visits to the newspapers were over. When we reached home, we found Grace and Harlan getting ready for the Naw-Rúz Feast, and we joined them. It was midnight. We retired a few hours later, thankful that no longer would we have to get up at six o'clock for early breakfast and prayers. The Fast was at an end and this is how I remember that Feast.

Grace and I were filled with holiday spirit and we enjoyed the work of preparing the enormous pilau. It was a privilege to be with Grace while her thoughts were drifting happily on the Master's hospitality. In the afternoon, other "maidservants of the Merciful" arrived, bringing contributions. Said Bessie, in her blustering way, "I might have known I would be asked to bring the onions. I cried my eyes out!"

Everyone worked with the intention of dressing dull Tilbury in festive garb. There were always plants in the Ober house: our yellow lilies, ferns and ivy. Now even the goldfish and canary were commandeered to add charm to the rooms. Mabel had brought pink hyacinths in pale green frills. There was an Easter lily. Tables were extended through the archway between the living room and the dining room. They were spread with white cloths, trimmed with paper ribbons and set with lovely silver and china that Emily and Ruth had brought. Mr Payne's funeral chairs were drawn up in a phalanx on one side, later to be placed around the tables. It was now seven o'clock. The candles were lit, and the guests began to arrive.

"This place is heaven!" sighed little Mr Glinka, our Hungarian follower of John Huss.

"So enter in then, all ye angels," boomed Harlan. "Find your place cards."

A bell tinkled and the canary trilled as Grace and Willard entered from the kitchen, each bearing a serving tray piled high with the ornamental pilau. The repast was trimmed with vegetable and fruit designs that were Grace's specialty, designs which testified to courses that Grace had taken in Art School. Each presentation was a masterpiece soon to be demolished and eaten. The pilaus were placed one at each end of the long table. Willard and Harlan stood ready to serve the guests as, plates in hand, they filed past.

Harlan asked a young Bahá'í, "Can you tell me, in one sentence, what is the Bahá'í Faith?"

The young Bahá'í answered well: "Can you hold the ocean in a cup?"

Harlan grinned at me. Encouraged by her success, she continued, "We are interreligious, international, interracial; in fact, we are intereverything."

"These pilaus," said our host, "are symbols of the Unity of Mankind. They are composed of the blending of many gifts from God's kingdoms (mineral, animal, vegetable). They are, indeed 'intereverything'! The result, I think you will agree, is a unique and delectable flavour. It is not the taste of any one ingredient; it is the blend."

After the food on the trays and side dishes had greatly diminished, Grace rose with her familiar gesture of opening wide her arms and said, "The lower worlds of the animal and vegetable have now been promoted to the human kingdom. The cycle is complete." We laughed. "But spiritually," she went on, "it seems to me that this special Naw-Rúz Feast is delectable because of the blending here of our racial and national inheritance. Let's move our chairs back and be confidential about our own contribution to the flavour of this gathering, starting with Willard."

Willard complied. "My four grandparents were McKays, Judds, Willards and VanDuesens. Scottish, English, Welsh and Dutch."

"And mine," volunteered Walter Buchannan, "were African Scottish."

Forty-one people had come to our Feast. About twenty-five were recent acquaintances made during the last three months of our organized meetings: first, the Wednesday evening study class at Alice Parker's and then, the advertised public meetings at Utility Hall. From these meetings a few firesides followed in people's homes where Howard, Grace or I had been invited to speak. Now, some of the ladies had brought their husbands. The collection of "ingredients" for our blend was interesting: Hungarian, Jewish, African, Russian, Canadian. As the disclosures of ancestry went around the circle, they looked at each other in astonishment.

It was a social miracle that we had a hilarious time and experienced universal love. The Bahá'í friends lingered to clean up the place and to exult together over the Feast's success. It was their Feast, too, for most of the food had been contributed, the people who still had incomes providing the more expensive items.

"It is an anniversary too," I reminded them. "It was a year ago today that we first met."

"We yall, you mean," corrected Walter.

On the weekend after Naw-Rúz, Willard was invited to speak in Washington. His expenses would be paid. On the 26th, he left on an Easter excursion which gave him two nights and a day in the capitol. I went with him to the trolley a little before ten, trying to put off my melancholy to give him a cheerful send-off. I stood on the curb waving to him as he rode away. "Willard's requirements for happiness are quite simple, he claims. He is happy if I am happy," I wrote. But for me, things were not that simple.

> The winds of God are buffeting us. All we know is that they are the winds of God. The Ives have found an opening for their work in a new town and are leaving April lst. The Obers' hold on Pittsburgh is being loosened by Fate also. The McKays have had an offer to return to New York state to work on a fruit farm, with old friends as hosts. Why is this offer so passionately unacceptable?

On the walk home after our good-byes and parting, it seemed that I was keyed emotionally to a state of apperception described better by artists and mystics. I felt an unexpected rapture in everything I beheld: the row of Kosher restaurants closed on this Saturday Sabbath, the wide-open Italian shops offering "fresh pastini" and the enticing Easter flower stands. I was absorbed with delightful sights. Others have called it the "innocent eye" of pure feeling or pure aesthetic.

"When the Bahá'ís talk of Oneness," I meditated, "it is much more than an intellectual concept. The Rose of Oneness is, for us, a transcendent emotion that can transform our lives in this outer plane. Jewish, European, American shops here before me, three in a row. Beautiful!"

When I reached home, the boys were waiting for me.

"Auntie Doris, are you going to help us with our Easter eggs?" David wanted to know.

"Do you need help?"

"Sure," said Aziz.

So we went out into the kitchen and made a terrible mess. The boys scrapped as usual, while I painted Harlan's and Willard's pictures on a couple of duck eggs.

Grace and Harlan were at the dinner table. Willard was still away. I was halfway between the table and the kitchen sink when Harlan said that if business did not pick up, they would have to leave for Eliot in a few weeks. We could go with them or return to New York state. I ran back to the kitchen to cry over the dishes and to wipe my tears on the dishtowel. I bounced back and said, "I think the Guardian wants Willard and me to stay in Pittsburgh."

The firm planks of the Crimson Ark withstood the battering of the winds of change.

I prayed until two in the morning, using the Guardian's name in supplication, and I awoke with those words sounding in my head. I felt my fixed desires relax and then could whisper, "I am not sure that I know what is best for us. How should I know?" The firm planks that steadied me? The daily cleaning of the house, washing and ironing Mabel's things before she packed them, having a scant but attractively served dinner ready when they came home at night. These, I felt, were the firm invariables.

In the afternoon I went out to give a talk to the Abundant Life Group. I had heard that some had said that Bahá'ís put Bahá'u'lláh ahead of Christ. I spoke about Christ and Christian mysticism, about eternity and time and about the need to be free in order to make others free. I prayed that these groping souls would catch a glimpse of the reality of the "abundant life" they were seeking so earnestly. Their faces were shining. Surely a sign.

A Patch of Sacred Ground

One felt affection for this room. It had its charm: the lovely oriental rug of tan and green with soft designs in rose and grey, a Victorian stained-glass window over the stairway with its polished newel. I felt affection for this room and mild regret at the thought of leaving it. The Tilbury community was at the point of dissolution.

When Grace and Harlan acknowledged that they would not need us after April 1, a wild elation took hold of me. And Willard began to beam like the sun. All tension broke and complexes untangled. Harlan was but our friend again and Tilbury was no longer a prison but a patch of sacred ground.

No one had, by his own volition, called out, "Enough!" We would have remained together had not circumstances prevented. Now the Obers were leaving for the same reasons that we had left our first home – the doors were closing to their remaining. They had tarried dangerously close to the margin of destitution.

The four graduates of the school that we called Tilbury Tenement looked back over their year in that house. The vows that had gone up from Tilbury, our combined emotions, the opening doors and the ones that closed, the attacks of illness, our moments of madness and of exalted sanity. If there are atmospheric colours created by the intense vibrations of the mind, as some will suggest, what a kaleidoscope hovered over that hallowed Bahá'í address. In my imagination I can see it like a rainbow sparkling with flashes of sunlight and the sky behind it rolling with black clouds. Tilbury. Place of our solemn Covenant with a company of His chosen ones. It had been made an arena for the testing of our unwavering resolve, a testing that had reached intensity. Someone, powerful and omniscient, knew the balance of negative and positive temperaments and knew, also, of our will to carry on.

As Harlan was pleased, we were too. He said, "Including the Ives, our being here together has resulted in the welfare of the Cause. We have got the Assembly organized for the first time, have a flourishing study class, downtown meetings, publicity – most of the work being done by the people in this house. A study group has been started in New Castle. Pittsburgh is now a fertile field for racial amity..."

We said our last prayers together, continuing our supplications for protection and guidance, the Remover of Difficulties elevating from Tilbury Tenement.

Joy Gives Us Wings

In the morning paper there were pages of advertisements offering "Rooms for Rent, Light Housekeeping". Emily Craighead was coming to take me to look at some of them. The rates were listed conveniently, and we would not need to waste gas on the expensive ones.

I remember the attic studio that I rented once when I went to teach art at Niagara Falls. That memory convinced me that one could make any place attractive with a few sticks of second-hand furniture and a paintbrush. "Why, this city must be full of such places," I thought exultantly as Emily and I started out that bright April morning. Instead, we were given a tour through the slums of what once had been called the richest city in the world.

One place did rather attract me, although Emily made no comment. In it there were two rooms which had been parlours in a well-designed house now backed up and mouldering against the rear of an old Greek Orthodox church that blocked the light. A cooker on a table occupied one corner. In another, a couch converted into a bed for two and in lieu of clothes closets, a section of wall was hung with hooks and drapes. "It has the charm of the Left Bank of Paris," my former self urged. "Emily, it's not far from Alice Parker's," I argued. "It's close to meetings, Schenley Park and the library. What an opportunity!"

But my newly cleansed eye rested on the greyness of the woodwork and the walls. I told the faded lady in charge that I might return later with my husband.

"Would you like me to drive you out to the address in East Liberty?" Emily suggested. "I know that street. There is not so much soot there and some of the houses are not so ancient." She took me to a place on North Negley Street, high up in the rear of a three-storey rooming house. The landlady was named Mrs Bowser.

I had never heard of a bed-dining room, but this was one. The bed, an odd-sized roll-away, dominated most of the wall space on one side, making a raised level like a mezzanine or balcony. The bedspread was white, spotless. The dining table and white kitchen chairs were across the room by the window. I saw a wardrobe and a chest of drawers with a mirror, and there was a kitchen. It had been a clothes closet, but now it had a gas plate and oven and a little square worktable on rollers. On the wall there were shelves with a coffee pot, saucepan and a few dishes. The running water was in the bathroom, and we were told that we could wash dishes there at quiet times of the day. Grace came out with me early the next day and gave it her approval, then Willard went to pay a week's rent.

Our Last Day at Tilbury: April 7, 1932

The Ober family was moving, too – not to Eliot, Maine, but, until the end of the school year, to temporary lodgings.

I wanted to capture and store away an image of that moment in my mind. I wrote:

> It is a bright spring day with a touch of elixir in the air. I am visiting, for the last time, my 'palais royale' and relaxing on the little sofa by the window. My yellow curtains are blowing out and the sunshine falls warm on my hands. Our room is torn up, the bed sitting rakishly in the alcove. The cleaning lady has washed the rug with Austin's Cleaner and it smells wet.

We had been washing, ironing, and packing all day when Bahiyyih, Ruth Brown and the baby, Beth, came to call at four. We sat in the bare room and talked with Bahiyyih, who, with Edvard, was moving to Pittsburgh to stay with the Browns. I was telling them about the tiny apartment that we were moving into that very night. "The best thing about it," I said to them, "is that it is on the third floor and we can look out through the east window and see, first, the sunrise, then the treetops and then the outline of the hills."

We Arrive at North Negley

Ten-thirty on a Saturday night and the food stores were still doing business when the streetcar let us off at Negley Avenue. There were bargains to be had and we were pleased with the bag of food we purchased for five dollars. There was another package, which I bought without comment. We climbed the stairs, took out our new key, let ourselves in and turned on the droplight. We unpacked, found places for the groceries and lit the gas plate. Exclaimed Willard, "This place is Heaven on Earth!"

I opened the other "package" for which I had paid the price of seven loaves of stale bread – thirty-five cents. It was a marigold blooming in a pot. "This is our flower garden," I announced to Willard. He took the plant in his hand.

"Much more than you thought," he observed. "It comes with a weed and a ladybug. It is a whole estate!"

"And if we don't hurt the ladybug," I replied, remembering the nursery story, "she will bring us good luck."

With a castle of our own, we began to practise hospitality. Guests invited to our Sunday morning breakfasts were illustrious. Bahiyyih (Margaret) and Edvard Lindstrum[25] were our first.

"We shall be living in Pittsburgh," explained Bahiyyih, "with my mother, Ruth, and Bishop (Brown) until Edvard gets settled financially. I have been going through the Egypt of the spirit," she confided.

---

25 During my first visit to Green Acre, we called at the Randalls' summer residence. I met Mr Harry Randall, who had distinguished himself as Martha Root's co-worker. He was ill at the time. Ruth and Bahiyyih were not at home, but I remember seeing a good-looking blond young man sitting on the lawn. This was Edvard, the man engaged to Bahiyyih.

Edvard was boyish and genial, a little too high-keyed. Bahíyyih resembled Harry Randall in appearance. She had been taken to 'Akká on a pilgrimage when she was a little girl and had been the beloved child of the party on whom the Master had showered His bounties. She was now a devoted Bahá'í, mature, and a worker for the Cause. At this time, Bahíyyih and Edvard's own child, Beth, was about a year old. We knew that we would love this couple. Our hours together during this Sunday breakfast were delightful. They had to leave at twelve, but Edvard came back in the afternoon to take us to the Feast.

Alice Parker

"Your heaven is high up," said Alice, panting a little after her long climb. "I suppose I should call it an ascent, rather than a climb. How do you manage to run up and down all those stairs?" she sighed.

"This is the time when 'joy give us wings',[26] to use the Master's own words," I replied.

Alice responded with one of her habitual expressions. "You sweet thing."

The marigold sat on the windowsill. Here was a picture with the sky for background. A breeze came from outside and set the little plant to quivering. One of us commented, "Isn't this like our hearts when animated by the breezes of God?" After lunch and a tour of all the features of our Castle, we rested on the bed while waiting for Bishop to call for Alice. I confessed to her, "The Lord has been paying so much attention to our training this year that I have come to look on all material happiness as fleeting. The kind of effervescence Willard and I are having right now is 'bubble stuff'. We are swimming around like minnows in a lake of joy, with a vague uneasiness that another wave may come and sweep us back on the pebbles again."

Alice looked amused. "If 'Abdu'l-Bahá had asked His favour-

---

26 'Abdu'l-Bahá, *Paris Talks* (London: Bahá'í Publishing Trust, 1969), p. 109.

ite question, 'Are you happy?' and you responded, 'Very happy', what would He say?"

"He would say, 'Khayli Khub'. That means 'very good.'"

"Joy gives us wings," she said, "and wings have been provided to us – to fly above the gloomy atmosphere of Pittsburgh. Dear Doris, think only of that and be exhilarated. . . Here's Bishop!"

Howard Drops By

Howard Ives was in town and he and Grace came to breakfast. It was evident that the man before us was another person to whom the Lord had given wings. I noted,

> Howard was full of spiritual dynamic. . . very wonderful. What he said inspired me. He is bubbling over with zeal. His personality is flooded with power from on high. After the events of last winter, he is a miracle confirmed.

But life in the sky-parlour of Negley Avenue, no matter how exalted, was not designed to be a perpetual breakfast party. Like the sudden clap of hands, the tensions of the first Pittsburgh year were over. I admit that my wing-giving joy rose first as a release from the numbing burden of housework. Somehow, Bahá'u'lláh and Harlan, my mentors, had accepted my contribution and, weak though I knew it to be, had made me feel good about it. Now we knew that the days before us would be filled to overflowing with a variety of interesting activities.

There would be more writing. I had been appointed Associate Editor of the Bahá'í magazine. The Thirty-Six Lessons Course on the Bahá'í Teachings was in circulation and Willard and I were appointed by the National Teaching Committee to handle the sales and correspondence. The Local Assembly had adopted the Course and put me in charge as teacher of the weekly study meetings. Then I was elected Chairman of the Assembly, an honour that overwhelmed me.

The crown for Negley Avenue hospitality arrived when Lorna Tasker came for a week during a school holiday.

April 15th

I could tell when Lorna got up in the morning, for she put her pillow to air in the window of her rented room across the street. I would watch her as she walked over, limping a little from an ankle broken last year. In a way, Lorna reminded me of Martha Root: she was not so much a personality as she was a presence. Not that I had not seen her as a strong personality while she was teaching, but sometimes when we met after an absence there seemed to be a "third person" shared by both of us – our united Self, devoid of personality. St. Teresa in her Interior Castle might have accorded us a moment's sojourn in that "little chamber where great stillness reigns". This inestimable bounty, this nothingness that Lorna and I called The Place. It was a condition, a realm described by the prayer "that shall rise above words and letters and transcend the murmur of syllables and sounds – that all things may be merged into nothingness before the revelation of Thy splendor."[27] We felt this to be a confirmation of the covenant we had made four years ago on her first visit – the covenant to reach out to people with universal love, to pray for them and to seek unity with them.

Lorna wrote ninety pages in her journal to describe that week in which we worked together. Emily Craighead took us to the Browns', Eve Kerin's, the Sekers' and Mrs Payne's. On the evening of the Study Class, there seemed to be a special atmosphere of aid from on high. Two ladies at that meeting were from the social class at one time rich, but now in need and dimly aware of their poverty of spirit. One of them, the elegant and gracious Mrs D, had been very friendly to me. On this night she extended an invitation to a dinner party to meet her friends. Lorna was quite attracted to her and was delighted that she had asked both of us to speak. A letter from Lorna describes what took place:

---

27 *Bahá'í Prayers*, p. 71.

At the luncheon all the eyes around the table were [socially] veiled. Afterward I read some of my poems. Then you spoke and told them about our dedication to a new way of life on the night of The Blazing Log, and how our own lives had grown richer and happier.

It seemed to me that as you spoke, the whole meeting opened out full like one of the roses in the bowl on the table. The Spirit descended into our midst and we were all one. It was a new dedication. This time it had come, not as a dream and a promise, but as a fulfilment and actuality. We had worked together.

We Search for Wider Fields

Lorna's visit and the rebirth of our aims opened fields of activity that had been entered before but not sufficiently explored. How to help the people who were trying to help the world? Some were agitating for a Bahá'í principle without awareness or acknowledgment of its Source. These were people who campaigned for Universal Peace or Social Justice. Others were interested in the search for man's hidden powers. Black organizations rose up for the advancement of their race. The apostolic energy of the churches was stirred up.

"They are unconsciously answering the Call of Bahá'u'lláh," I exclaimed. "We must get closer to the people, Willard. These partially awake people need more than 'a mere set of principles'; they need contact with Universal Love. But how to reach them?"

"Well, if 'joy gives us wings,'" quipped Willard, "we will have to fly to them."

His teasing remark reminded me that it had been two months since we had found happiness in the tiny space that was all ours. What bliss it had been! Willard was thinking of our uncertain future when he said, with determined optimism, "No matter what happens to us, we can look back on this time of heaven on earth."

There had been only one casualty. A sudden windstorm had

blown our symbolic marigold out of the window down onto the pavement below. The flowerpot was broken, of course. Willard begged a jelly glass from Mrs Bowser and brought the plant back to me. It did not seem possible, but the ladybug was still clinging to it. When we left, we gave both to Mrs Bowser.

In the weeks that followed, I joined the Women's International League for Peace and Freedom (WIL) and Willard and I gave a joint talk on "The Bahá'í Plan for Universal Peace". This was my Bahá'í bow to the more than three hundred women in the organization. Over half were educated, aggressive and Jewish. Many had relatives or friends in Hitler-persecuted Germany. Mrs Norman W. Storer, at whose home Martha had spoken in December, was President. The American members were ardent sympathizers. Our talks were informative and, to judge by the interested questions asked, seemed to be well received. The meeting was in a room in the Chamber of Commerce building and the League was going to have lunch there. Willard left and I remained.

There were reports of new atrocities in Germany and it was hard for Mrs Storer to keep the meeting in order. I sat in the midst of a bubbling cauldron of explosives and quaked. I was uncomfortable and I knew why – my elbows were digging nervously into my ribs. I wanted to be anywhere but there. I asked myself, "Should I leave?"

"No," said the voice within. "You are a Bahá'í teacher, sent here to represent Bahá'u'lláh. When you call on the mercy of God, waiting to reinforce you, your strength will be tenfold."[28] How often to some other aspiring soul had I quoted that line from 'Abdu'l-Bahá?

That helped. I found myself relaxing the way a cat does when it feels at home. I loved the people universally. I even stayed to have lunch with Mrs Storer at the big round table and heard myself talking Peace.

From my journal:

> Now that the Obers and the Ives are gone, the community says that they are depending on us, the McKays. I must stop feeling

---

28 *Paris Talks*, pp. 38–39.

little and unimportant and accept the responsibility of study of the Writings and prayer. And I must strive for faith, initiative and responsibility. I am such a sloppy person, so vacillating, so limited. It is hopeless! My efforts are those of a bird carrying a grain of sand to some glorious foundation that is being erected.

'Yes, that is true,' I told my lesser Self. 'Of ourselves, we can do nothing.' But what of Bahá'u'lláh's statement, 'God doeth whatsoever He willeth'? Even in our noonday prayer we testify each day to our poverty and His riches, to our powerlessness and to His strength. As Willard would have said: 'Our human negative reactions are an expression of self – not worthy of mention, if we truly desire to serve Bahá'u'lláh.'

On the eve of the Feast of Núr (Light) we had readings and prayers and later discussed the departure of the Obers and the coming of the Lindstrums. There was talk, too, about 'survival'. The member we affectionately called 'Blackie' was silent. We did not question him. Instead, we invited him to dinner with each household, rotating different nights of the week. He accepted, with his humorous twinkle.

Then someone said to us, "Are you all right?"

Willard told the community, "Simply great – so far. Except that the work I have now won't last much longer. But we are sure something will show up. It always does."

At this point Bessie Seker created a sensation, first by raising her hand and then by standing up to emphasize what she had to say. "Perhaps something has shown up, although I am not prepared to say what. I took it upon myself to write the Guardian about the work you were doing and about your affairs. The answer has come back. He said about you, Doris and Willard, 'They are well versed in the Teachings and have the Bahá'í spirit and that is all the capital a Bahá'í needs.'"

"And in some mysterious way, our Guardian knows," added Ruth Brown. "Sometimes when we were sitting at the dinner table in Haifa, a faraway look would come into his eyes. There might be minutes of withdrawal when we were sure that he was responding to urgent prayers poured out to him from different parts of the world, in accordance with the promise 'God will answer every servant, if that prayer is urgent.'" Ruth went on, "We are too tepid in our prayers. Beyond a mild reaction, what do they accomplish? Concentration, purity of intention and detachment from the outcome – these are the attributes of prayer."

From my journal: June 6th

> Tonight we are going to bring our affairs before the Local Spiritual Assembly. Willard's work has about come to an end. The city still has a faint pulse and a reflex of breathing, but in reality, she is quite dead.
>
> The Sekers have offered us a free apartment, so if we can find twenty-five dollars a month for electricity and gas, food and car fare, we can still subsist.
>
> The Bahá'í work is booming as never before. When Grace left for Green Acre, she turned her contacts over to me. We have temporarily given up the downtown meetings because of the heat, but the Study Class is flourishing. Willard is chairman of a Teaching Committee of nine.

Another example of our efforts while still living in Negley to reach the heart of this strange, perilous, fascinating city of Pittsburgh I described:

> Somehow, I have associated myself with the Lucy Stone League for Colored Women. I have just come back from a tea given for the League. The Crafts of the YMCA are leaving the city for work in the new "Y" in Harlem. Mrs Lampkin informed me that I was to speak. Mrs Craft, a delightful woman in a pink silk dress and a white fur piece, introduced me as "someone a little different from most people – a Bahá'í." I spoke for ten minutes on our interracial contacts in Harlem saying that the Bahá'ís believe in one religion and one God and one race – the human race.
>
> After the meeting, Mrs Lampkin said I might have said more about the Bahá'í Cause. She spoke as a field secretary of

the NAACP about the cooperation of the Baháʼís and that she is very pleased and that Mrs Craft is very near to acceptance of the Faith. This was news to me as the Crafts were our first contacts for the interracial work in Pittsburgh. Although we had come well introduced, they had seemed quite determined not to be coaxed into friendship.

And now, the beautiful coffee-colored Mrs Craft gave me a farewell kiss, while everyone looked on in astonishment. 'I love you,' she declared, 'in spite of all appearances – and you are not to say I don't.'

She was going and probably we would not be seeing each other again. In Harlem she will meet my friend, Lois Allen, who I hear, has become a Baháʼí.

A few days later, I noted in my journal:

Willard has been taken on as a salesman for a firm that does business with little parking coupons. The Sekers have moved to an apartment on the top floor. Their building, recently covered with imitation brick, looks like a shoebox stood on end in this environment of single and two-storey structures. It is topped by a flat roof enclosed by a two-foot-high brick wall. Bessie has been up there to pray under the stars and at dawn. She is so near to Baháʼu'lláh up there that she speaks to Him with more familiarity than I would dare. 'Baháʼu'lláh, what are you going to do about Henry's gambling?' she says. And the prayer is answered. When Henry heard that Baháʼu'lláh had been called in, he never gambled again. . . 'A real penthouse for evening meetings,' I told Bessie.

June 10th

We have come here to live in the madding crowd. This congested three or four streets of provision stores is a famous market section. The street and sidewalks are so narrow it is almost impossible to slide through the crowd. . .

We parked at the curb with the Sekers, while Bessie entertained us with histories of some of the people who were our neighbours. Homewood is an intimate neighbourhood, like a small town. The setting is a vast network of narrow streets and alleys littered and smeared with rained-on soot. We float in a sea of slums, yet with our own civic pride we have a branch Post Office, a bank, a branch library, and a small park.

At eleven o'clock, Henry stopped the motor and Willard and I followed Bessie's lead and disembarked. We walked around to the entrance of a former wallpaper store, an entrance which was now the front door to our home. The windows were pasted over with newspaper, but there was a light switch on the inside woodwork. We turned it on and it lit up an aisle which ran the length of the store – half a block long by Homewood Avenue standards. There were still odd remnants of wallpaper, some partially unrolled, hanging over the shelf edges like neglected drapery. Up a step, then, to the door of the apartment. The square living room was bare of furniture. There we set down our bags, which contained the food, books and kitchen things we had bought at Negley. Bessie announced cordially, "The kitchen and the bathroom are ready for you and your bed is made up. We'll go at it again in the morning. In the meantime, welcome to your new home."

"Thank you, Bessie. It's going to be great!" Willard hugged Bessie and I kissed her. She went out through the kitchen door and we heard her trudging up the two flights of wooden steps to their own apartment.

The bathroom had expensive fixtures. The water was hot, always hot, as Bessie had promised. Because of the limited space the tub was only four feet long.

"A tub of our own," I enthused.

It was four o'clock in the morning when the clamour broke out. (I remember seeing the little ivory and red wall clock.) Our bed was plumb against a lath-and-wallpaper partition that quivered and shook. We felt the movement of heavy objects being thrown against it from the other side. A babble of voices shouting in foreign tongues could be heard through the wall, sometimes wild with laughter, sometimes bawling in anger. At last, the body – or whatever it was – was rolled out on heavy wheels, loaded onto a truck and borne away.

Later in the morning we found Bessie. "Did you hear the riot last night?" we asked. Called Bessie, "Listen to this, Henry."

Henry showed us, for the first time, how hard he could laugh. When he regained control of his voice, he told us, "It's them Eyetalian fellows next door. The press sends out a load of morning papers and they sort them. The news chaps come and take out a bunch to deliver and sometimes there aren't enough and the chaps fight for them. If there are some left over, they're sent back on the truck. I promise you," Henry waxed emphatic, "you'll get used to them, same as we did."

Our first day in Homewood began with an effrontery to our ears when the early morning newsboys piled in. Following this, our spirits were dampened by a week of steamy and rainy weather. Most of our daylight came from the alley between Homewood Avenue and Zenith Way, where, for three storeys, the apartment balconies were built side by side and on top of one another. We were embedded in a section of space called "the Court", which wrapped us in a smothering blanket of dimness, dampness and dirt.

My depression grew by progressive stages. The Court, the air we breathed, the smell of the community trash box, Willard's slow start with work and the swearing of Mrs Wells. She had a flat on the second floor and, from time to time, would suspend her cursing to sing gospel hymns.

Once again I had struck bottom, but for Bessie and Henry's kindness, I wore a bright smile facade. Although I do not mind sharing their contents now, the notes I wrote then were private, secret. There had begun a series of dashings out to the library or to the Park, or even out of town. My running away had the pretext of winning back the nearness to reality, the lack of which is also a peculiar feature of nightmares. This is subtle torture for a Bahá'í; the remoteness is really from God.

Only a week away from the peace of Negley Avenue and what of the 'wings of joy' now? I asked myself in the coolness of the library, "The wings supporting our spirits, have they become already only an image of faded delight? Yes, they were real, but evidently only lent to us here. Have we lost them?"

I asked Willard that question on the night we went out to find the hills. He said firmly, almost automatically, "Take refuge in God! Seek the 'inner invariability'! I don't need to tell you that."

"But how I need to hear you say it! However, I will answer my own question next. How to do it? Your answer is 'Walk thou above the world by the power of The Most Great Name.'"[29] And that was what he was doing then, breathing "Alláh-u-Abhá" as we walked a few blocks and began to climb a series of hills ascending from level to level, finally by wooden stairs, until we balanced on a street called Apple Avenue. From there we could look out over seven miles of Pittsburgh and its boroughs. In the late sunset we could see the two synagogues on Squirrel Hill, the University buildings grouped around the Temple of Learning where Bishop taught, the seven blast furnaces from which came the soot, and the lights outlining the fifty-seven bridges over the Ohio, Monongahela and Allegheny Rivers that shaped the Golden Triangle. We could look down at our own street, Homewood Avenue, a bright lavaliere of rhinestones as blue, red and yellow store signs and the moving flashes and glares of automobile lights crowded the beginning darkness. It was Saturday night, and within a mile of our lookout thousands of people were milling around those three or four blocks in search of food bargains.

We climbed higher on the tiers of streets. Each stairway would connect with a rutty unpaved road with a scattering of poor houses where Black people stared out with observant eyes. When we reached the top and turned again towards level

---

29 Bahá'u'lláh, *Tablets of Bahá'u'lláh revealed after the Kitáb-i-Aqdas*. Trans. Habib Taherzadeh (Haifa, Universal House of Justice, 1978) p. 142.

ground, I said conversationally, "'Joy gives us wings', but pain gives us feet to walk on. Sometime earth feet are needed, especially when walking with others. If I have never experienced how it feels to be depressed, how can I know what most of the people in Pittsburgh are feeling?"

Window in the Sky

On Sunday mornings there would be no noise in the newsroom next door. But today I awoke at four o'clock anyway and lay there with my eyes open. First there was nothing to see in our little dark dungeon. At this time of night in summer, I imagined the stirring wonder of the outside world. I felt helpless and deprived. All that I could see of the outside was offered by a small tipsy square of a window notched into the wall beneath the zigzag of a stairway. And all that I could see now was predawn sky. Suddenly I noticed that the moon was in my private plot of sky. It was an old moon shining with a mellow incandescence against the soft azure of the sky, its face turned away. Then there appeared a star, too, in the crook made by the moon. As a climax to my startled wonder, there appeared in my square the Sekers' cat, looking beautiful and weird with the moon irradiating her fur.

Now the sun was rising, and its rays struck the red chest. There had been some old furniture in the garage, which we were privileged to use, including this chest with two deep drawers. I decided to paint the chest a Chinese red. I found red paint and added a small can of orange. As I worked putting on two coats of colour in two days, some of that glorious tint got into my soul. Colour is cosmic, I had read somewhere; the capacity of the mind to perceive it is a faculty and a sign of God.

As I painted the chest, I became more interested in my little place. The rooms would be scoured bright and clean, the walls and carpets cleaned. We would put plants outside in the little junky court to make of it a Greenwich Village sort of place. Willard was pleased that I was nest building.

But now my thoughts were soaring to a higher nest – the Sekers' flat roof. "It would be like the roofs in Persia, away from the world and nearer to God. We could have our meetings there on hot summer evenings," I urged Bessie.

Bessie and Henry owned a house in the country about twenty miles from Pittsburgh. They had bought some furniture that came with it, furniture that was meant to be Victorian. One weekend Willard and I went with them to visit the house. Mine is an uneasy memory of a room that had an air, quite common in country homes, of wakes and funerals. There was an unusable fireplace, for example, trimmed with an old hymn book and a vase of artificial flowers. But the haunting impression of the room was caused actually by the massive black walnut furniture upholstered in lack-lustre black satin.

"The Elks," Henry had remarked. (The Elks Club was a men's social organization to which Henry belonged.) They had refurnished their meeting room. Could they have sold this old stuff to Henry? Perhaps this is backbiting. I stopped thinking.

There was a rather pretty wicker set. I expressed a liking for it and Bessie promised it to me for our still unfurnished parlour at the flat. My mind started dreamily fitting it into our nest. She said that a truck would bring it in. There were plants outside, too, which we transplanted and carried into town in pots.

We packed the car with an old matting rug, some low chairs and tools and a wide-spreading sun umbrella in gorgeous colours.

At home we set the plants around our penthouse pavilion, put down the old rug, two card tables and our seating arrangements. The effect was both spacious and gracious. There would be a cloth and tea things on one table, we said, and Bahá'í books on the other. In the chairs, our beloved Bahá'í friends.

Tuesday afternoon came and at supper time Henry would be coming in the truck with the furniture. Willard and I slipped in for a look at our living room. We had used Dic-aDoo, a wallpaper cleaner made in Geneva, which brought back the paper's true colour, a pale green with a tracery of flowers and a satin finish. Bessie had provided the paint for the woodwork and floor. There were no windows in the room, but we had the overhead light turned on and the blaze of the late sunset fell upon and fired the red chest in the next room.

Henry called Willard to help carry in the furniture. IT WAS THE MASSIVE, BLACK, PADDED SOFA AND GARGANTUAN LOUNGE CHAIRS FROM THE ELK'S CLUB. Henry was glowing, "This is the good stuff, not that riff-raff wicker you picked out. Thought you would like this best."

I told them, "Move it back into the corners against the walls. I shan't be able to shift it." Still beaming. Henry went to find Bessie.

Woe! Woe! I climbed up on the biggest of the monsters, the sofa, and began to cry. The other great monsters seemed to stare.

A half hour later we suddenly began to laugh. This was one of 'Abdu'l-Bahá's little jokes, with a lesson tied up with the gift. "If George Spendlove were here," Willard contributed, "he would remind us once again of the three Most Holy Words given by Bahá'u'lláh in the Persian Hidden Words: 'Prefer not your will to Mine, never desire that which I have not desired for you, and approach Me not with lifeless hearts, defiled with worldly desires and cravings.'"[30]

So, feeling rather weak with so much emotion and so much laughter, I began nest building again. "We can send back to Geneva for the floor-length blue and gold curtains that used to hang in the book room at the farm. We can drape them over those spectres. No need for curtains when a room has no windows. So we will hang the furniture instead!"

We laughed again, perhaps a little hysterically, and accepted 'Abdu'l-Bahá's gift... and Henry's too.

The second Sunday in June. There was a Bahá'í picnic in Youngstown, Ohio. Bahá'ís from Pittsburgh, Cleveland, New Castle and Youngstown convened in the rain in a fairyland of a park. A pavilion accommodated our considerable numbers. We

---

30 Bahá'u'lláh, *The Hidden Words of Bahá'u'lláh*. Trans. Shoghi Effendi (Wilmette, IL: Bahá'í Publishing Trust, 1971), Persian #19, p. 28.

spread our food out on tables and held our meeting in a rustic auditorium.

When the meeting was over, I said goodbye to Willard, the Sekers and the three guests we had brought with us and left to catch a ride to Rocky River. A friend, Lois, had rented a cabin there for a month. She had a job not far away in Cleveland and commuted back and forth daily by bus.

I was thus left alone for two incredible days, completely vacuous and at rest, as blissfully I tossed pebbles at a rock in the brook. On the third day I, too, caught the early bus to Cleveland.

Before store opening, I waited on a park bench by May's Department Store. The beauty of Rocky River was still with me as I viewed the landscaped flowerbeds and bushes planted around a fountain that was scattering diamonds in the early morning sunlight.

A flock of pigeons arrived for breakfast and several cars drew up. Boys and girls leapt out with bags of bread crusts and table scraps to feed the birds. Perhaps this bird feeding is a project of the private school where Kay Cole teaches, I thought. These children are well dressed and have come in big cars and are most lavish with their crusts. They tossed their scraps into a low-fenced enclosure where the birds were.

Watching this pleasant scene from his bed in the grass was a rumpled victim of Want. His eyes roved between the falling crusts and the manoeuvres of the birds. The children were laughing at the greediness of the pigeons.

"Don't you ever know when you've had enough?" one boy yelled at them.

Soon the boys and girls climbed back into the cars and were whisked away to school. The man stepped into the enclosure, picked up his dreadful breakfast of trampled and grass-stained bread and, crouching there, wolfed it down. When he saw others looking at him, he scooped up a handful and shuffled away.

Like the desperate man, the people passing in the park seemed, in their own way, to reflect the abnormality of the Depression. The shop girls hurried to work in single-minded concentration. Heads and shoulders thrust forward, they walked not with a free stride but with legs bent sharp at the knee. They were like the stick figures we children used to make at school. Action was shown by straight lines bent at elbows and knees. Round knobs were attached for heads and hips. Live little figures, but no grace.

As the flocks of girls hurried past, my thoughts went back to the picnic at Youngstown. Bishop Brown had read from a large book bound in green, the colour of the Báb's turban. It was the first time that any of us had seen the newly published *Dawnbreakers*, a translation by Shoghi Effendi of Nabíl's Narrative. One of the readings was of the story of how Quddús, the last Letter of the Living, had found the Báb and had recognized Him instantly by His gait.

Bishop had asked us to close our eyes for a moment and to meditate on the gait of the Báb. It would, we imagined, have been an unhurried stride and there would have been a unity of rhythm in the movement of His body, His head perhaps a little inclined. There would be signs of loftiness in His gait, loftiness tempered by humility.

But what of our own gait as Bahá'ís? Did it, I questioned, reveal truly our inner state of certainty?

May's big store was open now and I observed the mixture of human qualities manifested in the early shoppers. I joined them and spent an hour looking around the store before taking the bus to East Cleveland and lunch with Alice Dolittle.

Few of the western Bahá'ís had visited Haifa during these hard times. Most of us submitted to our deprivation, sustaining ourselves with the crumbs of plenty brought back to us by our more fortunate friends. These Travellers in the Path of God had taken on a special lustre because of their experience in the Holy Land. Alice Dolittle had made the pilgrimage and recently had returned.

I got off the bus and walked to the small house with its screened veranda. A neat sign advertised "HAIRDRESSING". I had gone twice, while visiting the Coles, to have my hair done by Alice. The first time was in winter and she told me jubilantly that over the years she had saved $400 to go to Haifa. But in May she said she was not going. "The Temple Dome," she explained. "I decided it was my duty to give my money to the Dome. All my customers wanted to know why I was not going, and of course I had to explain. They could tell that deep down, I was disappointed."

"But you did go, Alice. What happened?"

"It was this. My one wealthy customer gave me $400, but she said that I must use it on this trip only. When I talked to the others and asked, 'What shall I do?' they said, 'You must accept the gift, partly because of this generous soul. She will be hurt if you refuse. Also, you were meant to take this journey for the sake of God. Because of it, your services to the Cause will be increased.' So I went."

We had eaten lunch and were on our way to the Coles' house, four blocks away. As Alice was shorter and somewhat thick-set, I adjusted my long steps to fit her smaller stride. The wind was blowing noisily, and I bent over her to hear her talk as we walked along. She was a bit out of breath.

"You think I am excited? Blame the wind," she began. "Or perhaps it's that I am going to give my first talk to the Bahá'ís and I am nervous."

Impulsively she asked, "Do you think I have changed?"

"Yes, Alice, but I can't comprehend why."

"Our short time together is drawing to a close and I did promise myself to tell you this. . . "

"So why don't you start," I suggested, squeezing her arm.

"You see, my big fault when I started out on this trip was my inferiority complex. I was all wrapped up in myself. No one saw what was inside me. I thought of myself as an overlooked person. My fault, of course."

"I know that feeling," I put in.

"You do know how I am, Doris. No style, no looks, poor English. I'm nervous with people like the Coles with university degrees. 'Haifa,' I told myself, 'nobody will take notice of me there either.' But the Guardian must have known from the start. He singled me out and treated me like a queen. On the first night when I sat next to him, he asked me questions and showed great respect for me. I was in dreams!"

We checked our pace and Alice began to catch her breath.

"But still," she gasped, "I wasn't satisfied. You can see why I can't tell this to the others. In my folly I wanted Bahá'u'lláh Himself to take notice of me. Well, on the last day of my pilgrimage I went alone into the Holy of Holies [Bahá'u'lláh's resting place at Bahjí] and setting aside some flowers, I crossed over the Threshold to the inner room. How could I dare? I asked him for a sign."

She stopped and looked into my eyes as though to confirm her decision to tell me and continued. "I can remember the shaking – the walls, the floor and most of all, the atoms of my body. I felt thrown off my feet. Was it like wind, or waves or an earthquake, or was it like all three? I was on my knees, with my forehead pressed to the beautiful Persian rug, crying my heart out in gratitude to Bahá'u'lláh. I stood up suddenly, quaking with the fear of God. It's Awe, they say. It is not that you are AFRAID of God, but something different. And I knew that I was a new person, born again. Inside I could hear myself shouting, 'Bahá'u'lláh HAS TAKEN NOTICE OF ME!'"

Gazing off, she paused to savour an inner moment.

"Before I left," she continued, "I asked the Guardian what I could do to serve the Cause. He said, 'Teach. Speak.' 'But I am not a speaker,' I said. He told me to use my notes and the pictures I was taking and to speak to the other Bahá'ís about my pilgrimage. And that's what I'm trying to do."

In the Coles' house a roomful of Bahá'ís were waiting to take notice of the returned pilgrim. A sheet was hung on the wall and a table with a stereopticon lantern was set up at the opposite side of the room. Alice projected her pictures onto the sheet, and when she began to speak, she was at ease, in her element at last. The atmosphere expanded under the influence of her joy. The enlarged pictures bloomed on the sheet, and we were in Haifa with her. Later that evening Kay and I drove Alice to another meeting in a Cleveland home.

I came back from Cleveland a day early to a smouldering and unpalatable Homewood and, also, from being "up in the clouds". Key in the door of the shop with the papered windows, quick steps down the aisle with the flyspecked rolls of wallpaper, another step up to the dark room with the shrouded furniture and there, before me, was pure felicity – Willard eating fried green peppers at the kitchen table.

As if addressing an apparition, he sprang up and asked, "How did you get here?"

"On wings, my dear, wings of joy. A miracle happened in the days I was away. Homewood is suddenly HOME!"

My delight swept Willard, too. Our restored wings lifted us into a state of elation that we had known on so many occasions on our enchanted Emerald Hill farm. That state of elation was the joyous blending of souls; it was like a honeymoon.

"But where did you get all those green peppers?" I wanted to know.

"About midnight," Willard explained, "the grocer at the corner sold me a hamper full of them for twenty-five cents."

"We'll use them for barter," I gloated, "with Bessie and Mrs Mills."

". . . the matter of setting ablaze the cold and veiled souls. . ." I had heard words like that before and now they were saying themselves to me as I walked over to Mrs Norman W. Storer's on Women's International League for Peace and Freedom business. But when her big grey house loomed in front of me, my heart was in my mouth. This lady, with sharp steel-grey eyes and iron-grey hair cut short and strait, was my griffin. I prayed, "God, let the Holy Spirit work here. Let me stand out of the way!"

I pressed the button and heard the chime of bells inside. Mrs Storer opened the door, "Oh, it's you. I'll run upstairs and get that list." When she came downstairs it could be put off no longer. I kissed her firmly and convincingly and by that kiss told her things that words would have bungled. It was a kiss that promised Universal Love. In her astonishment, my frozen lady thawed. She asked me in for lunch, then to say Bahá'í prayers. The next day she telephoned inviting me to come and get flowers for our Feast that night. I had told her that we were hosting it on a roof.

Garden of the Heart

It was a garden of the heart on which Mrs Storer had lavished her loving care. While she had the assistance of a landscape gardener, only the commingling of her expertise and devotion could have coaxed a city garden plot into an effective illusion of leisured space. It was a rock garden whose foundation was a few boulders from Pennsylvania's Allegheny mountains. A spiral flagstone path led towards the top of a dramatic little man-made hill. Spaces were landscaped there for flats of growing plants, vines, flowering bushes and massed groupings of flowers. After soot-stained Homewood, I thought I must have died and gone to heaven.

She opened the screen doors to her plant rooms in the cool basement of the house. The rooms were furnished like a summer cottage but with the addition of tubs and sinks, filing cabinets and storage racks for the garden tools. Working in what I thought to be a chilly silence, she trimmed the armful of flowers she had picked and made them into a great bouquet for our meeting. Delphiniums and day lilies, late Darwin tulips and sprays of bridal wreath. She put the flowers in water and said, "There!"

Muttering, I told her that the flowers were lovely. Suddenly she spoke, her words exploding away a barrier.

"No one has guessed how I long to have friends – to be with people. People stand away from me and I can't go to them except through the work we do. I don't know what it is like to be close to anyone, not even my husband and son. There must be something left out of me or I'm inhibited. I'm really isolated and never happy except when I am with the flowers."

"Will it help you to know that there is one person who understands and would like to know you better? Besides, there are others: Alice Parker and Emily Craighead, and Mrs Bishop Brown."

"Why, I know all of them. Are they Baháʼís? Why are they different?"

"Because it is a religion of love, as was Christ's. You have heard the Baháʼí Principles. They offer Universal Love as the remedy for the ills of humanity. In one of our prayers we pray God to unite our hearts."

I think the thought struck us both that someday Ruth Storer would become a Baháʼí.

From my notes:

> Mrs Storer has invited me to come and live in her garden. She said we could come every day if we liked – Willard to play the grand piano and I to read or write or to tend the flowers. I think Mrs Storer is aware that the kiss was an offering to her of the Love of God. Between us there is a promise of an agreeable association. We could be a help to each other. Because I had prayed, I had been permitted to offer her a taste from the cup that is life indeed. The rational mind cannot explain the answer to our prayers. That we pray at all is a sign of His bounty.

The Feast of Raḥmat (Mercy), June 24th

As a whole, our community never before had entered the environs of Homewood. Tonight was hot, in the nineties, and we were asking the members to climb yet another flight of stairs to the roof. There were no comments, only sighs as they laboured skyward. The Buchannans had come, a new Black couple (the Smiths), Bahiyyih Lindstrum and the Browns, Eve Kerin and Blackie (Braydon Black). After following Henry through the Sekers' kitchen, they climbed a staircase at the right of our door.

Bessie and I were clad in our best and were standing to greet the Servants and Maidservants of the Merciful as, winded, they arrived on the roof. The taller men had to duck under the low doorway opening onto our makeshift terrace. There was a chorus of delighted exclamations as their eyes took in our collection of benches and chairs plumped up with sofa cushions, the green potted plants, the Bahá'í books (marked for reading) spread out on card tables under a strong overhead light and, in the centre of all, the umbrella stand holding Mrs Storer's flowers.

"We call it Paradise Penthouse," I told them.

"This has got to be magic," declared Walter.

"Or the entrance to the Kingdom of the Spirit." It was Bahiyyih's voice.

"How easy it is to get away from it all," said Eve. "Just climb up higher."

Now, with Feastly decorum, Bessie was calling us to order. "Welcome to the Feast of Mercy," she said. "Henry will read the opening prayer."

When the readings were finished, I begged Henry, "Oh, please put the light out so that we can see how AWAY from it all we really are."

He touched the light button and, quiet under the stars, we sat there, the street sounds muted and the air cool and pure. We said a round of Healing prayers and the prayer for the Remover of Difficulties. Willard said 'Abdu'l-Bahá's Tablet of Visitation.

The lights were on and now, knowing ourselves released, we clumped joyfully downstairs for cookies and a cold drink at the Sekers'.

An Assembly Problem

A loose-flung community of three million people like Pittsburgh and its environs had a point of oneness – an insistent commonality. And that was the unremitting predicament of the Depression. All of us were awake to instability and discomfort. It was not a local affliction but rather a creeping fungus that quickly had spread over the world. The Guardian had warned of the disappearance of the "islands of safety". It was apparent that minds which had once seemed balanced and secure were reeling. Thank God that Willard and I had come out from our year of Tilbury Tenement tests stronger and more seasoned. (I do not mean that the "maturity" I had once prayed for had been attained. Rather I was less hysterical than I had been last year!) We continued to be tested.

"Blackie" had come to the Local Assembly to say that he had no money except what he borrowed sometimes from other Bahá'ís. "Is there any Bahá'í agency to help me?" he asked. We wrote to the National Spiritual Assembly and were told that there was no fund as yet and that, regrettably, needy Bahá'ís should apply for public funds. Two of our members later went with Blackie for an interview with the Welfare.

The harassed worker, wanting to put our problem in its proper perspective, pointed out that others were trying to cope with starvation.

"Do you have any relatives, Mr Black?" he continued.

"Only some nephews and a niece."

"Where do they live?"

"On a farm near Grove City, but I haven't seen them for years."

"Well, we will contact them," said the social worker.

"But isn't there some other way? My family has always considered me a career man."

"Embarrassing," agreed the weary-looking worker, "but there is no other way. Please don't think of your case as unique. It happens every day."

His niece answered the letter and expressed delight and anticipation about having Uncle Braydon come to live with them. Just say the word, she wrote, and they would drive in for him and his things and bring him home.

The Assembly moved that Mr Black accept the invitation and decided also to write to the relatives, thanking them. The National Assembly would also be informed.

At home I said to Bessie, "Doesn't it seem as if an individual were being parcelled out?"

"It's an end to his worries, and ours too. He agreed, didn't he?"

A few days later, after a Wednesday-night Study Class, we gathered around Blackie. "When things get better, we'll see you back again. You have earned this rest with your young relatives."

We shook hands with him, and Eve Kerin put her arm around his thin shoulders. He was dressed in his respectable grey suit.

Ascension of the Greatest Holy Leaf

On July 15th, 1932, the cables from the Guardian had encircled the world like a despairing cry:

> GREATEST HOLY LEAF'S IMMORTAL SPIRIT WINGED ITS FLIGHT GREAT BEYOND. COUNTLESS LOVERS HER SAINTLY LIFE IN EAST AND WEST SEIZED WITH PANGS OF ANGUISH, PLUNGED IN UNUTTERABLE SORROW. HUMANITY SHALL ERE LONG RECOGNIZE ITS IRREPARABLE LOSS... I, FOR MY PART, BEWAIL SUDDEN REMOVAL OF MY SOLE EARTHLY SUSTAINER, THE JOY AND SOLACE OF MY LIFE...[31]

Shoghi Effendi sent to the National Spiritual Assembly his tribute to the Greatest Holy Leaf, and two days later the Sekers and the McKays, together with their fellow Bahá'ís, were climbing again the stairs to the meeting place on the roof.

As Ruth Brown read aloud the Guardian's words of passionate grief, some of us found his sorrow more overwhelming than the departure of Bahíyyih Khánum from this world. How to understand and feel deeply enough?

His message said, in part:

> The Community of the Most Great Name, in its entirety and to its very core, feels the sting of this cruel loss. Inevitable though this calamitous event appears to us all, however acute our apprehensions of its steady approach, the consciousness of its final consummation at this terrible hour leaves us, we whose souls have been impregnated by the energizing influence of her love, prostrated and disconsolate...[32]

---

31 *Bahíyyih Khánum: The Greatest Holy Leaf*, compilation (Haifa, World Centre Publications, 1982), p. 22.
32 ibid, p. 31.

Hundreds of words testified to the exalted station conferred on her by Bahá'u'lláh. In the conclusion of his message, Shoghi Effendi calls to her,

> Dearly beloved Greatest Holy Leaf! Through the mist of tears that fill my eyes I can clearly see, as I pen these lines, thy noble figure before me, and can recognize the serenity of thy kindly face. I can still gaze, though the shadows of the grave separate us, into thy blue, love-deep eyes and can feel in its calm intensity, the immense love thou didst bear for the Cause of thy Almighty Father... The memory of the ineffable beauty of thy smile shall ever continue to cheer and hearten me in the thorny path I am destined to pursue... The sweet magic of thy voice shall remind me, when the hour of adversity is at its darkest, to hold fast to the rope thou didst seize so firmly all the days of thy life.[33]

How the Guardian's bereavement, which he had started to share with us, put its test on the depth and sincerity of our own hearts! We had been so detached, so cool, so Western! We defended our poverty of spirit by saying, "But, we had not known her".

We appealed to Ruth and Bahíyyih Lindstrom, "You knew her. What did she mean to you?"

Ruth spoke thoughtfully. "I think she was most loved because of her understanding and sympathy for everyone; she had the true 'sin-covering eye'. Dear <u>Kh</u>ánum. She read in us the person we might have been and still could be."

"First, in my private thoughts," Bahíyyih continued, "she was Bahá'u'lláh's daughter, born to an exalted station. He was the 'Tree of Life', 'Abdu'l-Bahá, its 'Branch', and Bahíyyih <u>Kh</u>ánum, its 'Most Exalted Leaf'. In them the bounties of the All-Glorious overflowed. Now all are gone from this mortal world. That book is closed."

Eve Kerin, her eyes smouldering in her white face, had been stirring restlessly as if disturbing thoughts were racing through her mind. She now exploded in a rough and too-loud voice, "Do you think things can now be worse than they were?"

---

33 ibid, pp. 43–44.

Bishop answered, "They may be. We don't know. The Guardian seems to imply that with the ascension of the Greatest Holy Leaf we have stepped into a new stage in the evolving history of our Faith. It is like the cycle of the seasons. The spiritual springtime has passed. Next comes the season we call the Formative Period, a season of our maturing relationship with the Cause. The Guardian has called Bahíyyih Khánum 'the well-loved and treasured Remnant of Bahá'u'lláh.' Of His family she alone, over the years, had remained with us on our earthly plane. As His adored daughter, she had known Bahá'u'lláh's love. She had suffered with her family, had endured, had worked at every task and had remained selfless and tranquil. She had loved and served. She was the centre of God's bounty here among us. His Presence was here with Bahíyyih Khánum – one of the Mysteries."

"So, she is lost to us," said Eve despairingly.

"No, indeed, Eve. Now we must turn our thoughts to her and implore her intercession for our prayers."

I unfolded a brown silk handkerchief, a gift from the Greatest Holy Leaf to May Maxwell. In 1930 May had given it to us that we might, in our hoped-for time of growth in the Cause, have contact with the sacred atoms in its folds. The handkerchief had a Persian design in black on tones of brown and there was a brown silk fringe. As Bessie took it and passed it around, each one said the Greatest Name and recited a short prayer. It was a spontaneous response.

Ruth told us, "There were few servants in 'Akká or Bahjí. Khánum often cooked for the household and did the washing. Some American Bahá'ís, after their pilgrimage, gave her a washing machine. I have heard that she gave it away."

Photographs of her had been brought by the friends and were placed on a little table with Henry's spotlight shining on them against the darkness of the late evening sky. A favourite picture of her in which she had posed against a photographer's tasteful background, had been taken about 1895 when she was still youthful in appearance. The pose is regal, her features classically beautiful. The gaze of her eyes is far away. Her dress, worn with an embroidered jacket, was of flowered material with a draped skirt and worn with a little train. Her hands hung relaxed at her sides and, to my eyes, seemed to have a lyrical beauty like the angel hands modelled by Michelangelo.

Willard spoke, his voice husky with feeling, "We had a book for a time, an English publication called Unity Triumphant. There was a story in it about Bahá'u'lláh's buying flowered material to make pretty gowns for His daughter and His granddaughters as well as for Munírih Khánum (wife of 'Abdu'l-Bahá). He might have selected the material for the pink-flowered Robe of Bounty. It had panels of pink-flowered design like the one the Greatest Holy Leaf is wearing in the picture."

"Not all of you have heard about the Robe of Bounty," he went on. "It is now May Maxwell's, but once it was worn by the Greatest Holy Leaf. We have told you before that, on the last night of our visit in Montreal, May arranged for us to sleep in 'Abdu'l-Bahá's bed. She came in for a final prayer and spread the Robe of Bounty over the bed and left it with us all night."

"At a teaching committee meeting in New York," I concluded, "prayers for guidance were said on the Robe. May sent it to us in Geneva, where we had the privilege of keeping it for a few weeks."

We said the Tablet of Visitation and other prayers. Tonight we had felt the presence of the Greatest Holy Leaf and had drawn closer. In hushed silence we reflected. Then Henry spoke for us all. "When we went up there tonight, I knowed we'd find HER!"

After we descended Eve noted, "It disturbs me that Mr Black was not with us tonight. I, for one, miss him."

"He will be so much better in Grove City with his family, away from all his worries."

But I was troubled too. Justice is the responsibility of the Assembly, I remembered. But the requirement of the individual believer is to show love to the people. 'Abdu'l-Bahá is our example. Had we done enough?

The story is, as I heard it later, that Marion Little saw in a dream the entrance of the Greatest Holy Leaf into the Abhá Kingdom. Those whom Bahá'u'lláh calls the inhabitants of the cities of immortality were arrayed on each side of a shining aisle up which the ephemeral white-clad figure of Bahíyyih Khánum made its ascent in the direction of the Glory of God. The next day Marion was informed of the passing of the Greatest Holy Leaf at the very hour of the dream.

I Meet the Dawn-Breakers

We were having dinner at the Browns' on the eve of July 26th when Bishop, contributing to the table conversation, mentioned that he had received a surprise request to conduct a class on *The Dawn-Breakers* at the Flint (Louhelen) summer school.

"The committee," he said, "feels that the Guardian will be pleased if the study of the book can be started so soon after its publication. I agree. It is a wonderful idea, especially since the Bahá'ís are eager to get their hands on it. But why has this happened to me? The class starts in less than two weeks."

"Have you any plans?"

"Yes, Bahíyyih has agreed to make a set of question-and-answer quizzes on the principal figures. The information will be in the selected readings and in my talks."

Willard asked, "How many pages are in the book?"

"Six hundred of Nabil's Narrative besides the introductions, notes and epilog."

It seemed to me that the atmosphere around our pleasant supper table became suddenly electric. It was so still and yet so DYNAMIC. Could Bishop, Ruth and Bahíyyih all be holding their breath? Why were they all looking at me?

Bishop broke the silence. "Doris, we are asking you to write a synopsis of *The Dawn-Breakers* for me to introduce at Louhelen. You will have until August 5th."

"I too will be working hard on my outline lessons," defended Bahíyyih. "And Bishop will be organizing his course. We will all three meet and plan together quite often."

I did not pretend that I needed to be urged. I was ready to fall into their arms because of my hunger for the book. When we went home that night, tucked under my arm was Bishop's number two copy of *The Dawn-Breakers*, a copy that is still with me today.

Dark Entrance into a Different World

Morning. I awoke with my spirit bound by the fetters of sleep. I was alone. The subconscious again, call it what you will, had concocted temporarily a potent brew of incoherence that left me frightened and depressed. I had forgotten about last night.

My notes recall:

> I looked up at the tiny skylight to find out about the day to come. I thought, 'the rain is not only streaming; it is STEAMING. That man we found yesterday slouched in a chair at our wallpaper store apartment looked like a rate-collector in the London slums back in the time of Charles Dickens. He was stamped by his job, bulbous and unkempt. He asked us our names: 'Mr and Mrs Willard McKay.' How I hated the sound of our names then! He handed us an envelope.
>
> "Read this," he commanded. It was a paper stating that the part of our property called the Baker Farm, noted for its fruit growing acreage, had been seized by the bank.
>
> "Sign here." he said. We knew that the next time he came, Emerald Hill would be gone in the same way.

Still, we could joke a little because this must be happening to someone else. At the McKay farm the pickers would be stripping the last of the Montmorency crop of pie cherries from acres and acres of trees. I would soon write:

> It seems weeks since Willard has taken in any real cash. My ring is pawned again. We are adapting ourselves to two meals a day. We are becoming better and better hikers; it is the car fare that kills. But my shoes. . .

Willard is out early up at the stores. He is trying to rent parking lots to people who have lost their cars!

I shook off the fetters of sleep and could now see the green and gold cover of *The Dawn-Breakers* waiting on the red chest. The book covers were the gates to the world that lay inside. For ten days that world would be my world, my reality, too, my human thoughts discarded like the faded wallpaper in the abandoned shop.

I ignored the "Big Chairs" and soon moved into the den with my little Corona and a card table and put on the bright overhead light. I set up page one on Bishop's writing paper and divided the page in half with a line running from top to bottom. On the left side I listed names, dates, places and, on the right, the outline of the main events of the story.

Like other readers first approaching *The Dawn-Breakers*, I had to find my way through what seemed to be a forest of unpronounceable names. This difficulty was eased when I found that each name included the person's title and geographical origin. On the first page I met S̲h̲aykh (teacher) Aḥmad of Aḥsá'í (from Aḥsá, an island on the south side of the Persian Gulf). In Chapter 2, I met Siyyid (descendant of the Prophet) Káẓim-i-Ras̲h̲tí (from the city of Ras̲h̲t). Now that I knew and understood their titles, names and birthplaces as well as their surnames, they took shape as persons with real identities. I could even try to pronounce the names using the table on page 673. I could use their names and call upon them for inspiration.

My prayers for assistance were answered, and I found myself reading and taking notes with an unusual fixed concentration. At 4:30 p.m. the telephone rang. I jumped with a startle. It was Bishop asking how I was getting on with my work. I told him, "I am getting into it." "Getting into it" meant that suddenly I thought I knew what this book was about.

For my own pleasure, I scribbled from time to time in the margin of my notes. In one scribbling, I noted:

This is God's book. It records the stages by which He manifests through the Holy Spirit. From the beginning His Plan has never changed. This is the NOW stage of His Plan. It was time for the Rose to unfurl its petals again. And this time there were two Buds, not one. Two manifestations, the Báb and Bahá'u'lláh.

I read on through the week, about ten hours a day. Sometimes at night Bishop and Bahíyyih joined me, and we checked over our notes. There seemed to be a spell on all three of us. We were spared from wasting time on needless errors. Our Study Class continued to meet on Wednesday nights at Alice Parker's and we went there together, prepared to answer questions. In the minds of our friends there was a scent of the mysterious.

Walter Buchannan felt it and brought it out. "I seem to sense something out of this world."

Bishop responded, "It's probably this *Dawn-Breaker* work of ours. Doris, Bahíyyih and I have been living in another world with it and it is a mysterious other world.

"Who, indeed, could interpret the book as anything other than the mysterious? Even from page one of his Narrative, Nabíl records a book-long series of events best described as supernatural. Why? Because they all gave evidence of the operation of a Divine Will within the realm of men's minds. Not in miracles for all to see, but in the consciousness of His forerunners and His Chosen Ones – those who were to people the stage on which this greatest of dramas was to be performed. How shall I say this? There seemed to be a continuity of awareness that swept through their thoughts, namely that this is the day of the coming of the Promised One.

"These were incendiary thoughts," Bishop's quiet voice continued. "To have divulged this knowledge prematurely would have had the destructive effect of touching a lighted match to a piece of paper or, in this case, a sacred scroll. The pre-dawn period of the 'two wisemen', Shaykh Aḥmad and later Siyyid Káẓim, would last forty years."

"It seemed like a time," commented Willard, "for the protection and nurturing of the young Faith. When did events begin to happen that led to the disclosure of this knowledge to the outer world?"

"The synopsis we are working on deals with dates and events of an outer, physical world termed 'historic'. But the Divine Will operates first in the consciousness of men. It's a different category – a history of a God-infused inner world."

"Yes, that's it, you see," I added. "When <u>Sh</u>ay<u>kh</u> Aḥmad began to fulfil his ordained role, Bahá'u'lláh was not yet in this world. He wasn't even physically conceived at that time. But something, someone, was directing the operation of the Divine Will within the consciousness of his Forerunners. So who can say when it really began to unfold? Perhaps this is another mystery enshrined in the meaning of an eternal story."

For days *The Dawn-Breakers* became my world and the people in it, the realities with whom I conversed. I sat, clad lightly in the humid little room with the light on overhead which seemed to disdain the perpetual sunlight outside. Sometimes in the middle of the afternoon I would leave my work and stagger to the bedroom, fall on the bed and sleep for half an hour.

A week later I found myself back at the Wednesday night Study Class. I felt that I had become "older" in the Faith (I was going to say "centuries older"), not in age but in insight. Working for ten hours a day with attention fixed on the Chosen Ones of the Heroic Age was to be in their company. Forgetful of self, for a time I breathed the freedom of unhampered mind. It was a release like entering an empty room – empty except for a plenitude of sunlight and fresh air – after having been confined to one which is dark and crowded with the soiled relics of the past. In that freedom you breathe the qualities of the Chosen Ones who speak not, save by His permission.

The following Wednesday we were again at Alice Parker's for the Study Class. "In *The Dawn-Breakers*," I told the class, "Divine intervention becomes the proof to the doubters of the existence of God." Some of the faces stared blankly at me. I detected in others a yearning or even a hope. A few of the seekers that we had met at the Utility Hall meetings were there. The faces of Eve and Emily were smiling, encouraging me to go on. I asked if I might read them a few of my notes. (I did have, at least, the foresight to bring the notes with me!) At their wish I continued.

"Last week Bishop spoke of *The Dawn-Breakers* as a book of mystery. Bahá'u'lláh tells us 'There is a power in this Cause – a mysterious power – far, far, far away from the ken of men and angels...'"[34] I began to read from my notes:

> Because of the presence of that power in the unfolding of every event, in the decisions of every person, this marvellous story, like that told in the New Testament, describes how a supernatural knowledge of the presence of One Powerful and Great was infused into the mind of the forerunner Shaykh Ahmad and, later, into the soul of his youthful disciple Siyyid Kazim. A few chapters later we learn how a similar miracle illumined the minds of the Letters of the Living – eighteen minds which, independently of one another, became infused with that knowledge. Within God's creation of man are hidden capacities, including the capacity to know. There is another source of knowledge besides education. There is Divine guidance.
>
> Little by little I feel it more. There is a Being out there, an Essence elusive because of the limits of our rational minds, an Essence Who sent word to us that He created us to know Him and to adore Him. He is a Spirit, a Guide with angelic helpers. He is the eternal Manifestation of God, the Ancient of Days, the I AM that existed before Abraham, the Father to whom Jesus spoke, the Nightingale of Paradise in Bahá'u'lláh's Tablet of Ahmad. He is the Author of The Hidden Words. He spoke with the Voice of all the prophets, but only the Báb and Bahá'u'lláh wrote down the Words.
>
> And from their Writings we glimpse another mystery, the relationship between the Báb and Bahá'u'lláh. Never before were there two Divine youth growing up at the same time and in the same country. Both came from families of respect and wealth. Both had innate knowledge. Both were adored by the people. Both were idyllically happy in marriage. And to

---

34 *The Covenant of Bahá'u'lláh*, compilation (London, Bahá'í Publishing Trust, 1963), p. 70.

both came visions and intimations of Their Supreme Station. Although They never met on this earthly plane, we learn from *The Dawn-Breakers* of Their love for each other, and we are told of the letters They exchanged.[35] Both spoke the Word of God. Their voices are ONE voice, the voice of God itself. The day of the Dawn-Breakers was the appointed time for God's call to be universally sounded. It was the time for the revelation, the inauguration of His Plan. And as Christ knew that He would be crucified, the Báb knew that He would give up His life for Bahá'u'lláh, 'The One Whom God shall make Manifest'.

I selected one more scribbling to read:

> Like perfume, a knowledge drifts to us of a Divine Presence and a warmth touches our hearts.

On the morning of the tenth day, the telephone rang. It was Ruth Brown. I was able to say, "It's all over, Ruth. I am checking the last details."

She responded, "Something else is over, Doris. I'm calling to tell you that Blackie's body was taken out of the river early this morning. They found our address in his pocket and a letter from his niece in Grove City. She had written, 'Where are you, Uncle Braydon? We are waiting to hear from you. When do you want us to drive over to get you and your things? We are happily looking forward to your arrival.' That was all – our address, the letter, a quarter, a dime and a five-cent piece."

Eve Kerin, who had not wept for Charlie, was inconsolable. "He would sit for hours in the Fort Pitt Hotel," she told us. "He would read his newspaper and watch the people. I would sit with him for a while. We had a strange relationship, understood

---

35 The metaphor is given that if the oceans were turned into ink and the branches of the trees into pens, love could not be sufficiently expressed. To me the early Writings of Bahá'u'lláh and the Báb, in choice of word, in style of rhythmic prose and especially in the power to quicken the heart, demonstrate the product of a single mind – that single Voice.

each other. I guess we were meant to be a couple of outsiders. After Charlie died, I didn't feel sociable. I would just wave and pass on by."

"'Come back. Come back and let us be kind,'" I quoted. "We all feel we have failed, as Bahá'ís, I mean."

"No. It was a kindness to leave him to his private life. He chose that when he left his boyhood home in Grove City. To have people know that he was broke crushed him. We're not all alike, you know."

"In one way we are all alike," I murmured. "We are all too proud."

With Blackie to Grove City

We were in the Sekers' car, driving behind Mr Payne's hearse. Leila, with her husband, was sitting in front of the hearse. The slow-paced ride, after two turbulent days, was a balm to our spirits. Our untired gaze took in the wide valleys and encircling foothills. Streams sparkled down the sides of the hills and cut rivulets through fields of market vegetables: corn, beets, yellow beans and acres of harsh, bright green turnip leaves.

When we arrived in Grove City, the minister and a family of three (the two nephews and the niece) were waiting for us in the churchyard. The nephews helped Mr Payne with the coffin, and the minister beamed benevolently to the young relatives, "Your uncle has come home at last." We thanked Mr Payne and said goodbye to him, while Leila joined us to go to the farmhouse where we were invited to dinner. The eldest nephew gave him some bills in an envelope.

The Blacks' dinner table was usually a round one. Now the leaves had extended it and soon there was a feast spread out for us. Chicken with gravy and dumplings, an array of vegetables, pickles, jellies and a mountain of homemade ice cream. "Perfectly delicious," said Willard after a few moments of joyful assimilation, "and I think it was all raised on your farm."

Soon we were all sharing one of those rare incredible moments of release from tension when spirits rise up over tragedy. At the table, the whole group reached an oasis in a desert of despair. That group even seemed now to include Braydon. His Pittsburgh Bahá'í friends had never really known him before.

"Would you like to see some early pictures of Uncle?"

"Yes, we would." And we saw him from childhood into his youth. We saw his stern father and his comforting-looking mother.

"We all looked up to Uncle," one of the nephews said. "We looked to him as somebody who had made a success in the city – carved a life out for himself."

"Yes, he called himself a career man when he was talking to the Welfare worker."

When it was time to return to the cemetery, we went. We went as the family of Braydon Black. The townspeople were already there. The minister and I gave a short talk on "The World to Come". Leila Payne's high-voiced invocation opened eyes and turned faces. There were men of seventy who had gone to school with Braydon. One said, "It's religion, whatever they are calling it."

The trip home was the morning's landscape in reverse. The sunlight, rather than raining down from overhead, slanted from the West and gave a richness to every colour. It was as though we were moving through a book of paintings by Constable. Bessie and Henry were quiet, a little drowsy. We held on to our dream mood while praying, thinking of Blackie. "O Lord, perpetuate his existence in Thine exalted rose garden, that he may plunge into the sea of light in the world of mysteries. . . "

Overlapping Worlds

Back in Homewood again, Willard and I mused on the psychological mileage between the different worlds of Pittsburgh and Grove City.

"A world is more than an environment," we agreed. "It

can be also a state of heart, a condition of mind." True to our covenant of the Burning Log made with Lorna, we had been paying deeper attention to other people and less to ourselves. We had been praying to convey to others even the faintest scent of Universal Love, offering our own hearts as channels for the Ocean of God's grace.

"The variety of souls we have thus beheld," I exclaimed, "is a fabric of overlapping worlds." Think of them: the world of the man stealing bread crusts from the pigeons; the world that Alice Dolittle found in Haifa; the cold grey castle of Mrs Storer, warmed only by her garden; the desperate mental realms of the Jewish Peace ladies worried about relatives in Germany as news of Hitler's atrocities is spread; and, lastly, Blackie's world. His last act on the cool, damp wharf near one of the bridges on the Allegheny River, the river a blaze of light, with not quite enough money in his pocket to buy a bus ride home. These were the worlds that flowed back through the channels of God's grace. To see more, even if not to know more, draws us closer to people.

Little Girl Dead

One night, about ten o'clock, someone pounded on the shop door. It was George Washington, the Black welfare worker to whom Willard had volunteered work for four mornings a week and to whom he had talked about the Cause.

"I am asking you and your wife to come to our house and pray," he said.

"Anything wrong?" Willard asked.

"Linnie, my little girl – playing on the street after dark – has got hit and killed. We need you to come and pray at our house. You told me you could pray. I have my car here."

Willard raced back to the room for the prayer book, and we ran out and jumped into George's car. We sped through the streets to his house. A small crowd loitered at his apartment door and we pushed through. Upstairs, a chubby eight-year-old dressed in white lay in a white coffin on an ironing board by the window. She had white flowers in her hair and her complexion was blue-tinged.

George was shaky. His wife's face was stony with pain. The neighbours lamented noisily. This world was broken. "I told her," the mother said, "not to go out but she just laughed and ran out, just ran out." The room was buzzing with flies.

George introduced us. "Meet Mr McKay and his wife. They have come to pray for Linnie and to say a few words. Their hearts are with us."

We stood by the coffin and said Bahá'í prayers to guide the little newcomer to the "garden of happiness". We told the Washingtons that she would grow up in that world and become a beautiful maiden. And that someday they would find her and she would be their daughter forever. We then asked for a silent prayer so that our thoughts could rise and reach her and, for a moment, go with her There. Then there was no sound except the click of the mother's fan above the child's face.

At home Willard said, "George is like the students I met on the trip with Louis Gregory – graduate in Social Sciences from a Black university. Fiske, no doubt."

"Employed by the city at too low a wage to buy screens," I protested.

"Like the rest of us," Willard concluded sadly. "The city of Pittsburgh is bankrupt."

There was a world of high-pitched gaiety here too, especially among our Italian neighbours on Zenith Way. Their back wall spanned the left side of our "court". A mother and her five children ate their meals outside on an open porch. It was sunless there, but they would turn on a lamp with a red shade. They had also put out a red tablecloth. Their radio was always playing catchy music from the local stations. Our gospel-warbling neighbour at the second-floor front criticized the family for having the radio. We could hear the children laughing or squabbling in Sicilian, the language of our cherry pickers at the Geneva farm. The smell of garlic from their stews wafted into the court. We loved all this.

Remover of Difficulties

I withdrew from the contemplation of our empty kitchen shelves to admit our young friend Lois. Our connection with her had begun in Geneva when, in 1928, the Obers had brought her to our Blossom Picnic. Lois Halderman was not a Bahá'í, although she would listen to us talk. Others had found her very reserved and hard to know but with us, Lois wasn't shy. Actually, I think her talking to us may have saved her sanity. She was one of three sisters in a once-comfortable family. Emma was the eldest and, until recently, a student at the university. Lois and Ellie were teenaged, but it was Emma and Ellie who had suffered mental breakdowns from the strain of having lost faith in the future. At first they had been angry, then confused. Now, they were mentally sick.

"The doctor has diagnosed Ellie's case as schizophrenia," Lois explained. "But she has something to love, which saves her, and that's her canary." Lois looked uneasy. "I can't go back to that dinner table tonight. I really can't. Oh, please let me come here!"

I sat down with her and asked her to explain, "What has happened, Lois?"

As though speaking through wooden lips she tonelessly explained, "Ellie reached into the cage today and killed her bird. She said she could not bear its singing."

"Well, as for coming here, Lois dear, what shall we eat?"

"I can give you twenty-five cents a meal if you will take me to board."

"Twenty-five cents is an absolute fortune," I exulted. "We can all three live sumptuously on that. Praise be to God!"

How was this to be done? Ground beef, which must be bought carefully, was ten cents a pound. Root vegetables were sold cheaply or even given away on the Saturday-night clearing of the stores. Day-old bread, currant buns or cake were available four blocks away on the corner of Penn Avenue, and often there was often a glut of fruit in the stores. Our food could be prepared in different ways: cooked, served raw, made into soups. I praised the year at Tilbury Tenement when I learned these ways with food.

Although Lois was not shy with us, we began to understand how some people had found her difficult to know. There was a depth lacking.

During one of our dinners, she told us, "There is so much warmth here between you that you must think I am frozen, and I am. It's like water in a flowerpot that freezes when it's left out all winter. The frost can break the pot. In this case it's my heart."

We sat nearer to her, looking expectant but saying little. "Six years ago, when I was twenty-five, I met and became engaged to my ideal man. As the wedding date approached, he fell in love with someone else and married her instead. My problem is that I can't stop loving him. When I accidentally meet him on the street, I want to die. I'm not interested in other men. What is the matter with me?"

"Sounds as if you have a fixation," Willard offered. "You need a healing."

We concluded the conversation by challenging Lois to say the Báb's prayer for the Remover of Difficulties nineteen times for nineteen days, starting that night. Using the powerful, bounty-imbued Words, we would pray for the healing of her ills and that she would "find someone else". Although not sharing our assurance, Lois agreed reluctantly to say the prayers with us.

Two weeks later Lois began the dinner conversation, "I don't think I ever told you about Marty. No? Three years ago, before the Depression, I took a trip to Buffalo and Niagara Falls by myself. I met Marty on the bus. We talked, had dinner together and went to look at the Falls. When we separated, we exchanged addresses but never used them; that is, until today. He wants to come to Pittsburgh and to visit me! Says he has some business here."

"What will you tell him?" I asked.

"Well, I shall be honest about the girls and that I never have company."

Marty wrote back to tell Lois that he was coming anyway. He showed up on the Haldermans' doorstep and was popular with the family. Early in his visit they came to see us. Marty's grandfather had emigrated from Norway and his family resided now in western Canada. Marty was honourable, secure and kind. He asked Lois to go to Canada to visit him and to meet his mother. Lois went and did not return. During that visit she married him.

Willard and I believe that the answering of those prayers was a miracle. But Bahá'u'lláh has not chosen to teach by miracles. Lois did not, to our knowledge, ever become a Bahá'í.

What do we do when our teaching efforts have not been rewarded? We pray for them and leave them to God.

Prisons of Self

One August night we sat sipping iced tea with Alice, the Browns and Emily Craighead. Most of our "seekers after truth" had left at the conclusion of yet another Study Class. Said Alice, "At this time of night you can see the ruffles on my curtains begin to move. It is a sign that a breeze is coming down from the atmosphere above the hills that hover about us on a hot night. Is it fanciful for me to say that the Holy Spirit blew upon this meeting, lifting, just a little, the stuffiness in the 'prisons of self where some of those friends are languishing?"

"Prisons of self!" cried Emily. "I felt like reading this to them." She opened to a marked passage in her *Wisdom of 'Abdu'l-Bahá*:

> Turn your faces away from the contemplation of your own finite selves and fix your eyes on the Everlasting Radiance; then will your souls receive in full measure the Divine Power of the Spirit and the blessings of the Infinite Bounty.[36]

"Why," wailed Emily, "do these beautiful people invite us to take part in their meetings and why do they come regularly to ours while, in a single breath, they talk about mind over matter, reincarnation, New Thought, the supernatural, and yet they will not even challenge the Message of Bahá'u'lláh? If they will not listen, why do they come?"

I suggested, "Is it because they sense that despite the world's

---

36 *The Wisdom of 'Abdu'l-Bahá*, p. 185.

confusion, we have found peace within? Our small and sometimes down-at-the-heel group of assorted people appears young at heart and one in spirit. For them, that is unusual. Our friends hide the fact that they are assailed by a thousand fears; their secret spectre is that the mind-over-matter schools of thought will not grant them immunity in this time of crisis."

"And we," observed Willard, "are the bearers of glad tidings, 'did they but know.' Take heart," he told us. "Occasionally someone listens!"

And then there was Dr Bryson. We had come to rely upon his continued presence as a seal of "respectability" to our meetings. He was a distinguished figure, elderly and dignified, clad with conservative elegance and an aura of being in charge. He was a retired doctor (Nose and Throat) and a prestigious leader of a popular New Thought group. Someone commented on Dr Bryson's appearance of peace within. "It seems that he has confidence in an unseen power."

"Yes, but what power? Where is the centre to which he turns?" questioned Emily.

"Couldn't his composure be the result of a disciplined willpower; disciplined, that is, in accordance with the precepts of New Thought."

"Very good!" replied Bishop, "But those precepts are not endorsed by the Word of the Founders of the world's religions which yield the human will to the Will of God. That's a different form of discipline. What we have is a discipline of detachment and renunciation. What we have is a Faith, not a cult of the mind."

It was to be expected that Dr Bryson and the people who came with him to our meetings should show signs of unrest when we referred to the Manifestation. Our study outline, as prepared by the Teaching Committee, dealt mostly with the history and the principles of the Faith but throughout, the station of Bahá'u'lláh proclaimed itself.

One evening as Dr Bryson rose to leave, Dr Mary Coffin, one of Pittsburgh's Scottish-Presbyterians and soon to become a Bahá'í, had to ask him: "Who was Christ?"

"Jesus," replied our doctor friend, "was a man to be respected and his example followed. But given more knowledge and a strong enough incentive, we could all be Christs. The soul of man is divine."

A few days later Ruth Brown telephoned to inform me that Dr Bryson was very ill and in hospital. He had fallen in his apartment, evidently striking his head on the cast-iron radiator, and all night he had lain unconscious on the floor.

I went to see him. The nurse at the desk said to me, "You may see him, but he may not be conscious. He keeps drifting in and out."

I went in and stood by his bed. He was conscious, recognized me, and spoke: "Last night I thought I was going to step out, but I am still here."

His eyelids were beginning to droop.

"Dr Bryson, I did not come to talk but just to sit with you a little and say some prayers."

"Thank you," he whispered. He was gone again into that opaque enveloping fog we call coma. And yet, I am told there is an extraordinary awareness of the soul at such moments.

I sat in a chair by the window and said the Greatest Name and the Healing Prayer, not so much for the man's body as for his soul. Then I rose quietly to slip away.

But no. He was beckoning to me, his eyes raised above the level of the pillow. He motioned for me to bring my ear closer to his lips and he whispered, "You have met the Manifestation."

Could this be a declaration of belief? I had to be sure and asked him to repeat. Again he said, "You have met the Manifestation."

"Do you mean Bahá'u'lláh?"

"Yes."

I took his hand, spectral and old, in my warm one. There was a weak pressure of his fingers and he was gone again into the calm of the spirit.

When I walked out again into the street I was walking "above the world by the power of the Most Great Name". There is no rapture to compare with even a momentary contact with the Abhá Kingdom. In a state of euphoria I called all the Bahá'ís to tell them that a miracle had happened to the doctor's soul.

In a few days I heard that he was better and that his daughter had come to take him home with her to California. He had forgotten his Moment of Eternity at the hospital. He had denied his acceptance of the station of Bahá'u'lláh. We never saw or heard again from Dr Bryson.

"Be happy," said Willard. "In his heart he was accepted. Later, when he goes, he will leave his veils behind."

A Lesson for Bessie

I sat in the Sekers' kitchen that special morning, watching Bessie slice beef to make sandwiches for our community picnic. We were discussing the other Bahá'ís. I watched her affectionately. How vital she was! How deft with her hands. And how aggressive was her whole person – but likeable, even if sometimes so pugnacious and loud. Bessie's heart, I thought, is another magnetized particle drawn by the power of love into the Unity of a Bahá'í group. We were diversified and yet we were one. If we were not tested so much by one another's egos, we could belong to the New Creation promised by Bahá'u'lláh.

But unfortunately, Bessie was letting off steam at the moment by scolding Bishop, whom actually she admired and adored.

"He's too NICE, I can't bear him," she raged. "I know he laughs at me. He's amused because I shout when I talk and I bounce when I walk. I always have. Sometimes, though, he makes me feel like DIRT. He makes me so mad that sometimes I'd like to . . . " Bessie emphasized her remarks by waving threateningly her long murderous-looking meat knife. It caught her left wrist and released an arc of bright arterial blood.

"Don't stand there with your mouth open," she yelled. "Get the first aid kit out of the bathroom. Help me bandage this wrist. Call emergency. Get Henry."

On the way to the hospital Bessie held up and looked at

her poorly bandaged and reddening wrist. Then she began to laugh. "This will teach me not to backbite Bishop. So help me, Bahá'u'lláh, I won't do that again!"

The dressing at the hospital cost eight dollars. Bessie broke out laughing again on the way home. Henry and I were still too shaken to manage more than a weak smile.

Bessie thought of Bahá'u'lláh and His guidance. "He sure is prompt!" she noted.

Race Relatives

At supper time Willard and I were in agreement about dropping in at the Buchannans'. Since becoming a Bahá'í, Walter's lighthearted questions and comments had enlightened our meetings. I picture, in my memory, a small, slim, laughing man, his eyes brown, a well-chiselled aristocratic nose, features delicate and Nordic, all enclosed in a coffee-coloured skin. We loved Walter and savoured with true relish his charm.

Ida was twice his size and of a warmer coffee colour. Laughing, loving and singing were in the depths of her personality. But Ida could be fierce and free, too – quick and fervent in her movements. Ida had a degree in music from Oberlin College, Ohio. Walter was a Princeton graduate. He was at Tuskegee Institute with Booker T. Washington and was later President of A & M College in Alabama. Now he had a little truck and was selling coal. "At least we keep warm," he laughed. And laughing delightedly, they opened their home to us.

Ida dramatized despair. "You know I have nothing but toast for our tea." She cut thick slices of homemade bread and we toasted them on forks over the coal embers in the fireplace. Spread with butter and honey, they were delicious. Ida served the tea in Limoges china cups with hand-wrought silver spoons. Tea at the Buchannans' was a ceremony from a culture born in the deep South.

We luxuriated in the knowledge of being "at home" with these friends. Rain streaked the windows, but I was warm before the fire, a warmth that reminded me of the earthly well-being and peace of the Geneva farm when applewood crackled on its hearths. The coal fire at the Buchannans' was a basket of red embers, the black chunks of cannel coal making explosive noises as they expanded in the heat, kerosene igniting and flaring up in the cracks.

I, the homeless one, watched Ida. I thought, "This is Ida's house. It is her habitat. Here, graciousness and warmth exude from her personality." Her soul relaxed in this atmosphere and for this reason, we were given a view of the emotional fire beneath the ash as she told us the story of her foray the night before.

"There was a Greta Garbo picture offered at the Homewood Theatre. I had to see it, but the man at the window said, 'Sorry, no seats.' 'But people are going in,' I said. 'Why not me?' 'No Coloured,' is what he said. I threw my money on his counter and stalked in carrying myself like an African Queen. And I had a very good view of the picture. I had the whole row to myself."

She had to make us understand how smothered her spirit had been. Dressed in a silk tunic of a print resembling tiger skin, she sank to the floor at my feet and pounded on the arms of my chair where I had been sitting so Whitely and privileged. And as quickly as she had made this gesture, she was up on her feet in a wide, dancing, sweep of the room.

"I heard this the other day," she announced. "'When de Lawd gave out hair, the Black folks hung back and de White ones got the best hair. Jes' a li'l wool left for us. So when de Lawd gave out feet, the Black folks was fust and we got the biggest.'"

Walter commented, "She makes fun of us, but she wouldn't let you do that. What would your brother say, Ida?"

"He would laugh too," she said firmly. "My brother is a professor at the University of Cairo. Do you know, when he came to see us last summer, he stood on the doorstep and boomed, 'Ya Bahá'u'l-Abhá.' Neither of us knew the other was a Bahá'í. I replied, 'Alláh-u-Abhá.' What a meeting we had! How we hugged each other!"

Willard asked for music and Ida went to the piano and began

to play the spirituals we loved. We joined into the magic spell of her voice.

Later when we were sitting more quietly, I startled myself by asking her, "Do you resent Willard and me because we happen to be White?" It sounded so funny that we were all laughing, then standing together in a gigantic hug. Walter exclaimed, "We used to talk about race relations, but we are race relatives."

September 1932

I look back on the Homewood days as glorious. At the time, the amount of work allotted to me was so bewilderingly overwhelming that I was obliged to turn it over to the Holy Spirit. I was beginning my chairmanship of the Local Assembly. I had responsibility for managing the advertised meetings at Harmony Hall and for teaching the weekly study class at Alice Parker's. I based the sessions on the thirty-six lessons which we had prepared for the National Teaching Committee. But this was not all. I have mentioned earlier the Women's International League for Peace and Freedom and Mrs Norman Storer. To her I offered myself as a "worker" and was more and more drawn into the lives of the League's members – American Jewish women, about four hundred of them.

All at once I seemed to have been put at the forefront of activity, going about to church and school groups to talk about peace. I have never been sorry, for I learned more about my own capacities and realized what skills I could impart to them. I offered to do their publicity. I had newspaper experience from the work of the Faith, and I knew the formalities. I could dispense with the preliminary stages of learning how to open the doors. With the League I met many important visitors from other countries who came to speak about peace. I attended many meetings and became even more at home in newspaper offices, offices in which Martha Root once had worked.

Back to Geneva

A brief recess came in the fall of 1932 when Emily Craighead offered to drive me back to Geneva for the Labor Day weekend. Beloved Geneva. In my memory, a peaceful college town, the fruit farm with its view of Seneca Lake framed by tall poplars and pines. That was the memory. We arrived late at night at the home of Rex and Mary Collison. The Collisons were born into the Faith with us, when Howard and Mabel Ives gave us the message seven years before in 1925.

I slipped out early the next morning to walk through the field which bordered our old Preemption Road, a border to our old life. Here were the mailbox and the little bridge over the stream where watercress was growing. There, the lane to the sweeping lawn of the house. The cherry crop still hung on the trees, a crop that had been sprayed against rot in anticipation of a June picking. The branches were loaded for a "bumper crop". The cherries were now as large as plums, tasteless. No need for the harvest. The markets were closed.

Geneva, beloved Geneva. I found the farm in relative ruin. The ancient smoke house, which had been built in the 1700s, had been torn down. The 25-foot dining room had been converted into a kitchen with a stove at one end. The back of the house had been torn off. Dido, my black cat was there, indifferent to my affections. Geneva. Emotion drained out of the dream. There was nothing left to hook on to. . . And it did not matter.

Winter came. In its "orchestra", the violin strings of economic pressure were tightened to a higher note, to the pitch of a shriek.

There was a street near us called Nadir Alley. That would have been a good name for the whole city, the whole country, perhaps the whole world – a world at its nadir, its lowest point. Willard and I were so in the habit of determined optimism that we refused to face the reality of our financial situation. One afternoon I came home to find a familiar slouching figure in our apartment. He had come once before to take part of the farm. He returned now with foreclosure papers to take the rest. The bank had taken over the Baker Farm for unpaid taxes and mortgages. The dream of ever going back was over. This was the emotional finality.

We had still a few antiques stored in the old Guest House, and now we were forced to sell some of them. Willard's brother Cecil helped with their disposal. A little money came in from their sale. Willard's grand piano earned $50. From time to time, help came from Lorna, who was teaching high school in Beverley, Massachusetts. She originated the concept of "Bahá'u'lláh's Money", which in critical moments came down like manna in the form of $5.00 and $10.00 cheques. With this bounty and Willard's sales of small gadgets, we were able to pay our utility bills and to buy groceries. Willard's only outer reaction to the pinch was that he was unusually hilarious. I tried to match his mood.

One night we reached the bottom of the purse. It contained a latch key and a dime. We said many prayers that night for God to sustain us. But God forgive me, I could not sleep.

It was an hysterical response to personify poverty as a beast stalking the streets. But sometimes one shivered. Mercifully, our affairs did not challenge our faith. We felt safe. I said, "Just remember what the Guardian wrote in his letter to Bessie about our coming here. 'They are well versed in the Faith and have the Bahá'í spirit, and that is all the capital a Bahá'í needs.'"

"Yes," Willard agreed, "we have had many proofs of this and will, no doubt, have many more."

I went on, "'Help over which we have no control' will sustain us. . . Here it is in the prayer book, in the words of 'Abdu'l-Bahá. 'Prepare for us the means of livelihood; give us bread through channels over which we have no control – Thy heavenly treasures.'"[37]

---

37 From the old black prayer book:

> O God! O God! Cause us to drink from the cup of Thy bestowal. Illumine our faces with the light of guidance; make us firm in Thine ancient Covenant. Suffer us to become thy sincere servants. Open before our eyes the doors of prosperity, prepare for us the means of livelihood, give us bread through channels over which we have no

No, I could not sleep. As I lay there praying, almost supernaturally alert, I thought of Emily Craighead. Something was wrong. I nudged Willard. "Wake up and help me pray for Emily. She is in trouble," I pleaded. After many more prayers, the need seemed to be over and we both slept.

The next morning the telephone rang. It was Dr Mary Coffin, one of our near-Bahá'í contacts. She said, "I have been with Emily Craighead. She had a heart attack last night at three o'clock. She is safe now, I think, especially if she has rest in bed for two or three weeks. Emily wants you to come and stay with her while her sister is away during the mornings. She will give you your dinner, your car fare and a dollar each day. Can you do this, Doris? Emily has faith that she will be healed."

Of course I stayed with her. I remembered placing my hands on May Maxwell's heart, feeling it race and when I said the healing prayers and repeated the Greatest Name, I felt it regain a more natural rhythm. I applied the same treatment to Emily, and in two weeks' time, she was on her feet.

Spring of 1933

The bottom was dropping out of Pittsburgh and out of the substance of society itself where, in the United States, it was estimated that thirty million people were out of work. The money I had made was spent and again we were face to face with real want. Yet the Guardian had promised us that we would not be forsaken by our angels. We were well versed in the Faith and had the Bahá'í spirit. That was all the capital we needed. On March 12th, I received a letter from my cousin Harry in Brooklyn. I had not had contact with him in years. He said the thought had

---

control – Thy heavenly treasures! Grant us power to turn our faces towards Thy merciful countenance and to be faithful in Thy Cause. O Thou Clement and Compassionate One! Verily Thou art gracious to those who are firm and steadfast in Thy strong and impregnable Covenant. Praise be to God, the Lord of the worlds.

'Abdu'l-Bahá

come into his mind that I might need help and he had enclosed a cheque for $5.00. Riches!

This was the day that Franklin Delano Roosevelt announced the closure of the banks throughout the country. Eleven o'clock that morning was to be the deadline. Willard joined the crowd before the wicket of our Homewood bank. As I peeped corner wise through the outside window, I saw him jostled to the counter. He was given his $5.00 and the window closed. This had been the first inspired move of FDR, the newly inaugurated President bringing with him the New Deal. He was soon to offer the WPA – public work projects and jobs for unemployed men. Willard landed one that involved taking statistics and measures of outside chimneys. Hundreds of men had applied for the job. Willard was paid $17.00 a week. Sometimes the work would stop and a new project commence. Once, when work reopened, he was made squad leader of seven men.

Roosevelt's strategy was to stimulate spending in the United States. The banks opened again, and people dared to redeposit the savings they had left – if any. There was a little life now and there was a new hope, a feeble one. The people on the Homewood streets were still in shock, however. They had no hope. God was lost out of their hearts.

It is unusual for me to remember dreams. One night, however, I had one in which I was standing on top of a pushcart at the intersection of Homewood Avenue and Nadir Alley, screaming passionately to moving crowds of unhearing people, "I preach Christ crucified. I say, I PREACH CHRIST CRUCIFIED!"

As Bahá'u'lláh said in the Tablet of Aḥmad, "for the people are wandering in the paths of delusion, bereft of discernment to see God with their own eyes or hear His melody with their own ears." Except for a few. A few for whom Christ had been crucified, and for whom Bahá'u'lláh had been made a prisoner. This day will pass, and another generation will be able to listen to His message.

Through Willard's employment and a Saturday job at Sears-Roebuck, we had enough to pay for an apartment by ourselves. It was in an old brick mansion near the store and I won it on the approval of a cat. When I interviewed its aristocratic and elderly owner, she said, "No, I want a single man there." She was quite firm until a big fluffy cat came in and suddenly jumped on my lap. Said Mrs Edmonds, "That cat never goes to strangers. I'll have to let you come after all." We lived in faded splendour for over a year, and when Mrs Edmonds died, I helped the nurse lay out her body. We stayed on with the approval of her daughter, who lived there too, an artist who had a studio in the tower of the house.

National Convention, 1933

The Coles in Cleveland gave me money to go to the 1933 Convention. Convention was in June that year to enable the friends to attend the Chicago World Fair. My bus ride from Cleveland to Chicago was interrupted frequently by Declaration Day parades in towns along the way. When the bus arrived, very late, Dale and Katherine Cole were waiting to take me home. Certainly, there was no place in the world that seemed as much like home as did their delightful suburban house set on a big lawn in Cleveland Heights. The next morning, Kay (Katherine) and I, with some other Cleveland people, drove to Wilmette.

Thoughts, like tendrils, pushed out ahead to Convention – a hazy dream of expectations. I was excited by the prospect of reunion with the bewildering assemblage of people who would be there, the amazing people who had been with 'Abdu'l-Bahá and had gone out as teachers with His light on their faces and beckoning smiles and gestures. Our dear friends, so accessible, later to become fabulous myths. May Maxwell, Louis Gregory, Roy Wilhelm, the Trues (mother and daughter), Loulie Mathews, Mabel and Howard Ives, Grace and Harlan Ober and 'Keith'.

But I had other expectations as well. My life had turned a corner when we moved into the new apartment. I told Lorna,

"Homewood was, in reality, a loathsome, nasty, little hole. The fact that it was a warm little hole, a cosy little hole, a convenient little hole, was ungratefully forgotten. I hope that I can seal up that book as I sealed up the book of Tilbury."

I tried to put that life behind me and began to branch out. In April I had taken three classes at the University – psychology, writing and figure drawing. The tuition fees then were especially low. Through those courses I fell in love again with learning and studying. I had never had a university education and I found that, gathering As and Bs, I was doing very well. I began to recover a lost confidence. I was studying a lot and beginning to write, doing extensive supplementary reading. I was busy, too, with publicity work for the Women's League. I felt better about myself but sometimes I wondered if I were frittering away my time. I began to see how scattered my activities were and to see the dissipation of energies by distractions, inadequacies, worries, monotonies and financial failures.

Lorna and I had talked often about "The Place". It is a state of spirit that can be maintained only through effort. "The Place" is a zone of nearness to God, a zone of "seeing naught save God". With my newfound excitement for learning and through the intensity of concentration on my classes, I went a little off the spiritual track. I came to experience the truth uttered by 'Abdu'l-Bahá when He said, "Knowledge is the greatest veil." It had removed me from the zone I had come to occupy and feel at home in. By the time of Convention, I knew of my need to get unified and to refocus myself on the Cause as the centre of activity. The Cause is our one claim to distinction, our one source of power. I needed a better connection to that power.

So many dear friends were there. During the first session of Convention, I sat as a delegate in one of the front rows with my head screwed on backwards watching those that entered. All my dear friends. I felt my separation from them. "These are not my people any longer," I thought. I felt the loss of "The Place" and I began to mourn.

I knew how Convention would open. The song of two sweet singers from Chicago, the scent of the masses of roses, the

Persian rugs on the wall. Ernest Harrison from Montreal was called to say the Prayer for Canada. Then the voice of Horace Holley giving his report of the Bahá'í year.

One of my last glimpses of the late comers caught sight of Dorothy, this radiant personality with sparkling eyes and a fun-seeking quirk on her lips. She saw me and waved an index finger of her raised hand. I felt a magnetic surge toward her which, after the session, brought us together for lunch. It was two years since we had met. Today she had come with a flock of new Bahá'ís from Lima, Ohio. She was teaching. She was healed of her physical ills. The Dorothy of two years ago was lost to me because I saw in her the beginning of the death of SELF. I saw it in the outline of her aura of spirit, the garment of the person of the "fifth kingdom", that infusion of the human world with the atmosphere of the "world to come" while still on earth. I, the friend, four years older than Dorothy, on whom Dorothy had leaned two years ago, now felt humility and immaturity in the face of this "being" who had bloomed in the interval.

After the afternoon session, I left Dorothy to search for May (Maxwell). May would be in her room, resting, as she must after long train journeys. Mary would be somewhere near. May reclined on pillows on her bed. She, too, I had not seen for two "Pittsburgh years"! I ran to her. Her motherly arm embraced me. She could be loving. But she said, "Doris, if you have to go to the washroom, don't be scared. There's a young alligator in the bathtub. Mary insisted on bringing it with her." I looked in the washroom and saw the alligator grinning at me with its long satirical jaws.

All of us were staying at a hotel in Evanston. Later that evening Kay Cole found me crying on my bed. My glorious friends! I felt separated from all of them. I felt as though I had lost my Cause. The Holy Spirit was gone. Kay understood. She brought me something special to eat and comforted me. After a few evenings spent in this way I was given back what I had lost. It was a gradual and rather unspectacular recovery. I can only credit it to my rededication and the refocusing of my efforts on the business of the Convention. It was the work of the Convention that took me out of my "prison of self" and slipped me back into "The Place".

After Convention, I began a new routine of sustained meditation and prayer. I remember the first morning. I was most restless, like a cat that wanted to get away, but I held myself down until the struggle ceased. It took fifty minutes. That's discipline – and it brought such a sense of achievement, a clearness, a groove to hold my wheels.

I went back to Rochester and Geneva in September. Some of our other friends had also returned to Geneva from distant part of the United States. It was a reunion of sorts. But this time, I felt a different kind of separation from my friends. Marguerite, Christine, the Collisons all seemed pretty impersonal and hard to get at. I realized that it was a habitual numbness of response. Everyone in the group was grand, but something was missing. One night at Dr Heist's home, I was called upon to speak. I took as my topic "What does it mean to be a Bahá'í in 1933?" I spoke of the Depression and its effects on all of us individually and collectively. I said, now that we were back together after three years, we ought to take stock together. What was our condition, I asked. Suddenly I flared up and demanded, "What about the wall between us and other people? Is it still higher and more impenetrable than three years ago? For a Bahá'í who is a representative of God's love, THE WALL MUST GO!"

Everyone began to talk at once, from out of their ghastly isolation, and began to bear witness to the wall and its devastating effect on their lives and the growth of the Cause. "What can we do?" they asked. I talked about the power of prayer and the need for courage to come out from our intellectual ramparts and begin loving. As we talked, we came together once more, truly united in the love of God. This talk and the one I gave in Rochester taught me something about letting go, of releasing the spirit.

As I mentioned earlier, during our early Bahá'í days in Geneva I had responded to an article that appeared in the *Atlantic Monthly* magazine. I wrote to the editors offering my thoughts and the Bahá'í teachings which inspired them. They published my letter. This was one thing that drew attention and put me on the floor at the National Convention and on my first National Committee, the Study Outline Committee that later prepared the Thirty-Six Lessons.

In November of 1933 I wrote to Stanwood Cobb suggesting that the Study Outlines be used as a correspondence course. I turned them into writing exercises. Students would write articles based on the material in the Outlines and send them to us. We would critique them and mail our comments back to them. I thought the articles might also prove useful to the *Bahá'í Magazine*. Between forty and fifty people took the course. I remember receiving a letter forwarded from Europe asking for the course materials. It was from George Townshend, who was then investigating the Faith. Mr Townshend later became a Bahá'í and a Hand of the Cause of God.

From my notes: December 21, 1933

> Where is it that Bahá'u'lláh tells us to appreciate the values of these fleeting days? I was struck, all of a sudden, while going through the kitchen door, by a bombardment of thoughts about the importance of day-to-day living and experience and how we should welcome opportunities to develop spiritual qualities through the exercise of living. How we ought to have perspective enough to know that certain things are dumbbell drills and sit-up exercises of squeezing out of each day every drop of growth, experience, colour and appreciation that it contains – storing it all up. It is the raw material of the fabric of the next life. I feel that we are wasteful of material, that we discriminate too much and really accept too little. That high rapture that comes over us at times is a fore-vision of the meaning of life eternal. It is for this potential rapture that the game is worth playing. That God has created us glorifies the verb "to be" out of its humdrum inescapableness. I want to proclaim against all nullification and deadness and half measures and compromise.

About this time, I began to see more clearly how I had been changed by the Pittsburgh experience. I was feeling a little victorious inside. I had become much more of a social being and I was praying for more love, more dynamics, to be exactly as 'Abdu'l-Bahá had encouraged – to show forth affection to every creature. Pittsburgh was the proving ground for my first attempts in practising universal love. Now I prayed to expand the practice. I wrote at the time, "If radiance is to be found in these streets, is it not better than acquiring it by the easy means of an orchard or a sunset? I cannot have my soul at ransom to the accident of environment." Another lesson had been learned.

One morning during the Fast, the inflation of our lives seemed to collapse. I related to Willard an exciting discovery. "I believe I'm ready to leave Pittsburgh at last. How about you?" Willard replied, "If a door opens, I'm ready, too." Dawn was rising over our three-storey aviary and we finished another round of the Remover of Difficulties, feeling strangely free and at a little loss.

Go Thou Straight On

Three and a half years and suddenly our work in Pittsburgh seemed redundant. My activities for the Women's League had grown out of proportion and had born little fruit for Bahá'u'lláh. A fruit would ripen later, however, when Mrs Norman Storer became a Bahá'í. But the Bahá'í group was assured. Alice Parker, a great teacher, was keeping up the Wednesday night study classes.

In three short weeks from the Fast and our prayers, we were on our way to Jamestown in the Sekers' commodious car, together with Henry and Bessie, their dog 'Noodles', the cat and canary – plus ourselves and all our earthly goods. The goods consisted of our books, clothes and a few dishes. For the first time since we left Geneva, we were to have a home that was not a furnished apartment.

We and the Sekers stayed the first night in a tourist house on Prendergast Avenue. I had a nightmare, screamed and threw myself out of bed. I thought the "prohibited" cat which was in our quarters was escaping into the house. Willard rescued me from under the bed. The next morning the landlady passed me on the stairs. I was covered with bruises and was limping. She said, "Did you hear the explosion last night? It shook the house." "Why, no," I replied, "I didn't hear one," and hastily passed by her. The cat, sleeping illicitly in the Sekers' room, was not discovered. Willard and I went out, found a clothing store, charged a new suit for him, then went up the street and rented the home where six years later the Jamestown Assembly was born.

Lucy Wilson

There was one Bahá'í town temporarily: Lucy Wilson, Martha Root's lifelong friend. Alice Parker had been my great friend in Pittsburgh and now Lucy, years older, was to become my new friend in this environment. When I think of Alice or Lucy, I feel a glow of warmth in my heart. They were twenty years older than we, perhaps then in their sixties. The personification of subtle wit, understanding, bravery, perceptiveness and loyalty – everything we loved in people – was given to us in Alice and Lucy. To be with them was heaven.

Lucy Wilson, we found, was not won easily from her own excessive shyness, a quality augmented by her physical appearance: small-boned, thin, very delicate. Her manner apologetic, she had an aura of humility and submission and of having suffered.

A trained musician, she had a very sensitive touch on the piano and had lived only by teaching music. She had no students now, no money and very few places to go.

Lucy was a flower that quivered in an atmosphere of love. Willard and I set out to win her, and we asked her to speak of Martha. Lucy opened up like a choice orchid whose inner petals were blue violet with a centre of gold. We persevered because it was evident that love was a part of the Bahá'í life she had been missing, and now she was learning to breathe in it, relax in it, swim in it.

The three of us had very little money. Materially minded people would say that we had no luck. But we knew, because of our love of Bahá'u'lláh, that we were rich. As part of our wealth, we counted Martha's letters to Lucy. The letters came regularly and when Lucy came up our walk, her eyes shining like stars and a smile on her lips, we knew another letter had been stuck in her bag. Precious Lucy. To write of her is to long to see her again.

Finding a New Home

To speak of Lucy first has been a digression. This is how we found our new home: We walked up the street looking for "FOR RENT" signs. There was one on a small duplex, a neat-looking house with brown shingles and white woodwork. No one was at home, so we followed a cobblestone path neatly bordered with flowers to the back of the house and waited on an old-fashioned school bench under a grape arbour. The back yard was enormous and seemed to be a whole street long. The neighbours, too, had great lawns and gardens, and since there were no fences, it was as though they were all one. The rear edging, a sharp incline, was bordered with tall trees. On our yard was a square of twelve fruit trees – cherry, pear and apple. The grape arbour was the size of a small house.

We waited, enjoying the sunshine, until a little grey man appeared. It was Mr Fretz, the owner of the house. He opened the door and we stepped into the house and looked around. On the first floor was a large living room – always an asset to Bahá'ís. There were also a small guest chamber, dining room, bathroom and kitchen. Upstairs we found a large room with a bed and another room with a locked door, behind which was the private world of Mr Fretz himself. We could have the house for $25 a month, if we would take Mr Fretz, too.

Eve Nicklin

At a time before the Guardian's instructions discouraged Bahá'í membership in churches, Eve Nicklin was a deaconess and a superintendent of a church-sponsored orphan asylum in Sheffield, Pennsylvania. Before learning of the Bahá'í Faith, Eve felt "ordained" as a Christian in the children's service. After reading the Word and talking to God, she became a Bahá'í and continued to work at the orphanage.

I had first seen her at the Sekers' while we were living in Pittsburgh. With an unconventional ease, Eve stretched out on the floor to listen to a reading of a newly received book from Shoghi Effendi, "The Goal of a New World Order."[38] She had the air of a gypsy, and we were wondering if she would become a Bahá'í. Howard Ives met her later and taught her more about the Cause.

A short time after we moved to Jamestown, she dropped in with her assistant, Wreatha Cranston,[39] and a few others.

"We brought our own refreshments," she announced. "All we would like is a cup of tea."

Willard and I were embarrassed because all of our cups had cracks in them. We prepared the tea and I set the table, while telling our visitors that our cups had had a very hard life. "If one of you should be so unlucky, you might get the cup that is cracked."

They came to the table and we sat on packing boxes. Our guests all shouted at once, "I've got the cup with the crack!"

Eve's uniform had such a stylish look. She refused, except on ceremonial occasions, to wear the bonnet with the white ties. She wore instead a daring black beret. On this visit, she wore dangling, bright red earrings and a bold plaid suit. The effect produced was picturesque, a bit theatrical. I called her "Garbo."

Eve had considered herself, for two years, a member of the Pittsburgh Bahá'í community, although an often absent one. I had met her on other occasions, but I had never before had the opportunity to get to know her. Not until October, that is, when she came to Jamestown to speak at the Methodist Church to a conference of church workers. I went with her on the first afternoon of the conference. She spoke to half a church full of women about her orphans and swayed them with real magic. She was telling them, in effect, "Abandon what perisheth for an everlasting dominion."

We sat that evening around the little "Cricket Herald" stove and talked until the late hours. Praising Eve, Willard said, "Here

---

38 Shoghi Effendi, *The World Order of Bahá'u'lláh* (Wilmette, IL, Bahá'í Publishing Trust, 1974), pp. 29–50.
39 I visited Eve at the asylum one day in February of 1935 and Wreatha joined the Cause that night. She was twenty-three.

is someone, at last, who comes near to being a real Bahá'í, and it is also a thrill for her to be staying in a Bahá'í home for the first time." With Eve there was not the customary expression of Bahá'í affection between us but rather a detachment so strong in concentration that when our paths crossed it was as though a messenger had been sent with a mystic scroll to be read. Eve Nicklin would return.

The Story Story

Mrs Margaret Story seemed to me to be so much more perfect than I. By her mere presence, she embarrassed me. She was of another class – good shoes, good clothes, good education, and in comparison, I was an example of apparent crudity. And yet, I think I fascinated her.

She was the wife of Mr Chester Story, Sr., Principal of Schenley School. She was President of the local chapter of the American Pen Women and a noted author, having written a book on style, as opposed to fashion. She had written another book and asked me to do the illustrations. I did them and they were approved by the editor, but unfortunately, the book was never published. Had it been, our financial problems would have been solved.

Our friendship began while Willard and I were still living in Pittsburgh. She had invited me to a tea back in early 1934. I had gone, feeling particularly uncomfortable. I was wanting to leave, but I told myself, "You're representing Bahá'u'lláh, not yourself," and with this sophisticated crowd I did not give up being myself. I remember watching Mrs Story and thinking, "This person needs love." Like Mrs Norman Storer of similar social background, I singled her out for the practice of universal love and prayed that I might be able to love her.

When the party broke up and the guests were departing, I summoned my nerve and kissed her. That kiss was the beginning of our friendship and the first of many answers to the prayers. Mrs Story opened up to me, later confiding in me and asking for advice in resolving personal problems. She told me that her friends did not stay with her, and I told her that I was her "Rock of Gibraltar". With me it really was her heart that had blossomed and responded.

We were at another meeting in April, which I described to Lorna:

> Mrs Story was looking rather hard and unapproachable, and I knew that she really was not. You see, I could look into her. I sat beside her after most of the others had gone, and she told me that I was beautiful because of the spiritual light in my face. . . I've become a mysterious person to her. I know something she does not. I'll tell her sometime – have been on the point of it twice, but something interrupted. I woke up last night, prayed for her and went back to sleep, and when I woke up, there she was inside. In a little while she called me – said she was thinking of me and had to call. Just think, my greatest Pittsburgh bugbear, this person who had the power to bruise and break my wings, being in this relationship through the working of 'love and will'! The splendour can be endless as long as there are people in the world to be loved and won.

Now that I was in Jamestown, Mrs Story wrote to me often:

> . . . Just a short time ago I came in from lunching with Alice Parker – so very happy to have her physically near again – How I long to see you with the physical eye as I so very often do in remembrance –
>
> Here in my hands is what I found on my return – a marked copy of "World Order" (what a splendid title – there is so much written on "World Chaos"!). "Through the Invisible" by Doris McKay is a classic – a poem. It is so beautiful it hurts – You were, as you always have been, priceless, in our loving friendship to have me share this, your individually love-inebriated, intuitively self-impregnated expression of a Divine vision. From the purple vault of Sacredly inspired emotion – or more than that, spiritually discerned Beauties, you fling the treasures of your Soul. Yes, darling, I am grateful.

Such a hunger for a visit with you – When are you coming?
Love and love,
    Margaret

About a year later, her husband, Chester, sent for me. It was urgent. She was very sick and had asked for me. I remember hearing in those days a tune on the radio called "Dream a Little Dream of Me". I took the bus to Pittsburgh, and when I arrived at their apartment, I was ushered into the dining room, where all the relatives, both close and distant, had gathered. All waited to be called to her bedside. Quite a formidable group. I sat with them, very much out of place and much looked at. This was not my crowd.

After a time, Mr Story came running out, quite excited and calling out my name. "Peggy is calling for Doris. She promised to come and hasn't arrived yet." Through the opened bedroom door, I could hear Mrs Story raving, screaming my name. Chester found me and escorted me to her bedside. She looked to be frightened and very far gone. I sat on her bed and began saying prayers from memory. I did not know then as many as I do now. I said all that I could, and after a while, she seemed satisfied and weary. While Mr Story and I waited, the minister came. He was from one of the fashionable churches with a socially sophisticated congregation. He came to pray for her soul, but Chester stopped him. "We've already had the service – Bahá'í prayers. Peggy requested Bahá'í prayers."

A few days later, Peggy died. Willard and I received this letter from Chester:

Dear Doris and Willard,
I wish I could write you all I feel about the wonderful help you have both been to me, and to us, for our family circle is not broken, though its best part now reaches into a more serene and lovelier somewhere. I am sorry, Doris, that you had to leave before I had my spiritual revelation of Peggy's soul. I must tell you of my experience. It came in the night as I was lying awake thinking. Somehow, I became conscious of Peggy's soul above me. I realized that in all my life with her I had known only

a tiny section of her spirit in all its beauty and strength and inspiring power. I could almost see her soul, like a great dome above me, sheltering not only me but big enough to cover a multitude. And the message came to me from that soul that it would be always near me to bless and inspire, that it was at peace and happier than ever on earth. Everything resolved, and I could even state it perfectly in words that satisfied me with their logic and sense of calm beauty. Then I fell asleep.

In the morning the words were gone. I have tried often but cannot state the solution as it came to me then – only grope vaguely towards the idea. But the calm feeling persists. All my bitterness and resentment of the summer have gone, all the fear and horror of death. To me now there is a gentleness, a wisdom about that opening of the door to a new and happier world that I can feel but not express. You understand, I believe, for your understanding is so far greater than my own. But I know you will be happy to know that you helped me to find the way to see the truth. And perhaps my experience will strengthen your own knowledge and beliefs...

Chester

Mr Story later told me that when Peggy had called for me asking for Bahá'í prayers, she had said of me, "She is the only one who knows that I have a soul." For me, that is sufficient confirmation of the power of universal love. Now and then that tune enters my head and I say a prayer for Peggy.

Mr Story would remarry in time, and we never heard from him again.

In September of 1934 I had written to Lorna my last impressions of Pittsburgh – of watching the stars from the balcony at 1:00 a.m., seeing the Pleiades. My first month in Jamestown, I was homesick and noted that Alice, Ruth, Eve, Bessie and Mrs Storer, anyone of them, would have looked now like an angel, a star of another heaven. "Here there is nobody," I had written. "Each day is a complete and endless blank. It seems as if bedtime will never come."

Aspects of that first month lingered. Jamestown was a very grey world during the first year. Evelyn Underhill had written in her book, *The Grey World*, "Want of faith in the improbable is really responsible for all that is deliberately dreary in our lives." The improbable that I fought with was the finding of new friends and of teaching. "Somewhere in this population of 45,000," I wrote, "there must be friendships and the conscious need of God. It is hard to break through if one is not very aggressive or to wait if one is not very patient. But I have come back to fight. I am going to find the jewels that He has hidden here."

Meanwhile I continued to give talks[40] and to teach, not in Jamestown, but in Rochester, Geneva, Pittsburgh and Cleveland. I turned forty and noticed the advance of my weight and dress size and felt the physical contrast I made with the younger students in the classes that I continued to take. Lucy Wilson was the only light in this grey world, and in June she would leave to return to Cambridge Springs. The prospect of her leaving was frightening.

The grey world, how I struggled with it! In the spring, I wrote:

> I have eaten all the food in my spiritual cupboard and stare now at bare shelves. Outside of the two Pittsburgh trips, there has been no replenishment for eight months. Now I see that what I had brought with me is gone. I must face an adjustment to the altered conditions. I must 'plow the rock until it bears.' My restlessness is of a vague desire to serve the Cause, not knowing how. Once I asked Mother Beecher what to do and she said, 'Prepare yourself and God will open the way.' Pray that the wisdom will be revealed.

On one of the Pittsburgh visits, replenishment had come from Emogene Hoagg. Those days were without flaw. Mrs Storer was away so it was decided that we were to stay with the Sekers at our old Homewood address. The Sekers gave us the warmest,

---

40 Many of those talks were given in the Black churches in Pittsburgh.

sweetest welcome and I enjoyed every minute of the two nights we were there.

On the first night, Emogene and I talked until three o'clock in the morning and found that we saw eye to eye in all matters mystical. We decided that "attainment" depends upon complete, constant and unflinching servitude. Servitude even in sleep, servitude in our prayers, in our work, in our going out and coming in. She was as delicate and pure as my intuition had told me. She was a passionate lover of the Beloved of the world and her heart seemed broken with her love for Him.

Emogene was very frail in body and she was not very eloquent or dynamic. Yet there was a blue fire in her eyes as she talked. Her three meetings in Pittsburgh were thoughtful and searching rather than brilliant. The people who came wanted to talk, and they asked many questions. We took turns in answering. We spent Friday and Saturday nights at the Browns', and I later stayed with Alice. My prayers then went west with Emogene. I wrote, "Now she will belong to me the way Alice and Lucy belong to me."

Mrs Storer returned before I went back to Jamestown. We had several long talks about the Cause, the law of cohesiveness bringing us into a closer relationship – part of the machinery of love.

After completing my first year in Jamestown, I looked back and observed:

> I have learned to be alone, to live happily on a little solid island in the midst of social nothingness. My occasional trips to the mainland have shown me an added power and poise. That study in the College Center is the only other gain. Willard has gotten on top of his work and made a good record for himself. We can't see far ahead, but this must be part of some big picture – one of those jigsaw pieces you can't fit in until you see some more of the design.

In November 1935, at the encouragement of my English teacher, I began to write a longer work. A novel, he called it. *Hole in the Wall* was about Homewood. Homewood had been a hole – a hole in which to hide and a hole to get out of. We all have a personal Homewood, and the theme of the novel was escape – escape from the living spiritual reality which lies one step beyond the day-to-day sordidness. It was about how we tend to submerge our inner life under outer interests which, in time, define for us our world. My schoolwork, for example. In hiding in our personal Homewood this way, we become less sensitive to beauty and become physically remote and somehow estranged from God. In the newly published translation of the *Gleanings* I read, "Know ye that by 'the world' is meant your unawareness of Him Who is your Maker, and your absorption in aught else but Him... Whatsoever deterreth you, in this Day, from loving God is nothing but the world."[41]

Gleanings. The book was a present from Neysa Bissell on her farewell visit. She responded early to the call of the first Seven Year Plan and pioneered to Rutland, Vermont. Willard and I started each day by reading a section of it at breakfast and when we were finished, we started again. During the first five days, I read until I reached the point where I not only wept but shook. These Writings filled me alternately with terror and with joy and with the presence of Bahá'u'lláh. His Words threw me into agonized self-searching such as would the prospect of death. Yes, that is it. If we truly read them, we face eternity, while at the same time we see the world with a lucidity that gives us a pain behind the eyes like that of too-bright sunshine on snow. Interspersed are essences of protection, of a great heart beating, and of loving helpful angels whose task is to inspire, answer our prayers, comfort and guide us. I was so moved by the import of the publication of the book that I saw it to be the "the big event" I had been waiting for. I told Lorna, "It is the Scriptures raised to the nth power."

---

41 *Gleanings from the Writings of Bahá'u'lláh.* Trans. Shoghi Effendi (Wilmette, IL, Bahá'í Publishing Trust, 1949), p. 276.

Martha Root: "Thou art ever pervading the universe."

On August 3rd, 1936, I wrote in my diary:

> Willard is away teaching at Louhelen summer school. Today I was meditating as I worked on some quotations to be used in the Green Acre devotions – quotations on the marked contrast between spiritual consciousness and our comfortable earthly reactions. I thought of the latter as the world of make-believe; children playing with dolls, getting frightened in the dark. An imaginary built-up existence with playhouse tasks and dark-corner boogies. People read novels, go to the movies and play games to escape still farther into the world of make-believe; it is a form of semi-life and few people dare to venture into the Real World.
>
> Then I thought of the spiritual world as a medium in which you have to learn to maintain yourself. You are ascending in a balloon. The cords are released. If you hover too near the tree-tops you throw out sandbags. To stay up you must not carry too much weight. We have to have the 'thinness' of air if we would penetrate, while still in the earth consciousness, 'the realms of the unseen'.
>
> Yet, miraculous as it may seem, we do belong to those transcendent heights. How to exist there? By forming habits of prayer, working with the spirit of worship, reading the Word, teaching the Faith by word and deed.
>
> A very lovely thing happened this afternoon. Martha Root and Lucy Wilson drove over from Cambridge Springs and we had an hour to visit together. With Martha's dear sympathetic presence, I felt expanded. I was simply on fire, happy beyond all belief, eloquent, loving, free of shyness. Oh, to be like that and to make others experience, if only for an hour, eternal life!
>
> Something BIG happened. 'Abdu'l-Bahá had said that He saw His Father's face in the faces of those who came to Him and that was the reason they came forth from His presence radiant. Martha did that to me today, and I know that she and Lucy carried away a picture of my true self that few see.

It was heavenly. Nothing must ever happen to make me forget.

Nothing has made me forget that time, and I need to say more about it.

On that afternoon I was sitting in the garden among the flowers. Except for the stimulation of my own thoughts and meditations, it was a rather typical Jamestown afternoon – rather boring. I looked up and saw two approaching figures, Lucy Wilson and Martha Root. I had known that Martha was coming sometime because of the letters Lucy had shared with us.

Martha had prayed that her work wouldn't be incapacitated by ill health. That was the word she used: "incapacitated". Now, in the opinion of the Guardian, Martha was incapacitated. She was worn out by a long struggle against ill health combined with tireless exertion. The Guardian left it now in the hands of a committee of the National Spiritual Assembly to decide when Martha, our most cherished teacher, was to be allowed to start on her trip to India. She was told to recuperate, to rest.

On the day that they visited, Martha seemed elated to have had a legitimate reason to rest. I was pleased that she was so relaxed and happy. Later I told Willard that she was like a little girl who needed pampering, and I felt a need to do things for her. I discovered that many people were feeling this way. People who were arranging her meetings. People who were working for her. All wanted to spoil her. Our feeling for her was tenderness. With her I felt that the spiritual powers were playing with us as though she were a window through which poured the "all-pervading influence". We experienced a different atmosphere, a different vibration. This was sheer magic. Everyone who had contact with her felt a rising spirit. We all seemed to be touched by her power. She looked at us with such love that we would have believed anything she said. She looked at everyone with a look that goes beyond acknowledgment. It was a look of recognition that made us know of ourselves as better than normally we thought we were. Her look and love elevated us. This was the atmosphere of the vibrating influence of the Holy Spirit released by her faith and actions. It was very much out of this world, and I only wish that I could express it more clearly and credibly.

Martha and Lucy were like two schoolgirls on vacation, joking and laughing on the start of a journey. They were looking for something to do that was fun and they invited me to come to Cambridge Springs. There, Martha could show me her life as it had been.

I stayed at Lucy's house but spent hours every day with Martha. In this little town in the Allegheny Hills were the roots of Martha's heart. She was devoted to her memories of her people and to her brother and his family. It had been a keen personal sacrifice to be away for years at a time from this environment, and now she was exultant and happy at being home again, so much so that she wanted to share her happiness with Lucy and me.

Early the first morning, Martha came to take me to the Polish college where she used to teach English in her pre-Pittsburgh days. This was one of two Polish institutions in the United States designed to keep the culture of the 'old country' alive by educating young men in the language and traditions of Poland. The buildings were in a wooded, hilly section, and we approached them by a wooden bridge crossing over a ravine. Martha was welcomed by her friend, the bearded principal, who explained that because of the summer vacation, the students and teachers were away. It was an unlikely and dreamlike environment with portraits of Polish heroes staring at us from the walls of the long corridors.

The next day we sat with Martha's brother and his wife in the Baptist church where, many years ago, Martha had been denounced publicly by the minister of those days – the very place, probably the very pew, where this shattering experience came to Martha. How her heart must have broken when her townspeople withdrew from her!

That night we went to supper at her home, and the neighbours were invited to a meeting. Martha, the world traveller, was treated now with honour and respect, even if the people still held to their old ways and did not accept Bahá'u'lláh. A few gathered in the country sitting room, but Martha became ill and asked me to speak to the people.

The next morning she started out on foot to show me more of the town. On the way to her brother's grocery store, again she became suddenly ill, had an attack and had to lean for a few minutes against a tree until her strength came back. Then we went on – the same cheerful, enthusiastic Martha! The next day there was dinner at Lucy's with two Bahá'ís from New Castle, Pennsylvania.

Twice during the fall and winter Martha came to Jamestown, a short train-ride from Cambridge Springs. She was with us about a month. That winter of 1936 may have been the most difficult test of her entire Bahá'í life. She felt impelled to go to India and was slowly getting to feel that perhaps this was not to be. She was disturbed. The lack of physical activity transformed that disturbance into rather unpleasant states. She became more and more depressed and increasingly restless as she waited to hear from the committee. The power of the spirit around her seemed to have relaxed a bit. She was not getting the rest she was supposed to have. Why was she not told to start, she wondered. Why had not Horace Holley and the others corresponded? Why did not the Guardian tell her to go? He had always advised her before.

On the visits to Jamestown, ever self-denying, Martha took the least expensive room in the hotel. She lived on buns and tea made with hot water from the bathroom tap. When I came to see her, I would bring some fruit and we would share the food lying on the bed talking about "the Beloved" and about the Guardian. I have heard that Martha's relationship to him was motherly. They, the two hard-driving workers, were concerned about each other's health. One day I found Martha shedding bitter tears. The hoped-for letter with the permission for her to be on her way still had not arrived. Martha Root wept in my arms.

Eve Nicklin returned in September. She had been with us for a few days in the spring, and while she was away from the orphan asylum, her supervisor had opened some of her Bahá'í mail. Eve was in trouble because her job was with the Methodist Church and the woman who had opened the mail was not very warm about it. She had called in Eve's two assistants, Wreatha (a Bahá'í) and Betty (about to become a Bahá'í). Eve eventually lost her job with the Church, the job for which she had been trained. Now she was living in Rochester, working as a housekeeper. She told us how she had been saving money from her paltry wages; how she had been preparing to offer herself as a pioneer to Peru. As she described her intentions, Willard and I exchanged a glance which needed no words. We gave Eve one of the two hairs of Bahá'u'lláh that Martha Root had given Willard after his southern tour with Louis Gregory. Eve was leaving Jamestown to consult with members of the National Assembly about pioneering. But this Eve, of the daring black beret and bright red earrings, had left her lipstick at home. She fretted, "I'm sure they won't take me without my lipstick." I made a concoction from cinnamon candy which worked as a poor substitute.

Eve was accepted and became the second pioneer to leave from Jamestown for South America. (John Stearns, whom I will introduce later, was the first.) I saw Eve several years ago in the movie *The Green Light Expedition*. Hand of the Cause Rúḥíyyih Khánum had called her "the Mother of Peru".

More Lessons in The Power of Prayer

January 29th, 1937

I credit the change to the prayers of Dorothy Baker. Of course, there had been my own, too. In the spring of 1936 I had prayed for a miracle. Something inhibited my love for the people, and I told myself, through my diary,

> I never want to be anywhere again where we are not known as Bahá'ís from the start. That is what made Pittsburgh such a happy hunting ground. It is a harmful thing to have to inhibit the Cause."

I was asking God for a miracle, to manipulate events that would break the spiritual ice in Jamestown. The miracle was given.

Dorothy came in January 1937, full of the spirit of faith and purity of aim and intention. Willard and I had been in Jamestown for more than three years. We had little money and were down in our inspiration. We were the "righteous", while Dorothy was of the "near ones."[42] We had had our fill of firesides and meetings to which no one responded, and we had had our fill of giving invitations to the unaccepting.

When we told Dorothy of our situation, she suggested that we say the invocation of "Yá Alláh El-Mustagháth." I hesitated, "But Dorothy, that prayer is to be used only in dire circumstances, life and death situations."

Dorothy looked at us and said, "What greater calamity than for Doris and Willard to have spent three years in this town with no result?"

Dorothy washed her hands, and she and Willard said the prayers. I had the flu so I did not go through all the prostrations with them. Ninety-five times they called, "Yá Alláh El-Mustagháth." We would know, in a relatively short time, the answers to the prayers.

Meanwhile Martha Root had returned from Cambridge Springs and was again staying at the hotel. The day before, I had invited Dorothy to meet her for lunch. Dorothy was stirred and excited at the prospect of meeting this Bahá'í teacher who was back from one of her trips. I planned to have them meet at the YMCA restaurant. Martha and I went there and watched for Dorothy.

She swept into the room looking lovely, triumphant, like an angel. I introduced them to each other in some ordinary way. "Martha, here is someone you would like to meet: Dorothy Baker." Visibly, Dorothy was the prominent one, distinctive in her dress. In contrast, Martha's style lacked style and was unassumingly plain.

---

42 "The good deeds of the righteous are the sins of the Near Ones." *Some Answered Questions*. Trans. Laura Clifford Barney (New Delhi, Bahá'í Publishing Trust, 1973), p. 126.

But Dorothy saw with the spiritual eye and recognized Martha's station, for she showed in her presence such a submission, such a humility of spirit. She watched Martha's every move and anticipated serving her in any way that she could. It was a very noticeable attitude, similar to that of 'Abdu'l-Bahá's in the Tablet of Visitation:

> Make me as dust in the pathway of Thy loved ones, and grant that I may offer up my soul for the earth ennobled by the footsteps of Thy chosen ones in Thy path, O Lord of Glory in the Highest.

Martha spoke at the YMCA. A cousin of Paul Haney's mother was on the Board, and we had used her name to get the room for the meeting. She spoke on Oneness or some other seemingly inoffensive subject, but later we were told that the Board was disturbed that we had held a Bahá'í meeting there. The Secretary said to us, "We thought you were Brahmans. Now that we have found out that you are Bahá'ís, we hope there won't be any more of your talks here." Ironically, I was a member of a social club of world-minded people devoted to the oneness of mankind, and as a member of that club I was later invited to speak at the YMCA and to give the Bahá'í message directly. I was not embarrassed at all, for I was not speaking under YMCA auspices. I guess Martha's prominence had caused more publicity than they wanted.

Last Sight of Martha

When it was decided at last that Martha was able to start out again, she flew like a bird from a cage.

I went down to the train station to see her off. She was there, and yet she wasn't. This was the atmosphere again. This was my one experience of the presence of another world of spiritual heat that the mystics talk about. It was a winter day, not at all warm, and yet I felt a heavenly and delightful rise of temperature within me as I searched for her face in the coach windows. I found her, and it was as though my physical heart was on fire. I boarded the train and joined her. Martha had her usual bunch of packages, seemingly excessive in number. We used to have bags that we put things into, paper bags with handles, and Martha had an unusual supply of them – a cheaper way to travel without luggage. I gave her a basket of fruit, and she told me that she was going to share it with the other passengers. I soon heard the warning of the conductor, bade her farewell and left the train.

Martha was going on an expedition more glorious than any she had taken before. Two years later, in Australasia, her legs gave out. Cancer had reached her bones and she died in terrible pain. I found a copy of a letter that I had written to her in which I had begged her to give her pain to Bahá'u'lláh as a martyr's ransom, that we might know, as she did, the fire of the love of God.

When she died, the editor of *The Bahá'í World* asked me to write about her. Martha Root. How ever was I to sum her up? I sat down at my writing table and asked, "Martha, what do you want me to say of your life?" And she answered, "Love. Write about love." After all, Martha was under obligation to spread the love of God among the Bahá'ís first, then among the nations. She had the experience of it and could not live without it. It was out of this world. Martha wrote the article through me, through the "interpenetration of spirit."[43]

After Dorothy and Martha left, I continued to suffer intensely, imagining all too clearly the futility of our lives in Jamestown. Later, we would see that the effects of Dorothy's prayers of El-Mustagháth were the beginnings of the Jamestown Assembly. The lives of at least four people were influenced dramatically at about the time the prayers were said.

---

43 It was May Maxwell who introduced me to the concept of interpenetration of spirits, but I believe its origins are with Evelyn Underhill, who wrote in one of her books, "The interpenetration of human spirits is a mere shadow of the deep and actual penetration and influence of God on souls."

The first was John Stearns. He had lost his wife through divorce and was mourning the loss of her love. John was looking for company and new ideas and told us that he was attracted to us by our happiness. (He had wondered how people so poorly dressed could be so cheerful!)

We contrived to ask John to drive us to Green Acre, offering to pay for his gas and oil, and he accepted. Once there, we let the atmosphere of the Bahá'í school work its magic. But John was distant, not an easy person to get to know. He was not very sociable and did not join us. One day I saw him sitting on his bed in one of the rooms at the Inn. He did not look like the rest of us. His eyes were like cold fish eyes. He was so forlorn. I went to my room and prayed that he would have soft eyes. Those prayers were answered. John started reading Bahá'í books that he took out from the library. He became fascinated with *The Dawn-Breakers* and took to carrying it around with him. He opened up, developed soft eyes and later became a Bahá'í. John would become Jamestown's first pioneer, moving to Ecuador. His fascination with *The Dawn-Breakers* attracted the attention of Greg Wooster, who later borrowed the book and became confirmed by reading it.

Freddy Reis was John's cousin. At the time of Dorothy's prayers, Freddy suffered the loss of his job. John hired him and introduced him and his wife, Audrey, to the Faith. Vivian ('Vivo') Lawson, a violin student, was number four. Her loss was that of her father. She became attracted to the Faith and began coming to meetings.

After Dorothy and Martha's visit, Willard and I began to say every evening 'Abdu'l-Bahá's Prayer for the Northeastern States. No matter what company we had or what event might be happening, we excused ourselves, retired from the living room, and said the prayer. Ken Christian was once visiting from Binghamton before pioneering to Greece. He claimed that the room shook, vibrated, when we were saying the prayer.

Doris and Horace Holley came in May 1937. There was a marked increase in warmth on the part of all who were present to hear Horace speak. We prayed for all the speakers. Before he was to talk, Horace asked me for suggestions. I told him, "Anything you say will be all right. All of the Bahá'ís will be praying for you." He gave his strange laugh and spoke to them. When he came back, I said it was a good talk. "Why shouldn't it have been? How could there have been any mistakes with everyone praying for it?" I had prayed that he would be inspired out of his intellectual and administrative reaction to the Faith, and I noted in my diary, "A delightful social contact was established. ... the minds had been stimulated. Now I want the hearts to be touched."[44]

The hosting of study classes had been a goal of mine since our first week in Jamestown. Now there were enough people interested in the Faith to invite to meetings. Wilfrid ("Willo") Barton, a believer from Detroit, had joined us. I remember the evening of our first study class.

On that night Willard, Willo and I sat for the holding of the meeting and, as usual, no one came. We had made some wonderful refreshments for the introduction of the study class. The house was polished and clean and surely, after all of those prayers, they would come. We waited, and they did not come. The appointed time passed, and they did not come. I was so disappointed, my spirit crashed and I began to cry. I talked of giving up. We had tried so hard, and this was to be a big occasion – so many had been invited. I was rescued by Willo's inspired power.

He grabbed me heartily in his arms and ordered me to have faith and to stop giving up and to stop crying. We looked out again from the little back porch. Sure enough, at eight o'clock, when it was getting dark, we saw a group of people – a small crowd – coming up the street. In it were John Stearns and

---

44 I had a similar incident in Toronto with John Robarts. He was just a good member of the community then, not a Hand of the Cause. I was asked to speak and had not had time to prepare or think about a talk. John said he would pray for me. I told him not to pray for me, but to pray for my audience. "They are the ones who need prayers," I said. In introducing me, John told them what I had said, and that became the life of the meeting.

Dorothy Ferguson, whom we had known at the College Center, and there were others. All of our contacts were coming at once! That was the beginning. Some of them declared later and became members of the "Jamestown Fireside" which grew to become a group of thirty people.

There was one woman who became a Bahá'í through the influence of a dream. She dreamt that we had surrounded her and were chanting "Bahá'í, Bahee, Baho, Bahum". Her dreams persisted until she declared. Later, that chant would become our Jamestown cheer, heard often at the end of our Feasts.

But the successes were less constant than my struggles – struggles which continued to search for a different, more interior, victory. There were many nights in which I experienced the "dark night of the soul". It was a time of severe testing for me, and I fought on by developing new ways of rededicating myself to God and by experimenting with Christian mysticism and the focus of my energies. I made schedules or programs of discipline that I would put myself on for periods of nineteen days, after which I would evaluate their effects, a practice I would long continue. Some of the schedules included physical exercise and times set aside for writing. All were founded on repetition of Bahá'í prayers and meditation. I remember one in which I would go up to the attic and prostrate myself in prayer, putting my head in literal dust. I wrote,

> It was the catnip my spirit wanted. I built more of a habitual attitude toward my spiritual goals with my head in the dust during those thirty minutes than I could have learned in a month of ordinary effort. The feel of it is in me, the feel of supplication and nothingness."

This became my "upper room", and soon I began trying to translate those special prayers into service. I experimented with the household tasks that I had always hated and had wanted to neglect. I tried to carry them out with the same spirit of supplication. In my relationships with others, I concentrated on the spirit of worship and on refusing to allow myself to descend to an ordinary human plane. My notes tell me that I found myself much more helpful to others. There is no mention of success with the home chores.

The personal struggle for discipline and the maintenance of an altitude of spirit and the practice of universal love is a theme I once described in this way: "Love is the wind in my sails, but now I am becalmed. I am drifting away from the use of love and falling back on ordinary practicality and logic and finding them inadequate." While I was acutely aware of and sensitive to my own lack of progress and failings, I was also unnecessarily aware of it in others. I felt like I did when I had overconfidently confronted May Maxwell with her intimidation of the two sisters. This is one self-awareness that always is accompanied by pain. This is my darker side, which often forgets events like the fireside that Dorothy Baker gave at the Woosters' in 1939.

Many were attracted to this meeting. Forty-one attended, twenty-six non-Bahá'ís. Dorothy's talk was so brilliant, I felt so humble. Evelyn found me afterward and said, "Dorothy's talk was inspired, but do you know that it is the love you have been showering upon us that moves our spirits." That, of course, is what I was needing to hear. We try to maintain a constant altitude of spirit and experience a roller coaster through troughs of despair and glorious heights of nearness.

After the fireside Dorothy and I sat up until four o'clock in the morning, and she revealed her heart to me. When we had said our 'good night' she threw me three or four kisses and slipped away to her room. Then she came running back to place 'Abdu'l-Bahá's prayer beads in my hand, the ones He used the day He died. She told me she had bared her heart to me as to no other human being.

The growth of the Cause in Jamestown would quicken in time. After a while it seemed that there were declarations at each Feast. Twenty new believers by the time we pioneered to Canada.

Finances

While we were in Jamestown, Willard worked at Sears Roebuck. He was now farm machinery and garden supplies manager, making a dollar a week more than he had in Pittsburgh. At one time his boss asked him if he would take on extra work, work which would require him to go to the store several evenings. "I won't have a lot of time," he said, and asked me what he should do. We were not without our financial worries, but I told Willard, "No." He disliked his job very much, and that was the answer he was hoping for. Ironically, it was I who would begin to work in the evenings. Earlier in the fall, I had offered to teach a class at the College Center in Commercial Art. I had written to the President enclosing a proposed course outline.

One day a simple-looking man came to our door. I greeted him by saying, "No, I don't want to buy a vacuum cleaner." There had been several salesmen calling that week. He said, "I am the College President, and I have come to discuss your application to teach." In spite of my welcome, he gave me the job. I would be earning a $1.00 an hour or $8.00 a week. I taught that class for four years. Willard's income was still low, but this extra money was reserved for Bahá'í purposes. We stored the bills in the pages of Maeterlinck's *The Treasure of the Humble*.

When twenty, thirty, or more people began showing up for meetings and firesides, all of the money went for refreshments. It takes a bit of planning to have tea and cookies or cake for so many people. Our contribution to the Fund was normally very, very low. I remember having some money left over once and being able to send a cheque for the enormous amount of four dollars to the Temple fund. I wrote to Horace Holley at one point. I told him that we were spending money for our firesides and asked, "What do you advise? We can't give to the Temple." He wrote back and said that the National Assembly was pleased that we were having the meetings and to continue them.

Our finances were small and tight, but we never became frantic. We were always assured. Normally others paid for, or assisted, our travel to this or that Bahá'í school or meeting where we were teaching. I still have a letter from Willard written to me from Louhelen, where he was giving a course. He had had an offer to teach elsewhere in Michigan. He wrote to ask if he would be justified in spending the six dollars required for the bus ticket. He felt he had to write to get my approval.

The Jamestown summers, summers of the late 1930s, followed a pattern. My classes would break. I would go to Convention and later teach at Green Acre. In 1936 I taught Public Speaking. My Creative Writing Outline was approved and published, and I used it at Green Acre in 1937, and in 1938, Willard and I taught Comparative Religion. Prayers and Meditations was the subject we taught in 1939. And for several years, Willard taught at Louhelen.

At nearby Lake Chatauqua there was a summer music program. We would go and enjoy performances such as Gilbert and Sullivan's *Gondaliers*. These summers were reminiscent of our cultural revellings in Geneva. Lorna Tasker came to visit in August 1937. She noted in her diary:

> August 1. John Stearns took us to see the Davises. Mrs Davis asked about our religion and we had a chance to talk about it.
>
> August 5. Mr Stearns took us to Chatauqua for a concert.
>
> August 6. Mrs Howes came and we had a lovely afternoon with her. She read some of her poems. That night I wrote 'The Perfect Answer'.
>
> August 7. Willard and Doris and I had a beautiful evening at home. Ate ice cream and peaches, played chess, read poetry and a chapter in Davis' *Capitalism and Its Culture*, also Willard read the Word, as he did every night...
>
> August 8. We had seen the movie *The Good Earth*. Eleanor Eckbert came after breakfast and talked about Christian Science...

August 14. We left Jamestown to go to Hartford.

August 18. We were in Beverly [Massachusetts]. Doris was working on her Creative Writing Course] which she will give at Green Acre.

National Convention, 1938: The Departure of Grace Ober

As soon as the 1938 Convention opened, I knew why Harlan had asked Lorna to pray for it. There was, he said, a "special reason". Some believers with weak heads for the Administration had been making trouble. They had sent a circular letter criticizing and accusing the National Spiritual Assembly and actually had travelled to many local Assemblies with the intention of broadcasting their views. The Guardian had cabled and had called it a crisis. Before the Convention proceeded, this matter had to be brought out and the delegates had to speak their minds. It took nearly two days.

It was the third time I had been present when this spirit of opposition swept all business out of the way. It made me feel as if the earth might quake and the stars tremble in heaven! The second day I heard that two older, wonderful Bahá'ís had been mixed up in it. 'Abdu'l-Bahá had known them and had honoured them. That night in bed I wept, suffering with deep disillusion. But I prayed on till peace came.

After the election on Friday, tension cleared. Earlier, one of the women had been handing out a list of names of people to vote for. Now, the voting over, the agitation quieted. But the delegates were muddled and confused, and we never did get much business done. We had to learn, belatedly, that Bahá'í laws are to be obeyed. We felt our condition to be a divine rebuke. Then, on Saturday morning, just as we were leaving for lunch, came the news of the death of Munírih Khánum, wife of 'Abdu'l-Bahá. The Riḍván Feast was called off and for once, we were still and quiet before the Throne.

At the end of the afternoon session, Grace Ober took her departure to the celestial realm. It was time for reports from the travelling teachers, and Grace was called to report of her work in Louisville, Kentucky. She flared up in the brilliant way she had and called for pioneers. She told funny stories and coaxed the people. She took us with her as she described her teaching activities. It was as if her soul were a ransom that we might be awakened. She finished the talk, sat down and slumped over in her chair.

She was carried out, and the Convention continued. Harlan, chairing the session, called for more reports. Then Dr True came to the door of the hall and called for healing prayers, and Harlan leapt down from the platform and raced out of the hall. Grace was taken into a small room and the door closed. We could hear Harlan chanting the Greatest Name in a powerful voice. A Black girl fainted. The Convention sat obediently in its seats, prayed and wept and at last experienced unity. Dr True was addressing us from the doorway. "Friends, will you say the prayer for the departed?" I was then standing with my arm around Mabel Ives. It was if an electric shock went through her. But she rallied and so did Harlan, who had exchanged a few words with Grace before she left him.

Another event also marked the 1938 Convention. On the 25th of March, 1937, Shoghi Effendi announced his marriage to Mary Maxwell. Her mother, May, had come back from Haifa to attend the Convention. The first session was waiting to begin when she and her niece, Jeanne Bolles, entered the hall. We stood until they were seated. Now, more than ever, May was our mystery. Whatever had been her inner experience, she had moved away from us into a realm of detachment. At least it seemed that way to me. When I talked to her, I knew no longer how she was feeling.

May seemed to glide rather than walk as she moved through the ranks of her friends. She had moved away from us. My instinctive practice of detachment from the temptation of being dazed by her and thus forgetting God was a protection.

It allowed me to realize that her personality had withdrawn. Someone wrote to me weeks later commenting that she was still "the same May", but I was never to see this. Our paths lay in different directions. My eyes were on her lovingly, from afar, and I was resigned to the distance between us, resigned except for a sadness.

I recalled that May had said once that Lua [Getsinger], her teacher, was really great because she never deserted a soul to whom she had given birth. She was there as long as that soul needed her.

On the last morning of the Convention I stood with the other leave-taking Bahá'ís in the corridor of Foundation Hall. May, walking alone, was coming toward us. We stood silent. For a moment she stopped by my side and whispered in my ear, "Doris, our hearts will never be separated!" Even now, I write these words with tears of gratitude and praise to God.

1939 Was Different

I looked at the people in Foundation Hall. So many of them, filling that great nine-sided room. I thought, "Suppose every one of us should become ablaze and, by the grace of God, drop off all our limitations and all sense of the lower self? Could we ever do it?" Already the pressure of the Divine World was painful in its insistence. I noted:

> I am seeing in a few people the apostolic spirit. It flashes suddenly like sunlight on a keen flexible sword. It is not a soft light.
> Saturday was the anniversary of Grace Ober's passing. In the afternoon I was sitting by myself on one of the seats along the wall. As I sat alone, I had the experience of smelling attar of roses. This heavenly fragrance came and went in waves. It wasn't steady. It was a moving fragrance coming in gusts. I looked up at the clock and noted that it was three o'clock. Mabel Ives was sitting as a delegate, and I passed her a note: 'Grace died at this hour a year ago. Please stop the Convention and ask for a

prayer mentioning her name.' Mabel stood up, raising her hand with a commanding signal to stop, and called for the prayer. The delegates sat in silent prayer and then quietly went on with their business. The mysterious fragrance faded gently away, and I knew that Grace said, "Thank you." About four hours later, the fragrance of attar returned while I was having dinner with Mabel and some friends from Toronto. We were talking about Grace – how at one of the Conventions of the Depression, the difficult appeal was made for funds for the temple dome. It was Grace who spoke. She stood with arms raised, hands together above her head and she pleaded for the temple, "Clothe me, clothe me." That was the year that Fred Schopflocher responded with a gift of $100,000. Again the rose perfume enveloped me. It was incredibly strong. My eyes met those of the Toronto girls. They were having the same experience.

The big thing I got from this Convention was that at last, the Bahá'ís, in general, were fully awake, dedicated and hard-working. And that these were very precious days for the immediate spreading of the Teachings.

After Convention I rode with Dorothy Baker to Cleveland. We felt a strong tie between us, and she commented that I was like her twin. We did not understand each other particularly well; we just wanted to cry when we heard the other's name mentioned. Dorothy was then a thoroughly awake and radiant maidservant of God, soaring in a continuous and swift flight in the heavenly atmosphere.

I stayed with the Coles in Cleveland and visited with Emogene Hoagg.

These were precious days. 1939 was a boom year of intense activity and fruitful writing. Before going to Convention, I had noted how precious they were. I wrote to Lorna:

> [Jan. 1939] My writing for the Cause is being confirmed. Efforts meeting with enthusiastic approval. I have six private drawing pupils and two more starting Saturday. Everything seems to move without effort or stress: the writing, the artwork, the fan-

ning of the Assembly. And why not, if it is the Divine Power that is allowed to manifest?

[Feb.] We have had fourteen at our last two study classes, all possible prospects. I have had an article on 'The Bahá'í Faith: What Is It?' in the first column, first page, of *The Graccian Magazine*, which is passed out to at least six centres of businessmen who club together to study one another's ideas. They live in six different towns around here. 'Time does not fly, it flows.' Snowed under with people coming to see us, and with things I have to write. No time...

[March] After starting this letter to you, the telephone rang and events just tumbled over one another like puppies from 11:00 a.m. to midnight... Life is so strenuous, sometimes I feel all stretched out...

[April] Since Christmas I have done ten book reviews for the Publicity Committee and four *World Order* articles. I am going to try hard to write six radio talks for Mrs Morton before Convention, but I am afraid there isn't time. Have been asked to speak in Geneva and Canadargia, so will dash over and right back for the forming of our Assembly on the 21st. What great and wonderful days these are...

On April 21st, Riḍván, we elected the first Spiritual Assembly of Jamestown. Mabel Ives came clown from Toronto to join the celebration.

First International Picnic, July 1939

We crossed the lake on a steamer. Seventy-two people gathered near Brock's Monument (Brockville, Ontario); more than half were either new Bahá'ís or newly attracted. Howard, very feeble and greatly aged, came down from Toronto in his longing to meet his Jamestown grandchildren. It seemed as if the living

Presence had moved into him, like the Friend into His house. He had lived so much with the Word in his writing of *Portals to Freedom* this year and last that, almost unconsciously, he spoke the Word instead of his own language. He took the Jamestown people aside and poured out his love, tenderness and counsel on all of us. We had invited a middle-aged Syrian rug dealer, Namaan Hadbeh, to go with us. He used to live in Haifa and had met 'Abdu'l-Bahá. Howard took him in his arms, called him by his first name and questioned him tenderly. He told all the Jamestown Bahá'ís that he knew all of them by name and was eagerly interested in all of them. He said that he thought the sense of kinship he felt was because of the special closeness that he and I had between us. Howard told them that he prayed every day for all of them. They loved him. He took down the walls of his heart and gave them his whole life in those brief moments.

The picnic was a typical Ives idea. It was a real "get together" in other significant ways, too. There was some consultation, and it was agreed that the travel teacher circuit, which included Pennsylvania and New York, would be extended to include neighbouring Canadian Bahá'í communities and that we would concentrate on exchanging teachers. It was also an occasion for the Bahá'í youth of both countries to meet one another, and at this picnic the first youth conference was planned. It would be held later in Jamestown. I think that it was at this picnic that I met the youthful Lloyd Gardner and his brother Cliff. They taught me how to make "proper" tea. Another youth, Grace Ober's nephew, was also there – John Robarts. The picnic was truly a cross-border event signalling an increase in shared teaching activity.

Prelude to Pioneering

The sequence of events that led to our becoming Canadian pioneers began in 1939. Howard and Mabel Ives were then living and teaching in Toronto. Because of her enthusiasm, Mabel was a genius at finding work for other Bahá'ís. In July, I wrote to Lorna:

I have said 'yes' to an as yet unofficial proposal to take charge of the Bahá'í booth at the Toronto Fair [Canadian National Exhibition or CNE] for two weeks starting Aug. 25th. Mabel Ives says the Committee will write me, offering me a room – in the house with the Ives – and $35.00 to cover other expenses. Rosemary Sala is to be asked also. It seems to be taken out of my hands with the expenses covered that way, and already I am anticipating the experience.

With the exception of our teaching trip of 1928 and our visit with the Maxwells in Montreal, I had never been in a Canadian city. I was starry-eyed about the opportunity to serve in a "foreign" land. The Canadian Union Jack flags were floating – and before this I had known only the 'Stars and Stripes'! And there was a difference in the people which I found charming, a story-book quality. I was to stay at Laura Davis' house at 44 Chestnut Park, where the Ives had a living arrangement and there were other Bahá'í roomers in the three-storey brick mansion.

Every morning after breakfast, it was like going out to work, taking a trolley for the long ride to the Fair grounds. In a leisurely way, the public walked past our booth. There was an exhibit of washing machines across the aisle, which represented for us the "worldly things" in contrast to what we had to offer. Against a backdrop of a rising sun, a white model of the Wilmette Temple sat on a table. There was a table with flowers, cases with Bahá'í books displayed. As each group of stragglers came by, I thought, "What will they choose, this life or the next?"

I remember one night when a small group formed opposite the booth. It was led by someone from an evangelical rally. I knew I had cause to be nervous when the "mob" started to move toward the booth.

The leader approached and asked me, "Who is the prophet of the Bahá'ís?"

"Bahá'u'lláh, the Glory of God," I replied.

"Is Bahá'u'lláh buried?"

"Yes, He died in 1892."

"But is He still buried?" he demanded.

"Why yes, of course."

"Well, Christ is not! Christ ROSE from the dead. Your prophet cannot be who He claims to be, because He is buried."

Fortunately, a policeman arrived who ordered the group to move on.

At Chestnut Park I expanded under the loving concern of the four hosts: Howard and Mabel, and Laura and Victor Davis. Another member of the family was Laura's mother, Mrs Violet Romsey. There was a painting in the house by Romsey, the famous English artist of the last century – a connection of which her family was proud. Mrs Romsey was a member of the first Bahá'ís group in Toronto, years before George Spendlove moved there.

On the first afternoon I was weary from standing all day at the Exhibition and was glad to be back to Chestnut Park. Howard invited me to rest on the couch. Placing pillows lovingly at my head he said, "I have just finished the last chapter of *Portals to Freedom*. How would you like me to read it to you while you rest?" The sound of Howard's reading voice enjoyed the same effect as Willard's Washington speech. In a few minutes I was ungratefully asleep. When I awoke with a guilty start, Howard was sitting beside me with the palms of his upturned hands raised to receive heavenly blessing as he prayed earnestly that I might be refreshed.

The Hidden Gift

I have said that 1939 was different. Our experience in teaching at Green Acre that year was special, too. The Green Acre committee had asked Willard and me to consider the subject of *Prayers and Meditations*, a new book of Bahá'u'lláh's Writings translated by Shoghi Effendi. We had been thrilled by the appearance of *Gleanings* a few years earlier, and now we were being asked to give a week-long course to introduce this new book to the friends, most of whom had not yet seen it. We prepared, from our notes of the Christian mystics, what was meant to be an intellectual introduction to the general subjects of prayer and meditation. Willard had taken a large notebook page and had single spaced the different names of God mentioned in the book's invocations.

Green Acre was such an ideal place to discuss this book. Bahá'u'lláh's Writings, as given to us through Shoghi Effendi's precise choice of words, are poetic. *Prayers and Meditations* beckons some previously unaroused faculty within us to answer the eloquent call of the Word. That faculty awakens to an impression which is not of this world, yet one which has been communicated and transcribed for us on this plane by God Himself. Green Acre's atmosphere is a reflection of that impression, something special – not quite of this world. Here, at Green Acre, was to be found "a draught of soft-flowing waters of Thy knowledge" on the "shores of the ocean of Thy nearness". In the pines warbled "the birds of the hearts of them that are nigh unto Thee," that we "may listen to the melodies of the Dove of Thy transcendent oneness". At Green Acre were "the wonders of Thy perfect tranquillity" and the "fragrant breezes of Thy joy," the perfume which was "the fragrance of the raiment of Thy Revelation". At Green Acre, if you are not an artist or a poet, you may find yourself wanting to become one.

This was our fourth year with the same people who gathered there, and we were very much at home with them. There was the crowd that had come up from Boston. Louis and Louise Gregory were there and Marguerite Reimer, who one day would marry Bill Sears. We had brought with us a few women from Jamestown who later would become Bahá'ís. Really, this was an extraordinary group, the Green Acre community, and awaiting it was an extraordinary experience.

The classroom filled up at nine o'clock on the morning of the first day. About thirty came. We entered with our notebooks and a copy of *Prayers and Meditations*. I remember Willard, notebook in hand, standing behind my chair. In our preparations we had selected some Writings from the book and distributed them for readings. We began our class speaking rather academically and drily from our notes. The students scribbled in their notebooks. When I turned to my list of quotations, I decided that after each reading we would sit for one or two minutes in silent meditation. And so began our experience of *Prayers and Meditations*.

In the silence that followed each of the readings, an extraordinary power became apparent in the room. It was sensed by many, sensed as a combination of bliss and uneasiness. A sense, a power, that grew and intensified. Marguerite was sitting next to me, and our chairs were shaking so much that they were squeaking. The unleashed power of the Word was becoming a group experience. As one of the teachers, I was aware of my responsibility to keep the class from becoming hysterical. It reminded me of some of the old camp meetings we had had as children. I knew that the excitement must be guarded against. I think we were all relieved when we returned to our everyday notes and gave people something that could be copied down and understood.

It was a group of excited people who walked for lunch up to the Inn. There was much comment about our experience. Some of the Boston people said that what they had experienced was not spiritual but psychic and that we needed to be careful with our investigations. Others said that it was the presence of the Holy Spirit. A friend of ours, who was teaching in the Stanwood Cobb day school, joined our class late. She came in with a raging headache and claimed that it disappeared the minute she joined us.

Another Green Acre visitor was inspired to tell me of an experience she had had with 'Abdu'l-Bahá. She remembered that when He visited the United States her mother had taken her to see the Master off on the train. She was but a little girl of about seven at the time and was sitting on a stairway which the Master was about to descend. She said that He approached and stepped on her shoulder and that He had not had any weight, nor did He hurt her. It was her own experience and she said that whenever she had doubts about her faith, she recalled that memory.

Willard explained that 'Abdu'l-Bahá tells us not to tamper with psychic forces. Yet the Master had said, ". . . the power of the Holy Spirit is your assistant. Above and over physical forces, phenomenal forces, the Holy Spirit itself shall aid you."[45] We talked about these differences.

When I was asked for my opinion of our experience, all I could say was that SOMETHING had come into the room and a power was added which had not been present before. I told them that these stories of people's reactions are side effects. Let us not become so fascinated with them that we lose sight of the reason. It was the reading of the Word that released the power. Bahá'u'lláh has told us of the power of reading the Word, a Word that is meant to be read aloud. He says:

> Intone, O My servant, the verses of God that have been received by thee, as intoned by them who have drawn nigh unto Him, that the sweetness of thy melody may kindle thine own soul, and attract the hearts of all men. Whoso reciteth, in the privacy of his chamber. The verses revealed by God, the scattering angels of the Almighty shall scatter abroad the fragrance of the words uttered by his mouth, and shall cause the heart of every righteous man to throb. Though he may, at first, remain unaware of its effect, yet the virtue of the grace vouchsafed unto him must needs sooner or later exercise its influence upon his soul.[46]

As I attached energies to new hopes, the separation from Jamestown was beginning. In November I was back in Canada, scheduled to give talks in Toronto and Hamilton, where I was making new friends. The Ives had also asked us to go with them to Memphis, Tennessee, where, it was hoped, I would look after Howard and assist with Mabel's teaching. In the months ahead, I would be travelling most of the time.

Jamestown was my testing ground. I had had my own spiritual struggles and I had been in the company of spiritual powerhouses. I must have learned something, for now it seemed

---

45 'Abdu'l-Bahá, *Star of the West*, Vol. 8, No. 8, p. 103.
46 *Bahá'í Prayers*, frontispiece

I was called out for greater service. Martha once wrote to Lucy, "We can't all be called to be Hands of the Cause. But we can all dedicate ourselves as if we were." When I look back, I see that every moment in the Faith has been a moment of history, a moment of vital importance. Nothing we ever give to the Faith is enough. So little is given all the time, and we are sleepy Bahá'ís called upon to awaken and give all that we have, to donate our spirits to the Faith. The greatness of Dorothy, Martha and Howard was that they became slaves to giving.

Before leaving on another trip to Hamilton, Lorna had written to me a letter in which she restated our Covenant of the Burning Log – our promise to practice universal love. She had said:

> The whole message now seems to be a call to come out from behind these walls that have held us in, to give of the reality we are – deep within; to be to the world what we are in our hearts, with all the tenderness and wonder and shining, all the unexpressed and unlived things, like poems – to give them all, as Philemon and Baucis gave of their hospitality to a stranger, only to find that, unaware, they had entertained a god.

I replied by saying:

> I accept it, and I will try to arise to its challenge. Part of my failure to do so is inertia; some of it is pride and withdrawal; some of it is fear of making hurtful contacts with people who fray my wings. I should have to make myself over to live by such lines; they are like a searchlight piercing into the sincerity of all our words and stated goals.

The Jamestown community was full of problems. Each member faced some serious difficulty in his or her personal life. Before I left again, Willard and I said some very intense prayers for them.

Lorna shared in my teaching trips, a silent spiritual partner, my "Bahá'í twin". If I had any success, certainly she and Willard shared in it. My letters to her tell as much about our relationship and finances as they do of my teaching activities.

Letters to Lorna

On the train [near Buffalo, New York] Feb. 8, 1940:

. . . I am full of anticipation. A letter from Hamilton has announced that four new people believe in Bahá'u'lláh. What a privilege is being given to me. If these join, there will be eight and there are several others that I should have thought nearer. I am meeting with about fifteen of them tonight and a Feast is being held.

I had a letter from the Teaching Committee yesterday, encouraging me in my work and offering more funds to carry on this Canadian work. I am going to support Willard's going next time. He has one day of vacation left which he could combine with a Sunday. Pray the prayer for Canada, if you want to help. . .

April 15, 1940, Jamestown:

Thursday night in Hamilton at a pilau supper at which I entertained ten Toronto people and the Hamilton friends, six people formally joined the Cause making a wee trembling little community of ten. I was pressed for time and sleep when I left. I went, held nine major meetings, got swollen glands, achieved an Assembly, got over the cold, slept an average of about five hours a night, and here I am feeling a little apologetic for skipping out this afternoon. In an hour I'll be hurrying downtown. Tonight I'll teach my last class at the College Center. I leave for Convention next week. I am churned inwardly by the new phases of the war. I am haunted by a sense of the dipping motion of airplanes that I saw in a newsreel. . .

May 25

Thanks for sending so promptly the cheque to Willard. What a hand-to-mouth existence we live – but I don't know how we could do otherwise without curtailing our Bahá'í work. I did not take my private pupils this year because of the many calls out of town. Fourteen Bahá'í trips, my dear! But how glorious to have the opportunity.

May 29

I am waiting for my train and will soon start to write my customary report to the Ives of my Canadian doings. I had thirteen meetings in ten days and half a dozen special appointments with people who wanted to talk with me. Every afternoon and evening and some mornings were filled. In all my spare moments I visited with Laura Davis, whose house was my headquarters. I wish you could meet all my wonderful friends in Toronto. I never saw so many adorable people in one place.

September 23

I am filling every day to brimming over. I keep saying that, don't I? When I went to Toronto this time it was more or less grim duty; my face over my shoulder. I am ashamed of that. I came back in an entirely different mood after the resplendent confirmations at Hamilton.

September 27

Your pale-green surprise cheque is already adorning my back! I was fortunate enough to get a really warm and good-looking fall coat for $10.88. I don't know how it happened. The thrift shop in Bigelows. The other coats were almost twice as expensive.

What a lift! Two days before I had said to Bahá'u'lláh, 'If I am going to be clothed adequately, I shall have a little help, dear God!' The ten helped me to reinstate my credit at the store. I had already paid one ten when I returned from Canada. Usually I take care of that with night school money, and now I can go and do my fall teaching work with a feeling of looking all right. I ought not to mind shabby, chilly, spring coats in autumn. I haven't had a good between-season coat since the year we had a good cherry crop, and that was 1927 or 1928! Now I am snug and comforted in my very soul. You know what a coat can mean. It was an unbelievable piece of good fortune finding one for ten. It was the only one on the rack and it was perfect.

Mabel Ives and I continued our separate teaching trips to Hamilton. We had helped the Bahá'í community there to grow close to the required nine for the Assembly, an Assembly which formed in 1940. I remember that Laura Davis and John Robarts drove from Toronto on a stormy night for the occasion. Mr and Mrs McGregor were there, too, and I happened to ask them what had confirmed them in the Faith. They answered by recalling an earlier Hamilton meeting at which I spoke about life after death – a meeting which I had mentally labelled as "very discouraging" as I had rarely felt less inspired as I did on that night. Mrs McGregor said, "I always thought that when you were dead, you were dead. But after that meeting I KNEW you weren't!"

The strength of the Jamestown community was also developing. Freddie Reis had started a class in "Bahá'í Administration", and I held one called "Bahá'í Expression". It was much like the "Practice in Speaking" sessions that we had had when we were new believers. For this class, however, the practice was in answering questions. One night that spring Audrey, Freddie and Onolee came. There were three seekers who asked some very good questions. The new believers took turns in answering and the anticipated 45-minute class expanded to an hour and a half. It was live wire! Onolee [Eddy] walked home with me and we talked until 2:00 a.m. She was reading every Bahá'í book she could get her hands on and was beginning to dream of being a "pioneer teacher". She said she would not want to attempt it "without having the facts at her tongue's end."

The Death of May Maxwell

I was at another meeting that spring, probably in March. I wrote to Lorna:

> I was at a friend's house. As I was leaving my hostess brought out a clipping, a New York newspaper notice of May Maxwell's death in Buenos Aires. It was as if I were under a cold shower. I took a step backward as I felt an icy current flow over me.
>
> My hostess witnessed my shock, 'Did you know her? Oh, I am so very sorry.'
>
> I hurried home to tell Willard, who said, 'Whatever we are, May Maxwell helped to make us that way. She certainly influenced our lives.'

I remember how she whispered to me at the 1938 Convention, "Our hearts will never be separated." As I write this, waves of an ocean of ineffable tenderness wash over me from another realm, and I know she is near. I do not have to understand this with my mind, but I know that the rainbow swirling of my atoms has expanded and heightened just now. My infant soul seems rocked in its own atoms. It comes and goes as I write of her.

It was with May that we talked often about the "interpenetration of spirits" between friends who are in unity. It was May who taught us that unity was a hidden mystery, "the key to the treasure house to be worn next to our hearts." It was May who opened our comprehension to the mysteries of the spirit. This was not the last time that I would feel the presence of May and the connection of our hearts.

National Convention, 1940

I went to Convention in May. The Bahá'ís at the 1940 Convention were, as a whole, just their lesser selves, their regular everyday selves, living in the little things they had done for the Cause the last year. They gave signs that unity at home was needed – as it was needed here. The mischief of some troubled person had been the cause of difficulties, and our unity was beclouded. It seemed to be that way in many assemblies. The ingredient UNITY was not yet with us in realization. Yet, 'Abdu'l-Bahá had said that if even two would unite, they might save us all – release the divine forces.

Except for the stir created by the attendance of Georgie Wiles and a new group of Black Bahá'ís from Nashville, the Convention moved slowly. People seemed to be in a daze. There was almost no mention of the war. We did not face that reality and there was a lull over us all.

I had been reading an article, "Out of This Agony" by Horace Holley in the October 1939 *World Order Magazine*. Horace wrote,

> The vast spectacle proceeds, whilst we fear for the fate of the few we love, or shed tears because one tree falls, one home burns, one child lies crushed beneath the wheel...

But for the prospect of war and of a grief for more massive losses Horace said, "Human feeling was not created to mourn the death of a world." But Bahá'í feeling was.

In the summer I returned to the Canadian National Exhibition in Toronto to preside a second year at the Bahá'í booth. Canada had joined the United Kingdom in entering the war and a new song "There'll Always Be An England" seemed constantly to be in the air. It was heard everywhere, and everyone seemed happy to be united in a common cause. How the bands played it at the "Ex"!

At the time, the National Spiritual Assembly of the Bahá'ís of the United States and Canada was meeting at the King Edward Hotel. On the last day, the Bahá'ís were invited to an open meeting to discuss the sending of pioneers to complete the first Seven Year Plan. It called for a Local Assembly in every province and state by the spring of 1944. The members of the National Assembly spoke urgently on this theme, and we were invited to respond with comments of our own. Dorothy Baker gave a rousing call to action in which she said the Bahá'ís needed the equivalent of a pentecostal baptism in the Faith. I raised my voice and made a talk in a similar vein. I said that we needed a "holocaust which would consume our lesser selves in a spiritual flame." I made it sound so HOT that I think they laughed. I was a little rattled at my own nerve and, with a red face, collapsed into my seat. Did I see a loving gleam of amusement in Dorothy's eyes?

I shared a hotel room with Dorothy, and we talked most of the night. She confided to me how Loulie Mathews had told her that she must take off the "Princely Cloak" and put on the "Robe of Light". For her, the robe of light was to mean "freedom from love and hate," a detachment from emotional involvement with people who were attracted to her personality. It represented the lonesome road she had been walking, one of separation for months at a time from her adoring family in Ohio. Dorothy had become a person with a special duty, a special destiny. In her heart was a special kind of martyrdom. She had a martyr's spirit. She had prayed for it years ago in the dome of the Temple. I would write later to Lorna:

> I have concluded that we have to take one role only – the one where we do the most effective work. Dorothy Baker has done that. She is like a candle sacrificing herself to the Light. We had breakfast together in Toronto and again she laid bare her heart to me. She told me about riding home in the car with Frank and Louise and loving them and knowing that again she must leave them. In thinking about it, she unconsciously moaned so that they heard her. Their glad chatter was stilled until she reassured them that she was all right. But Frank knew. He just patted her shoulder.

With that fiery little talk of mine I should not have been surprised when, after our stint at Green Acre, the National Assembly asked me to make a teaching trip to New Brunswick. Amidst great uncertainty about indefinite plans, I left in October and, after a day in Rochester, New York, a day in Hamilton, two in Toronto and two in Montreal, arrived in Moncton on the 22nd.

The presence of May Maxwell joined me when I was in Montreal. Montreal would have been a homecoming, only no one was home. I was feeling the absence keenly, the actual loss of May. All of the Maxwells were gone. Mary was now Rúḥíyyih Khánum, wife of Shoghi Effendi. She and her father, Sutherland Maxwell, were living in Haifa. And May, my mentor and close friend, had died that spring. Early in the morning, around dawn, as I felt this absence, pondered the unknown land that was before me and wondered about the experiences I would have, she came to me and I heard her whisper again, audibly, "You know, dear heart, our hearts will never be separated."

The weeks in Moncton followed a pattern of social rounds and meetings not unlike those in Hamilton and Toronto. The fledgling community there was the child of Mabel Ives' efforts, and the purpose of my own visit was to deepen and consolidate the believers. I wrote to Willard,

> My personal work with the Bahá'ís absorbs a great deal of attention. They pass me around and around like a box of candy and it is like a perpetual love feast. I am associating with them constantly, praying for them and trying to lift them all into a self-sufficient band who will do their own teaching. A number of the people here are natural born teachers...

With some, the practice of universal love would be confirmed. The practice was not limited to the enlisted members of the Bahá'í community. Leila Wells joined the Cause and soon after wrote to me of how she saw the attraction of others to the Faith, "not for anything that we of ourselves could do, but just that the light might be so bright that the lamp would not be obscured."

I stayed with different people in Moncton, but 32 Ralph Street, the home of the Gearys, would become headquarters. Here was an attraction of kindred spirits. Irving had a talented subtle turn of wit, a talent possessed also by Willard. I felt that I had been bottled up and serious for too long, and we spent our first afternoon together in delightful gales of laughter. We enjoyed much companionship and had an intimate exchange of personal histories. We laughed and we cried. I found Irving and Grace to be the loveliest people and took to calling them "the Dearys".

Being with the Gearys would be a confirmation of another sort, a confirmation that was to be the start of a special Canadian relationship. As had Leila, Grace described her experience in a letter she wrote to me:

> I tell you that I have had a spiritual renewal, and you tell me that you have been evoking power though prayer. But I think what has happened has been my spiritual birth into the Cause. For three years I have sincerely believed the Teachings, I have tried to live them, but I see now it has been a cold, formal, intellectual acceptance and only vaguely and at rare intervals has my heart been stirred. I remember hearing Mabel Ives speak of someone who had suddenly become a 'flaming Baháʼí' and wondering rather wistfully how that miracle was accomplished and then concluding that things like that happened to some people but not to me. Then last week came that rushing Tide of Spirit that flooded my heart and melted the ice of indifference and swept away the mud of self, and now prayer is a reality. The Cause is real, and everything is bathed in a new light. The winter of my spirit is over, and spring has come. And now Irving and I are able to ascend to that plane together and we are truly united at last. When I surrendered to your love, I opened every door in my heart. There is no nook or cranny that does not belong to you. If you find any riches there, you must help me to bring them to the surface, that they may be used in the service of Baháʼu'lláh, for all that I have or am is dedicated to His Cause.
>
> Sometimes I tremble when I think of where this experience may lead me. I am so weak and feeble. But I have put my hand in yours and where you go I will dare follow.

There were brief trips to Saint John and Halifax. Six of us piled into a car and went to Halifax for two nights. It was more a scouting trip of looking up the believers, sandwiched between a lot of driving and my marvelling at the landscape. I remember leaving at dawn, seeing the ships in the harbour and thinking that I should sometime go back to Halifax. Somehow I felt the field of Bahá'í work was greater there.

I returned to Jamestown in December to find letters from Mabel and Dorothy insisting that I go to Memphis right after the New Year. I was all "hollowed out", and I seemed to have few feelings about it one way or another. I remembered a tradition attributed to Muhammad: "Pass through this world as if you were already dead."

Letter to Lorna, Dec. 24, 1940

Willard is working tonight, and I have been trimming my little Christmas tree. I am not in a 'merry' mood this Christmas, I have to admit it. I have been sad today almost to tears. The holiday time makes so much more poignant the world conditions, the confused and wilful humanity, even the Bahá'ís themselves. Why is it that there are not others as qualified to go 'way down there to Memphis? Why must it be I, when my Canadian teaching work in Hamilton and Toronto will suffer by my not returning to them after this long absence. I long to answer Hamilton's request, and yet I must turn and go the other way. Dorothy Baker, Mabel Ives and Horace Holley are so sure, what else can I do but comply? The final arrangements are not made, but I think I'll be leaving the end of the first week in January to go first to Cleveland, which I promised in October, then to Lima to confer with Dorothy. My days at home with Willard are so precious and so fleeting. He is so perfect.

Dear Willard, he showers such love upon me because he feels I may be leaving him soon. He follows me around the house. The other night I ran upstairs to get a book and he came with me, just to go along.

It is interesting how my non-Bahá'í friends are flocking around me and wanting me. I could lead an intensely social life, with very fine intelligent people, if I had the time to spend in Jamestown...

Preparations

The Guardian had written to us,

> As to racial prejudice, the corrosion of which, for well nigh a century, has bitten into the fibre, and attacked the whole social structure of American society, it should be regarded as constituting the most vital and challenging issue confronting the Bahá'í community at the present stage of its evolution.[47]

Memphis was called "the Gateway to the South". Its racial situation had been described as "unusually acute." I was briefed on a situation which found two Bahá'í groups: a White one and a Black one. My assignment was to bring them together into one administrative unit. Memphis would be a real test of sincerity.

My Memphis assignment began and ended with visits with Dorothy Baker. From Jamestown I went first to Cleveland. An afternoon fireside was given at the Coles' and that evening I shared the platform with Louis Gregory at the Bahá'í Room downtown. Many of the Cleveland friends were Black and were eager to offer their prayers for my work in Memphis. The next evening I took the Nickel Plate Line #9 to Lima, Ohio. I had a lovely visit. That night Frank Baker laid the table in the breakfast nook with crackers, five kinds of cheese and coffee. And there was "Heavenly Hash" – a concoction of jams. Frank Baker was very human, down-to-earth and in a wonderful expansive and beaming mood – a mood which was contagious. The Dorothy of that night was so much the homebody. She had all of Frank's qualities, but she was the one who had to sacrifice them. This night, however, she was warm and responsive to friendship and thriving on her own hospitality. It was a view of her that few had seen.

---

47 Shoghi Effendi, *The Advent of Divine Justice* (Wilmette IL: Bahá'í Publishing Trust, 1973), p. 28.

Dorothy and I shared a room with twin beds and talked until 3:00 a.m. The next day she and I escaped from the lively house for another two-or-three-hour conference and prayer session as we drove in the sunshine throughout surrounding countryside to Mother Beecher's grave site. Dorothy, who took a special interest in the Memphis situation, told me a little of what I was about to enter and the problems she perceived. Dorothy was so wonderful to me. She fluffed me up by calling me her "superior officer". She said she was Mullá Ḥusayn and I, Quddús! In her humility she really meant it. She saw such a vision of me while I thought of myself as "Lot's wife", insecure in my capacities to give to the Cause in this soul-stirring field. I had to put on my armour and go bravely into the battle, and to do so, I had to be detached. I had to be a real Bahá'í.

Horace Holley came to Lima for supper on the last night of my visit. He discussed with me the Memphis situation before going to the Hotel where he gave a brilliant talk to about a hundred people. It would have been a classic had it been transcribed into a printed article. I left early and caught the train for Memphis. It would be an eight-and-a-half-hour run with a stopover in St. Louis. Lima had been an out-of-the-way and costly routing. But now I economized by renting a pillow and taking a day coach. In Memphis, Howard and Mabel met me at the station.

The First Day – Tuesday, January 14, 1941

Carlotta Pittman and another lady came with a car and took me to a panel discussion of H. G. Wells' *Bill of Rights*. Before I knew it, I was seated in the front of the Church Women's Council room with the five others on the panel! Before us were about a hundred fine-looking southern representatives and the minister. For me it was "sink or swim". I plunged into the discussion, offering Bahá'í-ish remarks and making a hit with the liberal minister. He asked me if I would like to be his secretary and said that he needed someone "on her toes intellectually" and, as he put it, "full of the idea of oneness". I could not accept, but I did agree to address his Council in a month's time. I followed up by going to his church the next Sunday.

I was soon to meet the White Baháʼí group. Three of the seven came from a Unitarian background, one had been a Jew and it did not seem to me that the others had been anything. Most of these people had been taught by Mabel. This was her group. A Feast was held at the apartment of Miss Pittman, a retired schoolteacher and sister of a judge. Mrs Kelly was there. She had a big house, and she was willing to use it for future meetings. Mrs Clara Keller, who had gone with Mabel to the Black business college, was present also. Mrs Bogan, the newest member, was ill and facing an operation. Miss Johanna Zimmerman was the first Memphian Baháʼí of Mabel's group. She told me at this meeting that she had given the Faith her "academic approval" but after a year in the Cause hadn't found any life or heartfelt excitement. After that first meeting I thought all of the White Baháʼís were in that condition. The other missing member was Alvin Blum, a travelling salesman who was out of town.

Some decisions were made. Their regular Tuesday night meetings were to be turned over to me, and I was to give them the McKay course in comparative religion and in *Prayers and Meditations*. They had been reading together *The Kitáb-i-Íqán* and had not really been enjoying it. It was decided also that those interested in an afternoon study class in Baháʼí metaphysics would gather for tea the next Thursday at Mrs Florence Kelly's. During the whole time of this Feast no mention was made of the Black Baháʼís.

Mabel departed a day or so later, and I was left to care for Howard and to carry on the Baháʼí work. I soon realized that Mabel's trip to Little Rock was an important teaching campaign and that it could not have happened without me or someone else coming here to look after Howard. Her pioneer venture in the south was just the sort of thing the Guardian would have stressed most. If I had not done another thing but just keep house so that Mabel, with a free mind, could open up the southern cities, I would have been giving Baháʼu'lláh sufficient service. I was getting more and more into the habit of accepting service by envisioning my response not as one of reacting to a person or a committee but to Bahá'u'lláh Himself. In that way I found it easier to render a full and agreeable service. At first, I tried to put my heart completely into the care of Howard, whose delicate health made him so dependent. Something could have happened at any time to snap his hold on life. I prayed that should such an emergency occur, my chicken heart would turn into that of a lion. I told Willard to remember the position of this man who had taught us the Faith and asked him to see in all the housework chores he was doing in Jamestown, the things I was now doing for Howard in Memphis.

To Lorna:

> I have been desperately homesick. I am busy building bridges to a number of people but when I get there it will be merely to deliver a gift and go. I have decided that I am on a kind of Fast and these attacks of desperate loneliness are hunger pangs of the heart.
>
> I had a letter from Willard today and its tenderness nearly capsized my frail craft. I said to Howard, 'Should I pray to have this homesickness taken away?' 'No,' he said. I guess he is right. I know I am winning through to a new sensitiveness. When I sit quiet for a moment, my 'particles' begin to float and I sway as if on a gentle swelling tide. I feel as if a slow fire were burning in my human self. Howard is right. I will not try to extinguish that fire. 'Create in the hearts of Thy beloved, the fire of Thy love, that it may turn away the thought of everything save Thee.' I know what to pray for. The ME dies hard!

My first contact with the Black group was through Professor Henderson, who conducted a Business College. Call it innocence or call it ignorance, I wasn't aware that I was being tested by him. I called him on several occasions to arrange a meeting and was put off. I persisted, and finally he offered a date. He told me that he would send a car for me. Well, when the day arrived a car was sent indeed. It was a dilapidated and battered hulk of a taxi that probably would compare to the one driven by Amos 'n'

Andy. The chauffeur was a Black cabby in shirt sleeves. I got in and rode in regal style to the Business College.

Thirty or so bright and neat girls were tapping away at typewriters to the strains of Victrola rhythms. Stepping into the school was like stepping onto a well-propped stage. It was positively theatre! Ruby Jenkins, the secretary, greeted me and took me to Professor Henderson's office. Here was a dapper person, more than well dressed, with a flower in his lapel and a white silk kerchief tied in a bow under his chin. He introduced me to the Dean and then had Ruby escort me around the school, upstairs and down. It had been waxed until it shone and was the model of cleanliness. I saw the rooms in the girls' dormitory. Back downstairs they put on an exhibition of typing coordinated to music. It sounded exactly like tap dancing. As a show alone, this tour was worth the price of a ticket. The Professor joined us and introduced me to all of the students, and I made a short Bahá'í talk. I remember how bright some of the faces looked and how at ease and intimate I felt with them all. Professor Henderson then donned a light overcoat, throwing it around his shoulders like a cape, and put on a wide-brimmed hat. All of us were marshalled outside to pose for what seemed like an hour of picture taking.

When we went back in, Professor Henderson played and sang some delightful music for me until a few of the girls served us a sumptuous repast in the office. There was beefsteak, sandwiches, tea, toast, nuts and candy. We were joined by the Dean, Ruby Jenkins and Corella Grey. Corella was one of the teachers. Ruby and Corella would be two of the students in my Bahá'í classes. Only one knife had been brought, so the Professor cut up all of our beefsteak and buttered all of our toast. We called it the "family knife".

Then we got into a real discussion of the Black situation in Memphis. Both men were highly intelligent. Professor Henderson was a member of the Urban League and said that if I desired, he would introduce me to the secretary. The Dean was a member of an interracial committee to which prominent citizens of both races belonged. He told me that he could arrange for me to speak at a Black high school where there were thousands.

I was tempted by having too many doors open for me. I realized that with time enough, I could spend all my time in teaching the Blacks. At any rate, my job was not to throw my energies to one side exclusively. We arranged for a class that I would give in "Bahá'í Qualifications", a small informal class which I would continue each week until the Regional Committee was satisfied with the Black students' eligibility for enrolment.

I would learn later that I had passed my tests. In my ignorance I had not seen them as tests at all. It was all matter of fact for me to accept the offer of the taxi, for me to have my photograph taken in public with them and, especially, to "break bread" together. I would discover that some of these things had not been done before in Memphis. The next week I went back and gave my first class on the station of the Báb.

To Lorna, January 22:

> I've just got back from a meeting [with the White Bahá'ís] in which I have been talking all the evening on metaphysics. A nice old lady and her daughter brought me home, and as I left the car, the old lady said innocently, 'The Negroes are a lower race. God created them to be servants. It says so in the Bible.'

I continued my consolidation work with the separate Bahá'í groups. I found through my social activities many doors opening for teaching. I worked also on developing relationships with the individual friends.

Grace Bogan

Mrs Grace Bogan was a new Bahá'í, not too well established in her faith – something that could be said as well of most of the other, older believers. Grace was from Mississippi and well rooted in a southern tradition of fear of the Black race, a fear that was amplified by a natural desire to protect two attractive daughters. Grace would soon learn that to join the Bahá'í Faith was to invite contact with her source of fear.

Grace was ill, and before meeting her I considered her to be "out of the running" for active participation. I visited her and said healing prayers for her. She told me she had "inside" trouble that she had ignored for some years. It was cancer. From time to time, she would be examined by the doctors and the examinations would leave her in pain.

She called me a few days after my visit. It seemed the doctors had examined her again and had found the cancer had reached an acute stage. They told her that it demanded immediate attention. She telephoned me to ask for prayers, hoping that I would encourage her to use the prayers as a substitute for medical treatment. Somehow, I was given credit for getting her to go to the hospital. While ostensibly giving her an examination while she was under anaesthetic, the doctors cut her open and removed some of the diseased tissue. After a brief stay Grace went home, and the doctors gave her a favourable report. "No cancer!" The results of the biopsy had the physicians puzzled. Not only had the growth disappeared, but Grace reported no pain from the surgery although earlier examinations had left her distressed. Word of my efforts and the confirmation of the prayers spread. One of the friends told me that if this healing were the only thing that happened as a result of my coming to Memphis, then that alone was enough to justify the effort and sacrifice involved.

To Willard:

> I go through every door that opens a crack, even a hospital door as today [with Grace Bogan]. Everything is considered a possible lead when you are in the employ of Bahá'u'lláh.

Mrs Watkins

Mrs Watkins was another seemingly isolated Bahá'í with whom I spent time. She had been ill when I first arrived and had been "unseeable." She telephoned later and gave me a date on which to pay her a visit. As it turned out, she was a doctor's wife and, if I remember correctly, had been educated at A & M College and knew Walter and Ida Buchannan. Both she and her husband had been taught by Louis Gregory so many years ago, they must have been children then. I began to see Mrs Watkins as a vital link and prayed that she would use her influence to encourage the friends at the Business College. I offered to give her daughters drawing lessons on a weekly basis. For me it was so important to set up regularly scheduled events – my meetings with the Whites, my classes at the Business College and the drawing lessons. That was how I fought disorganization.

After my first visit with Mrs Watkins, I wrote to Willard,

> This sense of belonging to the 'untouchables' does devastating things to the Coloured psychology – Jim Crow regulations and all the rest! It is insidious, takes away self-respect and the sense of responsibility that is part of self-respect and personal validity.

The Feast of Dominion (Mulk)

On Friday, February 7th, I went to the Feast. It was a White one, of course, but it signalled a turn of events. I was given the floor and asked to talk on Bahá'í Administration. The people were attentive, intellectually mature and had no difficulty with the words I was using. For some, however, the concepts would later prove difficult to swallow. Essentially, this is what I told the White Memphian Bahá'ís:

"The Feast is more than a community meeting. It is an Institution, a convention of spirit in which each member is a delegate, regardless of whether he is on the Assembly or not. Each member has the opportunity to bring forward recommendations to the local Assembly or, through its Secretary, to the National Assembly. Local Bahá'í administration, as it could come to exist in Memphis, could be a small working model of the World State. 'Abdu'l-Bahá had said, 'Those Assemblies are the emblems of the Supreme Concourse and the prototypes of the congregations of the spirits in the Kingdom of Abhá.'"[48]

---

48 *Bahá'í Scriptures* # 889, p. 472.

When I began to talk about true Bahá'í consultation being a form of prayer in which the group begs for the power of Bahá'u'lláh to reveal His Will, the members realized that we had not started with prayer. Someone then read the prayer for those who take counsel together, and it produced a deeply spiritual effect. After the prayer, I spoke about the qualifications of those who take counsel together, and the effect deepened in intensity. Then came the questions about forming the Assembly: "Should we have an Assembly this spring? Are we ready for it?" I gave them the list of believers that Marion Little from the Regional Committee had sent. The list included Professor Henderson and Mrs Watkins. I told them that if there were nine eligible Bahá'ís at the beginning of the administrative year, April 21st, the formation became a necessity and that the National Assembly would expect it. 'Abdu'l-Bahá had concluded his comment about the Assemblies by saying, "Avail yourselves of the opportunities of this time, neither let the occasion slip by unheeded."[49] Someone then asked, "Could we hold Feasts separate from the Coloured members?" The consultation pursued this point, cautiously and gently and to the extent that they were able to think it through for themselves.

The concept foremost in this discussion was this: that Bahá'í Institutions are divine and that nothing can injure or retard the Cause as much as a disregard of its requirements; that the institution, in its form, centres in the Feast as an inclusive community meeting. It is through this institution that we demonstrate the oneness of mankind to a sceptical world made up of warring nations. It is through the Feast that we prove that we are not just one more selective society but a unit truly composed of diverse elements which have learned to function together. In its spirit, the "breaking of bread" together with a feeling of love and fellowship becomes a sacrament, something which would represent the appearance of the New Day in our southern states. . .

Then I went around and asked each member, one by one, for an expression of feeling. Clara Keller and Johanna Zimmerman were the first to respond. "If we are going to call ourselves

---

49   ibid., p. 472.

Bahá'ís, let us BE Bahá'ís." Some of the others were worried, but the decisions that came out of the Feast were:

1. The Assembly would be formed if there were nine believers of any colour.
2. A suitable place of meeting would be found and all Bahá'ís would be notified of administrative activities.

I went home and prayed.

The following Tuesday I was back at the Business College, conducting my class in "Bahá'í Qualifications". My lessons focused on the Will of 'Abdu'l-Bahá and its provisions. In those days the reading of the Will was a prerequisite to becoming a Bahá'í.

Professor Henderson asked me about the forming of the Assembly and the eligibility of the three people studying with me. I told him that I expected them all to be eligible and that I expected the Assembly to form.

I had written to Willard,

> One girl has not been able to attend the classes, but the other two are stars, Irene Gleadon and Corilla Grey. I am proud of them. We are sailing right into Administration full tilt; going to put on a trial consultation next week.

With Howard

From my diary:

> I am out to make use of this opportunity to harvest the late autumn crop of the wisdom of Howard Ives. I offer him some provocative questions as we meet at mealtime and pray silently while he answers. At times I take down a note or two. I have great faith in his inspiration. He has always had the ability to open new worlds to me, and I know that it was written in the stars that I should have had the bounty of being with him again.

I will try to reconstruct with some of my own comments a conversation I had with him the other night, beginning with 'What is the love of God – our love for God?' My sense of his answer is that God is for us a sense of the atmosphere of the Manifestation. We yearn to be in that atmosphere and, when it is attained, rise to an nth degree of elation.

Then I asked, 'Where does our love for people come in?' He said that in our fellow men, we see our Master's face. That when we attain to the love of another, that relationship is a symbol of our life on the next plane of existence, a foretaste of the joys and release that will be ours. It transports us to heaven. He quoted from *Gleanings* that knowing our own selves is the same as knowing Himself and that this can also be true if we really know the reality of another soul. In other words, if we love that soul, it becomes the mirror of the qualities of the Beloved.

I said, 'Should we expect to love all people alike?' He said, 'Certainly not! There are as many kinds of love as there are people.' Then he quoted the Bhagavad Gita to the effect that 'if you lose discrimination, you lose everything.' Everyone speaks to us in a different way and reveals a different degree of reality. I suppose destiny determines who shall speak to us in the most thrilling of voices. The quality of our love, says Howard, is determined by our loss of the consciousness of self. If we can lose ourselves in the object of our affection, be it an intermediary human spirit or the Divine Beloved, we merge or fuse ourselves with it. The loss of self is that fluidity we mention – the softening of outlines, evanescence. The mystics sought thus to merge and lose themselves when they meditated on 'a little thing the quality of an hazel nut.'

Then he told the story about Grace Ober's conversation with an elderly lady. The woman said: 'I hear that the Bahá'ís believe in free love.'

Grace: 'We do!'

Lady: 'Oh!'

Grace: 'Do not mistake me. I said love, not lust.'

Upsetting the Apple Cart

Believing myself to be in accord with the decisions arrived at the last Feast, I told the friends that I intended to host the Feast of Loftiness ('Alá') at the Ives' and that I would be inviting the Black believers. I felt supported by the National Assembly, especially after receiving a letter from Horace Holley in which he said,

> The situation in Memphis seems to be unusually important as it is part of the fundamental race work being done in the southern states, and therefore our success in Memphis is vital to the progress of the Cause. [Feb. 24]

Two days before the Feast I was invited to dinner at the home of two White Bahá'ís. The husband had been ill and had not attended any of the Feasts since I had arrived. The subject of the Feast came up. "Out of the question!" he insisted. The "breaking of bread" with the Blacks, he said, "will ruin us and the Cause." And as far as forming the Assembly went, "we should not try it until we have a thousand members." And he meant White members. I began to explain some of the principles of administration that I had shared at the Feast. His wife piped in and said that she realized that she could not be a Bahá'í because she could not accept any authority other than her own self – no other authority whatsoever, even if it came from God. A third member was also present, who, although she had earlier expressed support for the spiritual principle, now stood behind the husband and wife. I was shocked by her present change of attitude and denial. A division was beginning to crystallize as these three people thought that my presentation of Bahá'í Administration was simply one of my personal interpretation. For me the situation was made even more delicate because these were people who had been taught by Mabel and were loyal to her. The situation would put Howard between two fires: Mabel and me.

Prayers had always been an essential, but extra efforts were needed now. I wrote to Lorna:

I am having one of my intense prayer times – two or three hours each night after going to bed. I am able to go a little earlier than at home. I am praying for a spiritual heat that will fuse these diverse racial elements. It will take a spiritual bonfire...

I have Martha Root's picture (1938) propped up where it makes her my daily companion. Her eyes and smile speak to me and test my sincerity. I doubt if any going forth will ever strike as hard as this one has...

Since the beginning, Willard and the Jamestown community, Lorna, Dorothy and a number of others had been praying with me for these efforts. I had told Willard, "Don't forget the prayer squads are pioneering with me right over the top of the colour line. I am holding my breath in order to maintain a nicety of balance, as if I were walking on a very narrow path and must not fall off on either side." I felt particularly vulnerable now and wired Jamestown for additional prayers from the squads there. And then I wrote to Horace:

Last night I was invited to the [ ] home for dinner and [ ] was also present... Mrs [ ] said that my proposal to invite the coloured friends to the Feast had met with Mr [ ]'s emphatic disapproval. He came in at this point and we reviewed the necessity of preparing our community to take the two steps mentioned above (the two decisions from the previous Feast), a need which we now had to face because of the approach of April 21st. [ ]'s comments were:
1.   that any such moves would be ruinous to the social and business position of the White Bahá'ís,
2.   that no inkling of this situation was made clear to him when his name was included on the list of Bahá'ís...

... He said that they had known of the coloured believers but had thought of them as a group that could go on indefinitely operating separately. Also that they had supposed that the time of forming the Assembly was optional, and that it was much too soon to form it.

Miss [ ] and Mr and Mrs [ ] were unanimous in their

support of all these ideas, all elaborating the point that the 'breaking of bread' at the Feast is social dynamite, that it would inevitably become known and that the prospects of the Cause in Memphis would be blighted. For at least an hour they suggested alternatives, including asking the Guardian's permission to indefinitely postpone the Assembly.

The legal end of it was brought up. Anything, they said, may constitute a 'nuisance', according to definition by a judge. Someone offered to look in the city records to find examples of cases where Coloured-White association has been so considered. If we can prove this point, they said, would it not be our obligation to comply with the law (written or unwritten) of the City of Memphis? Please answer this point, Horace. I admit that the race situation here is very bad. The enclosed clipping from yesterday's paper is an example of the unfortunate publicity that has been in the papers recently.

[The heading of the article was 'Preacher of Racial Equality Shooed from Jail and City'. They had kept him locked up for fourteen days without a formal charge.]

. . . [since] four out of seven registered White believers here were not qualified by understanding or belief to function under our Administration, may I emphasize what seems to me the necessity for tightening up on the membership qualifications of those still under group administration. . .

The Jamestown friends wired back, "Render thy Lord victorious by that which is within thy Power." I had also written to Mabel and shared the situation with her. Howard, who was deeply upset by this turn of events, agreed to meet with the group. I dropped the idea of hosting the interracial Feast until I heard back from Horace, and I went to the Black Bahá'ís and told them that I had been unable to arrange it. On March 2nd we held another White Feast. We sat there bright and cordial but as dead souls, avoiding argumentative issues. The atmosphere would not lift.

From my diary, March 12:

Yesterday I was reading 'Abdu'l-Bahá's Will with two of my Coloured students and I came to this:

> ... Should other peoples and nations be unfaithful to you show your fidelity unto them, should they be unjust toward you show justice towards them, should they keep aloof from you attract them to yourselves, should they show their enmity be friendly towards them, should they poison your lives, sweeten their souls, should they inflict a wound on you, be a salve to their sores. Such are the attributes of the sincere![50]

I saw something in their faces and my eyes filled with tears. I said, 'Girls, these things have already happened to you because of racial prejudice, isn't that so?' And they said 'Yes.' We had a deep talk and they told me they were ready to accept the Bahá'í consciousness and to live by that rule. It was beautiful, that talk. None of us will forget it...

The response of the National Assembly came, one which re-emphasized the import of the Guardian's statements about "the Most Challenging Issue" and the need to push on toward consolidation. According to Horace, there was no alternative. We had received also the support of Miss Nellie Roche in Nashville. She wrote that they had ten Black and five White Bahá'ís there and that they had had Feasts in the homes of the Blacks because the White members weren't 'keeping house'. She also said that they were having an interracial Naw-Rúz. I called Mrs [ ] and asked her if the White group could meet at their house and read the statements prepared by Horace. She said, "No." It had all been settled as far as she was concerned. She and her husband had never intended to join a "legislative religion", and it was necessary for them to remain "free agents".

A few day later Clara and I went to visit Professor Henderson. I shared with him the Jamestown telegram, and he shared a letter

---

50 *The Will and Testament of 'Abdu'l-Bahá* (Wilmette, IL, Bahá'í Publishing Trust, 1971, p. 14.

he had recently received from Louis Gregory. This sharing was a moment of unity of spirits, made even more magical when the Professor began to recite:

> Bowed by the weight of centuries he leans
> Upon his hoe and gazes on the ground,
> The emptiness of ages in his face,
> And on his back the burden of the world.
> Who made him dead to rapture and despair,
> A thing that grieves not and that never hopes,
> Stolid and stunned, a brother to the ox?
> Who loosened and let down this brutal jaw?
> Whose was the hand that slanted back this brow?
> Whose breath blew out the light within this brain?
> Is this the Thing the Lord God made and gave
> To have dominion over sea and land;
> To trace the stars and search the heavens for power;
> To feel the passion of Eternity?
> Is this the Dream He dreamed who shaped the suns
> And pillared the blue firmament with light?
> Down all the stretch of Hell to its last gulf
> There is no shape more terrible than this –
> More tongued with censure of the world's blind greed –
> More filled with signs and portents for the soul –
> More fraught with menace to the universe.
>
> What gulfs between him and the seraphim!
> Slave of the wheel of labor, what to him
> Are Plato and the swing of Pleiades?
> What the long reaches of the peaks of song,
> The rift of dawn, the reddening of the rose?
> Through this dread shape the suffering ages look;
> Time's tragedy is in that aching stoop;
> Through this dread shape humanity betrayed,
> Plundered, profaned and disinherited,
> Cries protest to the Judges of the World,
> A protest that is also prophecy.

O masters, lords and rulers in all lands,
Is this the handiwork you give to God,
This monstrous thing distorted and soul-quenched?
How will you ever straighten up this shape;
Touch it again with immortality;
Give back the upward looking and the light;
Rebuild in it the music and the dream;
Make right the immemorial infamies,
Perfidious wrongs, immedicable woes?

O masters, lords and rulers in all lands,
How will the Future reckon with this Man?
How answer his brute question in that hour
When whirlwinds of rebellion shake the world?
How will it be with kingdoms and with kings –

With those who shaped him to the thing he is –
When this dumb Terror shall reply to God,
After the silence of the centuries?[51]

It was a beautiful and inspired recitation. We were all elated and when I rose to leave, I asked him, "Professor Henderson, may we bring our Feast to you at six o'clock a week from today [Thursday, March 20th]?" He agreed. Corilla Grey, one of the teachers at the Business College and one of my students, signed her enrolment card that day.

The announcement was given. The Feast of Naw-Rúz for the Memphian Bahá'ís of both races would be held at Professor Henderson's Business College.

The time was approaching when Marion Little would be coming to test my students and to evaluate their eligibility for Bahá'í membership. She inspired within me a fear of being dis-

---

51 Edwin Markham, *The Man with the Hoe and Other Poems* (New York, Doubleday & McClure Company, 1899) p. 15. "The Man with the Hoe" was written after seeing Millet's painting of the same name.

appointed because she carried with her the power to kill these efforts. Here she was, a society woman and looking very much like one in a very correct dark suit and stylish hat. This was the woman who took my students and grilled them with questions about the Faith and its Administration. Howard came to hear Marion's report. He comprehended the situation and shared Marion's unspoken concerns. Loyal to Mabel and fearing the downfall of my hopes, he summoned me and said, "You know that 'Abdu'l-Bahá has said that no sincere effort is ever lost. No matter what happens, you mustn't feel too badly about how things work out." We waited. When Marion came back to us, she told us that she had to accept the Black girls as Bahá'ís. There was no doubt. They all knew what they were getting into. But what I remember most was Marion herself. As we left, this woman so properly and conservatively dressed danced down the street, responding to a spontaneous and ecstatic heart.

What was lost in the White group was gained in the Black. Dr Watkins said that he would "go with us 100 per cent," and that, if necessary, he would sign another card. He had believed in Bahá'u'lláh for seventeen years after hearing about the Faith from Louis Gregory. I went to Grace Bogan, who was entrenched in the social values of the "old south" and had doubts about her ability to accept these new values. I gave her a copy of "Bahá'í Procedure" and told her that when she had read it, she would know whether she should attend and continue to call herself a Bahá'í.

On the day of the Feast, I called the White members and reminded them of the exact hour. The girls from the Business College and I planned the details and went out and bought refreshments to be delivered to the school. Dr and Mrs Watkins came to help us set up the tables and to prepare sandwiches and a fruit salad. Alvin Blum came back from a long trip. Clara and Johanna came. Surprise of surprises, Grace Bogan came. Counting Howard and myself, there were twelve confirmed adult Bahá'ís and two youth members. Howard said a prayer, and the silence persisted as we 'broke bread' together. After the feasting, the reading of messages from absent friends, the taking of a group photograph, reading from the sacred Writings and music, members of the Baháʼí Community and future Assembly of Memphis elected temporary officers. We discussed the Nineteen-day Feasts, the National Fund and the obligations of the Local Spiritual Assembly.

My job was over. The amalgamation of the White and Black groups had happened, and we discovered that we were not oil and water. We had mixed and were all enriched by that event. The evening was not exuberant, but the flow of the spirit was authentic and many of us were quiet in the significance of our act. After all, this was history.

Grace Bogan called me the next day and said, "When you saw me there, what did you think?" She told me that she had followed my advice, read the book and had prayed for guidance. The answer had come. She told me how her inner voice had said, "Baháʼu'lláh has done so much for you, now you must do something for Him!" For her, there was no longer any doubt. It was not only tradition that she had to put aside, but her fear of Blacks and the rejection of White society. She put that fear aside. We "fear no one save God". I would meet Grace in a year's time, as a delegate to the National Convention.

The Memphis community was now one, and the Assembly was on its way. The credit needs to be shared with Georgie Wiles. One day I lunched with Alvin Blum. He had known Georgie very well and told me about her sudden and almost incomprehensible death. (She had died from a haemorrhage from a relatively simple operation.) Alvin said, "She had reached her limit on this earth." As he was telling me this, I remembered suddenly how Georgie had begged me to come to Tennessee to work with her. I told Alvin, "Georgie Wiles is still working in the southern states!" With my prayers, her confirming influence had found a channel.

I left Memphis on the 28th and met Alvin Blum in Nashville. He drove me across the state of Kentucky to Cincinnati. It was a beautiful trip on a bright day. The Race Amity Committee was meeting there, and I was to report on my work in Memphis.

They were thrilled, and I received from the National Assembly a letter expressing their great appreciation of my "remarkable piece of teaching work." Work assisted by my prayer squads.

Dorothy was at that meeting and we spent together another night in conversation, picking up where we had left off two months ago. As we lay down in the hotel room, it filled with the fragrances of spring flowers. Neither of us was wearing perfume, but for an hour we inhaled a divine aroma.

I later went with her to Lima, and I remember a day when, after driving around, we returned to the house to rest. At the end of that time Dorothy arose and prayed the long obligatory prayer. I watched her until I could bear it no more, and I lay blinded by my tears. Something was happening to Dorothy as she prayed. She explained later that through her own tears, she had come to know the meaning of the tears of adoration that the Báb had shed when He addressed His Lord.

In her own strange way, Dorothy was offering me a love in that far clime where she had her being. Martha Root had turned to me, too, giving me her most intimate heart. She had wept in my arms, and I had comforted her. Literally, I had laid my hand on May Maxwell's heart. In thinking over these great gifts of friendship with the chosen ones of God, I realize that Bahá'u'lláh has used this way of awakening me. Certainly I have never been worthy of equal association with those who have chosen the station of martyrdom, yet they have given their hearts to me as if I were one of them in that sisterhood.

A woman I met in Lima told me that when she had met Dorothy in Pittsburgh, she did not believe that Dorothy could be real. She moved to Lima and worked for Dorothy for three years. This woman said that in all that time Dorothy never failed, not even for a moment, to exemplify the station that she had elected to occupy.

I remember the afternoon when Dorothy told me what I had meant to her. I had responded, "But I thought you were the one who didn't need a friend." She said, "I did think so once, but now I know that I do."

I shared the room in Lima with her for two nights, and I

watched her retire in exhaustion. I heard the alarm clock awaken her before dawn.

I returned from Memphis, but Jamestown was still more a point of departure than a home, the home of my affectionate dreams, the home Willard and I called McKaydia. Grace Geary came to visit us in Jamestown and to share the atmosphere of McKaydia. We had a wonderful time, our friendship deepened and she said that she had become thirty years younger. In the late spring and early summer I returned to Toronto and Hamilton and was asked by the Teaching Committee to make the rounds of the western New York "circuit".

We went again to Green Acre and repeated our course on *Prayers and Meditations*. I remember talking to Doris and Horace Holley about Canada and the fields of work there. Horace responded by suggesting that if the doors should open, we should pioneer to the Maritimes. Soon after, the National Assembly received the recommendation for me to make another extended trip to the Maritimes, concentrating in Halifax.

"There never was such a teaching challenge as these Maritimes."

On the last day of August, 1941, I was back in Canada. I spent a week on a holiday with Irving and Grace. We drove to Halifax and met Beulah Proctor and then went on to Peggy's Cove, where Irving and I did a lot of sketching. We returned to New Brunswick and spent a most enjoyable three or four days at their cottage, called "the Hideout", at Point de Chene. I bought a book of foolscap, took my fountain pen, labelled it "Maritime Diary 1941" and began to write.

Sunday, September 7th, The Feast of Might

Suddenly it was warmer and the sun shone, and we went to the beach. Grace and Irving had gone 'in' on a day when it was simply awful – raining and cold, oof! What a hardy people the Maritimes raise up. This day I wore first my 'play suit' to the beach then came back and changed to the all-out bathing suit that I had purchased for a dollar at J.C. Penney's in Jamestown. I got a little wet, then went, clinging to Grace and Irving, for a little ocean walk. The clouds overshadowed us again and we returned to our little house after our play. I'm glad we did, because the radio music was exquisite that afternoon – Sibelius' 2nd Symphony seemed to be full of the purpose of my coming out here. That night I was to meet the Moncton friends at a Feast at Leila Wells'. They are now old and tried friends, and I was delighted to see them again.

After the Feast we drove back to Moncton and our holiday was at an end. Irving parked the car, but we were not ready to go in. I said I wanted to see The [Tidal] Bore. As the Bore appears, quite ostentatiously, on schedule, it was a preposterous suggestion. But Irving said, 'Very well, we will make it come in now.' We drove down to the park and there, at twenty minutes of midnight, was a row of people lined up and waiting for the spectacle. In five minutes a nice big bore rippled in and filled up the brown banks of mud with swirling tidewater. Triumphantly, we returned home.

The next day I went back to work in earnest, began seeing people, getting my clothes in order, going out to tea or lunch, holding meetings. On Friday, September 12th, I mounted a bus and started out for a trial two weeks in Halifax.

During that time I toured the ingenious and complicated beds of flowers in the famous Public Gardens. I went up Citadel Hill one night and saw a dazzling display of northern lights. But for me, so much of Halifax was permeated by a brooding sense of coming disaster, an uptight fatalism. The fleets were leaving the harbour under convoy and people were alert for spies. The Bahá'ís with their talk of Universal Peace were deemed impractical, harmless.

Max Mosher was one of the Bahá'ís then in Halifax. I remember meeting him later and being taken by him for a drive out to the Northwest Arm and along the road through the white birch wood called The Dingle. Glimpses of the Arm and the harbour were beautifully framed by the trees. On this trip, "Mac" spoke of the Halifax Explosion, which occurred in 1917 when he was a boy of nine. Usually, he did not like to talk about it, and this moment was a rare one. He told us enough to convey the sense of shock and 'awful' activity that accompanied the disaster – the dead and injured, the burning houses, the refugees gathering in the parks and open spaces and the unseasonably heavy snowstorm that enveloped them. The story was vivid because it was usually locked away, a complex resulting from the shock given to a young boy. This submerged shock, now twenty-five years past, coloured the psychology of the city. I realized that this event, now legend, gave rise to the war fears of that time. Instead of saying "This can't happen to us," like the citizens of many other cities, Haligonians knew that war-related disaster had happened and could happen again. They were fully awake to the perils that existed. We continued our ride to a park where an anchor from one of the vessels which exploded in the harbour in 1917 had landed and lay embedded in the ground. Halifax. I was told that it was a Mecca for German spies and full of ammunition of one form or another.

Beulah Proctor conducted a boarding house on Morris Street and while her contacts were mostly with transients, she was an active teacher. Her distinction comes from being the first pioneer to Nova Scotia during that Seven Year Plan, answering a personal appeal of May Maxwell. She had emigrated from Worcester, Massachusetts, and was responsible for attracting a youthful Muriel Sheppard [later Muriel McLeod]. It seems to me that Beulah was also managing a canteen at the military base at Debert. One time she and I took the ferry to Dartmouth. We went up on deck and were admiring the beauty of the harbour – the vessels in a grey mist, the irregular line of the city and the islands, the distant expanse of water. Beulah was very much moved and said, "It is all so beautiful, and we may never again see it like this."

This trip was like most of the others in that my days were

filled to the brim with the making of social contacts and the hosting of meetings, study classes and firesides. But this trip was especially significant for two events: the first public meeting to be held in Halifax (and perhaps all of Nova Scotia) and the organization of the Halifax Bahá'í Group.

On Monday, September 22nd, Emeric and Rosemary Sala arrived. Dorothy Wade picked them up and we had supper together at her apartment. That evening we went to Eve Morley's and they spoke to ten who gathered there. The next night Emeric would speak at the Nova Scotian Hotel. The title of his talk was "Out of Venezuela". We had prepared publicity, which appeared in the three newspapers, and we had advertised it on the YMCA bulletin board. Salon E of the Hotel had been reserved. That night nineteen attended, ten of whom were non-Bahá'ís. Two men came from the Y, one of whom was a Hungarian from Emeric's hometown. We had a good discussion period and collected the names and addresses of a number of people to follow up. Three carloads went back to Dorothy Wade's for coffee and cookies.

Toward the end of that week, on the 26th, we held a supper and celebrated the Feast of Will (Ma<u>sh</u>íyyat) at the Wades'.

REPORT OF TWO WEEKS' PRELIMINARY WORK DONE IN HALIFAX
SEPT. 12 TO SEPT. 26

On the night of Sept. 26 a supper Feast was held there at which Beulah and I, five Halifax Bahá'ís and Eve and Pat [non-Bahá'í guests] were present. After supper and a discussion of teaching plans, our two guests excused themselves and we proceeded to a move which we all felt most momentous, that of consolidating our ranks by discussion of Bahá'í Administration and the election of officers. In a talk full of inspiration, Beulah summed up the purposes of her stay in Halifax and pointed out to them that the next step was to establish a working unity in accordance with the Administrative pattern. Individuals were now to be merged into a new concept of group activity. I gave a further talk on Bahá'í Administration, sharing with them my experi-

ence in a number of other Baháʼí communities. We then elected the following officers:
Sec. Maxon Mosher, 51 Vernon St.
Chairman Dorothy Wade, Pinehurst Apts.
Treasurer Wm. Laurie, Prince Arthur St.

With the election of the Treasurer, the Baháʼí fund was forthwith established. We are sorry to say that we will have to elect another Treasurer because Bill has been transferred to Montreal. Dorothy Wade was appointed Convener of Feasts.

The next morning Beulah and I drove out of Halifax, leaving the work in the hands of our newly elected officers. We parted at Masstown, Nova Scotia, where I took a bus for Amherst. I was met there by Grace and Irving, and we departed on a two-day scouting trip to Prince Edward Island.

Prince Edward Island: First Glimpse and a Birthday

From my diary:

> Irving and Grace were waiting for me at the bus stop. When I saw them after my brief two weeks, I realized what a strain I had been working under in Halifax. All at once I was so tired from relief of being out of that war-jittery spot and embarking on an expedition to the peaceful Island that I felt wobbly in the knees and tongueless for at least fifteen minutes.
>
> It was a perfectly pale day with the foliage at its most gorgeous hue, reddish purple of the oaks, orange and red of the maples, yellow orange of the beech trees and the dark blue green of the pines. Before I got off the bus, I was drunk with the beauty of the Nova Scotian landscape. Now the three of us good friends and jolly companions were off to catch the ferry at Cape Tormentine...
>
> We had coffee on the ferry and watched the sunset from the upper deck. From here the lights of Summerside made a

brilliant frontage. It was completely dark when we reached the Island side. We found the tourist cabins we were looking for and the proprietor told Irving, looking at the two women [Grace and me], that he would leave the sleeping arrangements to him. Grace and I slept in one bed and Irving slept on the other side of a rather flimsy curtain.

The next morning was sunny again and, in the direct sun, quite warm. I was filled with anticipation now that I was actually on PEI. Prince Edward Island is a dimpled darling, there is no doubt of that, 'rolling agricultural paradise with lakes and woods and sea vistas' [quoted from tourist book]. We stopped at Summerside and met Rosemary Sala's sister, then we drove on about one o'clock in the direction of Charlottetown. We visited Green Gables, scene of L.M. Montgomery's famous stories, and signed ourselves in a register where 4,000 tourists had inscribed their names. We drove to a great sweep of beach and sea. The wind was now blowing a gale with a slight wintery edge in it – warning of what to expect later. . .

It was late afternoon when we reached our tourist-lodge destination about a half hour outside of Charlottetown. There was a curving row of little houses facing a field. In front of our cabin was the aerial tower of the CFCY radio broadcasting station. We took a little rest and drove on to Charlottetown, arriving in the town in the late twilight. It has a fine old hotel, The Charlottetown, with a high pillared entrance, the mansion-style of building with a wide hall, parlours and dining room – very dignified. This was the eve of my birthday, [Sept.] the 28th, and I was given a birthday dinner in the beautiful old room. It was served quite elaborately – Malpeque oysters on the half shell, local to the Island, duckling, empress potatoes. We sat later in the main salon and listened to the Sunday evening concert, which was interrupted rudely by the war news turned up too loud. The guests of the hotel came in to listen – men in uniform and well-dressed, conservative-looking, middle-aged men or couples. We went out and drove by lamp-light around the town, then went back to our cabin home, parked near the red and green-lighted broadcast tower, and said some potent Bahá'í prayers for the work on the Island.

When we awoke the next morning, the 29th, the wind was blowing almost at hurricane speed. We had visions of our cabin rolling around the field, but, mercifully, this did not happen. We drove to Charlottetown, shopped, studied the agricultural situation – then back to the cabin. There is a cabin with a kitchenette and in it, my birthday dinner of chicken 'à la king' was prepared and eaten on crackers. Grace had brought the things in cans from Moncton. A small stove supplied the warmth, and we ran out in the streaming wind for wood. It was a novel birthday party. I had also been given some presents at breakfast. Later we washed up, repacked the basket of food and dishes and returned to Charlottetown.

We revisited Province House and met the Archivist, who guided our inspection of the 'Cradle of Confederation'. We were taken to the room where the representatives of the colonies had convened in 1864, saw their pictures, the chairs where they sat, the table...

PEI is a 'pocket' province. This city, its capital and metropolis, has a population of 16,000, the size of Geneva, New York. The stones in front of Province House and its stairs are worn into hollows by the tread of perhaps a hundred years. We signed our names in the register where at various times royalty had been given an entire page. The Duke of Kent had passed that way a few days before.

Irving and Grace left me at the public library, sunk in a book of Maritime history. About an hour later, they returned to take me to their friends', the Sinclairs', for tea. Mrs Sinclair had been told about my birthday, and my cake came in with a lighted candle on its top. After a very jolly time we emerged into a landscape calm in the rosy light of a marvellous sunset. We would be on our way back to take the ferry for Tormentine. The ride through the hills and valleys of this pastoral country was never to be forgotten. The light would be purple in the valleys and fiery red and orange on the hilltops. The farm people were doing their chores. There were dark pine woods and the shining waters of coves and inlets and, everywhere, a bewildering amount of space.

In November I went back to Halifax for a month, accompanied by Grace, her first foray into the field of travel teaching. Grace and Irving were not so accustomed to prolonged separations as were Willard and I. I wrote to Willard,

> I hope you write to Irving and commiserate with him from the Bahá'í husband viewpoint. He is being as generous in his attitude as you are. He writes grand letters to Grace...

Grace and I established a regular Monday night study group which met in a basement-level apartment that we rented at 346 Quinpool Road. Sometimes we would meet at the Wades'. We made as many contacts as we could, turned over every stone. I noted that Halifax needed a "real resident teacher".

Thoughts of Farming

The earlier trip to PEI had, for Irving, been more than holiday. He began to investigate farming on the Island and checked with the real estate brokers for a listing of farms and prices. He was beginning to consider buying a farm in the spring. The effects of the war made us think that this kind of investment in self-sufficiency could be the means of creating a Bahá'í community and a self-contained refuge where work could be found and would be needed.

To Willard, November 11, 1941:

> Your letter was forwarded to us by Irving, who has put an ad in the paper advertising for a farm! If you and I join in Moncton in April, they will have their nine [to form the local Assembly] by Convention time. We start from there, and a very good beginning. I will stick around here as long as I can, but plan to be home on or about Dec. 15th and won't it seem like heaven.

Irving had written to Willard about the prospect of farming.

This would be one way in which, to facilitate our emigration to Canada, work could be offered to Willard. Willard was most practical in his response. He wrote to me:

> . . . apparently the farm idea right next to Moncton is taking shape in his [Irving's] mind. I should think that might be an all-right idea. I could make a dandy garden and put in a few acres of sweet corn and cabbage. It seems to me that a part-time farm job would help get the farm into good shape against the time when we might need it as a Bahá'í refuge. Here again is the thought that if we have livestock on the farm they might be postponed for a year or so, because someone has to tend them every day. If the four of us were actually living on a farm we would want some animals. To make money on a farm calls for a considerable investment and an all-out expenditure of determined effort. It would not be necessary to get a farm merely for me to enter Canada as a visitor for a few months. By the way, I suppose the farm season does not open up so early in New Brunswick.

For almost a year now, while I was called away on other trips, Willard had been making visits to Hamilton. During this time he went back to Hamilton again, and I suggested that he enquire about immigration with the officials face to face. He was also developing, through correspondence, a relationship with Irving.

Bill Laurie was another Bahá'í, then in the Royal Canadian Navy as a non-combatant electrician. I had met him on my earlier visit, and he had been elected Treasurer of the Halifax Bahá'í group. When I had said prayers with him during that trip, he said that, through me, he had heard the voice of May Maxwell whom he had known in Montreal.

By this time Bill had shipped out for England on a Corvette. He had said his goodbyes a few weeks ago. I remember sitting with his new bride, Margaret Mosher, in the apartment on Quinpool Road. Her brother Max was also present. There was a blackout, and we sat in our little subterranean shelter imagining what the 'real thing' would be like. A bomber flew overhead and they set off a few booming guns, but no one was scared. After the blackout we had a discussion about protection, and we read from *The Promulgation of Universal Peace* about the Titanic disaster:

> ... these events have deeper reasons. Their object and purpose is to teach man certain lessons. We are living in a day of reliance upon material conditions. Men imagine that the great size and strength of a ship, the perfection of machinery or the skill of a navigator will ensure safety, but these disasters sometimes take place that men may know that God is the real Protector. If it be the will of God to protect man, a little ship may escape destruction, whereas the greatest and most perfectly constructed vessel with the best and most skilful navigator may not survive a danger such was present on the ocean. The purpose is that the people of the world may turn to God, the One Protector; that human souls may rely upon His preservation and know that He is the real safety".[52]

We said prayers and read the *Tablet of Aḥmad* for the protection of Halifax and for Bill. Three day later we learned that Bill had lost his life with the sinking of his Corvette.

The work in Halifax was different from Memphis and western New York State. I found it much more difficult to get started and, once started, to assess my progress. The population was so transient and the work, at best, could be described as "vague". Yet I knew I was pioneering. I wrote,

> Pioneer work is slower gauged and the station of one's apostlehood is more often assailed. I do not feel satisfied with my efforts, even though I am apparently doing all that I can.

Teaching in the Maritimes was both an inner and outer struggle. Outwardly I found that if ever there were a heavy atmospheric

---

52 'Abdu'l-Bahá, *The Promulgation of Universal Peace* (Wilmette, IL: Bahá'í Publishing Trust, 1982), p. 48.

pressure that needed to be lifted, then here was its spiritual equivalent. When urgent opportunities to teach are available at every turn, there is not so much an inner struggle as there is a struggle to summon additional energies. Those opportunities seemed to be non-existent here and needed to be created. I confided to Lorna, "My work here calls for a constant exercise of the will to climb – the need for 'brass-like feet' and an 'adamant' soul. This is a most subtle requirement... in times of lull."

Muriel Sheppard asked us to go with her to the Victoria General Hospital to visit her mother, Rebecca, who was ill. Rebecca had a strong, beautiful and careworn face. She related to us that Muriel had told her about the Faith and that we had come as teachers. Would we, she asked, answer her questions? We had been starving for an occasion to teach 'deeply' and here was a wonderful, 'prepared' soul who was asking to be taught. What a joy! Rebecca accepted the Faith that night and we learned later that another of her teen-aged daughters, Audrey [now Audrey Raine] had become a Bahá'í, too.

We arranged for another public meeting and on November 25, I was the speaker. The press clipping began:

BASIS FOR WORLD ORDER IS OUTLINED

Mrs Willard McKay, Jamestown, NY, international lecturer for the Bahá'í Faith, spoke last night at the Nova Scotian Hotel, her topic being 'Our New World Destiny.'

Soon afterwards I left Halifax and went home via Boston and Beverly, Massachusetts, where I visited Lorna. I remember listening to the radio with her on December 7th. Pearl Harbor had been bombed and the United States was at war. I returned to Jamestown, where the friends were gathering to make a voice recording to send to John Stearns, our pioneer in South America. I returned to Jamestown, but not for long.

To Lorna Tasker, Jamestown, January 20, 1942

We are going, dear! Willard got a letter from the Immigration Commissioner at Ottawa and then over a week ago now he took a trip to Fort Erie, Ontario, and straightened out the rest of our doubts. Since then things have moved so fast that I am in a state of perpetual amazement so that I tweak my whiskers in wonder. I am being most extravertish in order to cope with two 'Ps' that now dominate my life – people and packing. You know how hard it has always been for me to get away anywhere. Well, now that the news is out, I am constantly answering the phone and the doorbell. People who have had me filed away somewhere are now frantically trying to catch up in a week or two, the Bahá'ís are trying to extract the last drop, parties are being planned, and dinners given.

Yes, I suppose it is destiny calling me to Canada. The call has been there ever since my Canadian National Exhibition experience. When we went to Convention in the spring of 1940 after the Hamilton Assembly was born and I heard myself called a 'Canadian Pioneer', it was like a strain of music to my ears. Then Grace and Irving opened the door. There has been divine guidance all along. I remember so eagerly, staring out of the window on my first trip to Toronto, feeling the heightened sense of Place'. I felt ready to go in accordance with the Will of Bahá'u'lláh.

We are leaving Jamestown in a blaze of glory. Bahá'ís and non-Bahá'ís are rushing out to touch us with their love. I'm like a 'bride' in the midst of presents, parties, teas – a very exciting, thrilling, touching leave-taking.

I am to speak Sunday afternoon at the Hotel Jamestown, a last call to any who will hear. We had our last fireside last night with over thirty attending.

We entered Canada as landed immigrants at Fort Erie. Irving had written a letter to accompany our documents stating that he would accept responsibility for us. He was our 'sponsor'. We stopped in Toronto to visit Laura and Victor Davis, went on to spend a week with Rosemary and Emeric Sala in St. Lambert and had a meeting with the Canadian Teaching Committee in Montreal. Then on to Moncton.

Years later, Willard would write to the Jamestown community:

> It is twenty-three years ago this month since Doris and I left you and 'landed' as they call it, as immigrants at Fort Erie, Ontario, in Canada. I had three reasons for wanting to tear up our Jamestown roots: one was a desire for a change in occupation after eight years with Sears, Roebuck and Co. Another was the feeling (fostered by John Stearns) that my Bahá'í work in Jamestown was completed; and, finally, if I was ever to see anything more of Doris it would only be if she and I went pioneering together.

Willard didn't write of his real sacrifice. In coming to Canada both of us gave up invitations to continue race amity work in the south – work for which we were better qualified and probably would have been much more successful. The need in Canada, however, was urgent.

In Moncton, Irving had renovated the upstairs of their house at 32 Ralph Street into an apartment with a bedsitting room and kitchen. Willard was able to find some work, and we began to host firesides and other meetings. It was a beautiful beginning, and the Moncton Assembly reformed on April 21st. John Stearns sent us a postcard from Quito, Ecuador, which read, "Welcome to Moncton. Place your whole faith in God and never look back." We had consulted with the Assembly about extension teaching and in two weeks' time, Grace and I were on the road again, back to Prince Edward Island.

"The situation is not rosy..."

Charles Murray was the first pioneer to Prince Edward Island. He had moved to the Island from the United States sometime in the 1930's and had remained for about ten years. When I first began visiting PEI, Charles was employed at the airport near Summerside.

To Willard, May 17, 1942:

> Charles Murray came to the house about 8 Saturday night and we held, in the following way, the first 19-day Feast ever held in Charlottetown. We walked over to Victoria Park and consulted until the sun dropped below the line; then, we sat on a park bench and read and said prayers for half an hour or more. After that, we carried on a more formal consultation. Charles brought a bag of cookies which we took with us on our further perambulation. We continued our visit in the Charlottetown Hotel writing room and went over the telephone book for a list of names. Then we walked around another park and ate our cookies, hilarious at our very funny way of holding a feast with no place on which to light. We, speaking of the dove sent out by Noah, decided to call this the Feast of Ararat instead of Azamat!
>
> I got a lot of practical information and advice from Charles. He knows the people very well and the situation is not rosy. I am established well enough here now to go ahead and do a few things – let the chips fall where they will. I am going to advertise and hold a public meeting about the middle of next week, sending out cards to a certain list of people. It will be centered on my Confederation studies carried on so ostentatiously at the public library. I am sure I can get some people, at least, and follow up with publicity. Having proclaimed the Cause in Charlottetown, I will hope for some follow up leads, enough to keep us here a little longer.
>
> I will be quite busy this week working up my Confederation article mornings when I wake up early and doing direct-contact work with some of the people I have met already and

some others that Charles or Mrs Coles have suggested. This is all routine. If nothing comes of it directly, perhaps a secondary opening will come, one thing leading to another. At least, having gone through the schedule, I will feel that my duty has been formally done.

The more I think about it, the more it seems as if a number of Bahá'ís will have to move here. . . perhaps come from the United States. It is encouraging that the long deadlock as to jobs for 'foreigners' promises to lift from sheer necessity – or perhaps a farm project to raise food and provide shelter, similar to the Elgin plan, will attract the number as the need increases. I do not feel that PEI is our responsibility as far as residence goes because New Brunswick needs us almost as much. But others might come from somewhere if it were put up to them. The nine do not seem inherent in this soil.

Charles' cookies were rather tasteless, and I pretended to eat them while quietly stuffing them down through the cracks of the park bench we shared in Rochford Square.

During the administrative part of the Feast we planned the first public meeting, which was given in the Charlottetown Hotel a week or so later, about the time of the fiftieth anniversary of Bahá'u'lláh's Ascension, May 29th. Grace chaired the event, and I was the speaker. I talked about World Federation, basing my comments on my research on Canadian Confederation. I entitled the talk after an Island assessment, "They builded better than they knew." Four people came. We were complimented by one of that audience who noted that we were not discouraged at so small a turnout, proceeding as if the hall had been filled. Discouraged? How could we be discouraged with four souls sitting there! One was Flora Rogers, whose husband owned the CFCY radio station. She would give us, throughout her life, her friendship and support. Another was a corporal in the Royal Canadian Mounted Police.

Charles Murray had taken Grace and me to the "Mounties" and introduced us to Corporal MacArthur, who was responsible for investigating "queer ducks and geese" and other war-time visitors like ourselves. He seemed to be glad to "get in on the ground floor". Whether he came to the meeting out of interest or duty, I would not know.

There might have been more people out for our meeting if there had not been, that night, a War Defense Rally at Prince of Wales College.

The audience was curious and plied us with questions until after eleven o'clock. Mrs Rogers asked, "How long ago did Bahá'u'lláh die?" She was told, "Fifty years ago tonight." The audience was curious, but the response was one of polite interest. They neither accepted nor rejected.

Grace and I returned to Moncton via Summerside, where we held the overdue Feast of Núr with Charles. We had, before leaving the Island, an interview with the editor of *The Journal Pioneer* newspaper.

In June we found ourselves at Elgin, New Brunswick. The DeMilles were friends of the Gearys. They were not Bahá'ís then. Mrs DeMille had a rustic camp which she rented to groups of summer tourists, mostly from the United States. Camp Hermit Thrush was big, with several log cabins, a large central building with a fireplace and an open-air pavilion for eating; it was perfect for a Bahá'í summer school. Mrs DeMille offered the camp for our use. About fifteen people attended with Harlan Ober as the featured teacher. Mrs DeMille[53] declared herself soon after, as did an Amy Weir of Moncton.

I returned to PEI in the fall. Rosemary Sala accompanied me, and Emeric later offered to sponsor regular travel trips to the Island. I rekindled my friendship with Mrs Rogers and, through her, was swept into an active social life.

Tonight we are going to have The Authors Club meeting at

---

53 Mrs DeMille's daughter, Priscilla Waugh, learned of the Faith in Ontario and declared her belief there. She later pioneered with her husband Bill to the Magdalen Islands.

Dorothy Duchemin's. I am going to give them some exercises in writing and I hope they will rally and turn out some good results. I do feel very much at home here now – kind of on the inside, and anything might happen. At least my potential mailing [contacts] list is growing by leaps and bounds, and I have been very active considering that I have been here only four whole days. But what next? That is the problem we have to pray about...

Rosemary spoke at the Duchemins' the next day on "The History of the Bahá'í Faith". My darker side offered another perspective. It found that my social rounds on the Island were not so productive as they had been in Memphis. I even felt that they were hampering my efforts:

> In a way it's too bad I struck this whirl because the mood has had to be extravertish ever since I came, with practically no opportunities for the talks I had on my last visit – that and social doings like the wedding and the teas and the clubs [Art Club] have taken up so much time. Last night a big local concert for Russian relief for which Flora was playing came off...

On the Day of Covenant, 1942, Grace and I were staying in Charlottetown at the Blair Athol House at 19 Euston St. We had recited 'Abdu'l-Bahá's Tablet of Visitation with a very real sense of His presence. Then I remembered, "We have forgotten to provide for the material Feast." Almost at once a knock sounded on our door, and in the lighted doorway stood one of the daughters of the landlord with a tray of delicious refreshments. For all the times that we would stay at the Blair Athol House, this would be the only time that food would be offered to us. It seemed as if 'Abdu'l-Bahá had sent it Himself.

Harlan Ober met us in PEI twice during that late fall. He gave a fireside to about fifteen people, gave a radio broadcast and was guest speaker at the Rotary Club. He spoke on World Order.

Willard and I were in the Moncton community for a year and

a half. This was the fourth Assembly we had helped to build – the others: Jamestown, Hamilton and Memphis. We were the only 'qualified' speakers in the area, and we continued for several years to make travel teaching trips. I gave another course at Green Acre entitled "Fathoming the Most Great Ocean" and taught at the Rice Lake school in Ontario. Willard made several teaching trips to communities in western New York, Halifax and Saint John. The objectives of the Seven Year Plan wanted local Spiritual Assemblies in every state and province of the United States and Canada. In July of 1943 the National Teaching Committee, then far off on the American west coast, realized that Prince Edward Island was, of itself, a province. In accordance with the Plan, it would have to have an Assembly by Riḍván 1944. While at breakfast with Grace and Irving Geary, the wire arrived: "Would the McKays leave Moncton and re-pioneer to P.E.I. at the earliest possible date?" A letter followed with the news that the Guardian had cabled the National Assembly saying that, due to the insularity of the people, PEI was a most difficult place to teach. The letter posed the question, would we settle there, planning to remain, if necessary, the rest of our lives? We wired back, "Yes, we would."

Pioneering: "Plowing the Rock…"

In the early 1980s the National Spiritual Assembly [of Canada] asked three people to write their descriptions of my pioneering efforts in PEI. Those three were close friends all: Louise Mould, then pioneering in Zaire; Ann Boyles, working on her doctorate at the University of New Brunswick and Linda McMahon, pioneering in Madagascar. Linda sent me a copy of her account, and I responded with my concerns:

> But please, since it is my image you are dealing with, let me help you keep it more realistic and true. My first years here, I'll admit, had their ghastly tests and crushing disappointments, but I praise them for the lessons they taught me and the proofs

they gave of our own persistent strength and purpose. The later pioneers, too, were up against the problem of growth. We all functioned actively for a dozen years with only one declaration of an Islander, Leila Morris in 1956.

But how do you assess 'evident failure' when we, the pioneers involved, would never accept it? While we were digging the soil and heaving the foundation stones, none of us ever succumbed to the thought that we were digging a grave!

I remember eating lunch at the Inn at Green Acre one day. A very large lady from New York City came over to my table and knelt on the floor, insisting, 'Come back, Doris. You belong to the world!' I could smile and shake my head and realize how deeply rooted I was already in Canada's untilled soil.

The McKays moved to Charlottetown, renting Alfred Duchemin's house at 279 Richmond Street. The Gearys came with us, and others responded to the call as well: Helen Gidden, from Toronto; Christine McKay, Willard's sister, moved from Rochester, New York. Edna Halloway came from Dorothy Baker's community in Lima, Ohio.

We met Edna at the station and brought her "home". I remember how Edna became suddenly quiet and withdrawn as we approached the house. The next day she told us that she had had a dream in which she saw the house and everything in it before coming to the Island.

Agnes McKinnon, originally from Scotland, pioneered from Lorna's town of Beverly, Massachusetts. Elizabeth Cowles moved from Montreal, but just before Naw-Rúz she had to return, and Elsa Ventu arrived to take her place. On April 21, 1944, we formed the first Local Spiritual Assembly on Prince Edward Island in Charlottetown.

Sometimes we do not care what happens to us in the service of Bahá'u'lláh. And sometimes we do care but go anyway. It helps to be reminded that painful sacrifice is acceptable, and, if it is met with prayers and meekness, it leaves an impression upon the spiritual soil of the region.

There were hard times ahead for the pioneers who had left

everything to answer the call of PEI. The trained people who came took menial jobs, when they could get them. Some took on housework, others farm labour. We were not young, our average age about fifty. Helen, a skilled stenographer, took a job handing out ice cream cones at the Pure Milk Company. Edna, who had sold out a private hairdressing business and her house, worked six days a week babysitting twins. She received six dollars a week and a meal a day. Christine and Agnes shared accommodation in two rooms heated by a Franklin stove and an antique oil cooker. Both did housework, and their combined weekly income totalled ten dollars plus meals while working. Elsa Ventu, the Finnish newspaper woman, was another to take a housekeeping job. She slept in a damp basement, which aggravated her arthritis.

Elsa's health suffered, and after six months she had to return to Toronto. But her influence was felt. Years later when Trinity Church was holding a discussion series on non-Christian sects and religions, the Bahá'í Faith came up for consideration. Some of our friends spoke out in our favour. "But," replied the minister, "at least it is not Christian." At this point Elsa's former employer arose and said that the Bahá'ís were not anti-Christian and that her Finnish maid had been very religious and quoted her Bible frequently and to good effect. Elsa's father, by the way, was a minister in Finland.

One day during our first year on the Island, Irving received a call from a lawyer in town advising him of a farm going up for public auction. The four of us gathered at Vernon Bridge and met with the people who owned it, talked with them and decided to put in a bid. We were able to secure the farm for about three thousand dollars. Irving had sacrificed his pension with Eaton's to pioneer. But they did agree to give him a fixed amount for a year after he left. For us, the farm became the primary economic focus. When Irving and Willard could not find work in town, they worked at the farm. I remember Willard applying for a labourer's job in town and being turned down. They worked very hard because neither of them knew anything about "dirt" farming.

To children I gave art lessons after school and on Saturdays. The children would come to the house, and I charged them twenty-five cents a lesson – thirty-five if two came together. I started with four students, two of whom were nieces of Rosemary Sala. Rosemary's sister lived in Summerside, and I would meet her daughters at the bus. In time I had about forty-five students, and I earned about ten dollars a week that way. I remember seeing a group of children standing outside the window, watching us do our art and thinking, "Oh, if I could only get art to all these children." That wish was to come true later.

Charlottetown was a joint teaching responsibility. There were nine, and sometimes as many as eleven, pioneers. We became a composite functioning body, helped by many visiting Bahá'ís. Our teaching efforts were financed by the National Assembly and the Teaching Committee, and whatever we did to proclaim the Faith was a credit to their support. We could not have accomplished it on our own. Teaching campaigns with public meetings, newspaper publicity and radio interviews were launched. Travelling teachers flocked here, and we found speaking engagements for them with the service clubs. John Robarts almost "commuted" from Toronto. Harlan Ober, William Sears and the Salas ventured here. Ruth Moffett came for several consecutive "campaigns", and Jamie Bond, then a student at the University of Toronto, came for an entire summer, taking a job as a newspaper reporter.

Tony and Mamie Seto were early teachers, coming for five weeks in November of 1943. They had offered themselves as pioneers, but the Guardian had advised them, because of Tony's important business connections in San Francisco, to make this a temporary teaching visit. The Setos engaged rooms at the Charlottetown Hotel and, with the utmost dignity and style, afforded the townspeople a model of American-Chinese marriage. For a time, they met people at firesides and teas and made contacts of their own. Tony addressed The Authors Club and different men's discussion groups. Then they were ready for their "campaign", as they called it. It began with very impressive newspaper spreads which they financed and were to be followed by three public meetings at the Queen Hotel on January 3rd, 4th and 5th. Twenty-five or so attended the first. Shortly after this, the Setos left to visit Moncton. While they were away, the news came that Tony's San Francisco partner had died suddenly. The Setos had to leave with their plans unfulfilled. Tony came back for one night only to gather their belongings and to check out of the hotel. We voted to hold follow-up meetings at the Queen Hotel on January 13th, 26th and February 4th with Willard and I speakers on those dates. For several years we would use 'the Queen'. Emeric Sala, John Robarts and Dorothy Baker would later speak there.

In 1945 Mrs Florence Cox was sent to the Island by the Teaching Committee. Florence, a very ardent, older Bahá'í, had a small income and rented a room on Rochford Street opposite the Square. She got permission from the Assembly to rent the living room of the house as a Bahá'í Reading Room, an effort the Assembly agreed to try for four months, from June to October. Books were provided, a sign, BAHÁ'Í READING ROOM, was put up and a schedule of hours posted. There was an opening reception and Thursday night meetings were advertised weekly. If no sincere effort is ever wasted, this venture had its reward, but since the visible response was almost nil, we suspended the activity and tried other plans.

We were still being supported by funds from the Teaching Committee. A special contribution had been earmarked for broadcasts, and together we went and tried out our voices on a tape recorder at CFCY. Elizabeth Cowles, back on a visit, Christine, Irving and Willard had the best. Grace and I wrote a script every week, which was broadcast on Sunday afternoons. In those days a fifteen-minute talk cost seven dollars.

We held the Maritime Summer Conference in Keppoch, PEI, that year with Doris Richardson as teacher. About fifteen attended, and Fred Izzard of Halifax announced his intentions to join the Faith. Doris stayed on to speak at the Queen in July.

In the fall of 1945, the National Assembly sent in a "bulldozer" to break up the hard soil of Maritime resistance. That bulldozer was Ruth Moffett. She gave a series of five seminars at the Queen Hotel. There were afternoon and evening meetings daily. A great many people were canvassed by letter and telephone, and there was extensive newspaper publicity. The opening response saw about twenty-five in attendance. After the campaign we could count about fifty to sixty different people who had come out for a meeting. Toward the end of the campaign, however, attendance dropped off. In the beginning it had been hoped that one or two series of seminars would attract sufficient people. This not being the case, we pressed on desperately until sometime in March. Most of the people who came were older and well entrenched in their own church life. They had come out of curiosity and had been attracted more by Ruth's personality than by the Message of the Faith.

In October I sent for Dorothy Baker. I had been introduced around and had joined two clubs, one for art and the other literary. I found the members of these groups friendly and marked with the social stamp, willing to listen but not to get involved. In my wishful thinking, I set my hopes on Dorothy Baker's magic ability to create a spiritual atmosphere. Sure that she would confirm them in a single meeting, I delivered my invitations in person at a number of homes, beseeching people to come and meet this wonderful speaker who was also my personal friend.

I asked Dorothy to speak on The Seven Valleys at our tea. People filled the room, sitting in a circle around the fireplace. I was never so happy! Until Dorothy gave her talk, that is. She spoke only to their minds. The ladies were charmed, but Dorothy's heart was not in it. Later I asked, "Dorothy, WHY did not you give them 'the works'?" She shook her head, "Did you think I would cast my Beloved at the feet of those women?"

She wrote to me from the train, "At first I thought all those people were dead! But this morning, on second thought, I think they may have been asleep. But I would have to work there six months to make any impression on them."

Dorothy had also spoken on radio, CFCY. Keith Rogers and the staff were astonished when she went on the air without any notes.

When John Robarts came, he worked like a person trying to "close a deal" with the fourteen or so people he contacted. He was the one who introduced *Bahá'u'lláh and the New Era* to Margery Patterson, who would later lift our hearts greatly.

For the small band of pioneers, it was a well-intentioned treat to be entertained by John at the Charlottetown Hotel. He was then chairman of the new Canadian Teaching Committee and came often to the Island. At times it seemed to me that John personally adopted the young Charlottetown Assembly. I remember a particularly hard period when most of us were relatively poor and feeling somewhat "homeless." When Christmas approached, John sent the community twenty-five dollars with which to celebrate, and the Bahá'ís got dressed up and went to a show together.

When the Guardian died in 1957, it was a different story. John came to the Island to talk to us about the problems the Hands of the Cause were having with Mason Remey. He asked Willard and me to have lunch with him at the Charlottetown Hotel. But this time, it was ham sandwiches sent to his room. John told us then about the search for the Guardian's will. It was not a time for celebration.

The Cause is indebted to the loyal friendships of the Rogers and Duchemin families. They fought battles for us with some of the suspicious people in town. In fact, they said later that we would never know how much they had had to defend us. One day Corporal MacArthur called at 279 Richmond Street. He had known us from our first visits, had attended the first public meeting and had come to hear the Setos speak, but this call was a police matter. He said that he had told enquirers that the RCMP knew all about the Bahá'í Faith and that it was entirely acceptable to the police. But now he had been called to ask if a Miss Christine McKay working at a house on North River Road was Willard's sister. People in an adjoining apartment, an English physician and his wife, had noted to the police that Christine was "suspiciously superior" for a housemaid – perhaps a spy! Later the Corporal reported to us that all was well. The doctor's wife became friends with Christine and was entertained by her at tea. Quite an experience to relate back home in England, that the doctor's wife had gone to tea with the housemaid!

I now think that we pushed it too hard. The Island people are not pushable. But we thought we had to try as hard as we did because of money. Everyone was running low on funds. The time came when some of the pioneers had to call on the newly created Canadian Bahá'í Fund for help. There were only a few hundred Canadian Bahá'ís to contribute to that Fund, and a drive was on for the ornamentation of the Wilmette temple. The Secretary of the National Assembly called us to put on more steam to teach and confirm the Island people so the pioneers could leave. How we laboured to plant the Faith! Our very lives were ebbing away with the discouraging years. Some of us watered the seeds with our tears, some got sick and left and some were replaced by others.

After three years (in 1946), our friend Margery Patterson came to the house and declared herself a Bahá'í. We had come to know her when Willard met George Patterson at a talk he gave to a discussion group made up mostly of Prince of Wales College faculty. George taught mathematics there, and he must have mentioned the Faith to his wife. Later he ordered some apples from our farm, and when Irving went to deliver them, Margery asked a lot of questions. Before coming to visit and to announce her intentions, she had, on this day, seen the minister and resigned from the church. She came every Wednesday for a month to study the Will of 'Abdu'l-Bahá and to deepen in the Teachings. She said, "Whenever you say I am ready, I will sign my card." When she did sign, she was a fully confirmed Bahá'í. You can imagine how our hopes rose.

One soul like Margery was worth it all. She was the hidden jewel "beyond the seven seas". There were other people, too, who had been exposed to the Faith as much as Margery, and I think some of them accepted it logically. These people would defend and stand up for the Bahá'ís and even lend their homes for meetings and offer lifelong friendships. They were called, but not chosen. Only Margery had the courage and the integrity to stand with us. How different it might have been! And how different it might have been had Margery been an Islander.

Speaker after speaker, firesides and public seminars, radio broadcasts, the Reading Room and the "bulldozer." Our beleaguered little band had thought that with Margery, better days had come at last. But soon the hopes that we had clung to for the past three years would be crushed. The very reason for our Island existence would be pulled from underneath us. Laura Davis was Secretary of the National Spiritual Assembly. At its request she had written us a letter but had waited five days before summoning up the courage to mail it. Because of our drain on the Fund, the National Assembly was asking us to disband the Charlottetown Assembly. The sudden interruption to the momentum of our efforts, which had become our way of life, overwhelmed us with what then seemed to be an irrational sense of defeat. Most of the pioneers had little or nothing to return to. It seemed that Bahá'u'lláh had turned us down, had rejected our efforts. The group of pioneers who were the first Island Assembly broke up. Our companions went back to Rochester, New York, to Lima, Ohio, to Toronto and to Montreal. The Gearys and McKays moved on a more permanent basis to the little farmhouse at Vernon Bridge. There were many out there who had heard Bahá'í talks given by Willard or Irving, and it was known as "the Bahá'í Farm".

In Charlottetown, Margery was left on her own. She started firesides, and we helped when we could. The next spring the Gearys left to aid the Halifax community. Later, they moved to Cape Breton, where they became "Knights of Bahá'u'lláh" for opening up that virgin territory.

This relatively short period in the 1940s I have described as one of "isolation, deprivation and evident failure". I remember being uplifted then by the words of one of the Tablets of the Divine Plan addressed to the pioneers:

> The darkness of this gloomy night shall pass away. Again the Sun of Reality will dawn from the horizon of the hearts. Have

patience, wait but do not sit idle; work while you are waiting; smile when you are wearied by monotony; be firm while everything around you is being shaken; be joyous while the ugly face of despair grins at you; speak aloud while the malevolent forces of the nether world try to crush your mind... The trees of hope will become verdant."[54]

Vernon

For the first time since we became Bahá'ís in Geneva, New York, Willard and I were alone. I'll admit that a passing wave of desolation struck us on that October morning when our friends Grace and Irving drove away. The nervous depression that had assailed Grace in Charlottetown had not lifted when we moved to the country. Although they had left their part of the house furnished for a probable return, we knew that they would not be back. The parting was tearful, and the sadness lingered for a time. But our temperament was to be positive and hopeful. I recalled John Stearns' postcard from Ecuador: "Never look back." Well, there are worse places to live in than the present! But the future was a blank.

We continued to proclaim the Faith. In Charlottetown we used publicity and in Vernon, contact with the people. I joined the Women's Institute and held Saturday art classes with children. Later the Institute engaged me to teach art two days a week in the country school.

I had learned that 99½% of the Islanders were church members. The church was more than a religion; it was a culture, a way of life. Here in the country as well as in Charlottetown, people were interested in us but closed their minds to our Faith. There did not seem to be many young people on the Island in those days of war; we knew people only of our own age or older. They would listen with an inhibited curiosity, never a question expressed. They were afraid of knowing something that would set them apart from the social norm, something that threatened an older sense of unity.

---

54 *Bahá'í Scriptures* #990, p. 548.

Willard and I laboured on the farm, managing to keep out of debt and enjoying our independence. We grew vegetables and small fruits and raised chickens – subsistence farming. Willard drove a horse and two-wheeled cart. Later we bought an old car that got us to town. Our ancestors had been "settlers", too, back in the 1700s in the United States. Perhaps that is why there were so many periods of "radiant acquiescence" in our lives.

I cannot bear to be pitied or praised for these years. There were always ways to serve the Faith in spite of our difficulties. Uppermost was our fixed commitment. We had given ourselves to Bahá'u'lláh for this undeveloped territory. What did He want us to do?

Well, at the time we were the only Bahá'ís in the Atlantic provinces who had speaking experience. We had a deep comprehension of the Covenant, taught by the great early Bahá'ís. We had the experience of applying the Administration. We taught at every summer school from the beginning, and we were on call for public meetings in Moncton and Halifax, expenses paid.

And we had company. There were a number of friends in town who were lifelong in their loyalty. I painted and artists came to paint our beautiful landscapes. Old Bahá'í friends came from the United States. The Salas, always involved with their interest in the Bahá'í Farm, came often. John and Audrey Robarts did not forget us.

In 1952, the National Bahá'í Convention was held in Moncton, and I was invited to chair one of the meetings. Shirley and Bob Donnelly were there on their honeymoon. Bob sought me out to talk about Charlottetown. The Guardian had cabled, "Charlottetown must be maintained at any cost." It was his second cable regarding the Island. The first pioneers had scattered, and now new ones had to be found. Bob and Shirley drove to Charlottetown and in one day secured jobs for which they had had recent training. They spent their first days on the Island with us in Vernon, and the McKays were enchanted. Seven Bahá'ís followed, and we were in business again. Margery Patterson, the first declarant, stood out like a landmark.

Our fortunes changed with the new upsurge of life. Dr Ken Parker, Superintendent of Schools, was interested in putting art into the curriculum. He asked me to speak to the Rotary Club about my experiences in teaching art to children, and there were present about a hundred men who heard me support Dr Parker's ideas. The decision to include art in the public schools was made, and although I was in my fifties, I got a job that turned into quite a dazzling career. I was teaching the teachers in art instruction and was going monthly into seventy-five classrooms to demonstrate the lessons. I had been given the authority to work out my own plans, and the plans were for Bahá'u'lláh, built out of prayer and inspiration. It seemed as if the creative power were fresh from the next world. I was in a space capsule with access to unusual energy, my mind full of ideas and ambitious projects including a book, *Art in the Schools*. It was used throughout the province and saw three printings. I blazed on with undiminished enthusiasm for sixteen years, retired, then took another school in Sherwood for a year and stopped at seventy-four.

Because of my school work in the Charlottetown area, I kept an address in town – an address that qualified me to become a member of the Charlottetown Bahá'í community. In the spring of 1954, I filled the vacancy on the Local Spiritual Assembly as the needed ninth member. The teaching impasse had not changed over the years. More pioneers came, including the return of the Gearys, and yet I was the needed ninth member for fifteen years.

Over those years I was home three nights out of seven and on holidays. Willard's heart was failing, and he had lost most of his hearing. I stayed with him, instead of travelling, but I continued to be a combination settler (in Vernon) and pioneer (in Charlottetown) and a career lady. Willard died in 1966, and I came home to stay in 1969. The house was and still is a shrine for Willard. People who come feel his presence here. He was the real settler, still much beloved by the older Vernon neighbours. He never wanted to move, a saint in that place with his garden, his fruits, his prayers, recitations and teaching.

"Plowing the Rock": Summation

I can sum my early years on PEI this way: The first pioneers were crushed between the urgencies of material existence and an unyielding wall of public apathy. The more secure we had felt in our earlier American teaching work, the worse we felt here. When I went out on errands, walking alone on the streets of Charlottetown, I would often feel the tears running down my cheeks, and I would fight them back to conceal them from others.

We were faithful. We had many meetings among ourselves, studied the Word, held firesides and observed the anniversaries and Feasts. We had lists of people to telephone. In the evenings the shabby Bahá'ís would go to one another's houses to hold weekly business meetings and to pray. But the heat would begin to fade out of the mystic coil of our isolated unity that held us together until we would have another visitor from "away." For a week the glow would brighten, and we would warm our hearts and be near.

When Dorothy Baker had visited in the late 1940s, she inspected my black cloth "pioneer's coat", then showing a greenish grey at the elbows and collar. She said, "I will make you some cuffs and a collar with some fur I have at home." In her closely programmed life, Dorothy found the time to cut the fur and to make neat circular cuffs and a collar stitched on a dark wool. In the box I received from Lima, Ohio, there were two housecoats that I had seen her wear at her home. One was a rose-coloured chenille. In 1954, on a snapping cold night in Vernon, came the telephoned news of Dorothy's death. I was stunned. I sat down on the stairs and cried for her – and noticed that I was wearing the rose housecoat that she had sent.

Second Childhood

When I came back to Vernon to live, there was yet time allotted generously to me for another life. It was a rebirth of sorts, in which I found my old friends again. My early days in the Faith had begun four short years after the passing of 'Abdu'l-Bahá – early days that had a storybook quality. There were few Bahá'ís in 1925, and our first teachers were like apostles sent out to deliver the Message. These delightful and inspired teachers were destined to become our intimate and loving friends, promising an eternal relationship with us "in all the worlds of God". For years, their radiance was like stardust that brushed off on our young souls. It was now forty years since I had known them: Howard Colby Ives and Mabel, Grace and Harlan Ober, May Maxwell, Martha Root, Louis Gregory. Now, even Dorothy Baker had slipped through the door to the next world, although she was younger than I. While still in Charlottetown, I began to write my stories. I took them to the Magdalen Islands and later on a teaching circuit in New Brunswick. At that time, biographies of these people had not been written and the young Bahá'ís were eager for "real-life" stories about the heroes and heroines I had known. It seemed as if at the mention of their names, these angelic beings came and joined us. I remember telling the stories in one place where the people stayed all night and we continued at breakfast the next morning.

I used the stories for a series of fireside talks that I gave at Bob and Shirley Donnelly's. Young people were there now and music and a magic hospitality. Then, one night, it happened: All those years of Bahá'í Administration and school teaching and all the scar tissue of a childless life of pioneering were swept away by a waterfall of universal love. I had surrounded myself with fences, and now they were being washed away. I was "in my second childhood" in the Bahá'í Faith. "The more you love, the nearer you will be to God."

That night I found a spiritual son, cold and isolated, critical, perhaps in self-defence, a youth from another province and new to the Faith. "He needs to be loved," whispered the inner counsel, and I remembered how May Maxwell, of whom we had been speaking that night, had rescued ME from the prison of self. What had she done? What any of us can do if we care for one another. With a warm regard she had encouraged me to talk, and she had listened – not talking much but with sometimes a quiet question. She did not veil her eyes. This was her way of teaching. She reached out for the soul, at the same time saying inwardly the Greatest Name to establish the rhythm of the spirit.

So much is said about Love in the Teachings. It is a great and vital power, a worker of miracles because it is the key to the heart of the True One. It is, to recall the short obligatory prayer, the reason why we were created.

Bahá'í love is phenomenal; it is only partially of this world. The person facing you is a dwelling with two windows, the eyes. Sometimes these windows are veiled. You whisper the Greatest Name – the intimate one, "Yá Bahá'u'l-Abhá" (O Thou Glory of the Most Glorious); you ask for a contact between yourself, the person or persons to whom you are guided and the Beloved of the divine world. You ask that the Holy Spirit vaporize the veils and that the fragrance of the divine attar be diffused. You offer yourself to the network of helpers between this world and the next. Helpers like Howard, May, Martha and Dorothy.

Who shall we love? Some people are known intuitively, as I was known to Howard and May and Martha – people who knew me before I knew myself. You sense the capacity of the listener, a capacity which is from God. You ardently seek for a meeting of souls and are illumined.

That night I realized what I had lost in my years of faithfulness to the obvious duties of the Faith and knew, at nearly eighty, that life had just begun again.

In another year that young friend left this house in Vernon to start a brilliant career as a pioneer in the land he called "overseas".

The years since been hae wonderful. I am welcomed back to love. It is a concentration of love power that goes out like an arrow to certain hearts and seems to enter them. There have been many hearts – youths of more than usual capacity that I have come close to. They have borne me along on their young, strong wings.

They have taken me with them to their pioneer posts in Finland, Vanuatu, Madagascar, Haiti, Macau and French Guyana. They have said prayers for me on their pilgrimages, deepened with me in their search for Bahá'u'lláh. The thoughts of my days are magnetized by a bond between my heart and the souls I have come to know since my rebirth into spiritual childhood. To these magnificent souls, who are the lights of my life, I want to say that the bond between us, wherever we are, is charged with a redeeming power. If I had not stayed on Prince Edward Island, I should never have known you; you are all iridescent motes in the atmosphere I breathe. I pray with you more than for you.

This book is also a result of that love power. It began with Howard Colby Ives. He had not veiled his eyes when we gathered to hear him speak in 1925. He gave us the gift of a message that became life indeed. Howard Colby Ives, who had been taught the lesson of Love by the Master Himself, was truly "a lighter of fires in many hearts". As one of his spiritual daughters, I aspire to be a link in the love-chain, passing on that heritage.

Dear Doris,

... Your gift for capturing the essence of personalities in a few sentences, and of evoking those very wonderful days of the 1920s and the activities of the friends is unequalled; I have never read a more exciting, poetic or detailed chronicle. Its value to the Faith will grow with every passing year. Of special interest, I found, was your uncanny capacity to depict – dare one call them "mystical" experiences: the epiphanic and transcendental moments in the lives of the Bahá'ís. . . The facts are almost always retrievable, and anyone with a Sherlock Holmes inclination can usually dig them out; but what you have preserved is that much rarer thing – the feeling, atmosphere, texture and spiritual shape of the events you describe. . .

Roger White

www.ingramcontent.com/pod-product-compliance
Lightning Source LLC
Chambersburg PA
CBHW070933230426
43666CB00011B/2423